THE BOTTOM LINE

READER

A FINANCIAL HANDBOOK FOR LIBRARIANS

Edited by
BETTY-CAROL SELLEN
and
BETTY J. TUROCK

NEAL-SCHUMAN PUBLISHERS
NEW YORK   LONDON

Published by Neal-Schuman Publishers, Inc. 23 Leonard Street New York, NY 10013

Copyright © 1990 by Neal-Schuman Publishers, Inc.

Printed and bound in the United States of America

Library of Congress Cataloging-in-Publication Data

The Bottom line reader : a financial handbook for librarians / edited by Betty-Carol
    Sellen and Betty J. Turock.
        p. cm.
    ISBN 1-55570-057-8
        1. Library finance—Handbooks, manuals, etc. I. Sellen, Betty-Carol. II. Turock,
    Betty J. Z683.B694 1990   90-5754
    025.1'1—dc20   CIP

CONTENTS

SALARIES MATTER

PREFACE

Government funding for libraries remains low, while costs of books, AV, and library supplies continue to soar. Libraries must compete with other institutions for funding from less traditional sources of support. Expensive new technology becomes more and more of a necessity if libraries are to keep up with advances in cataloging, interlibrary loan, and online reference.

It is hard times indeed for libraries in the latter part of the 20th century. In the 1960's and early 1970's there was government and social commitment to supporting public services. Since then, an economic decline coupled with a shift in values has resulted in dramatically reduced funding for these services, including libraries. During these lean days it is necessary for librarians to consider every means possible to use money efficiently, to attract revenue, and to find alternative sources for library support. No matter how dedicated and hard-working the staff, for the library to thrive—sometimes even to continue—the bottom line is money.

In response to this economic environment, Neal-Schuman Publishers created *The Bottom Line* journal, under the editorial guidance of Betty J. Turock at Rutgers University. Now in its fourth year, this journal has published critically acclaimed articles and features of practical use to librarians. *The Bottom Line Reader* brings together in one volume the articles that the editors view as of outstanding quality and continuing instructive value to library managers and administrators. This collection is meant to serve as a pragmatic resource for those librarians seeking to do the most with the least in planning library programs and services.

This book is organized into several sections, each one devoted to a specific area of financial concern. The first section, "The Economic Environment," contains six articles that place library issues and concerns within the larger social context. For the next section, "Financial Planning and Reporting," we chose articles on how to prepare a budget that will influence funding agencies to allocate money and several articles on how to apply accounting theory to library operations.

The need to know what goods and services really cost is considered in the chapter, "Understanding Costs" by authors who know the difference between "cost" and "price" and by those who have analyzed their own library operations. "Financing Programs and Services" deals with experiences, and the information gained, of several librarians engaged in raising money for automation; carrying out adult programming; planning photocopy services; managing overdues; and funding a literary project. Also there are articles in this section on the pros and cons of fees for library service.

Finding alternative sources for fundraising is a big concern for libraries. Evidence of this can be found in many of the advertisements in professional journals that seek a library director with experience in fundraising. In this section of *The Reader* topics include fundraising; staging special events to raise money; direct-mail campaigns; holding a successful referendum; and obtaining grants.

The final section, last but certainly not least, is called, quite to the point, "Salaries Matter." Personnel issues covered here include pay equity, employee benefits, and salaries.

The editors hope this book will be useful to its readers on a very practical level and that the information gathered will help librarians continue on with their fine public service to their various communities.

Betty-Carol Sellen

INTRODUCTION

Since we launched *The Bottom Line* in 1986, we have kept the spotlight on major financial issues and techniques in library and information centers. Our intent is to provide some practical guidance for library managers in the internal fiscal operations of their institutions. At the same time, through quarterly editorials, we have attempted to frame local concerns within the broader external context of the federal scene. As we look back to chart the course for the future, some major issues still clamor for attention, if libraries are to be fiscally secure in the decade ahead.

Libraries in the Zero Sum Society

When Patricia Schuman and I began to discuss the initiation of *The Bottom Line*, libraries were coming face to face with the Zero-Sum Society. In December of that year, at the federal level, the Balanced Budget and Emergency Deficit Control Act was approved by Congress and signed into effect by the President. Known as the Gramm-Rudman-Hollings amendment, after its chief Senate sponsors, its goal was to balance the budget by automatically sequestering, or impounding, program funds. Approximately 73 percent of the federal budget was exempt from cuts; half of the cuts were to come from the remaining domestic programs and half from defense. Library programs were not exempt.

At that time, MIT's Lester Thurow was at the forefront of those economists calling attention to the economic problems facing the United States. In two best-selling books, *The Zero-Sum Society* and *The Zero-Sum Solution*, he had focused on what the budget deficit meant to the future of this country as a world-class power. While predicting the effects a decline in status would have on our standard of living, he also pointed out that zero-sums meant no new money to support federal programs. Competition for scarce resources .would reach new proportions: more money for one institution or service would mean less money for another.

The 1988 Presidential campaign focused attention on a compelling issue: that future generations would pay the price if we left today's crucial economic problems unsolved. Unfortunately, that forecast did not stimulate meaningful discussion of national economic policy. At the same time, West Germany and Japan surpassed us in economic productivity, and other nations were catching up. In 1980, our $2 billion surplus had made us a competitor in world markets; in 1990 we are mired in trade deficits that have placed us among the world's highest debtor nations. The growing national financial mess led to the Gramm-Rudman-Hollings Act, which is still with us. The Zero-Sum Society is in high gear.

Positioning Library Programs in the Federal Hierarchy

While the financial future of libraries is heavily governed by the national economy, it is in the political sphere that the magnitude of the zero-sum game will be decided. That sphere is influenced by positioning, that is closeness to power, which translates into interest and action.

While I was working in the U.S. Department of Education, Office of Educational Research and Improvement (OERI), Library Programs during a year's academic leave from Rutgers University, I had numerous opportunities to observe action on behalf of the country's libraries in the federal hierarchy. The experience left me unconvinced that George Bush's "Kinder, more gentle America" would protect libraries' tenuous fiscal appropriations in a zero-sum economy. Two events proved most enlightening: attending hearings in the House and Senate on budgets for both Library Programs and the National Commission on Libraries and Information Science (NCLIS) and witnessing the level of knowledge about library programs on the part of top executives in OERI.

If attendance at the budget hearings was any indication of interest, and it usually is, then libraries are in trouble. When the House Labor, Health, and

Human Services Education Appropriations Subcommittee conducted the Budget Hearings for Library programs, besides the Chair, only three of the 13 Congressmen were present for that part of the session.

At the NCLIS Hearing before the Subcommittee on Labor, Health and Human Services, Education and Related Agencies of the Senate Committee on Appropriations, attendance got worse. When the session began, two of the possible 15 senators were present. Little more than one and one-half hours into the Hearing only one remained to listen to the supplicants. Fifteen minutes later even the Chair had more important business elsewhere, and those assembled were treated to the embarrassing sight of testimony being addressed to an empty platform. When I was reminded that testimony is for the record, I found it hard to believe that those who couldn't find time to attend the Hearings would take the time to wade through their printed version.

For the most part, in both the House and the Senate, the legislators' questions were directed to issues that reflected the immediate concerns of constituents back home—not the information needs of the diverse national populace.

But any remaining doubts about the level of interest in libraries were dispelled by the response of the media. Throughout the Hearings, when Public Broadcasting and the Commission on Comprehensive Health Care presented their budget requests, media lights were flashing. When the testimony for library support was introduced, drapes were opened and TV cameras were disassembled for travel. It was lights out for libraries!

That same lack of interest was in evidence on a daily basis as officials in Library Programs tried to integrate their charge into the mainstream of the Department of Education. One example serves the point: when the Bushes made it clear that their ongoing interest in literacy would not dim in their new capacity as the nation's First Couple, plans for bigger and better literacy programs were hatched all around. One neophyte, placed in charge of coordinating OERI's ongoing initiatives and developing new directions, visited with Library Program's senior staff and was surprised that libraries were involved in the plans and programs at all. He had no idea of what the library's role in literacy had been in the past or might be in the future.

Questions arise as a result of these experiences. In the United States, the American Library Association (ALA) represents the most powerful lobbying voice for the nation's libraries. But with the pres-

ent size of the ALA's Washington Office, how can we hope to educate the Congress to the importance of libraries in a democracy? Is OERI the most appropriate home for Library Programs? Do we need the Office raised to the stature of programs headed by an Assistant Secretary who reports directly to the Secretary of Education?

A Political Strategy for the 1990s

But the political power necessary to stimulate national attention not only reverberates in Washington, it also arrives there from local action. The federal agenda being built from statewide grassroots planning for the upcoming second White House Conference on Libraries and Information Services (WHCLIS II) is a current example. Other bright spots have appeared in the states as they have developed their own strategies for the 1990s. California, where a $75 million bond issue for construction and renovation passed, has demonstrated resounding success when libraries take funding directly to the people.

That success came slowly, by courting legislators, forging coalitions, and creating a Political Action Committee (PAC). It was led in large measure by the Government Relations Committee of the California Library Association, which later separated from the parent organization to form Californians for Community Libraries, the PAC that raised the money to support the campaign. Californians for Community Libraries hired a campaign director, conducted a telephone campaign, and attracted endorsements from organizations like the American Association of University Women, the California Taxpayers Association, League of California Cities, and California State PTA.

Supporters did not magically appear at the mention of libraries' special needs. There was real opposition in the Assembly, where a two-thirds vote was needed to get a statewide proposition on the ballot. Close to election time, polls showed that only 55%-56% of the electorate were reported in favor of passage, a slim and uncertain margin.

Proponents of the bond issue knew the political campaign was a high-risk, high-reward effort. Although they might need only a simple majority to pass, they were fully aware that, if the measure failed, it would be difficult to get further funding. Political decision-makers could base their reluctance on a claim that the voters didn't care about libraries. But these are high-risk, high-reward times. Californians won their battle, and residents of other states might be well advised to follow their lead.

The Feds in the Fiscal Life of the Library

As we review the first years of *The Bottom Line*, we are convinced that the most crucial issue libraries face as we enter this new decade amalgamates questions surrounding economy, positioning, and political action. It is not a new issue. For over 30 years the profession has debated the role of the federal government in the life of the library. We first alluded to it in an editorial in *The Bottom Line*'s second year. This latest resurgence of interest occurred when a redefinition of federal spending was unveiled, as the Library Services and Construction Act moved toward its deadline for reauthorization. Money for LSCA and the Higher Education Act was out and the Library Improvement Act, crafted behind closed doors by administration officials, was in. The tactic didn't work. Congress kept LSCA and HEA on the books as the major sources of federal funding for libraries, and Senator Harkins of Iowa worked hard to see that library construction money did not disappear from the legislation. Once again the importance of political action was obvious as ALA's Washington Office, NCLIS, and the Chief Officers of State Library Agencies (COSLA) worked together to stem cuts.

A recent Public Library Association (PLA) effort produced a paper that could move us toward the redefinition we seek—one that would secure a more sound fiscal future for libraries. Although politically naive in some of the solutions, PLA's work does offer a position which, with widespread exposure and discussion in the profession, might lead to compromises and modifications that could transform it into a palatable action plan for the future. In the past, voices and papers have come from single sources or represented splinter groups which failed to do the tiresome work of action planning, beginning with consensus building. That work remains before PLA.

Our profession has shown an ambivalence toward establishing a political infrastructure of significant magnitude to ensure political action. Why are there no task forces in our major professional associations working on fiscal action plans, including a comprehensive definition of nonredundant roles for federal, state, and local government in library support? Shouldn't the following issues have a place on the national agenda? The future of library funding in a zero-sum economy, better positioning of library programs in the federal hierarchy, and redefining federal government's role in the life of the library. Isn't WHCLIS II the obvious place to take steps that would weld local and national professional and constituent views into the political coalition necessary for libraries to survive—and thrive—in the chill of today's financial climate?

The 1990's promises to be a decade of exciting challenge, and *The Bottom Line* will continue in its mission to offer librarians practical advice and provide a forum for discussion of the practical and theoretical fiscal issues that affect the success, and even the survival, of our profession.

Betty J. Turock
Editor
"The Bottom Line"

THE
ECONOMIC
ENVIRONMENT

HARD HEADS, SOFT HEARTS

As part of the social conciousness that flourished during the Sixties, librarians reached out to client groups previously unserved and devised innovative approaches to better meet the information needs of the underserved.

During the Eighties, with the drive to bring greater fiscal accountability to public institutions, these nontraditional library programs were among the first to get the ax. While the reasons for their early demise run the gamut, we suspect that a primary cause is our profession's failure to prove the case for their continued support.

We are now caught between our mandate to serve our constituencies and our need to survive in an era of tight money. At least we are not alone. In our nation's capital, the book that has caused the greatest stir over the past six months is *Hard Heads, Soft Hearts* by economist Alan S. Blinder (Addison-Wesley). Blinder critiques the actions of Congress, but his observations could equally be applied to librarians.

He defines the problem as vacillation between two opposing points of view. Traditional liberal policies are "soft-headed and soft-hearted." They result in simply throwing good money at social programs. No one then thinks to ask how effectively they actually work. Traditional conservative policies, on the other hand, are "hard-headed and hard-hearted." They are long on economic rationalization and short on compassion.

Blinder proposes a new approach that is hard-headed and soft-hearted—policies that are neither liberal nor conservative. This change of direction would require those who establish public policy to focus less on powerful special interests and more on the constitutional injunction to "promote the general welfare." He warns that those who do not make the shift will continue to be part of our economic problems, not part of their solution.

Specifically, he is concerned with two types of policy-makers: those who focus only on their own locale, who fail to formulate long-term, broad-based strategies that would contribute to the economic well-being of the nation as a whole, and those who bend to the wishes of in-office political groups without learning the needs of their diverse constituencies.

The hard-headed, soft-hearted policies are based on two principles: efficiency and equity. Efficiency is the key to delivering more services to constituencies when resources are scarce—in other words, to increasing our productivity. At the same time, an efficiency-oriented marketplace is unfair to those who are not equally equipped to play the economic game. Equity principles are necessary, therefore, to add fairness into the equation.

The application of Blinder's reasoning to libraries would give us a modus vivendi for the 1990s.

The principles of efficiency and equity can lead us to accountability from a number of perspectives. Fiscal accountability means that we consider whether our services are economically sound. Administrative accountability focuses on compliance with operational requirements. Performance accountability is concerned with the consequences of funding—the effects of programs on the audiences for which they were intended.

But accountability mechanisms are not ends in themselves. Before we can undertake a more stringent accountability approach, we need information to fairly assess service impact. Is library funding directed at the most appropriate recipients? Are services effectively meeting constituents' needs? Are there incentives in place that reward good performances and seek to change those that are ineffective?

All too frequently, accountability assessments have led libraries to the conclusion that innovative library programs cost too much and serve too few. But those conclusions merely underline one of the major issues in evaluation: What are the appropriate measures?

Librarians have too often fixated first on input measurement, then on output measurement without regard to whether the numbers present the most accurate picture of the programs in question. Neither input nor output measurements are necessarily related to dollars and cents, yet productivity and accountability must be tied closely to cost.

A hard-headed, soft-hearted approach could ensure that we develop effective new means and measure to fairly evaluate our non-traditional as well as traditional services. It could stop us from rushing to quantify impact before we understand all of the factors at work in a new program of service. That means that we assess the intended—as well as the unintended—consequences.

If libraries are to be truly accountable librarians must learn to evaluate programs in such a way that we express the true picture of the service under scrutiny. Qualitative evaluation for innovative services is essential *before* we turn to quantification. Only with the understanding that qualitiative measures provide can we calculate costs and measure impact based on valid standards and appropriate criteria. Those of us who don't combine hard heads with soft hearts may very well find the Nineties just more of the same—or even less.

ON THEIR TERMS
Preparing Libraries for a Competitive Environment

W. David Penniman

All libraries, whether in the public or private sector, operate in a competitive arena. They compete with other organizations for finite and scarce resources in a zero-sum game. Unfortunately, there are winners and losers. The losers are not necessarily the organizations that have the least to offer; they are often the organizations least prepared to express their value and contribution in terms understood by their funders.

In business, government, and educational institutions, the universal terms that make a difference to decision makers are costs and benefits. Lord Kelvin said that "...when you can measure what you are speaking about, and express it in numbers, you know something about it; but when you cannot express it in numbers, your knowledge is of a meagre and unsatisfactory kind..."[1] The modern executive says, on a similar note, "show me the numbers."

Librarians often come to this arena with an orientation and mindset that leaves them ill-prepared for the contest. They have been self-selected and educationally reinforced to emphasize service. And this service emphasis has too often been equated with the inappropriateness of measuring the monetary value of a service.

With the current tight economy in the United States and elsewhere, librarians are beginning to look at strategies for joining forces to be heard in the arenas of power (for example, see Betty Turock's editorial "Libraries and the Zero Sum Society" in the charter issue of *The Bottom Line*).[2] But librarians are new to this arena and must learn the tools of the trade if they are to compete effectively. This requires understanding the techniques of business strategy development and presentation oriented toward a highly quantitative environment.

Incompatible Philosophies

Information service providers operate under one of two basically incompatible philosophies regarding the value of their services. The philosophy most common among traditional library leaders is: *information organizations are institutions providing services of immeasurable value.* The philosophy *required* in the information sector of business is: *information services/products have a measurable value.*

In the immeasurable-value approach, the organization is justified by qualitative assertions. The resources required are quantified, output measures are de-emphasized, and productivity is not (and cannot be) measured. The link between mission and output is subjective. Budgets grow or shrink incrementally and accountability focuses on the resources used. Using the measurable-value approach, the organization is justified by quantitative assertions. Resources and output are quantified and productivity is measured. The link between mission and output is objective. Budgets are constructed programmatically and accountability focuses on input and output measures.

The real test of which philosophy is prevalent in an information organization can be found in considering the following questions:

- Are the information services considered part of the mainstream of the organization or are they viewed as part of the quality of worklife environment?
- Are the information facilities (i.e., libraries) viewed as information delivery mechanisms or as warehouses of knowledge waiting to be accessed?
- Are the *managers* of these facilities working closely with key decision makers or hoping not to be too directly visible in such power arenas?
- Are the information facilities openly competing for resources from the same pool as the computing centers, management information systems, and other related information providers in their institutions or trying to stay out of that fray?

The implications of these questions are obvious. Once information service value is accepted as measurable, the positioning of the services, the infrastructure of the service organizations, and the skills needed for its leaders all become quite different from what is considered traditional in the library profession.

Given the significant change in orientation that is required, how does a leader begin the process of transforming an organization from one philosophy to the other — from immeasurable to measurable?

Quantifying & Measuring

The best approach to initiate the change process is to create a business plan,* the very process of which results in the *transformation* of an information service organization into a more business-oriented entity. (See box on pages 7 and 8 for definitions of asterisked words.)

To start, it is essential to understand the mission* of the organization. The mission statement* defines the present function, scope, and purpose of the organization in terms

understood by its members and those it serves. Creating the mission statement helps to develop a mutual understanding among the managers of the products/services* provided by the information organization and begins the process of change. Next, it is necessary to determine the positioning* of the organization with regard to populations served and those organizations providing competitive services.* This means that a thorough understanding of all products/ services offered by the organization

---

Information service providers operate under one of two basically incompatible philosophies regarding the value of their services. The philosophy most common among traditional library leaders is: **information organizations are institutions providing services of immeasurable value.** *The philosophy* **required in the information sector of business is:** **information services/ products have a measurable value.**

---

must be developed. These products/ services must then be compared to those organizations competing in the same arena in terms of comprehensiveness, cost, speed, quality, and complexity. For example, a private information broker might compete with the online search services of a library. Both must be compared for cost, speed, and end-user satisfaction.

Forcing an organization to compare *all* of its products and services to other competitive products/serv-

ices in this manner provides several desirable results:

- A comprehensive list of *all* products/services is developed.
- The costs* of each product/service are computed and compared to other (sometimes commercially available) competitors.
- Attributes considered important in determining distinguishing characteristics are quantified.
- True costs of products/services are realized by the staff providing these services and they no longer think of them as free or sunk-cost* items.
- Incremental cost* and variable cost* concepts can be introduced to understand the influence of economies of scale.*

In addition to understanding the products/services, it is also important to understand the user segments* served, the size of each segment, the needs of each segment, the sources of funding to support products/services for each segment, and the dynamics of these segments. In many cases, the segments served are not connected directly to the funding sources for libraries. This is a case where the buyers* are not the same as the customers.* Then, it is important to segment and understand *both* populations and any indirect linkages between the two.

Once the mission, products/services currently offered, and market or user segments served have been analyzed, it is time to explore the driving force* of the organization.[3] Fundamentally, the driving force of an organization is the central or unifying concept to guide strategy*-setting at the highest organizational

**TABLE 1
POTENTIAL DRIVING FORCES**

Category	Strategic Area
Products/Markets	Products/Services Offered Market Needs
Capabilities	Technology Production Capability Method of Sale Method of Distribution Natural Resources
Results	Size/Growth Return/Profit

level and at the subcomponent level. The driving force is derived from one of the nine strategic areas in three categories shown in Table 1.

Librarians often argue that their institutions exist because of the benefit they provide, but find it difficult to accept any measure of this in terms that might be quantified — especially in terms of return* or profit.* Yet, the social cost of an illiterate child growing up to become an illiterate adult *can* be quantified. The savings or cost avoidance* resulting from an investment in a community literacy program offered by a local library *can be measured in monetary terms* if the program actually teaches people to read. Consequently, it is not unrealistic to accept return or profit as the driving force for libraries. If this is the driving force, then a library manager will introduce new products/services or offer services to new markets* in order to gain the desired benefit. If bound to its current products/services or unable to offer services to new user groups (e.g., the business community for a public library), then return is not the library's driving force. In most cases, library managers accept their current products/services as the major philosophical constraint (and thus the driving force) of their institution. In some cases, they change their facilities and collections to respond to changing market needs (e.g., creating a computer room, or building a videotape collection). When this is the overwhelming focus of the library leadership, then market needs is the driving force.

The importance of the driving force concept is the idea of focus. An organization cannot develop a coherent set of strategies unless it has focus, and the concept of driving force provides this coherence. The strategy at the top of an organization must be compatible with the strategies of each subunit. The overall strategy is the framework which guides the choices that determine the nature and direction of an organization.

In other words, once the library knows its mission and has analyzed its current competitive posture, it can begin to chart a course for effectively expressing its goals* and objectives* in terms that can be understood by numbers-oriented decision makers. These concepts provide the framework for major organizational change in culture and leadership philosophy.

Librarians often argue that their institutions exist because of the benefit they provide, but find it difficult to accept any measure of this in terms that might be quantified — especially in terms of return or profit. Yet, the social cost of an illiterate child growing up to become an illiterate adult can be quantified. The savings or cost avoidance resulting from an investment in a community literacy program offered by a local library can be measured in monetary terms.

Many librarians would argue they already have a strategic planning process. But too often this is a long-range plan* generated by incremental projections of short-range or annual plans or budgets.

A true strategic approach begins with fundamental questions of organizational purpose and then builds on the driving-force concept. This approach recognizes the need for strategies developing from the top down and tactics from the bottom up. When this approach is accepted, it is then possible to talk about developing an annual business plan* for the organization that involves a coherent set of strategies.

Business Planning

The numerous components of a business plan have already been discussed in terms of the current state of affairs and the current and desired driving force. The following is a description of the various components of the business planning process, adapted from Leza and Placencia[4] (see also Figure 1).

An *organizational analysis* includes understanding the history, purpose, and key players within your organization. Significant events, current structure and staffing, historical and current trends in funding and service levels, current/new service plans, and current and new user groups to be served must also be studied. Take into account your organization's strengths and weakness. Are any technologies used or planned? Compare the organization's costs with similar institutions. Understand what resources are required to provide services.

A *competitive analysis* of other sources for similar services is essential. What are the advantages of your institution's and your competitor's? Rate competitors strong/average/weak.

Using a *market analysis*, take into account the geographic scope of users served and the demographics

FIGURE 1
COMPONENTS IN BUSINESS
PLANNING PROCESS

Organizational Analysis		
Competitive Analysis	Institution-wide Analysis	Market Analysis
	Strategy Setting	
	Management Analysis	
	Financial Analysis	
	Monitor Results	
	Generate Annual Report	

CONCEPTS AND MEASURES COMMON
TO THE BUSINESS WORLD

Annual Report A statement covering a 12-month period and providing details on accomplishments achieved and resources consumed. The backbone of this report is the financial statement showing income and expenses in profit and loss statement form. Further financial details can be presented as a balance sheet comparing assets and liabilities. In addition, performance measures are presented for each product/service and compared to previous reporting periods.

Assets Everything owned or due to an organization.

Assets, fixed Those things acquired for long-term use that are not quickly turned to cash.

Business plan A document created (or updated) annually presenting the financial and products/services objectives of an organization and the resource requirements to achieve those objectives.

Business planning Process involving a wide range of planning documents. Starting at the top there is strategic planning that is concerned with the broadest of conceptual planning and often involves very little quantification except to set overall goals or objectives for an organization. This level involves time frames of 10 or more years. Long range plans are often extrapolations of annual plans and extend from five to 10 years. Business plans usually cover one to three years and are quite specific in terms of actions to be taken, expenses incurred, and expected outcomes.

Buyers The individuals or groups who provide funds in exchange for products/services. *See also* Customers.

Competitive Services and/or Products Those alternative services that customers choose in lieu of the ones you would like them to. In the broadest sense, those things that consume resources you would prefer to have invested in your products/services.

Cost avoidance Costs which are not incurred due to specific actions taken, e.g., a change in the way a process is done or a change in product/service configuration.

Costs Outlay incurred including depreciation and amortization.

Costs, fixed Costs which do not change over the near term as the result of a small variation in such things as production rate or machine time.

Cost, incremental The net change in cost resulting from a change in production rate. Sometimes also referred to as marginal cost.

Costs, sunk Costs already incurred which will not be affected by subsequent actions.

Costs, variable Operating costs which when traced vary in a linear fashion with fluctuations in production rate for the same time period.

Customers Individuals or groups who use the product/service offered. They may or may not be the same as the buyers.

Driving Force The central or unifying concept that guides strategy setting.

Economies of scale Reduction in per unit costs as the result of increased level of consumption of product/service. Usually due to fixed cost being spread across a greater number of units and variable cost being a smaller proportion of total cost than fixed cost.

Goals The desired long-term accomplishments hoped for by an organization. Often not entirely achievable, but can be pursued continually with beneficial results.

Inventory The materials and products owned by the organization prior to consumption by customers. There are three basic types of inventory: raw material, work in progress, and finished goods. (With a little imagination the materials needed to create information products can be viewed in this sense.)

Liabilities All claims against an organization including salaries payable, unused vacation, taxes payable. Long-term liabilities include mortgages and bank loans.

Term	Definition	Term	Definition
Long-range plan	An extension of the annual plan to indicate long-term expectations (i.e, 5–10 years).		maintenance. These may be defined individually or in logical groupings.
Market or market segments	A group of customers who share a set of common characteristics that distinguish them from other customers. (May also be applied to the buyers or funders of services.)	Profit	The difference in income from buyers and the expenses involved in producing and providing products/services. The income can include interest and other nonoperating sources and expenses can include taxes and other nonservice related costs.
Mission	The chief function or responsibility of an institution. It should be clear, unambiguous and understood by all who contribute their time and resources to the organization.	Return on investment (ROI)	The ratio of profit (or cost avoidance) to investment required for that return. Can be measured as return on annual expenditure, or assets, or equity in the case of stockholder organizations.
Mission statement	A formal written representation of the chief function or responsibility of the information service. Serves as a bridge between the information service organization and the institution in which it resides.	Segmentation	The process by which user populations or markets are divided into homogeneous subsets along one or more dimensions to aid in identifying needs and behavior patterns.
Objectives	Specific and measurable accomplishments hoped to be achieved in a finite, measured period of time.	Segmentation, user	Division of the user population into homogeneous groups by factors such as geography, demographics, psychographics, and product/service preference.
Positioning	Locating an organization or product/service on a "map" (usually two-dimensional) with respect to similar competing organizations or products/services. Dimensions for such maps include cost, quality, comprehensiveness, timeliness, share of market, and market growth.	Strategy	A collection of decisions in areas of products/services, markets, resources, required and organizational structures.
Products/ Services	Anything offered to the markets served by the institution including ongoing support or	Value	The worth of a good or service to an individual or organization expressed in quantitative terms, usually money. Value depends on two elements: desirability and scarcity.

of the users. How can they be segmented (by life style, economics, etc.)? What distribution channels are used? What promotional strategies are employed? Also analyze the volume of services delivered, the rate of growth of services, and the share of market served by you versus your competitors.

Strategy setting for specific long-term objectives is also important. This includes performance indicators to measure objective achievement. What are the assumptions? Which strengths can be exploited? Are there weaknesses to overcome? Risks? Set specific strategies to be used involving technology, users, services, operations, finances, and back-up alternatives.

A *management analysis* identifies key functions and personnel responsible for each area (e.g., public relations, service promotion, etc.)

The *financial analysis* should include a profit-and-loss statement, a balance sheet, and a break-even analysis. The profit-and-loss statement is a detailed description of revenue (from grants, taxes, sale of services) and operating expenses. The balance sheet lists all assets and liabilities. A break-even analysis will show fixed and variable costs versus revenues for various levels of service.

Monitoring results is also crucial. Compare results to commitments made in the business plan and adjust accordingly. Report results in an annual report comparing objectives to achievements.

This brief outline of the steps involved in business planning indicates the nature and extent of analysis necessary to characterize libraries in the terms that business-oriented decision makers understand. The effort required is significant — the "return on investment" of that effort is also significant. ▬

References

1. William Thomas Kelvin, *Popular Lectures and Addresses* (New York: Macmillan), pp. 1891–94.
2. Betty J. Turock, "Libraries and the Zero Sum Society," *The Bottom Line*, Charter Issue, 1986, p. 3.
3. Benjamin B. Trego and John W. Zimmerman, *Top Management Strategy - What It is and How to Make it Work* (New York: Simon and Shuster, 1980).
4. Richard L. Leza and Jose F. Placencia, *Develop Your Business Plan* (Sunnyvale, Calif.: Oasis Press, 1982).

REVENUE PLANNING
A Vital Tool for Public Libraries

Blue Wooldridge

"The politics and processes of local government face substantial change because of Federal action on taxes and the budget deficit as well as court and Congressional challenges to local authority, according to officials at every level of government around the country.

Hundreds of counties, small cities and towns as well as some old large cities are increasing taxes and reducing services to cope with the loss of money from the $4 billion-a-year program of general revenue sharing that Congress ended to help reduce the Federal deficit."[1]

When tough financial times hit the public library, it may seem as though options that allow continued quality library services have disappeared. However, *Improving Productivity in State and Local Government*, a report of the Committee for Economic Development assures us that in times of scarcity, a public manager has available at least three possible strategies:

- Cut services. This requires the ability to identify priorities, to rank them, and to make reductions in a rational manner.
- Increase organizational productivity. This challenge, perhaps new to many public libraries, is extremely viable in a time of retrenchment.
- Expanding the use of existing financial resources or identifying new resources to supplement existing ones.[2]

While an understanding of, and the ability to apply, all three strategies are of vital importance, this article focuses on the third strategy—the enhancement of a library's revenue base through a systematic approach to revenue planning.

The recognition of the need for a systematic approach to revenue planning is not new. For some time, students of local government finance have decried the predominant procedure for revenue planning:

> For far too long, revenue planning at the municipal level has been oriented towards hindsight, and the "property tax principle." The traditional method has consisted of first, using last year's receipts plus a conservative increase as the basis for estimating non-property tax revenue for the up-coming fiscal year. Then, second, whatever the difference between the estimated non-property tax yield and expenditure budget becomes the amount to be raised by the property tax.[3]

The dysfunctions of this approach have long been recognized. In 1915 Milton Loomis pointed out:

> Up to the present time, cities have been depending largely upon increasing returns from the general property tax, either by raising the rates or, if that was not legally possible, by raising the basis of assessment to some point nearer the true valuation. Other sources of revenues are only occasionally considered as available to meet the requirements for money.[4]

Knowing the steps involved in revenue planning is important to public library managers.[5] If we are to be guided by the research identified by Prentice[6] we can expect that the local resources allocated to libraries are directly related to the per capita expenditures for other municipal services. Thus, advocates of better support for library services are well advised to insure that their local government is maximizing its total revenue potential. It also would appear that all public library managers have some control over their resources. Careful revenue planning would increase the probability that the library is realizing its revenue potential. Finally, if library trustees and other community leaders were made aware of specific sources of revenues that might benefit the public library, they could do a much better job of advocating increased financial support for library services.

There are four major steps in revenue planning:
- Review the existing revenue program
- Analyze all available revenue sources
- Propose criteria for selecting revenue sources
- Recommend a revenue program

Review the Existing Revenue Program

The first step in reviewing the existing revenue program is to *list and describe each existing revenue source* currently used by the library (or for the local government if the revenue plan is being conducted at that level). Such a task requires almost unlimited resources in both time and skills. With limited resources and numerous sources, a public manager might decide to aggregate some revenues, but this can reduce the plan's accuracy and utility. Revenues should be categorized into groups, either those required by your local or state government or perhaps the categories used by the U.S. Bureau of the Census.

1. For each revenue source, list the base, the rate, the amount anticipated for the period in question (for the property tax this would be the levy), the amount actually collected, the delinquency rate (or "revenue shortfall"), and the amount collected per capita. Repeat this exercise for a period of perhaps 5 to 10 years, identifying the year-to-year changes. Identifying the so-called "revenue shortfall" might lead to the revealing conclusion that the local system does not need new revenues, but just has to do a better job of collecting existing ones! Determine the percentage composition of the existing revenue program—that is,

the relative importance of each revenue source.

2. Repeat this process while "cleaning" the revenues of any change in productivity brought about by discretionary policy changes. Select the earliest year under consideration, and examine each revenue for every subsequent year; identifying any policy actions that would have affected the yield of any of the revenues (for example, a decision to increase the duplicating charge from 10 cents per copy to 25, or the reserve fee from 50 cents to 75). Factor out the effects of these discretionary changes on the yield of the revenue. These "cleaned" revenue data will let you detect the natural growth of each component of the existing revenue base.

3. Repeat #1 using constant monetary units to factor out the effects of inflation. While carrying out a similar exercise in the State of Connecticut, it was found that many local governments had fewer monetary resources in constant purchasing power in 1982 than in 1978!

4. Review the local revenue program for each of the years, making comparisons between the current list of revenues used and that of previous years, examining the principal changes in the relationships of one revenue source to another, and evaluating trends. The effects of local economic indicators on yields from various sources should be studied:
- Examine very closely any change in the relative importance of the existing revenue sources.
- Make sure you understand and are satisfied with the cause of any changes.
- Make sure that your library is utilizing each revenue source to its fullest extent.

Obtain similar data from other jurisdictions both in and outside the region/state to compare the characteristics and trends of your existing revenue program with those of other communities. What can be more exciting than finding a tax, fine, or other revenue source that other comparable libraries are using to better advantage. Such material can be obtained from professional associations, state auditors of public accounts, departments of community affairs, municipal leagues, or institutes of local government at state universities.

Analyze All Available Revenue Sources

After reviewing the existing revenue program, the next step is to carry out an extensive survey of all existing and available sources of revenue; even sources not currently used should be analyzed. The study might uncover reasons why a new source should be incorporated into your library's revenue base or might simply reinforce previous decisions to omit it. There are a wide variety of revenue sources available to local governments and other institutions providing services at the local level, but there is also a tremendous variation in the use of these revenue sources by local governments.[7] For ease of convenience, this article divides revenue sources into three types: taxes, charges, and miscellaneous revenues.

Taxes While taxes are taken for granted as the major source of public library funds, the types of taxes levied are seldom analyzed to determine whether possible revenue options are being overlooked. Of the wide range of nonproperty taxes currently utilized by local governments, there are three basic types of income taxes. The *broad-based individual income tax*, used by local governments in more than 4000 municipalities in 11 states, attempts to tax most of an individual's income including that from rents, dividends, and interest, in addition to income gained from salaries, wages, and profits. At least 16 of the nation's largest cities levy a *corporation income tax*, and several others utilize the *payroll tax*, a tax levied on the wages and salaries that appear on local payrolls.

The types of general and selected sales taxes used by local governments are even more extensive. More than 5,000 local governments in 26 states make some use of the general sales tax. Selected sales taxes used by local governments include the *admissions tax, alcoholic beverage tax, hotel-motel occupancy tax, insurance premiums tax, motor vehicle fuels taxes,* taxes on *parimutuel and other gambling events.* There are also such stand-bys as the tax on *tobacco products, business and occupation tax, excise tax on utility consumption*, and the *service tax*, a sales tax levied on services to individuals or to businesses. Other types of selected sales taxes used by local governments include the *financial institutions tax* (this "bank tax" allows local governments to impose a tax on local bank stock); the *motor vehicle tax,* and a *recordation tax*, which is an excise tax on the recording of property transfer.

A public librarian would be wise to examine the revenue base of his or her community to determine if appropriate use is being made of the variety of those taxes available to the library.

Charges and Miscellaneous Revenues Local governments have always made use of nontax revenues, but with the advent of the Tax-Expenditures Limitations (TELS), such as Proposition 13 in California and Proposition 2 1/2 in Massachusetts during the 1970s and early '80s, the importance of the nontax portion of the local revenue base reached new significance.[8] User charges made up more than 21 percent of all locally raised general fund revenue in 1980. Charges are different from taxes since they involve a direct exchange—a service is performed for which a fee is paid. In addition to generating revenues, user charges also ration output by limiting the use of public services to those willing (*and able*) to pay for them—they allocate the financial burden of paying for services to those individuals who enjoy the benefits. These individuals bear the burden in close relationship to the amount of services consumed. Charges provide the additional service of signaling how much service is wanted; that is, charges indicate which users value additional units of service as much as or more than the per unit price being charged.

The work of Professor Larry White of New York University advocating a greater use of charges for library service has generated much concern and controversy within the public library community. I would urge you to carefully assess the full array of library services to determine for which users charges/fees could be assessed without adversely affecting the library's clientele.

The types of **miscellaneous revenues** available to local public institutions are limited only by the imagination of public officials. This revenue category, including special assessments, sale of property, interest earnings, and "other," made up approximately 10 percent of local "own source" revenues by 1980.[9] The sale of disposable property by libraries can be an important "one-time" source of revenue. High interest rates of the late 1970s, early 1980s, combined with a cutback in federal funds and limitations on other revenue sources, led many local government institutions to recognize the value of the investment of "temporary idle" funds. Careful cash management, including cash budgeting, prompt collection of revenues, delayed disbursement, and investment with a view to maximize yield, proved that money can "make"

If library trustees and other community leaders were made aware of specific sources of revenues that might benefit the public library, they could do a much better job of advocating increased financial support for library services.

---

money. All public librarians should carefully assess their cash management practices to determine what improvements can be made to enhance this revenue source.

The "other" category of miscellaneous revenues covers a multitude of possible financial resources. The "entrepreneurial" public manager can find many ways to raise funds to serve public purposes. For instance, in Mt. Lebanon, Pennsylvania, pro shops are operated by the town's recreational facilities, selling products at prices competitive with private sporting goods stores and offering sales, selling advertisements, and accepting credit cards; forestry by-products also are sold by Mt. Lebanon, both for firewood and mulch.[10] Other communities sell advertising space on public buildings, and other facilities and in annual reports and other public documents; sponsor benefit functions, such as dinners honoring outstanding local citizens, ear marking the proceeds to support local public services, such as the library; rent out surplus space for commercial offices; and "contract in," that is, sell an inhouse service such as printing or data-processing to outside users. In Switzerland, local governments run government-owned car washes.[11] Some local governments in other countries operate car rental agencies and government-owned restaurants, bars, and hotels. Of course, not all of these ideas can be adopted by every local library. Legal authority, political pressures, and other considerations may preclude their use. Public librarians must be aware, however, of the numerous nontraditional sources of revenue that can be considered.

Propose Criteria for Selecting Revenue Sources

Developing criteria for evaluating the potential revenue sources generated above is the third step in a systematic approach to revenue planning. Since there may be many reasons why a local public library would not want to avail itself of a specific potential revenue source, a systematic assessment using a set of carefully developed criteria will bring to the surface the relative advantages and disadvantages of each potential source.

Almost every writer in the field of public finance has something to say about the criteria that a revenue system should meet. Pechman feels that taxation has two basic goals: to distribute the cost of government fairly by income class and among people in approximately the same economic circumstances, and to promote economic growth.[12] Rostvold discusses what he calls "maxims of a socially acceptable revenue system":

● The revenue system should be compatible with the social value criteria which governs the general social process.
● The revenue system should be fiscally adequate, broadly based, stable in its yield, and balanced in its final incidence.

- The revenue system should be administratively simple, economic to administer, with clearly defined base and rate structures.
- Revenues should have minimum adverse effects on economic productivity, resource allocation, and the levels of employment, income, and output.[13]

Eckstein emphasizes the need for a tax system to display sound administrative qualities as well as fairness. Two other desirable administrative characteristics are enforceability (a good revenue system does not impose taxes which are impossible to enforce) and, again, acceptability.[14]

Schultz and Harriss provide one of the most comprehensive of all listings of characteristics of a sound tax system. While including most of the criteria offered above, they mention a very important additional factor—constitutional compatibility. As they put it so clearly, "No matter how desirable from an economic, social, or administrative viewpoint, a tax may not be levied if it is held to contravene constitutional limitations."[15] In summary, this author suggests that the following 11 criteria be used in assessing proposed revenue sources: legality, administrative feasibility, social and political acceptability, productivity, horizontal and vertical equity, elasticity, stability, certainty, neutrality; compatibility to community goals and objectives, and vertical and horizontal overlapping.

Regardless of the strength of its economic, social, or administrative attributes, a revenue source cannot be levied if it contravenes **legal** limitations. Public librarians working at the local level will have to be cognizant of federal, state, and local constitutional and statutory limitations, both as to the type of revenue source that can be used and the degree to which it can be used. (For example, many states limit the charge a local government can place on a good or service to the actual cost of providing that good or service.) In addition, an effective revenue system must display sound **administrative** qualities. A "good"—administratively feasible—revenue source is economic to administer (that is, collection costs are a relatively small percentage of the revenue produced and its compliance costs are low). A "good" revenue system is administratively simple, with a clearly defined base and rate schedule. Furthermore, the revenue is enforceable.

The public must consider the revenue system **acceptable** and consistent with their notion of fair play. It cannot be considered too onerous as compared to the public's perception of what they get for their revenue dollar.

Since revenues produce at different rates, their **productivity** depends on the base, the effective rate, and the related economic effects of the revenue and its administrative costs. Even at moderate rates, a revenue source with a large base can potentially produce large sums of money. By comparison, the yield of a revenue with a narrow base is slight. All exemptions, no matter how otherwise laudable, that narrow the base reduce the productivity of a revenue source.

What is meant by an **equitable** revenue system is not a question of technical economics but of personal philosophy. Vertical equity refers to a "fair" distribution of the revenue burden on people of different income. What is "fair" generally follows one of two major schools of thought. The benefit principle calls for a distribution of revenue burden in accordance with the benefits received from the expenditures which the revenue funds (obviously, user charges, if set at full cost, follow this principle). The other standard of "fairness" is "ability-to-pay." Many people take it for granted that a "fair" revenue system calls on the richer members of the community to pay more than the poor.

Revenue **elasticity** is a term used to describe the responsiveness of a revenue to changing economic conditions. A revenue can be either elastic, inelastic, or uni-elastic. In a growth economy, the yield of a revenue that has relatively high elasticity increases faster than community income. However, if community income declines, the yield from highly elastic revenues decreases proportionately.

Stability of revenue payments in the face of exogenous economic changes is considered a very desirable element in state or local government revenue systems. At these levels of government, financial security depends upon maintaining a close balance of receipts and expenditures. Stability of expected revenues, or their steady growth, not only alleviates worries about fiscal insolvency, it simplifies planning and reduces the administrative costs of making expenditure commitments.

As important as stability is to the public institution, **certainty** is to the revenue paying citizen. Citizens should know (or be able to find out) what their revenue burden is, when it is due, and be able to make a reasonably dependable estimate of what is owed as it is earned. Revenue certainty eases administrative problems and, in many cases, it increases revenue.

Otto Eckstein considers **neutrality** one of the virtues of a good revenue system. By this he means that private production and consumption decisions should not be affected by the burden of the revenue. He and other fiscal scholars, while endorsing fiscal neutrality, are not questioning whether or not the burden of revenues does modify the economic structure. There is general agreement with the Shultz and Harriss statement: "Broadly speaking, every tax which touches business relationships is 'regulatory.'"[16] The debate lies in whether or not this modification of the economic structure should be deliberate. The fact that the burden of most revenue sources influences the behavior of individuals and businesses—that it is not neutral—makes it even more important that local public librarians consider the next criterion.

Each revenue source must be considered in light of the **compatibility** of its consequences with the overall goals of the community. If one goal is to increase the housing opportunities for low-income individuals, then a heavy reliance on the residential property tax or development fees might not make a lot of sense. Similarly, high user charges for all library services might be incompatible with a community goal to maximize the accessibility of these services to all citizens, regardless of income status.

Horizontal overlapping occurs when governments at the same level impose similar taxes: at the local level, schools, special districts, and the general government all tax the same property tax revenue base. In some localities, the federal, state, and local governments practice **vertical overlapping,** when they all tax personal income.

Recommend a Revenue Program

The public librarian who also makes—or suggests—financial policy must examine each possible new source of revenue and evaluate it against the proposed criteria (weighed in light of community values) in order to develop a sound revenue program. The allocation of money at the local level is the mainstay of public library income. With no change expected in that base in the near future because of our tight economic situation, public librarians can continue serving their clients adequately only by applying the systematic approach to revenue planning outlined here. Combined with improved productivity and better budgeting, it can assist public librarians in responding to the needs of their communities during these times of fiscal stress, and perhaps help to improve the fiscal outlook.

REFERENCES

1. John Herbers, "Local Government in U.S. is Reshaped by Federal Moves", *The New York Times*, November 30, 1986, p.1.
2. Committee for Economic Development, *Improving Productivity in State and Local Government* (New York: CED, 1976) p. 11.
3. Municipal Finance Officers Association, *Special Bulletin-Revenue Planning* (Chicago: MFOA, 1972).
4. Milton Loomis, *Annals American Academy of Political & Social Science*, vol. 60–62 (Philadelphia: July-November, 1915).
5. Blue Wooldridge, "The Public Administrator's Perspective," in *Financial Choices for Public Libraries*, Proceedings of the Public Library Association Program. American Library Association Annual Conference, New York, 1980.
6. Ann E. Prentice, *Public Library Finance* (Chicago: American Library Association, 1977), p. 35.
7. Catherine L. Spain and Blue Wooldridge, "The Role of Non-Property Taxes and Charges" in *State and Local Finances in the 1980's*, Norman Walzer and David Chicoine, eds. (Cambridge, Mass.: Oelgeschlager, Guinn and Hain Publishers, 1981).
8. Ibid., 116-117.
9. Ibid.
10. H. Edward Wesemann, "Innovative Revenue Sources, the Entrepreneurial Municipality," *The Pennsylvanian* (Harrisburg, Pa.: The Pennsylvania Municipal League, January 1980).
11. Blue Wooldridge, "Exemplary Practices in Local Financial Management: An International Perspective," *Public Administration Review* (Washington, D.C.: American Society for Public Administration, March/April 1984), p. 155. This article contains other examples of revenue sources used by local governments in other countries.
12. Joseph Pechman, *Federal Tax Policy* (New York: W.W. North and Company, 1971), p. 5.
13. Gerhard Rostvold, *Financing California Government* (Belmont, Calif.: Dickinson, 1967).
14. Otto Eckstein, *Public Finance* (Englewood Cliffs, N.J.: Prentice-Hall, 1973).
15. William J. Schultz and C. Lowell Harriss, *American Public Finance* (Englewood Cliffs, N.J.: Prentice-Hall, 1965), p. 123.
16. Ibid, p. 173.

LIBRARY AND MUNICIPAL OFFICIALS: THE GREAT DIVIDE

Virgil L. P. Blake

How are public libraries fairing in this era of tight money? Investigations into sources of financing have made two things clear. The first is the predominantly local nature of public library support, despite the attention given the array of federal and state programs implemented since the passage in 1956 of the Library Service Act, later the Library Services and Construction Act (LSCA).

Cecil Beach has found that "after at least two decades of sound and fury promoting state and federal funds, 82% of the cost of operating the nation's public libraries still comes from local taxes."[1]

This is in line with Paxton Price's earlier documentation that public libraries received 87.6% of their support from local governments in 1939, 87.8% in 1945, 87.4% in 1950, and 87.3% in 1956. In the face of this evidence, Beach concludes that "perhaps the time has come for ... public library supporters to concentrate ... efforts where they will be most effective—on local government."[2]

A second fact that emerges is the minute amount of support the public library actually receives. In the most comprehensive study to date, Faubel and Brandes report that "state and local government appropriations to support the public library in 1982-83 were less than half of 1% of the total governmental expenditures at these two levels of government."[3] It is no wonder that, in her review of the past 50 years of public library support, Ann Prentice concluded that "the golden days of library funding weren't all that golden. We never got our fair share."[4]

Over the past two decades, numerous sources have outlined strategies librarians can use to shore up funding. Suggestions were made that public libraries might adopt user fees to augment public support. This fee strategy was rejected by many as a fundamental change in the public nature of the public library. While all would agree that librarians should seek out other funding sources, they were divided about whether keeping faith with its traditional roles meant that the public library ought to be primarily supported by public funds. Politicians, on the other hand, who prefer to support good library service without voting taxes to support that service, encourage raising money from any source except the treasury.[5]

Because the public library is just one of many agencies competing for the community's public funds, "librarians and trustees need to understand the political structure of the community, the sources of power, points at which pressure can be applied effectively—and they must be willing to apply pressure."[6] Manheimer has added that "librarians must be politically aware and politically adept in order to survive in the [future]."[7]

Fred Glazer has advocated the development of a strong public relations program to generate citizen support for the public library. He has argued that to "effectively campaign for improved funding of our institutions we must 'promote or perish.' "[8] Only when this is done, Glazer contends, will it be possible for public libraries to cease being "a birthmark on the body politic ... powdered over, removed, or allowed to exist in place as long as we do not become bothersome."[9]

A more focused variation of this approach, suggested by Frieser, is backed up by successful case studies. He cited a strong community base developed through years of service to the public and the careful cultivation of a network of strong connections between the library and individuals within the community as the key factors in the Wellsley (Mass.) Public Library's efforts to maintain its level of support in the face of Proposition 2 1/2. This course has been advocated by librarians for many decades.[10]

Library trustees bear a major share of the responsibility for increasing public library funding. One of their important roles is to keep the library's needs before governmental officials. The library director and trustees, working together, can combine superior service and strong connections to the community leaders to develop a network of alliances among community organizations.

In reality, however, there is a gap between theory and practice. Individual public librarians counsel development of a strong community base, but in day-to-day practice, the librarian and the library are often isolated from others in the city.[11] Wheeler and Goldhor, some 20 years later, still lamented that isolation, scolding that "many library trustees and librarians, instead of being acquainted with real public opinion, i.e. all classes and interests, are in fact limited by personal acquaintance and preference within a small business, professional, cultural circle."[12]

Political Activity and Public Support

To gather evidence on whether isolation persists today between library and municipal officials, other than during the development and approval of the public library budget request, a survey was developed to measure seven municipalities. Questions addressed the numbers and types of community organizations to which library and municipal officials belonged, the local community organizations consulted about the public library's budget, attendance at meetings of the library trustees and municipal council, and methods of communication between the public library and city hall. The survey covered library directors, trustees, and municipal officials in a single Northeastern state. The urban communities they represented had populations ranging from 50,000 to 99,999. All of the library directors had served in their present positions for at least five years. Approximately 50% of those surveyed responded.

The Directors' Profile

The directors of these seven public libraries were not unique. In education, years of experience, gender, and prior position, they were quite like the directors described earlier by Alvarez[13] and Wasserman[14]. Five of the seven were male. Two were in their 40s, the rest in their 50s and 60s. Six had earned the M.L.S., the seventh another master's degree; two held second master's degrees. As undergraduates, all had majors and minors within the social sciences and humanities. Their professional experience ranged from ten to 30 years, with an average of 20.6 years.

These directors reported that not much information was sought or received from local community organizations as the library's budget request was developed. Only one of the directors made this a practice. Most spoke to local community organizations on the public library's behalf, but one director was singly responsible for 11 of the 49 instances reported.

Trustees' Profile

Like the directors', the portrait drawn of 27 public library trustees responding to the survey was familiar. In terms of age, occupations, education, and years of service they are quite like those described over the years by Joeckel,[15] Garceau,[16] Kroll,[17] Prentice,[18] and Carter.[19] Only seven of the trustees were under 50. Of the remaining 20, eight were in their 50s, five in their 60s, and seven in their 70s. They were all well-educated. Three held Ph.D.s, one an M.D., seven a master's degree, and four a bachelor's degree; others had law degrees, and one held a professional actuarial credential.

The trustees' occupations were typical as well. Nine of the 26 responding were in business or sales. Four were educators; three were clergymen. Seven held professional positions: two attorneys and a physician. Those remaining were an editor, a librarian, an actuary, a health sciences researcher, and a communication specialist. Two identified themselves as housewives, but one of them had ten years of teaching experience. The average tenure of the 26 trustees replying was 10.23 years, with a range of three to 30 years. Half of these trustees had served on their boards ten years or more.

Interaction in Social Settings

Although the library directors limited their membership to service groups and literary, artistic, discussion or study groups, the trustees belonged to a wide range of local community organizations. The most popular organizations were church-affiliated. The trustees also belonged to professional/academic societies, service groups such as Lions and Rotary clubs and the PTA, and citizen support organizations. They worked with youth groups and held memberships in veterans' organizations and sports groups. Only seven trustees (26%) listed membership in political organizations.

Unlike most of the directors, trustees were not likely to speak to local community organizations on behalf of the public library. Fifteen had not done so in the last three or more years. Only one had met with political clubs. Clearly, the directors have assumed the primary responsibility in this regard.

Talking to Municipal Officials

Table 3 indicates the number of local community organization types consulted by the director in drafting the public library budget request, by the library board of trustees, by municipal council members, by both the director and at least one member of the municipal council, and by at least one member of the board of trustees and at least one member of the municipal council.

Neither the directors nor the library trustees made local community organization opinion a regular feature of the process of preparing the library's budget request. Members of the municipal council did consult local community organizations, but, given the activities of the directors and trustees, there was limited overlap in information sources used by municipal council members on the one hand and library officials on the other. That left little chance of local organizations passing informed opinion from library officials to government officials.

This study suggests that library directors are not very likely to encounter members of the municipal council in a social setting. There were only three instances in which a director, at least one library trustee, and one responding municipal council member held memberships in the same local community organization. Overall, the directors did not seem to move in the same social circles as the politicians, and what limited contacts there were between the library and municipal officials developed from library trustee memberships in local community organizations.

Municipal administrators had a community activity profile similar to that of the library directors: they belonged to few local organizations. There were no common memberships with the library directors or trustees. Only one mayor belonged to an organization to which the library director belonged, and there were only two instances of common memberships involving a mayor and at least one library trustee.

Interaction in Municipal Settings

To determine the degree of official but not exclusively budget-centered interaction, the survey included items concerning director and/or trustee attendance at municipal council meetings, the status of the library director in relation to other municipal department heads, the procedures followed in each community to inform municipal officials of meetings of the library board of trustees, and the frequency with which municipal officials attended meetings of the library board.

The library director and trustees are no more involved with municipal officials in these settings than they are in more social ones. Library directors and library trustees alike attended meetings of the municipal council rarely, if at all. In all cases the library director was recognized as the head of an equal municipal department, regularly invited to both regular formal and informal meetings of all municipal department heads. In four of the seven munici-

---

The question is whether the public library can afford this splendid isolation as it competes for scarce public funds. There is some evidence that it cannot.

---

palities the directors always attended such meetings; in the fifth community the library director did so frequently.

The legal requirement to post notices of meetings of the library board of trustees was followed, but in three communities this was the only effort made to encourage municipal officials to attend. The mayors were more likely to receive personal notification of library board meetings, members of the municipal council usually less. In only one of the study communities was there evidence of an effort to specifically inform other municipal department heads. Mayoral attendance was unusual. Nor did members of the municipal councils attend library board meetings with any degree of regularity. In short, the library and its representatives do not seem to be deeply involved with other municipal officials. The two different worlds that exist in regard to local community organizations reappear in the more official setting.

Library directors and trustees were questioned about who received notification of special events held in or sponsored by the public library and about the distribution of minutes of library board meetings in order to determine the degree to which the public library communicated with others in the municipal government.

While the chief municipal administrator is likely to be informed of

special events, members of the municipal council are less likely to be, and other municipal department heads are not very likely to be informed. Nor is attending special events in the library a usual occurrence. In four of the seven communities the mayor, members of the municipal council, and other municipal department heads were rarely, if ever, present. In a fifth community the mayor rarely attended. Members of the municipal council and other municipal department heads never did. In only one instance did a municipal official—a mayor—regularly receive copies of the minutes of library board meetings.

How Officials Use the Library

A final measure of the interaction between municipal officials and the public library was the frequency with which officials used library services. Nineteen of the 25 responding members of the municipal council describe their use as either occasional or rare; their direct experience with the public library and its services was minimal. Only a distinct minority of six used the library frequently—about once a month. The chief administrators presented a slightly more encouraging picture—two were frequent users of the library.

Can the Library Afford Isolation?

On the basis of responses from library and municipal authorities, it would appear that the level of interaction between them is minimal. Library directors and trustees do not consult local community organizations on the public library budget request and so may not get the information from these organizations that is gathered by members of the municipal council as they consider the library's budget request. There is little mutual membership in local community organization types. Neither the library director nor the library trustees attend municipal council meetings. Nor do members of the municipal council attend library board meetings. Efforts to inform municipal officials of library board meetings are not impressive; minutes from library board meetings are not widely distributed. There are more regular attempts to inform municipal officials of special library events, but attendance is sporadic at best. In short, the library and municipal officials operate in two different worlds, a situation quite like that described more than 40 years ago by Miles and Martin.

The question is whether the public library can afford this splendid isolation as it competes for today's scarce public funds. There is some evidence that it cannot. A study of 38 California public libraries by E. Oakes[20] suggested that libraries with strong publicity programs and broad personal contacts received better tax support. When Berger examined the relationship between public relations programs and local support for the public library in Connecticut communities with a population of 25,000 or more, she found a statistically significant association; those with extensive interaction between library and municipal officials and with active public relations programs received greater local tax support.[21]

Clearly, in 1989 there is still a good deal of work needed to reframe the jobs of the library director and library trustee in the political context. If social and official interaction bring greater funding, then a new avenue of activity is added to the professional agenda of the library director and trustee alike. ═

References

1. Cecil Beach. "Local Funding of Public Libraries," *Library Journal*, 110 (June 15, 1985) p. 27.
2. *Ibid*, p. 28.
3. Betsy Faubel and Jean Brandes, "Public Library Expenditures in the U.S. Fiscal Year 1982-1983," *Public Libraries*, 25 (Spring, 1986), p. 18.
4. *Funding Choices for Public Libraries* (Chicago: American Library Association, 1980) p. 13.
5. Ervin J. Gaines, "Public Responsibility for a Public Library," *Public Library Quarterly*, 6 (Spring, 1985), p. 51.
6. Ann E. Prentice, *Public Library Finance* (Chicago: American Library Association, 1977) p. 90.
7. Ethel Manheimer, "Librarians as Political Activists," *School Library Journal*, 27 (January, 1981), p. 31.
8. Frederic J. Glazer, "Promote or Perish," *Arkansas Libraries* 36 (December, 1979), p. 13.
9. *Ibid*.
10. Frieser, Leonard H. "Fundraising and the Meaning of Public Support." *Library Journal*, 110 (June 15, 1985), p. 29–31.
11. Arnold Miles and Lowell, Martin. *Public Administration and the Library* Chicago: University of Chicago Press, 1941.
12. Joseph Wheeler and Herbert Goldhor, *Practical Administration of Public Libraries* (New York: Harper & Row, 1962) p. 230.
13. Robert S. Alvarez, "Profile of Public Library Chiefs": A Serious Survey with Some Comic Relief," *Wilson Library Bulletin*, 47 (March, 1973), p. 573–575.
14. Mary Lee Bundy and Paul Wasserman, *The Public Library Administrator and His Situation* (College Park, MD: Urban Information Interpreters, 1972.)
15. Carlton Joeckel, *The Government of the American Public Library* (Chicago: University of Chicago Press, 1935).
16. Oliver Garceau, *The Public Library in the Political Process* (New York: Columbia University Press, 1949).
17. Martin Kroll, Editor, "Public Library Boards of Trustees," *The Public Libraries of the Pacific Northwest* (Seattle: University of Washington Press, 1960).
18. Ann E. Prentice, *The Public Library Trustee: Image and Performance on Funding* (Metuchen, N.J.: Scarecrow Press, 1973).
19. Jane Carter, *Citizen Participation in Public Library Policy Making* (Metuchen, N.J.: Scarecrow Press, 1975).
20. E. Oakes, "An Investigation of the Relationship Between Library Promotional Activities and Tax Support in Medium Sized Public Libraries in California," Unpublished Master's thesis, University of Southern California, 1971.
21. Patricia Berger, "An Investigation of the Relationship Between Public Relations Activities and Budget Allocation in Public Libraries." *Information Processing and Management*, 15 (November, 1979) p. 179–193.

STAGNANT BUDGETS
Their Effects on Academic Libraries

Murray S. Martin

For many years, academic librarians worked in a fiscal environment of rapidly increasing budgets. Management of growth was the major problem. Today, though, most academic librarians face "steady-state" — or stagnant — budgets. This situation, more pronounced in recent years, has been with us for more than a decade, a fact most librarians and university administrators have been slow to recognize.[1] These budgets require new fiscal management techniques whose key words are cost containment, substitution, choice, and priorities.

While librarians are adjusting to these new realities, they must also face substantial changes in the information environment. They must not simply plan to buy fewer books and journals — an approach which, though fraught with problems, does not change the library's basic mission and its support structure. They must also cope with the introduction and maintenance of new technologies which expand and change both mission and structure.

Before considering these changes, we must explore the meaning of a steady-state budget. The phrase usually implies a budget with increases sufficient to cover the effects of inflation. It assumes that most parent institutions will provide enough money to cover increases in salary and the costs of supplies, books, and other materials. The result is a larger dollar amount, but unchanged purchasing power. Unfortunately, the institutional definition of inflation does not always match the reality.[2] The result is more likely to be a decline in purchasing power.

Several variations in this type of budget can have an even more severe impact. The first is an actual budget freeze. This may or may not be accompanied by frozen salaries. If not, the budget will appear to increase, concealing an increasing divergence in the buying power of various segments of the budget.

The second is a selective freeze, usually the product of program budgeting. Portions of the budget hold steady, while others expand or contract. If this process is carried out in consultation with library management, the effects can be controlled. If not, the library has to implement changes after the fact, often disrupting programs.

Finally, the effect of any budget decision is determined by the size of the library budget, its distribution, its position within the spectrum of automation — beginning, partway along, or fully implemented — and its relation to the goals of the library and the parent institution.

In summary, steady-state includes a wide range of budgetary strategies — from one that allows for inflation to one that freezes a budget at the existing level. For this reason, I prefer the term *stagnant*, since there is no visible direction of flow from one state to another and stirring the pool seems simply to raise the detritus of the past to the surface.

Causes of Budget Problems

The present budget crisis in libraries arises from three basic causes. The first, about which libraries can do little, is the budget problems of higher education in general. A declining enrollment pool, rapidly increasing costs, and loss of revenue (either from state sources or from static tuition fees) combine to force institutional parsimony. As a major budget item, the library has to bear its share of the cutbacks — and sometimes more than its share, since the institution must maintain its academic programs to attract students.[3]

Price Increases

The other two causes relate directly to the library and its programs. First, 24%–33% of a library's budget goes for materials. Historically, the annual cost increase for materials has exceeded inflation, frequently by a very wide margin. Beginning in 1986, and accentuated by the decline in the value of the dollar, the prices for foreign and sci-tech periodicals have risen rapidly — by an average of 15 percent a year. No university, no library budget has proved adaptable enough to meet such increases.[4]

Technological Changes

Second, changes in the nature of information exchange have increasingly forced libraries to turn to automation. But while automation has undoubtedly increased productivity and improved services, it has not proved the source of operating economies so confidently predicted by its early proponents.[5] Another external effect of automation is represented by CD-ROM or the database terminal. These new data retrieval mechanisms offer great benefits, but their costs have had to be borne by budgets constructed before their coming. Are they a type of library material? Are they automation? Are they equipment? Where do their costs come from? Should the user pay? All such questions are asked of budgets which did not include the existence of such services.[6]

Convergence of Forces for Change

Any one of these changes could be handled, but all three together have tilted the delicately balanced library mechanism. The results are as varied as the players. Some institutions, frightened by the prospect of massive subscriptions cancellations, have found emergency funds to enable them to hold on for another year. Some have accepted them as a fait accompli. Others have enforced alternate cuts or slow-downs. Few, however, have sought to address the underlying need — a clear definition of the institution's expec-

> *Stagnant budgets require new fiscal management techniques whose key words are cost containment, substitution, choice, and priorities*

tation of its library.[7] Without such a definition, mutually set and agreed upon, all other courses of action are palliative.

In order to reach such a definition, more knowledge of the interaction between budgets and programs is essential. While many libraries have begun such an investigation, the process is, inevitably, slow. *The Economics of Academic Libraries*[8] sets out some basic facts, which have not changed greatly since 1973. The Fifth International Conference on Academic and Research Libraries[9] discussed many of these concerns in detail, and several of the papers subsequently published presented a first groping towards solutions.

Studies of costs abound, particularly in discrete areas such as interlibrary loan,[10] but general studies of budgetary theory are lacking. ACRL has sponsored a research project to develop performance measures, building on the work of Paul Kantor and others. In time, these efforts will help both institution and library to develop realistic goals and the bud-

getary strategies to support them. In the meantime, though, the need is to handle wisely a very different budget problem — how to make do with less.

Library Materials

What is the current situation? The first and most obvious problem is the massive realignment of expenditures on library materials. Whereas libraries have, for years, aimed at a distribution that would hold periodical subscriptions at about 50%-60% of the total, the increases of the past few years have driven that total well over 60 percent. When standing orders and binding are taken into account, the committed portion of the library materials budget for most academic libraries now exceeds 70 percent. The result has been a severe reduction in book purchases.[11]

To mitigate the effects of budget shifts, many libraries have undertaken cancellation projects. Though essential for fiscal survival, these projects have had little effect. The underlying reasons are simple: there is generally little fat to remove. And there is likely to be even less fat to cut in smaller libraries, whose already low level of funding makes them even more vulnerable to price increases. Moreover, essential subscriptions are those most likely to be subject to high price increases. The publishers' argument that both the quality and quantity of the contents has been improved does nothing to reduce the cost.

Inspection of any list of titles by discipline quickly reveals that a major cut (say, ten percent or more) would entail cancelling either all the less expensive titles or the key titles. Neither option accords with the library's goal of providing information to its users.

Cooperation

At this point the possible solution of cooperative or coordinated projects is usually raised. Such projects have never been truly fruitful in the past. The present crisis may improve their probability of success, but any major effort is likely to take years. Each library must first serve its own constituency and, in rare instances only, cooperative access may provide a major portion of that service. The real problems relate to the cost of *basic* periodicals. Not only are these often the most expensive, but their importance to scholars would prevent libraries from relying on interlibrary loan to provide them, even if there were no legal problems with copyright in doing so.[12] If cooperative projects can relate only to marginal or little-used titles, the resulting savings will also be marginal.

Cooperation of this kind also bears a cost: first, the cost of agreeing to maintain jointly-owned titles; second, the added staff cost of providing interlibrary loan or telefacsimile transmission. In a controlled setting, though, cooperative ventures can be useful.[13]

A more promising avenue is the coordinating of subject specialities. The earlier Farmington Plan addressed this topic, as does the current RLG collection development project. Such large-scale ventures have great governance problems, and their pay-off is delayed.[14] Less far-reaching goals, as with local consortia, may prove more beneficial, since contact is close and users are more likely to be able to go to the resources. These projects still carry with them the cost of meeting external user needs, which may involve special procedures or modified hours of opening.

The Library Materials Budget

The most serious repercussion of the serial price increases of the past few years is not the realignment of the library materials budget (which could, with adequate funding, be corrected over the next few years) but its effects on already-reduced book budgets. In the same way that population distribution diagrams can show the effects of wars and plagues, the purchasing records of libraries will show a severe thinning over the period. In the absence of increased, dedicated funding, the late 1980s are likely to be severely underrepresented in library collections. One-time shots in the arm cannot overcome such problems. Their effects will be felt not only by present but future scholars who attempt to retrieve the works of that period.

Electronic Information Resources

Proponents of the new automated technologies feel that they have an answer. They suggest that libraries rely on access through terminal or CD-ROM. The presentation closely parallels earlier claims for cost and space savings from using microform, which never met expectations. Even though the new media will eventually have a place in the range of library materials, that place remains unclear.[15] Dictionaries, encyclopedias, and other similar types of publications may find their home in CD-ROM. It will be easier to judge the future when the CD-ROM escapes from the prison format of one station, one terminal, one user, (i.e. an automated book).

There are two budgetary effects related to CD-ROM that must be taken into account: the initial capital expenditure and the ongoing maintenance costs. Setting up CD-ROM stations is not cheap, and the donors who earlier funded such experiments now tend to regard them not as innovative, but routine. More outside funding is likely to link them to Local Area Networks or to automated bibliographic systems.

Most installations are leased rather than purchased, which, in effect, simply adds the cost to existing subscriptions. Any lease or purchase must be funded from somewhere and so is largely in competition with other library materials—a situation it was intended to relieve—or with the purchase of other essential equipment. Once installed, the stations require maintenance (part of the lease agreement) and supplies of paper, along with staff time to supervise use, to provide catalog access, and to call the vendor or effect repairs.[16] The staff time required is considerable and competes with time needed for other services, a situation not unlike that caused by microforms.

While database searching and online delivery of materials do offer extensions of library capacity, they also require staff support, frequently one-on-one with the user. That kind of time is very expensive and stretches the reference staff across yet another mode of service.[17] If—as also appears likely, given the problem with the maintenance of existing subscriptions—these services tend to replace subscriptions, they pose further ethical dilemmas. There are costs involved with each search. Are they to be passed on to the user? If not, can the library budget absorb them? What if they also include royalty payments that would not be incurred by using interlibrary loan?

If, maintaining that these are alternative information costs caused by library policy, the library elects to pay them, the expenditure must be balanced by a decrease elsewhere in the budget. If not, the library ventures into a business style by charging for services. While some libraries are already doing this, there is no general model for such a transformation and it is in conflict with the institutional model. Typically, a student expects, in return for tuition, to take courses, use the library, etc., without paying extra fees.

Access technology is expected to expand and to become more attractive. The rapid growth of faculty and student work stations has decentralized activity to the level that individual initiative has replaced institutional strategy. Few institutions, if any, can determine what is being spent, and by whom, on these technologies. Nor can they, except in defiance of general educational goals, seek to limit their use. Libraries find themselves in a situation where any response is likely to cause budget or program problems, none of which is understood by the parent institution. These innovations thus become yet one more decision point, where libraries must choose between economic goods because the budget cannot sustain both.

These issues require a reconsideration both of the information-based world within which the library operates and of the library's institutional role. Different institutional solutions are likely, ranging from aligning all information services under the library to branching off yet one more element. None of these solutions will solve the cost and service problems involved; they will simply be transferred to another locus. For libraries, any competition for or division of funds will affect their ability to sustain traditional programs and, especially, to innovate.

Automation

The third major factor contributing to library budget problems is automation itself. Most academic libraries either use bibliographic utilities or have fully installed operating systems. The first adds to the operating budget an item whose cost structure is externally determined, a good example of the loss of internal control. The second bears not only operating costs, but substantial capital costs. Most of the capital cost has come from a combination of grants, redirected internal savings, institutional reserves, or loans.[18] As systems become more common, donors tend to move on to other fields, which means that libraries still looking to install systems will find funding more difficult to obtain. The extent of expenditure will, therefore, be determined by the institution's ability to raise money. In short, the library must compete with other institutional agencies for risk capital.

Operating costs, however, rest squarely within the institution. Early claims that automation would result in sufficient internal savings to make up for the added costs proved to be overstated. Libraries have had to seek budget increases, raise funds, or cut other services.

One cost element in particular has wide implications. Systems require new skills to operate and, while these may be found among existing staff, they require nurturing. Automation causes shifts in priorities and may well result in shifts of staff if no new personnel are available. This adds costs—first the cost of training (including time lost from regular tasks) and then the cost of rewarding new skills and duties.

New hardware and software entail maintenance costs and, eventually, capital costs for replacement. Universities have never practiced depreciation funding on an adequate scale, making deferred maintenance a major problem. Tinkering with automated systems is the equivalent of minor building repairs when total renovation is required. Libraries now face five- to seven-year cycles of system replacement. These considerations add yet another budget cycle to libraries that already operate in several budget worlds.

Costs and Benefits

While system costs are only too visible, system benefits are diffused and often intangible. We have not yet found a way to measure the benefits of better catalogs or quicker circulation. Demand for library services is elastic in some respects. For example, in the early days of automation, circulation is likely to increase due to the enhanced access and ease of use its offers. Similarly,

the use of the catalog from distant stations may well increase.

As the novelty wears off, though, users tend to revert to earlier patterns. A good example is the reserve book system. While automation may make access and use easier, students are already reading as much as they are likely to read for their courses. Total time available has not changed; there are still only 24 hours in the day and many other things to do. If more books are borrowed, more time

Apparent budget increases conceal an increasing divergence in the buying power of various segments of the budget

is needed to read them. Although distant use of the catalog reduces travel time, other demands have not slackened, and not all students will opt to spend the time gained in library-related pursuits. The statistics will not increase. Observers will then claim that library service is dropping off and that automation was a failure. The staff may know that the use made of the library is more efficient, but costly surveys are needed to validate such a claim.

Staff

In all these discussions, the needs of and for library staff have been key, but they are seldom drawn together into a coherent, budget-directed statement. The old 60:30:10 division (60 percent staff, 30 percent books, 10 percent other) has been changed by automation and warped by differential cost increases. It did testify that libraries are labor-intensive,[19] and it serves to remind budget officers that changes in the proportions will do violence to the programs offered. More work on the direct and indirect relationships between acquisition rates and staff (including

shelving and circulation), on the best ratios of reference staff to user numbers, and on the effects of multiple service points will help to clarify budgets.

Some institutions have attempted to impose program budgets without allowing for their crossover effect on other areas of service. Nor do they take into account that library programs do not correspond with library organizations. There has also been little research on library budget theory. It is not surprising that administrators are unsympathetic to requests for staff, yet libraries face staff needs to meet continually changing needs and expanding services.[20]

Responses

While the problems are obvious, their solutions are not. The first and most important step towards a resolution is to engage the academic institution in the process. Frequently, it has, after all, been a part of the problem, taking the library for granted, paying little attention to the shifts that have changed the nature of the library. Librarians, for their part, have too often wanted to be left alone. This lack of common understanding on goals and needs has led to budget stand-offs and, worse, scapegoating. The dialogue must include not only those who provide the financing, but those who use it—faculty and students—and the librarians.

One-time relief in the shape of year-end subsidies—the most common institutional response—only aggravates the longer-term problem. The second most common response has been to cut the budget across the board, leaving the details to the library administration. Both are an abdication of the institution's responsibility. But, in order to effect longer-term solutions which may take years to apply fully, it is vital to plan carefully and articulate needs and goals clearly. It is also critical that there be full institutional involvement in library development.

Limits to Growth

Clearly, the era of unchecked library growth is over. There was a time when, to meet increasing demands for resources and services, libraries incurred enormous capital and operating costs (e.g. new buildings). A key influence in changing this picture has been new technology. And the library of the future is likely to emerge as very different from today's. For one thing, the primacy of the stacks, with their thousands of unused books, is being challenged. Programs for the acquisition and retention of materials can no longer be seen as self-justifying. Instead, they must be linked much more clearly to academic objectives. And, importantly, institutions must recognize that shifts in academic programs have far-reaching library effects. They must also realize that changing direction is a slow and difficult process for a library.

Electronic Alternatives

In the future, alternative information sources will become more important and need to be seen as part of the collection management budget, along with the associated personnel and equipment costs.[21] In fact, together these items may account for as much as 70% of the library budget. This calls for administrative understanding as expenditures are realigned to reflect the provision of basic resources and services rather than the older line-item approach to budgeting, or even the more recent programmatic approach. The process involves the making of choices not only by the library but also by the parent institution. The latter must set academic priorities—a difficult process, but one that is essential to help the library apply its resources properly.

Cooperation

Cooperative collection development, which has received lip service for decades, must now be taken seriously. Such a path no longer means parcelling out library responsibilities by area or by title, but broader understanding about specializations, about access to resources and about sharing expertise. Like everything else, cooperation costs money and must be treated as a budget category. Not only are there membership fees, but transaction costs and the costs of maintaining group resources. There are also operating issues, since no library is able to cope with a widely extended clientele without added resources.

Interwoven with these concerns is the strand of automation, which can, over time, contribute to their resolution. We have all seen how the

bibliographic utilities facilitated, and therefore increased, interlibrary loan. In doing so, they imposed a lateral, or horizontal, pattern over a previously hierarchical, or vertical, one. Some larger libraries imposed fees to control traffic, while some smaller libraries assumed a greater share of the load. All of this resulted in changes in workload and, therefore, in staffing patterns.

With the many new networks and interconnected systems, the game is being played out again, at a lower level, through the use of shared circulation systems. In many such cases libraries are grappling seriously with the equalization of the burden, whether by carefully structured fees or systems of reimbursement for net lenders. The negotiations tend to be easier because the partners are closer and more similar to one another. Nevertheless, there will be long, sometimes acrimonious discussions before the new structures of fees and reimbursements are operating smoothly. There are also likely to be many more instances where libraries are paying other libraries for such services as the management of automated systems or specialized cataloging.

Administrators must be aware, however, that shared services cannot replace basic service at home, and that these costs, which may amount to 5%-10% of the total budget, are additional costs, not merely substitutes for old ones.

Offsite Storage

The same is true of offsite storage for less-used materials. The cost of housing library materials on campus has passed the limit of institutional budget support. Offsite locations are needed but must either be owned or rented; they will also result in added retrieval costs. In the long term they are justified by lower building maintenance costs on campus. In the short term they require capital investment. Now is the time to consider truly cooperative storage. The cost of having each library store separately much of the same material is prohibitive, yet the obsession with numbers, quite apart from legal limits on the disposition of materials, has prevented even existing cooperatives from considering the consolidation of collections. The time has come to reexamine this issue. Equally, libraries must face the fact

that material that can be stored offsite indefinitely, without being needed, may well be a candidate for disposal.

New Budget Elements

The library budget itself is undergoing massive change. The proportion spent for operations is growing rapidly and will contine to grow.[22] Its present treatment as "Other" is entirely inadequate. The increases relate directly to program but in a diffuse manner. For example, libraries in the age of automation need more money for maintenance, telecommunications, and new supplies such as bar-code labels. Smaller savings in the acquisition of catalog cards or from discontinuing existing paper records help to maintaining budget stability but cannot offset all new costs. Basic library needs cannot be arbitrarily contained, any more than reference staff costs can be reduced by imposing limits on the number of questions asked.

Most library budgets barely cover essentials. There is an urgent need to communicate to budget officers and other administrators that the millions of dollars they believe can cover all eventualities are in fact predicated. Ninety-five percent of all operating costs are committed from the beginning of each year. Nearly 75% of the book budget will go for subscriptions, standing orders, and binding. And the only way to reduce the expenditure on staff is to reduce staff numbers. This is the setting that turned a 15% increase in serial prices into a disaster.

Personnel

Despite the many studies on staff needs, activities, and workloads, there is little agreement on the fundamental personnel structure needed by libraries. The statistical reports from ARL and ACRL show clearly how diverse staffing patterns are, even in libraries that are very similar in size and purpose. The more detailed staff allocations available from medical libraries show no greater similarities.

The better definition of professional, semiprofessional, and clerical tasks shows promise for understanding staffing patterns. To date, this has proved easier in the more readily definable areas of technical services. In public service areas, where tasks are less easily segregated, there is a much greater need for individual expertise. The application of technical models often backfires, as in the clericalization of interlibrary loan, where too much reliance has been placed on automated systems and too little allowance made for the complexities of bibliographic research.

Although libraries have begun to understand the complex shifts of skill required to exploit fully automated systems, human resources departments have been slow to respond by opening up classifications or evaluating new skills. These new needs require a complete reexamination of personnel structures, a slow process when the replacement or attrition of staff, rather than its addition, is the general rule. Libraries must reevaluate each position as it becomes vacant, seek to import new skills and to move positions to the areas of greatest need. Again, this can only be done in the context of a fully thought-out mission.

Goal Definition

Goals must be redefined if major changes are to be made. Despite librarians' all-too-frequent reluctance to reexamine existing programs, this can be a good starting point. If reducing costs is a primary goal, consolidation of service points offers one solution, but this must be supported by the user. Another is to reduce hours of service, but students and administrators generally resist this. The cost of keeping the library open is much greater than usually recognized. Reducing that cost may require the redesign of some library areas to control access, and will certainly inhibit continued use of multiple-access points. Redistributing staff hours at some service points may allow better use of existing staff, but is unlikely to contribute much to savings.

In the long run, the only way to achieve substantial savings is to reduce spending or to restrict services, activities that can only be done successfully with the help of the institution. Lowering sights is a painful process, and some things of value are likely to be lost. Lessons can be learned from past experiences — for example, the study carried out at Lehigh University, demonstrated that selling off a special collection could be counterproductive.[23]

Other lessons can also be learned. Libraries have too long been re-garded as expensive overheads, divorced from the academic programs they serve. Recognition of the added value they produce is slow to come, largely because the direct relationship between library and learning is very difficult to demonstrate in budgetary terms.

Librarians will have to learn ways to demonstrate this fact, whether through use measures or by reference to actual use by professors and

> **The needs of and for staff have been key, but are seldom drawn together into a coherent, budget-directed statement**

students. They will also need to show the value of the educational programs they conduct.[24] These are being recognized by accrediting teams and others concerned with institutional outcomes, notably in seeking answers to questions about how well students are being prepared for their post-educational experience.[25] Libraries will have to rely on program evaluation using objective measures, not on subjective experiences.

Income

Most libraries have some small income. The most common sources are fines, book replacement costs, fees for searching or interlibrary loan photocopy. Although the library community has been debating "fees or free" for many years, a coherent philosophy has been slow to emerge. While it seems reasonable that the user should pay for any services beyond the general level, such a stand has serious educational implications. If the goal is simply to provide money to carry out services which the general budget cannot support, then those services — essential though they may be — will be limited to those who can pay.

The more profitable line to pursue seems to be the concept of charging for substitutional services, i.e. those already available in some other format. A good example would be payment for a list of acquisitions, since the information is already available in the catalog. This rationale has enabled libraries to develop fee schedules for database searching, usually with differential fees for outside users. Other services can be investigated similarly to determine when or whether charges can be levied.

Always, however, libraries must be wary of simply seeking income. If, for example, serial subscriptions are discontinued, charges for database searches, interlibrary loan, or purchase on demand are a kind of double tax on the user. Nor should charges simply be nuisance fees. If the service is offered on a business basis, then the full cost should be recovered. Half solutions contain the seeds of their own failure.

As a corollary, institutions must be willing to recognize the costs that go into producing the income. In many instances, the institution simply asks for a calculation of the likely income and then allows for it in setting up the budget. While the procedure may be justified from an accounting point of view, programmatically it makes no sense. It is impossible to balance income and expense unless the items in question are separately budgeted. For all such activities the library should maintain separate accounts and be prepared to defend them on a business basis.

Libraries should, however, be wary of venturing into real business endeavors. Unless there is a sufficient expert or resource base for the service offered, it will not be profitable. Marketing is also necessary, but seldom adequately supported. The total cost of offering fee-based services to the community is high and cannot be subsidized from the regular budget.

Fund-raising

Libraries are now much more active fund-raisers than in the past,[26] not simply for annual gifts or for special purchases of materials, but for projects, buildings, operating expenses, and endowments. This trend can be expected to intensify, but firm commitment is needed from the institution. Too often the institution simply seeks money for building and books, neglecting the essential infrastructure of people and operating costs. New fund-raising campaigns will have to tie these library needs into other approaches to donors. Institutions will also have to forego the practice of reducing the regular budget by the amount of money raised if such endeavors are to attain their stated purpose: the improvement of the library.

Again, there are costs — especially in staff time — associated with raising funds. Few libraries are in a position to allow much time for such endeavors. One way to gain more time is to recognize fund-raising as a legitimate library activity and incorporated it within the budget by allowing for mailing, function, etc. How this is done will vary with the institutional setting. What is essential is that the library have real power in determining fund-raising directions. Libraries should also set regular goals for smaller grants and gifts. For example, a simple first step would be to aim for gifts and grants equivalent to 1% of the library budget. With experience, that goal could be increased. As is done in some academic departments, the number of faculty can even be determined by the level of success in fund-raising.

One of the goals frequently overlooked by libraries is that of replacement funds. A few thousand dollars for a small project that pays part of a salary, while it will not increase the staff time available, frees up some funds for other uses, perhaps even a student scholarship, which can, in turn, lead to other funding support. This snowball effect is very important.

Stagnant budgets, far from simply preserving the status quo, have caused major turmoil. They are non-answers to the problem of providing information. The provision of adequate library service in a time of inadequate budgetary resources and poorly defined goals requires a complete reexamination of the library/university relationship. This process is inhibited by lack of knowledge, both of the real needs of libraries and of the real needs of scholarship. Until these issues are attacked directly, libraries will be asked to do more with less, even though more is already expected of them. ▬

References

1. Richard De Gennaro, "Austerity, Technology, and Resource Sharing: Research Libraries Face the Future" *Library Journal* 100 (1975): 917–23.
2. John F. Harvey and Peter Spyers-Duran, "The Effect of Inflation on Academic Libraries" *Austerity Management in Academic Libraries*, John F. Harvey and Peter Spyers-Duran, Editors (Metuchen, N.J.: Scarecrow Press 1984): 1–42.
3. F. G. Stanbrook, "Changing Climate of Opinion about University Libraries" *Canadian Library Journal* 40;5 (1983): 273–76 and Daniel Sullivan, "Libraries and Liberal Arts Colleges: Tough Times in the Eighties" *College and Research Libraries* 43;2 (1982): 119–23.
4. Richard M. Dougherty, "Are Libraries Hostage to Rising Serial Prices?" *Bottom Line* 2;4 (1988): 25–7.
5. Herman H. Fussler, *Research Libraries and Technology* (Chicago: University of Chicago Press., 1973): 1. Also Michael Gorman, "On doing Away with Technical Services Departments" *American Librarier* 10 (1979): 4366–437.
6. Ann Bristow Beltran, "Funding Computer-Assisted Reference in Academic Research Libraries" *Journal of Academic Librarianship* 13;1 (1987): 4–7, poses these questions in response to earlier articles advocating and opposing funding such services from the materials budget. The discussion has scarcely begun, and so far no consensus has been reached.
7. Dennis P. Carrigan, "The Political Economy of the Academic Library" *College and Research Libraries* 49;(4) (1988): 325–31. See also the numerous references in the revised University Library Standards approved by ACRL in 1989.
8. William J. Baumol and Matityahu Marcus, *Economics of Academic Libraries* (Washington, D.C.: American Council on Education, 1973). In fact, these patterns have been in existence for much longer, and may be seen as persisting. An earlier study commissioned by the National Advisory Commission on Libraries, *Libraries at Large*, Douglas M. Knight and E. Sheply Nourse, Editors (New York: R. R. Bowker, 1969) especially Chapter 5, sets out the same concerns.
9. The theme of the Conference, held at Boulder, Colo., February 28–March 1, 1984, was "Contemporary Issues in Academic and Research Libraries." The papers were published under the title *Financing Information Services*, Peter Spyers-Duran and Thomas W. Mann Jr., Editors (Westport, Conn.: Greenwood, 1985).
10. J. E. Herstand, "Interlibrary Loan Cost Study and Comparison," *RQ* 20 (Spring 1981): 249–56.
11. Robert L. Houbeck, Jr., "If Present Trends Continue: Responding to Journal Price Increases" *Journal of Academic Librarianship* 13;4 (1987): 214–20, and "Paying the Piper: ARL Libraries Respond to Skyrocketing Subscription Prices" *Journal of Academic Librarianship* 14;1 (1988): 4–9.
12. Noelene P. Martin, "Interlibrary Loan and Resource Sharing: New Approaches" *Financial Planning for Libraries*. Murray S. Martin, Editor (New York: Haworth Press, 1983): 99–108.
13. Eva Martin Sartori, "Regional Collection Development of Serials" *Collection Management* 11;1/2 (1989): 69–76.
14. David Henige, "Epistemological Dead End and Ergonomic Disaster? The North American Collections Inventory Project" *Journal of Academic Librarianship* 14;4 (1987): 209–13.
15. Michael K. Buckland, "Library Materials: Paper Microform, Databases" *College and Research Libraries* 49;2 (1988): 117–22.
16. Brian Aveny, "Electronic Publishing and Library Technical Services" *Library Resources and Technical Services* 28;1 (1984): 68–75; Brownrigg, Edwin and others, "Technical Services in the Age of Electronic Publishing" *Library Resources and Technical Services* 28;1: 59–67; Meredith Butler, "Electron Publishing and its Impact on Libraries: A Literauture Review" *Library Resources and Technical Services* 28;1: 41–58; Gordon B. Neavill, "Electronic Publishing, Libraries and the Survival of Information" 28;1 (1984): 76–89.
17. Jane P. Kleiner, "The Configuration of Reference in and Electronic Environment" *College and Research Libraries* 48(4): 302–13, 1987.
18. Murray S. Martin, "Financing Library Automation" *Bottom Line* (Charter Issue 1986): 11–16.
19. William J. Baumol and S. A. Blackman, "Electronics, the Cost Disease, and the Operation of Libraries" *Journal of the American Society for Information Science* 34 (1983): 181–191. In this paper the authors stress that libraries are not only labor-intensive, but also labor inflexible, that is they have only limited ways of redirecting employee activities because they are dependent on human abilities which cannot be replaced by machines.
20. Barbara B. Moran, *Academic Libraries: The Changing Knowledge Centers of Colleges and Universities* (Washington, D.C.: Association for the Study of Higher Education, 1984). Also Paul Metz, "The Role of the Academic Library Director" *Journal of Academic Librarianship* 5 (1978): 148–52; "College and University Libraries" *The Bowker Annual of Library and Book Trade Information*, 29th ed. Julia Ehresmann, Editor (New York: R. R. Bowker, 1984): 80–81.
21. Murray S. Martin, "Financial Planning: New Needs, New Sources, New Styles" *Financing Information Services*: 91–108.
22. Moran, *op. cit.*, and Hugh F. Cline and Loraine T. Sinnott, *The Electronic Library* (Lexington, Mass: Lexington Books, 1983): 172.
23. Rebecca R. Martin, "Special Collections: Strategies for Support in an Era of Limited Resources" *College and Research Libraries* 48;3 (1987): 241–46.
24. For example: Jan Horner and David Thornwall, "Online Searching and the University Researcher" *Journal of Academic Librarianship* 14;4 (1988): 225–30, and Sonia Bodi, "Critical Thinking and Bibliographic Insturction: The Relationship" *Journal of Academic Librarianship* (1988): 150–53.
25. Correspondence from the North Central Association of Colleges and Schools and the Middle States Association of Colleges and Schools to Kent Hendrickson, Chair of the ACRL University Library Standards Revision Committee underlined this point, laying stress on outcomes rather than inputs.
26. Barbara F. Fischler, "Library Fund-Raising in the United States: A Preliminary Report" *Library Administration and Management* 1;1 (1987): 31–4.

ECONOMIC VITALITY
How Libraries Can Play a Key Role

Judith Foust

It is no myth that when major corporations consider a new business location the presence of a good library is one of the indicators they use in determining the local quality of life. If community services are not sufficiently attractive, corporations like IBM and AT&T may look elsewhere to avoid the difficulties in attracting a first-rate work force. At the other extreme, it is not news that when the economic base erodes, demands for information often increase as the jobless or dislocated seek assistance in discovering new employment opportunities. But until the 1980s the library has, for the most part, failed to capitalize on its importance to community economic vitality.

It is in this decade that librarianship, heeding the advice of longtime luminary Lowell Martin, has begun to redefine services to make obvious the significance of the library to small business owners seeking to understand the socioeconomic conditions they face, to high school drop-outs trying to enhance their employability through independent study, to the unemployed preparing for new jobs and new careers, and to neighborhood leaders devising community improvement projects.[1]

Martin has repeatedly admonished library managers to focus on contributing to their communities' drives for greater prosperity. Communities need the economic resources of industries, workers able to fill jobs, and neighborhoods in which people want to live. The library has a role to play in all three.[2]

One state, Pennsylvania, has been working hard to ensure that libraries play a role in economic revitalization. Like other states with a base of heavy industry, Pennsylvania experienced an economic slump in the early '80s that closed steel mills, manufacturing plants, and mines across the Commonwealth. These closings, in turn, forced the closings of services like groceries, cleaners, and department stores, which, in turn, threatened the survival of local government and the provision of essential services. With the better educated moving out of the region, the income level and general wealth were even more depressed. The poverty rate was increasing; unemployment was on the rise. At the same time that the fiscal base was eroding, citizens displaced by the loss of jobs put increasing demands on the resources of the libraries. The reduced local tax base, however, meant that library appropriations were slashed.

Another challenge to libraries resulted from the governor's decision that Pennsylvania's future lay in attracting new businesses to the state, rather than in supporting the so-called "smoke stack" industries. Small businesses offered more jobs, quicker start-ups, and lower financial commitment than new large manufacturing sites. He directed the Department of Commerce and all other state agencies to support revitalization by attracting and nurturing small business.

So it was that the State Library of Pennsylvania took the lead in ensuring that libraries became partners in revitalization. The State Library not only became a major supporter of the Department of Commerce, but also made participation in economic development a criterion for awarding LSCA grants funded by the U.S. Department of Education, Office of Library Programs.

In such a climate Pennsylvania's libraries became more conscious of their role in the economic vitality of their communities and began to stress innovative service roles. Library leaders reasoned that unless programs met economically based needs, the continued support of the library would become harder and harder to justify. Their communities could no longer afford to maintain facilities people "ought" to have but rarely used. Financial circumstances demanded a good return on tax dollars.

Pennsylvania's libraries began to plan on a broader scale, viewing the local community in competition with other communities for economic investment; they became major players in Pennsylvania's economic recovery.

Focusing on the Library's Role

While economic factors might have been enough for the State Library to initiate a program for economic vitality, two separate reports added more incentive. In the first, the Department of Commerce discovered that the single major cause of small business failure was lack of management information. While entrepreneurs had technical expertise, knew their product and their industry, they generally lacked knowledge of personnel management, accounting, marketing, and distribution. We quickly realized that all 600 public libraries across Pennsylvania could provide basic business texts.

The second study showed that libraries had a major public awareness problem. The Center for the Study of Rural Librarianship at Clarion University in Pennsylvania discovered that fully 95% of the businesses in Clarion County did not know that they could call the public library for answers to questions such as how to plan, find a potential market, organize a business, delegate work, or determine the current foreign exchange rate for the dollar.

Armed with this data, the State Library designed a multi-part program to support economic development. The plan included state funding for libraries serving economically distressed communities, and service to business and to the unemployed. We had two objectives: to attract businesspeople to public libraries and to assist libraries in serving this new constituency.

Local libraries needed money for books and staff for this service as well as to continue service to children, students, and others. In 1985, The Library Code in Pennsylvania was amended to make available at least $500,000 in additional state aid to libraries who were in most need as determined by unemployment rate, income per capita, or property values. Since continuation of local funding was a requirement, the law succeeded in maintaining local financial commitments to libraries while providing additional funds for books and service.

Attracting Business to libraries

We decided that the most effective method of attracting businesses to libraries was through state-level business organizations. In this way, we would reach people outside Harrisburg and central Pennsylvania as well as support local library outreach activities. The Department of Commerce provided entrée to the economic development councils and the state-funded Ben Franklin Partnership Centers. These groups helped define how library service could be most effective. The most important result of this coalition was a booklet, "Books for Business Success: A Guide to Library Resources for Your Small Business," sponsored jointly by the Department of Commerce and the Department of Education, with an introduction by the governor. The Department of Commerce has distributed over 10,000 of these booklets to businesses seeking assistance. Along with encouragement from Commonwealth staff, this booklet has persuaded businesspeople to call their public library for information services. Of course, public libraries throughout the state received advance copies of the bibliography, to prepare for an increase in questions.

In a further effort to reach out to the business community, the State Library and the Pennsylvania Chamber of Industry and Business co-sponsored a committee composed of business people and librarians. Committee meetings helped increase awareness of the rich resources in libraries, as well as how best to serve business.

Discussions with the Small Business Administration (SBA) regional office revealed that they were in need of facilities to hold their workshops. Several public libraries now host SBA workshops in their meeting rooms. Each workshop includes information about the library, and attracts new library users and supporters. These connections yielded an invitation for the Pennsylvania Library Association to exhibit at the White House conference for Small Business Preconference in Pennsylvania. The exhibit featured local reference librarians, a few books, and a telephone. Exhibit staff answered questions from their small collection, augmented by staff standing by at local public and academic libraries. Conference participants not only used the service, but they followed up later with more questions at their local public library.

Using information gleaned from discussions with the Department of Commerce and the State Chamber of Business, the State Library designed a bookmark to remind conference-goers of their public library. The bookmark was reprinted by the American Library Association for use at the White House Conference for Small Business and by the New York State Library.

In addition to increasing awareness and use of libraries by business, the State Library provided assistance to libraries to serve this new constituency. Many libraries received grants to buy books and develop programs. In addition, a workshop titled "Libraries, Business and Government, Strengthening the Partnership" was presented at three locations across the state. The program introduced participants to the library's role in the Commonwealth's economic development initiative and assisted them to develop a plan of service to business. The presenters were library directors, business reference librarians and Pennsylvania Department of Commerce staff.

One of the results of State library

leadership in Pennsylvania's revitalization, WORKPLACE is a program providing education and career counseling to displaced and unemployed adults. Funded through the Kellogg Foundation, it is currently located in nine libraries across the Commonwealth. Each site — Philadelphia, Pittsburgh (three libraries), Scranton, Washington, Monessen, and Chester County (two libraries) — serves a large population in need of job search assistance. They were willing to model a new level of service for this special group of people.

WORKPLACE is attracting a new constituency to the library. More than 5,000 people have used the service in the last year, and many libraries are reporting a 100% increase in circulation of guidance materials. It is also developing new links with state and local government and increasing the public's esteem for their library. At the Washington County site, the library has developed strong ties with county and state government and is part of the team which visits worksites prior to closing to counsel and assist employees.

ACCESS PENNSYLVANIA

The State Library's initiative, ACCESS PENNSYLVANIA, is another arm of Economic Vitality in Pennsylvania. The Statewide Library Card System, one component of ACCESS PENNSYLVANIA, makes it easier to visit any public library and borrow a book. Pennsylvanians can use their library card in more than 600 libraries across the state. Since the inception of the program, circulation has increased about 10%. This increase in reading directly relates to a better informed workforce and improved quality of life in the community.

The ACCESS PENNSYLVANIA database, a union catalog of more than 300 school, public, and academic libraries on CD-ROM, is also expanding the use of libraries. One rural school library experienced a 300% increase in use when students could search the catalog by key word using a microcomputer. The two delivery components of ACCESS PENNSYL-VANIA — the Interlibrary Delivery Service (IDS) for books and films, and a telefacsimile network for papers and periodicals — provide the means to deliver needed library resources across the state in a day or less. Many city and rural networks have designed their periodical service to provide articles while the patron is still in the library. Together these ACCESS PENNSYLVANIA programs are providing the right book at the right time to businesses, students and the general population.

As a result of these activities, libraries throughout the Commonwealth have been empowered to serve millions, increase the state's economic vitality, and enhance their own financial position, while the State Library is pioneering a model worthy of emulation. =

References

1. Martin, Lowell. *A Master Plan for the City of Philadelphia*. Philadelphia: The Free Public Library, 1981, p. iv.
2. Martin, p. 8.

FINANCIAL PLANNING AND REPORTING

BASIC BUDGET PRIMER:
Choosing the Best Budget for Your Library

Barry Devlin

The literature on budget preparation is almost redundant in pointing out that librarians insist on sticking with the line-item format despite evidence that it is the least effective means of developing the library's case for support. Perhaps we don't make the shift because we lack the understanding of the four major budgeting techniques—line item, program, performance, and zero-based—and thus can't evaluate their usefulness to our institutions.

A group of librarians at the Montclair Public Library decided to ferret out the facts about the budgeting process for our own edification as well as for popular professional consumption.

We began by settling on a definition of the budget that was acceptable to all of us and then setting out a series of questions. We asked: Is the line-item budget the frequent choice because of its easy applicability? Do program or performance budgets offer better avenues for fiscal control? How? Can zero-base provide the framework for ranking programs so that resources are allocated to the top priorities? When we knew enough to conclude that the answer to all of these questions was yes, the most basic question emerged: How do library managers decide what budget format is best for their organizations? We then got more specific: What are the distinguishing features of the four budget types? What are their notable differences? What are their advantages and disadvantages? What type of data is needed for each of the formats and how are they compiled?

Defining "Budget"

A budget is variously defined as an itemized summary of probable expenditures and income for a given time period, usually involving a systematic plan for meeting expenses; a planning document used by an organization, generally prepared and presented in standard accounting formats emphasizing dollar revenues, expenditures, and costs; or an assessment of revenues that can be realistically anticipated.[1,2] We agreed, though, that the most useful definition connects planning to control, by referring to budgeting as the process by which necessary resources are determined, allocated, and funded.

Line-Item Budgeting

The logic behind the traditional line-item budget generally involves three steps:

1) Last year's spending level is extrapolated into next year.

2) Last year's level is incremented for increases in costs.

3) The spending level is further incremented for new projects and programs. The underlying assumptions in the traditional approach are that all activities making up last year's spending level are essential to achieving the ongoing objectives, strategies, and mission of the organ-

ization; must be continued during the coming year; are now performed in the most cost-effective manner.

This budget format is accounting-oriented and directed toward answering the question "how much?" The line items, or objects of expenditure, serve as the focus for analysis, authorization, and control. Total amounts requested and expended for broad categories—such as personnel, supplies, and communications—are calculated for the entire library, as the excerpted budget in Figure 1 shows.

Incremental budgeting projects line-item numbers as derived from expenditures of the year before. In Figure 1, the 1988 funding request was calculated on a 7% across-the-board increase over 1987.

There are advantages to line-item budgeting. Line-item budgets are simpler to construct than other formats and are easy to compute. The individual lines are clearly defined; they emphasize control and tradition; they are comprehensible; little added explanation is necessary. But, on the downside, line-item budgets do not stress the library's services to the public. Rather, emphasis is on services or commodities to be purchased by the library. Cost centers are not identified. And there is not sufficient historical data with which to discern major cost trends.

The Program Budget

The program budget begins with the library's goals, and objectives and the derivative goals and objectives of each of the library's services.

Richard F. Wacht states, "The concept of program budgeting emphasizes the long-range perspective, or goals, in which the single year's budget allocation represents the results of specific short-range decisions, or objectives, made within the context of the multiyear plan."[3]

Program budgeting is a technique that formulates spending plans and then makes appropriations on the basis of expected results. Expenditures are plotted to reflect quantified objectives. The program budget is derived for each area of service within a department, then brought together for the department as a whole. Figure 2, for example, is built for Adult Services.

The department's budget is projected for the personnel, materials, supplies, communications, and other categories of expenditure necessary to meet objectives outlined for 1988. If one of the department's goals is to make service accessible to all community residents, it might be a good idea to initiate selection and delivery for the handicapped, aged, and shut-ins. The steps involved for that program budget might include:

1) *Defining the program objectives* for 1988 in terms of the output desired. For example: To establish within Adult Services a new selection and delivery service—called HAS—that reaches 20% of the community's handicapped, aged, and shut-in residents in the first 12 months of operation.

2) *Delineating the major activities* necessary to accomplish the objective. For example: Within the first month, assign the task of coordinating the service and initiate contacts with other agencies, including the Fire Department, to locate the target audience. Complete a needs assessment of the HAS clientele by the end of the second month. By the end of the third month, provide in-house staff training for those who will provide the service.

3) *Determining the nature and level of resources* needed to support the activity. For example: One new

FIGURE 1.
THE LINE-ITEM BUDGET

Account Code	Object	Actual Expenditure 1987	Request 1988
100300	Personnel		
100301	Full Time	$748,322	$800,705
100302	Part Time	110,218	117,933
100303	Overtime	8,240	8,817
200300	Benefits		
200301	Social Security	51,959	55,596
200302	Pension	75,345	80,619
200303	Health Insurance	32,000	34,240
	TOTAL PERSONNEL	$1,026,084	$1,097,910
300300	Materials		
300301	Books	26,250	28,046
300302	Periodicals	18,611	19,913
300303	Databases	21,816	23,343
300304	Documents	5,300	5,671
	TOTAL MATERIALS	$71,977	$77,015
400300	Supplies		
400301	Office	5,250	5,618
400302	Computer	3,190	3,413
500300	Communication		
500301	Postage	12,600	13,482
500302	Telephone	4,500	4,815
500303	Datalines	13,500	14,445
600300	Conferences & Dues	8,500	9,095
700300	Staff Development	4,000	4,280
	TOTAL OPERATING	$123,517	$132,163
	GRAND TOTAL	$1,149,601	$1,230,073

FIGURE 2.
THE PROGRAM BUDGET FOR ADULT SERVICES

Account Code	Object	Actual Expenditures, 1987	Request 1988
100300	Personnel		
100301	Full Time	$140,971	$150,839
100302	Part Time	29,680	46,758
100303	Overtime	—	—
200300	Benefits		
200301	Social Security	18,320	19,236
200302	Pension	13,840	14,532
200303	Health Insurance	10,503	11,028
	TOTAL PERSONNEL	$213,314	$242,393
300300	Materials		
300301	Books	24,600	24,950
300302	Periodicals	14,760	15,245
300303	Databases	16,810	15,731
300304	Documents	4,500	4,500
	TOTAL MATERIALS	$60,670	$60,426
400300	Supplies		
400301	Office	2,500	1,500
400302	Computer	2,109	1,100
500300	Communications		
500301	Postage	10,010	11,011
500302	Telephone	10,308	10,300
500303	Datalines	18,402	13,462
600300	Conferences & Dues	4,210	4,210
700300	Staff Development	4,200	4,200
800300	Programming	8,250	8,250
900300	Van Maintenance	—	500
	TOTAL OPERATING	$59,989	$54,533
	GRAND TOTAL	$353,973	$357,352

staff member, a part-time professional librarian, is projected, assigned one-half time to coordinate the service and assist in fulfilling requests, creating patron profiles, and recording materials received; staff training can be accommodated with no increase over the 1987 allocation; delivery can be accomplished by streamlining current Branch trips. The materials needed are already incorporated into the library's yearly acquisition program.

4) *Developing the budget requirements*, given the resources defined in step 3. For example: The salary request for a new half-time librarian is projected at $15,000; there is no benefit package since the job is 15 hours per week. The prorated share of van maintenance cost is $500.

5) *Stating the requirements* for all programs within Adult Services, using the same four-step process, as illustrated with HAS, then tallying the exact figures under categories common to all library operations and submitting them in one projected budget for the department.

Note that the program budget is not a formula approach. That is, unlike the line-item budget, the same percentage increase is not added to each 1987 line.

Program budgeting is a complex

FIGURE 3.
1987 PERFORMANCE AND UNIT COSTS FOR ADULT SERVICES

Input Allocated	Service	Program Objective	Output	Unit Cost
$171,032	Reference	Provide telephone and walk-in responses to queries	117,955	$1.45
$77,461	Readers Advisory	Provide assistance in selecting reading and other information sources	46,946	$1.65
$85,480	I & R	Provide information on and referral to community agencies	40,705	$2.10
TOTAL $333,973	Adult Services	Make services accessible to all community residents	295,604	$\bar{X}$ = $1.73

FIGURE 4.
ZERO BASE BUDGET (ZBB) DECISION PACKAGE

(1) Package Name   (2) Department   (3) Prepared By   (4) Date   (5) Rank
    Adult Services   Library   J. Jones   6/12/88   1
                                                    Department head

(6) Purpose/Objective
    To provide reference, readers advisory and information materials and services for community adults.

(7) Description of Actions (Operations) For This Level
    1. Staff all information services 65 hours per week.
    2. Provide timely, accurate responses to telephone and walk in queries.
    3. Develop and maintain an up-to-date database of community information and agencies for referral (I&R).
    4. Provide materials and databases to supply information needed.
    5. Initiate services for all community residents.

(8) Changes/Improvements From Current Operations
    Initiate service to the handicapped, aged and shut-in.

(9) Workload/Performance Measures	1987 Actual	1988 Projected	(10) Resources Required	1987 Actual	1988 Proposed
Reference Services	117,953	117,995	Positions — This level	7	7.5
Advisory Services	46,946	47,650	— Cumulative	7	.5
Referral Services	40,705	42,500	Expense — This level	$333,973	$357,352
HAS	—	12,500	— Cumulative	$317,425	$23,379
TOTAL	205,604	220,645	% of Prior Year	5.2%	7%
Increase	—	7.3%			

FIGURE 5.
DECISION PACKAGE RANKING

(1) RANK	(2) PACKAGE NAME Adult Services	(3) 1987 CUMULATIVE Positions	Total Expended (excl. cap.)	Change	(4) 1988 PROPOSED Pos.	Expense (excl. cap.)
1	Reference	4	171,032	0	4	$171,032
2	Readers Advisory	1	77,461	0	1	77,461
3	I & R	2	85,480	0	2	85,480
4	HAS	0	—	100%	.5	23,379
5						
6	TOTAL	7	$333,973	7%	7.5	$357,352
7						
8						
9						
10						
11						
12						
13						
14						
15						
16						
17						
18						
19						
20						
21						
22						

ORGANIZATION BEING RANKED	PREPARED BY	DATE	PAGE 1 of 1
Library	J. Jones, Department Head	6/12/88	

process. It is difficult to assign fiscal responsibility for programs that span several departments. And if goals and objectives are vague, the strength of the resulting data is vague.

But, clearly, when set out correctly, program budgeting can be much more useful than line-item budgeting. It not only provides the necessary data for costing out service based on objectives; it also pro-vides historic data with which to assess cost trends.

The Performance Budget

While program budgets look at the expected results of services, per-formance budgets define the work performed to provide that service. Performance budgets emphasize output measures. Calculation of unit cost is added. Services are subdi-vided so that they can be described in terms of work input and service output. Program elements are bro-ken down into their functions; activ-ities into their individual work components. As Ann E. Prentice notes, performance budgeting helps administrators to "assess the work efficiency of operating units by: a) casting the budget in functional terms and b) providing work-cost measurements to facilitate the efficient performance activities."[4]

One way to identify unit costs, as Figure 3 shows, is to divide the output totals for each program objective into the input costs. This is a simple but sometimes misleading method. A more accurate reflection takes painstaking measurements, as Michael Vinson's article on costing the acquisitions function, on page 70, demonstrates.

Because costing is explicit, performance budgets are useful in evaluating alternative means of carrying out the same activities. But, this technique does require a high level of accounting detail, time-consuming procedures to determine costs, and the capacity to handle more complex record keeping. Output measures must accurately reflect the key work performed in order to translate accurately into dollar requirements for support. For example, deriving unit cost for bookmobile service by dividing the number of stops into total bookmobile costs inflates the cost per unit of service and disregards the more important and meaningful statistic in meeting program objectives—namely, the number of people served. In many quarters, these difficulties are combined with skepticism about the impact of performance data in the budget process; there is doubt that the level of effort results in a concomitant level of budgetary benefit.

The Zero-Base Budget

The Zero-Base Budget (ZBB) is popularly defined as an operating plan through budgeting that requires managers to justify their entire budget in detail from scratch—hence zero-base or cut back management—and to show why they should spend any money at all. This approach requires that all activities are identified in decision packages that are evaluated systematically and ranked in order of importance.[5]

Wacht's presentation of ZBB directs library managers to ask three questions: Should your area of responsibility be abolished? Can its functions be performed at a lower level of activity and remain as productive as last year? If your budget increases next year, will the incremental costs outweigh the incremental benefits?

There are four basic steps in ZBB:

1) *Identifying decision unit.* Current departments, or major service components like Adult, Young Adult, Children's, Reference, and Technical Services, are frequently designated as the decision units.

2) *Formulating decision packages.* A decision package is a document that defines the activities of each decision unit, so that managers can compare it to other decision units competing for limited resources. Two types of alternatives are considered when formulating decision packages—different ways to perform the same functions and different levels of effort needed to perform the function. The levels are: the minimum necessary to achieve the most important objectives, usually calculated at 50% to 75% of the current level of support; the status quo, or support at the current level; the higher level, which projects an increase.

A series of questions is put to each of the library's major services in creating decision packages: How many ways can the library's objectives be accomplished? Which is the most effective way? What levels of functions and costs are possible? Following this review, the service's activities are segmented into one of the alternative service levels—minimal, status quo, or increased.

3) *Ranking decision packages.* Ranks are assigned by evaluating the cost of the decision packages and their order of importance in reaching the library's objectives.

4) *Priority ranking of all decision packages.* Following the initial ranking within the departments, the decision packages are forwarded to appropriate managers, who merge them into a single list of prioritized packages.

For example, under ZBB, the program managers within Adult Services would each prepare a decision package and submit it to the head of Adult Services, who would combine them into a budget request such as the one shown in Figure 4.

Then the head of Adult Services, together with his or her program managers, would rank all the Services' decision packages and send them to higher management in a prioritized format, such as the one shown in Figure 5.

Next, the heads of all major library programs, together with the li-

brary's top administrators, would look over the entire group of decision packages and reevaluate them to establish a single priority for support for the entire organization.

ZBB adds priorities to unit cost data, all of which are presented in relation to goals and objectives. This technique calls for setting priorities within the base of the budget as opposed to using an incremental approach. But while prioritizing is appealing to many library managers, its worth is offset by the amount of paperwork required and the difficulty in identifying and justifying each activity. A good deal of time is consumed in documenting programs and in reviewing the documentation.

Which Budget Is For Your Library?

In retrospect, the four budget types represent a hierarchy of decision-making information, planning, documentation, and record-keeping. The program budget focuses the process on the service aspect of librarianship by linking goals and objectives to fiscal requests. The performance budget adds measures of efficiency or productivity to supply current cost data. ZBB includes the strong points of the first two techniques and calls for priority ranking and the assumption that not all current programs are worthy of continued funding. Each of the three can be turned into a line-item budget with little added effort. If the library must submit a line-item budget to the ultimate funding decision-makers, it can employ any internal format it deems appropriate and then make the necessary translation.

After careful study, we would conclude all four approaches to budgeting are needed to meet the many requirements of successfully presenting the library's case for support. ▬

References

1. Richard E. Wacht, *Financial Management in Nonprofit Organizations*, Atlanta: College of Business Administration, Georgia State University, 1987, p. 480.
2. Ann E. Prentice, *Financial Planning for Libraries*, Metuchen, N.J.: Scarecrow, 1984, p. 27.
3. Wacht, p. 320.
4. Prentice, p. 96.
5. Peter Pyhrr, *Zero-Base Budgeting: A Practical Management Tool for Evaluating Expenses*, John Wiley, 1973, p. 5–7.

CREATIVE BUDGET PRESENTATION: Using Statistics to Prove Your Point

Robert Burgin

The fine art of budget presentation is based on a two-step process: the request for funds and the defense of that request. Although both steps use statistics, it is the budget defense that demands the creative use of statistics.

Establishing your library's needs and proving its good stewardship (also known as effectiveness) are the bulwarks of budget defense. First you must convince the governing body that the funds requested are necessary to meet a need. Second you must remind the funding body that the library has used effectively the money it has received in the past. In short, the library's case is that the money is needed and that it will be well spent.

The ideal of statistical collection can be summed up briefly: if the library does it, count it. Yet, although librarians en gage in a great variety of services and activities, few of these are counted. At budget time, however, any and all of these services and activities may be called into question by members of the funding body. If you can't produce the evidence—including statistical evidence—to justify these activities, not only is your particular argument lost, but confidence in your ability may be eroded. If statistics in a specific area have not been collected, support for budget proposals in that area will probably be weaker than it should be.

Overdue fines are an example of an activity where few statistics are kept. While all libraries devote staff time and effort in attempts to encourage the timely return of borrowed materials and to retrieve those that are not returned on time, few keep statistics concerning the effectiveness of their efforts. These statistics would be useful in defending a budget request for increasing the circulation staff or for automating the circulation system since studies show that libraries with automated circulation systems have lower overdues rates than do libraries with manual systems.[1]

At the Forsyth County (North Carolina) Public Library System, we used these data in our request for automated circulation (see Table 1). We compared our own overdues rate with the average for computerized libraries, estimated the drop in overdues that could be expected if we automated, and translated that percentage drop into books that would be returned and available for patrons. We found that if Forsyth County were automated, 2.59% or 41,019 more books would be available for the patrons to check out rather than being overdue.

Statistics for Decision Making

Realistically, few librarians have the time to exhaustively collect statistics. And so, the collection effort must be focused by the goals and objectives of the library. Statistics, after all, are tools and not ends in themselves. The connection between the library's goals and the statistics collection process cannot be overemphasized: statistics help in the formulation of reasonable goals, goals help focus the process of collecting statistical data. At the very least, then, the statistics collected should be relevant to the goals of the library and should enable you to determine whether the library's goals are being met and, if not, how serious is the shortfall.

Collecting statistics requires efficient data collection methods. It should be a continuing process since collecting all the statistical data needed for a typical budget presentation would be too great a task to undertake at one time. Using microcomputers and spreadsheets, statistical data can be collected and compiled efficiently and in a time-saving manner.[2] Gathered throughout the year, data should be saved on disk until needed at budget time.

Libraries with large automated systems for circulation and cataloging also can use these systems for gathering and manipulating a sophisticated range of data for decision and budget support, as Ken Dowlin and others have pointed out.[3] In fact, this may be one of their least utilized but most exciting capabilities.

Continually presenting statistical data to your funding board is as important as the continuous collection of the data. Funding officials should be accustomed to receiving status reports on the library regularly, as part of the monthly report, for example, and not just at budget time. Through this ongoing review you educate the funding officials, helping them to understand certain statistics by frequently presenting arguments that employ them. If this process of education has not been ongoing, it may be too late at budget time to not only present and defend a budget, but educate officials as to what these statistics mean.

Remember, statistics do not exist in a vacuum. They are a reference to something else—either an internal yardstick or an external one. Internal yardsticks can be goals and objectives and comparisons with historical data. External yardsticks are the performance of other libraries and library standards.

Internal Comparisons

Good data collection, guided by the goals and objectives of the library, will enable you to compare realities with possibilities. Comparing goals and statistics relates to the two arguments expressed in budget

defense: need and good stewardship. As a part of the needs argument you might note that the library's goals have not been met and cannot be met without the requested funds. For the good stewardship argument you can remind members of the funding body that the library has met its goals in the past and can be expected to spend the requested funds in an equally wise and effective fashion.

In Forsyth County, for example, the covering sheet of our budget presentation summarized the goals and objectives of our past budget year and noted which goals had been met and which still needed to be met. The presentation was based on relevant statistics that had been gathered.

Another approach is to compare the library's most recent performance with its past performance in order to show that the library is improving (in order to make the case for good, efficient use of funding) or that the situation is not as good as it once was (in order to establish that a need exists). At the Wayne County (North Carolina) Public Library, we were able to show the commissioners and city council members data (see Table 2) on growing circulation as evidence that the increased funding of recent years paid off and should be continued.

External Comparisons

External statistics—the performance of other libraries and library standards—provide a yardstick against which to measure performance. For example, book circulation statistics alone are meaningless. But they can be made meaningful by comparing them with internal data. For instance, how much has circulation increased over the past year? Even more meaning can be given to a level of activity by comparing it to the level of activity of other libraries or to an established standard. For instance, how does per capita circulation compare with other similar libraries?

There are a number of sources of statistics and standards for external comparisons, including national and regional data. Statewide statistical reports also are issued by most state library agencies.[4] Most important is to collect reasonably compatible statistics so that such external comparisons can be made. An argument

TABLE 1
PERCENTAGE OF BOOKS STILL OUT ON THE DATE THEY WERE DUE (1983)

Forsyth County	11.31%
Libraries with Automated Circulation	8.72%
Difference	2.59%
Number of Books Circulated in Forsyth County	1,583,755

TABLE 2
CIRCULATION CHANGE 1975–1981

	Wayne County Book Circulation	Wayne County Annual Increase	State Average Annual Increase
1975–76	143,853	--	--
1976–77	166,503	15.7 %	0.9 %
1977–78	202,559	21.7 %	4.3 %
1978–79	218,979	8.1 %	3.1 %
1979–80	221,243	1.0 %	3.1 %
1980–81	255,085	15.3 %	9.4 %
1975–76 to 1980–81	77.3 %		16.8 %

TABLE 3
BOOK COLLECTION CHANGE 1976–1981

	Wayne County Book Collection	Wayne County Annual Increase	State Average Annual Increase
1976–77	32,968	--	--
1977–78	41,434	25.7 %	3.9 %
1978–79	44,202	6.7 %	2.5 %
1979–80	53,255	20.5 %	3.1 %
1980–81	58,202	9.3 %	2.8 %
1976–77 to 1980–81	76.5 %		12.8 %

for the adoption of ALA's output measures is that they provide a common core of statistical data for use by libraries across the country. Or, since most state libraries require annual statistical reports, these reports can provide a shared set of data for use by libraries in an individual state and by libraries outside the state.

Making Comparisons

One way to present comparison data is to boast that the library is meeting its goals or improving its performance (using internal statistics), or to claim that the library is the best in some area (using external statistics). This approach generally serves the argument of effective stewardship—that the library has done an admirable job with funds provided in the past and can be counted on to continue the good work. There is an implied argument of need in this positive approach— the users are accustomed to this fine level of library service and need to have it continued.

Conversely, evidence of great need may be presented to the funding body based on the fact that the library is the worst in some area. When using such data, of course, try to avoid blaming or being blamed for the situation; instead, show that in spite of the worst you and your staff are trying; and constantly report progress to your funding body.

At the Wayne County Public Library we supported our request for additional book money by pointing out that the library was last in the state in the number of books per capita. We were quick to note why this was the case—that until recently, the library had not had the space to house many new books. We also reminded the commissioners and council members that this was no longer the case. Our new facility could house several times the collection of the old building and we were doing the best we could with out limited resources—our turnover rate was one of the highest in the state. We also shared with everyone the successful results of increased book funds: our book collection was the fastest growing in the state (see Table 3). We added more books in one year than did many libraries with larger overall budgets and we jumped out of last place in the state in books per capita.

Presenting Statistical Data

While statistical data are important, the way in which those data are presented is crucial. Although the ideal of statistical collection is the thorough enumeration of all library activities, the ideal of statistical presentation is brevity. Most funding bodies do not have the time to sift through an abundance of figures; they should have only the highlights presented to them. The general budget presentation—and the defense— should be succinct, using only a few relevant, core statistics—statistics that the funding officials have been educated to understand. But, the statistical arsenal should be thorough

in order to answer all possible questions and meet potential objections. You should be able to defend any specific budget area briefly and concisely.

Per Capita or Not

Should statistics be expressed as raw data or in per capita terms? There is a maxim in the legal profession that if the case is weak on facts, one should argue based on principle, and vice versa. And so, if your case is better presented using raw data, use raw data; if your case is better presented using per capita data, use per capita data.

Realistically, few librarians have the time to exhaustively collect statistics. And so, the collection effort must be focused by the goals and objectives of the library. Statistics, after all, are tools and not ends in themselves. The connection between the library's goals and the statistics collection process cannot be overemphasized.

Especially with larger systems, the sheer volume expressed by raw data will be sufficient to make a point or to allow a comparison. At the Forsyth County Public Library, we tended to base our presentations on our being the state's leading or second leading library in book circulation, reference services, and the like—all expressed in raw data. In Wayne County, however, the dearth of books could only be expressed adequately in per capita terms. We ranked an unexciting fortieth or so out of seventy public libraries in North Carolina in book holdings, and a deplorable last in the state in book holdings per capita.

How Much Is That In Service?

Budget presentations should translate everything into service— both requests for more money and potential cuts. In Wayne County, when we requested that the position of children's librarian be upgraded to a professional position and that our programs in that area be expanded, we could estimate the number of additional children who would be served. When we requested more book money, we were able to estimate how many books that money would buy, how many circulations would result, and how many people would be served:

In 1980, the average volume added cost the Wayne County Library $9.39.
In 1980, the average volume in Wayne County was checked out 4.4 times.
A $10,000 increase in the book budget in 1980 would have:
- purchased 1,065 more volumes
- resulted in 4,686 more circulations.

Funding cuts should also be translated into the effects they will have on services: Will hours be reduced? At what cost in circulation in materials? In people served? Talk in terms of constituents and voters. The members of the funding body are often elected officials. They understand that the individuals being served by the library are also the individuals who will cast votes for or against them or their party.

How Much Is That In Candy Bars?

Two years ago, the *Wall Street Journal* ran an article that pointed to a trend among the advertisers of America's largest corporations: "If Camel smokers had walked a mile for every Camel produced by R.J. Reynolds, they would have walked to the sun and back more than 17,000 times," claimed one ad. "Two ships the size of the Queen Elizabeth II could be floated in the ocean of Hawaiian Punch Americans consume annually," declared another.[5]

Outrageous presentations draw attention to the sheer volume of success of the particular company in terms that the consumer will remember. Three trillion cigarettes may be a lot of cigarettes, but that figure doesn't make the same impression as 17,000 trips to the sun and back.

You can also dress up your library's statistics in exciting terms. In reporting on the same *Wall Street Journal* article elsewhere, I suggested the following as examples of what could be done: "All the people who attended programs in North Carolina's public libraries last year could fill the Rose Bowl 60 times" and "Public libraries in North Carolina checked out enough books last year to line the road from Manteo to Murphy [the end points of the state] eight times."

The Politics of Budget Presentation

The budget process is not an entirely rational one. Where one set of commissioners will be proud of the library's standing as the best-funded in the state, another set will find this an indication that the library's budget can be cut. Where one group will think twice about cutting the library's budget if it means closing a certain branch, another will cut the budget and order the librarian to keep the branch open anyway.

The data used for budget presentations quite naturally vary from library to library and, within the same library, from budget presentation to budget presentation. For example, in Wayne County we made two budget presentations each year—one to the county commissioners and one to the city council. The statistical data needed for each presentation differed because the arguments that satisfied one group differed from those that satisfied the other.

What remains constant, however, is the need to use statistics when defending budget requests. Ideally, we should have a thorough arsenal of statistical tools and be able to use it in a flexible fashion in order to meet any contingency. We should be prepared.

For example, be aware of statistics that might argue against a point, but don't present statistics that won't help, the case. In addition to being aware of them, be prepared to explain the apparent discrepancy between what is being requested and the supposed evidence against the case.

The budget presentation and any related presentation of statistics should be rehearsed. Have a col-

Six Easy Statistical Formulas

1. **Annual % Increase** $= \dfrac{\text{This Yr's Figure}-\text{Last Yr's Figure}}{\text{Last Year's Figure}}$

Example: Forsyth County Public Library

1982–83 Operating Expenditures	$ 2,661,991
1983–84 Operating Expenditures	$ 2,782,764

Percentage Increase,

$$1982\text{–}83 \text{ to } 1983\text{–}84 = \frac{\$\,2,782,764-\$\,2,661,991}{\$\,2,661,991}$$

Annual % Increase = 4.54 %

2. **% Increase Over Several Years** $= \dfrac{\text{Final Yr's Figure}-\text{Beginning Yr's Figure}}{\text{Beginning Yr's Figure}}$

Example: Forsyth County Public Library

1978–79 Operating Expenditures	$ 1,463,907
1983–84 Operating Expenditures	$ 2,782,764

Percentage Increase,

$$1978\text{–}79 \text{ to } 1983\text{–}84 = \frac{\$\,2,782,764-\$\,1,463,907}{\$\,1,463,907}$$

% Increase Over Several Years = 90.1 %

3. **Service Level Per Capita** $= \dfrac{\text{Service Level}}{\text{Population Served}}$

Example: Forsyth County Public Library

1983–84 Book Circulation	1,583,755
1983–84 Population Served	249,172

$$\textit{Book Circulation Per Capita} = \frac{1,583,755}{249,172} = 6.36$$

4. **Service Level Per Unit** $= \dfrac{\text{Service Level}}{\text{Units Under Consideration}}$

Example: Forsyth County Public Library

1983–84 Book Circulation	1,583,755
1983–84 Staff (FTEs)	.95.3

$$\textit{Book Circulation Per Staff Member} = \frac{1,583,755}{95.3} = 16,618.6$$

5. **Collection Turnover** $= \dfrac{\text{Circulation of Collection}}{\text{Items in Collection}}$

Example: Forsyth County Public Library

1983–84 Book Circulation	1,583,755
1983–84 Book Collection	335,550

$$\textit{Book Collection Turnover} = \frac{1,583,755}{335,550} = 4.72$$

6. **Cost to Circulate an Item** $= \dfrac{\text{Operating Expenditures}}{\text{Items Circulated}}$

Example: Forsyth County Public Library

1983–84 Operating Expenditures	$ 2,782,764
1983–84 Book Circulation	1,583,755

$$\textit{Cost to Circulate a Book} = \frac{\$\,2,782,764}{1,583,755} = \$\,1.76$$

league play the devil's advocate by asking for statistical justification of budget requests, by pointing out which statistics seem irrelevant or poorly presented, and by using statistics to argue against what is being requested.

Finally, look at others' budget presentations, especially those from nonlibrary institutions. What statistics are they using to back up their funding requests? Which statistics were the most successful? Which were best received?

Easily Applied Statistical Formulas

Statistics need not be esoteric or complex to be effective. In fact, to help present the case for budget support, they should be just the opposite. The most useful formulas, such as those shown below, offer the opportunity for multiple variations on a theme.

Since there are physical limits to the amount of statistics that can be gathered, the library's goals must give direction to the statistics-gathering effort. The goals should help determine what data are collected and the statistics should help formulate the goals. Finally, of course, the library's goals should determine the development of its budget request.

References

1. Patsy Hansel and Robert Burgin, "Hard Facts About Overdues," *Library Journal* 108 (February 15, 1983): 349–352. Robert Burgin and Patsy Hansel, "More Hard Facts About Overdues," *Library & Archival Security* 6 (Summer/Fall 1984): 5–17.
2. Claudia Perry-Holmes, "LOTUS 1-2-3 and Decision Support: Allocating the Monograph Budget," *Library Software Review* (July-August 1985): 205–213. While the article focuses on the use of spreadsheet software in an academic library, the ideas presented can easily be translated into the public library's environment. *See also* Philip M. Clark, "Processing Numbers with Spreadsheet Programs," *New Jersey Libraries* 18 (Summer 1985): 17–19.
3. Kenneth C. Dowlin, "The Use of Standard Statistics in an On-Line Library Management System," *Public Library Quarterly* 3 (Spring/Summer 1982): 37–46.
4. On the variety of state statistics that are gathered, see Kenneth D. Shearer, *The Collection and Use of Public Library Statistics by State Library Agencies* (Chicago: American Library Association, 1978). For a look at regional statistical data, see Robert Burgin, "Regional Public Library Statistics: A Checklist," *Public Libraries* 21 (Winter 1982): 142–143.
5. "If All Our Reporters Are Laid End to End ... They Don't Report," *Wall Street Journal* 4 April 1983.
6. Robert Burgin, "Statistically Speaking," *Down East* 5 (August 1983): 3–4.

ON ACCOUNT

FUND ACCOUNTING BASICS

Sherman Hayes and Clifford D. Brown

It is a real challenge to summarize a major theoretical system such as fund accounting in two thousand words or less. We accept the challenge and hope to show why library managers should become more familiar with useful accounting practices and terminology, and why they should make the effort to understand fund accounting at all.

Financial accounting, as it evolves and changes daily, is based upon techniques, terminology, procedures and approaches useful in preparing financial statements for profit-making organizations. Fund accounting is a separate, but very similar, set of rules useful in creating an accounting system for not-for-profit organizations. A major distinction of fund accounting is the provision for setting up individual "funds" or "fund groups" to be tracked, accounted for and documented as separate self-balancing accounting entities. Each fund group can be reported separately, using financial reports unique to non-profits, to describe its activities. There is no requirement (as in financial accounting) for a single set of statements. In your work with not-for-profit organizations, you may have noticed that financial reports may be divided by fund type such as operating fund, endowment fund, and plant fund. We will discuss these fund types later.

Fund accounting evolved from the need to report and account for resources that can be treated differently, account for resources tied to specific functions, and, most important, account for resources whose use has been restricted by others, such as donors, or government. An endowment fund is typical of this last as it has restrictions on the use of both principal and proceeds. To help the not-for-profit entity track these restrictions and report financial activity within their limits, fund accounting systems were created.

Because the term fund is used in so many different ways in accounting, we need to define it. In fund accounting, each fund has a separate tracking system set up by function and is self-balancing. The name and reporting documents relate to the function of the resources and expenditures within the fund. The "funds" referred to when speaking of revenues or cash are not the same as the "fund" in fund accounting. Also, the term is not the same one frequently used to describe the division of materials expenditures (book fund, journals fund); the term fund raising is not the same as fund accounting. Now that you are thoroughly confused with the wealth of fund definitions, let's move on to the main funds in fund accounting which may help us understand the overall need for such a system.

Operating Funds

The major fund for most institutions is the operating fund, frequently called the current fund. Most of us working within a larger parent institution use the budget as the primary tool to manage and activate the operating fund. Usually the largest and most active fund, it is most familiar to librarians. The nature of the library determines the fund's revenues and other income sources — tuition or state appropriations for higher education; property or city tax funds for public libraries; or endowment income, fees and direct gifts for private libraries.

The three major reports prepared at the end of a fiscal period for an institution should be the Balance Sheet (assets and liabilities and fund balances); Statement of Revenue, Expense and Changes in Fund Balances; and the Statement of Changes in Cash, Sources of Cash, and Use of Cash. Because the operating fund is so large, it is common to have a separate, detailed statement of reve-

nues, expenditures and other changes related to this one fund. We wager that these statements are unfamiliar to many librarians.

Where does your budget fit into this maze of reports? If your library is a sub-unit of a much larger entity such as a university, you can read financial statements (or try to) and wonder where all of your budget effort and expenditures went! Our library's $1,500,000 expenditure to support the College's effort had one line in the financial statements under Educational and General Expenditures: Academic Support. If you are part of a separate public library, you may need to develop and use a full set of audited financial statements for your library. Remember, budgeting is a managerial tool to help plan and allocate resources and control their use. Fund accounting statements reflect an overview of total financial activity and do not report detailed use and distribution of resources throughout the organization as budget reports would.

Endowment Funds

A second major fund is the endowment fund or trust fund. This fund, or group of funds, is distinguished by the restrictions placed on its use and future disposition of resources by the donor of the resources. Although all funds can have restricted and unrestricted sources of revenue, the endowment fund is usually established to create ongoing sources of revenue by preventing use of the principal for current activity. The principal is usually protected and its gains in value and earned income are usually distributed by the institution according to a prior agreement between the managers of the institution, or perhaps the original donor. Proceeds may be transferred to another fund and then used for purposes within the restrictions of the new fund's guidelines. A typical transfer of proceeds might be for interest from an invested gift (principal stays in and perhaps one-half of interest for a year is designated) to be transferred to the operating fund to purchase books within a fiscal time period. A part of the ending fund balance of the endowment fund would be transferred as new revenue to another fund.

Endowments are critical for libraries in the future. As the operating fund comes under ever-increasing pressure from any number of crises (inflation, competing units within the institution, need for new materials and services or dwindling sources of taxes or tuition) it is very important to have additional resources set aside for future use. Fund accounting requires very close tracking of gifts and their restrictions as well as policies on their use and the transferability of resources. It is important to understand the gifts that might be received in an endowment fund such as life income, insurance policies, stocks, bonds, grants, cash, and physical items of value. Your parent institution might even have endowment resources given on your behalf of which you are unaware.

People reading the financial reports of an endowment look for very different items from those found in operating fund reports. These reports describe the value of principal (found in assets), additions to principal, earned income and any distribution of income to other funds. Restricted resources are usually noted and reported within the statement or as detailed footnotes to the statement.

Plant/Building Funds

A third major fund is the plant or building fund. This fund is probably treated less uniformly among different not-for-profit institutions than any other. In higher education, it might be divided into three sub-funds such as unexpended plant funds (reserve account or assigned for an upcoming building expenditure), retirement of indebtedness (to pay for a building financed with bonds), and investment in plant (the cost or fair value, if donated, placed on the physical assets of the institution). State and local governments use a variety of funds that may be called something slightly different but serve the same purpose. Sample subdivisions might be Capital Project Funds and Special Revenue Funds. Despite the title, these funds all revolve around the accounting concept of tracking and recording revenues and expenditures.

Because many institutions are empowered to acquire debt to finance facilities, there can be specific debt service and bonding restrictions on the use of such funds. In the aca-demic setting, particular streams of revenue may be committed to paying off construction debt. The librarian will most likely use this fund if there is major construction related to the library. Under a recent ruling by the Financial Accounting Standards Board (the rule-making body of the accounting profession) on handling of depreciation in not-for profits, you may be involved more heavily in determining the asset valuation of the library collection, furniture, and buildings for depreciation calculations. (See "There's Depreciation in Your Future," *Bottom Line: A Financial Magazine for Librarians*, Vol., 2, No. 2, 1988, pp. 27–28.) Management issues revolving around this fund include the need to understand the institution's definition of a capital asset, the concept of determining the length of life and the valuation of an asset, and the many restrictions that may be imposed on you as manager in acquiring and funding major asset purchases.

Governing boards may decide to use the accounting technique of reserves in determining the use of resources. The reserve is a particular amount of money set aside for anticipated changes affecting the institution. The plant fund is most commonly used to establish reserves for repair, maintenance or replacement of facilities or equipment. You must make several important determinations about such reserves: Should they continue as a constant source each year or are they just a one-time event? Are there hidden facility and equipment reserves available? Are there repair projects that might qualify through plant reserve resources that would be rejected out-of-hand if you requested operating funds? Is there an ongoing perpetual maintenance plant fund for your institution or library to systematically replace facilities and equipment before they wear out? Should there be such a fund?

Fiduciary Funds

There are other funds in fund accounting that are unique to each type of institution, such as fiduciary funds. This group is similar to but broader than endowment funds and includes pension trust funds, agency funds (you collect taxes for someone else and hold it for awhile), and loan funds (college setting in which you loan money to students through a revolving system). There are proprietary funds which have two major subdivisions: enterprise funds and internal service funds. Enterprise funds might be applicable to libraries whose unit activities are financed primarily by user charges. Examples in a city government would be parking garages, airports and convention centers.

Also in city government, internal service funds are established to account for services provided by a central service department to other governmental units where the services are charged back. Typical fund activities include motor pools, printing and duplication and data processing. One last type is a strike insurance fund that would be used by a labor union.

Finding More Information

There are several key bibliographic sources for more information pertinent to different kinds of libraries. A basic text with great detail on accounting systems for not-for-profits is available from the American Library Association, *Accounting for Librarians and Other Not-For-Profit Managers*, by G. Stevenson Smith, 1983, ALA. A more succinct overview from the accounting profession, formatted as a self-paced cassette set with workbook and answers to the problem set, is available from the AICPA, *Accounting and Auditing for Certain Nonprofit Organizations*, by Eugene Geiser and Clifford Brown, 1988, American Institute of Certified Public Accountants Continuing Professional Education. Technical publications addressing fund accounting issues for not-for-profits are: *Audits of Certain Nonprofit Organizations*, 1981, AICPA; *Audits of State and Local Governmental Units*, 1986, AICPA; *Audits of Colleges and Universities*, 1975, AICPA; *Statement of Financial Accounting Standards No. 93*, 1987, Financial Accounting Standards Board; *Statement of Financial Accounting Concepts No. 4*, 1980, Financial Accounting Standards Board.

Now that we have skimmed over many funds, we hope you are fired up to learn more accounting to better serve you in your management position. ▬

ON ACCOUNT

THERE'S DEPRECIATION IN YOUR FUTURE

Sherman Hayes and David R.L. Gabhart

Of all the issues confronting librarians in their daily activities, accounting for depreciation is most aptly described as a "shoulder shrugger." And in the recent past, a librarian would have been justified for having no interest in depreciation since it has had little impact on budgeting or financial decisions. However, with the release of the Statement of Financial Accounting Standards No. 93, *Recognition of Depreciation by Not-for-Profit Organizations*, we suggest that you consider taking a CPA to lunch.

Issued by the Financial Accounting Standards Board (FASB), private libraries, colleges, and universities now must disclose depreciation in their financial statements to receive an unqualified opinion from their auditors. An unqualified opinion is a "clean bill of health" in accounting parlance.

What Is Depreciation?

Most of us think of depreciation as a loss in value. For instance, when we buy a new car we contemplate how fast it will decline in value—or, depreciate.

Accounting's concept of depreciation, as used in the statement of operations, which is part of an institution's annual financial report, is quite different. It is not considered a loss in value but a means of matching the expenses of doing business for a period of time against the revenues for that period. The amount of depreciation an accountant recognizes in an asset, such as the library building or a piece of equipment, is not a function of a decline in market value (changes in market value are difficult to measure and costly to obtain). Rather, an accountant attempts to estimate the decline in the building or equipment's potential by allocating costs over a period of time.

As a result of Statement No. 93, libraries and other private institutions now have to compute depreciation to determine the value of such fixed assets as the building, collections, carpeting, shelving, library equipment (microfilm readers and binding equipment), and furniture.

Depreciation expense does not require an outlay of cash. It has little effect on cash budgeting.

How Accounting Standards Are Set

Standards such as Statement No. 93 are developed by the FASB through a "due process" system that gives interested persons the opportunity for input. Accounting problems and issues are identified and researched to assess alternative solutions and their effects. Then a discussion memorandum is written and released for comments, which usually are gathered through public hearings held around the country.

The issues are further deliberated after which an exposure draft of the potential standard is released. Additional public opinion is gathered for a period of at least 30 days and the Board reevaluates its position and reissues the standard if necessary. The Board then votes on a final standard. If adopted, the standard must be followed in the preparation of financial statements.

While attention is currently focused on nonprofit organizations, government agencies will soon face a similar requirement. The Governmental Accounting Standards Body (GASB) has released a draft statement that requires similar recognition of depreciation by governmental units.

GASB sets the standards for accounting and reporting of state and local government units. Its operational structure is similar to FASB.

The creation of a separate standard-setting body for government units was not without controversy. Many people believe there should only be one standard-setting body so that financial statements prepared by state and local government are comparable to those of private business.

How You Can Compute Depreciation

There are several recognized methods to compute depreciation, each with its own advantages. The most easily understood and simplest to compute is the "straight-line" method of depreciation. It considers three factors:

- the cost of the building or equipment (C)
- the estimated proceeds that will be received when the asset is retired, often called salvage value (SV)
- the number of years in the service life of assets (N)

Using the straight-line method, the amount of depreciation for any period of time is expressed as:

$$\frac{C - SV}{N}$$

For example, if you purchase a new photocopy machine for $16,000 and estimate that it can be sold for $1,000 five years later, the amount recognized for each of the five years is $3,000:

$$\frac{\$16,000 - \$1,000}{5} = \$3,000$$

At the end of the first year's use, the photocopy machine would be shown on the library's balance sheet as follows:

Equipment (at cost)	$16,000
Less accumulated depreciation	3,000
	$13,000

The 13,000 represents the estimated unused service potential of the photocopy machine. Also called its book value, this is the amount that can still be depreciated for the next four years. This is computed as follows:

Cost of Asset - Accumulated Depreciation

Remember, book value has nothing to do with market value, insurance value, or replacement cost.

Dealing with Statement No. 93

Because Statement No. 93 requires that depreciation be compiled and disclosed on the library or parent institution's statements on a retroactive basis, we suggest following a two-step approach to meeting its reporting requirements:

Step One. Make a complete list of all assets (equipment) under your control. Compare it to the list of equipment maintained in the administrative offices of your college, university, or government agency. Specific information should include the date the equipment was acquired, its original cost, and a description of its present condition. Any major repairs or improvements should also be recorded. If any of this information is missing, make estimates.

Step Two. Determine the original life and estimated remaining life of each piece of equipment and review these estimates with whomever does your financial statements. For example, if you purchased a typewriter five years ago whose original life was estimated at six years, its estimated remaining life is one year.

Taking Advantage of Statement No. 93

By applying Statement No. 93 you can systematize the need to predict equipment replacement. In addition, the information you gather for Statement No. 93 should prove valuable when preparing a capital budget or requesting a fixed asset acquisition. Finally, the information will drive future planning for services by showing what equipment is available and what must be acquired.

It is just good business practice to know what your library owns and to understand the financial implications of the library's assets. Adopting a process to meet this new reporting requirement will minimize the burden of work. But more importantly, you will find yourself speaking the same language as those who make the final financial decisions and so should find that you have a greater role in those decisions. =

LET ME COUNT THE WAYS: INFORMATION ACQUISITION ACCOUNTING

Sherman Hayes

As I once again go through the end-of-year analysis of my acquisitions accounts, it strikes me how much time I (and many others on the library staff) spend on accounting related to the acquisition of information. The library profession, like most, has developed a specialized language to help its members talk to each other. The information acquisition staff has to be adept at translating library terms into terms used by the business community they deal with. There are a number of accounting contact points in the acquisition process which are critical for almost every level of staff in the library.

As we use our specialized library definitions and language, we should not forget that much of what we do is really founded on basic business accounting practices. As we keep track of library acquisitions, most of our practices are similar to those of private industry. We can learn from the experiences of industry if we can see and translate the common elements into accounting jargon.

Since the library is in the wholesale and retail information business (albeit generally not for profit), we really shouldn't be surprised by the amount of cost accounting, bookkeeping, budgeting, purchasing, accounts payable, accounts receivable, cash management, and such that we do!

Strategic Accounting

The first use of accounting concepts is in our strategic definition of the library as a business. If we had to fill out a 10K report for the government, what would we list as our "line of business"?

Obviously, we do many things, but in information services we are mainly a retailer. As a service entity, libraries purchase the materials (read *information*), add value to them in many ways, and then offer them at the retail level for customer use. We provide a sales force and supply customer assistance.

One of the central products of library service is information in a wide variety of formats. This multitude of ever-changing formats is dictated by marketplace offerings and by customer demand. Information comes in the traditional book and journal formats, or in media such as video tapes and audio tapes, or on computer disks.

We serve the customer, as the for-profit retailer does, by keeping aware of marketplace offerings (selection of product inventory); by purchasing the product from a manufacturer or wholesaler (acquisitions); by enhancing access and maintaining an ever changing inventory; by sales assistance and promotion; by training customers; and more.

Our goal is to match customer needs with our stock of information holdings. The ultimate measure of success is judged by a number of criteria, generally excluding profit, but including such analogs to sales as circulation and other measures of usage, breadth and depth of inventory (strength of collection), preservation of information, access to information outside of facilities, service as an educational laboratory, recreation and entertainment.

The definition of *what we do* is as critical to strategic planning and judgment as to our success. Strategically, most libraries provide functions beyond straightforward retailing. These might include the original production of new information (publications), instruction and direct teaching, entertainment (showing films or telling stories), or the addition of research summaries to existing information.

However, information acquisitions, or the retail side of our business, is the major focus of libraries and the focus of this column. Besides just buying materials or providing access to information, we attempt to add value by arranging them in a specialized manner (classification system), by providing a full inventory (catalog), and by teaching people how to find and even use the materials. By looking at our "business" through the accountant's eyes, we can reevaluate the roles we play, the costs involved, and the opportunities for change and enhancement.

Using a business model and language, we can reexamine our cost-accounting analysis and determine what percentage of expenditures could be used for various parts of the retail business. Raw materials would be the purchase cost of information in its many formats. One of the ongoing debates in the library profession is the definition of information. A little more than a decade ago, it was safe to assume that our retail product was books or journals. Microforms and related nonprint media have been growing in number but are still relatively small players. Now with the advent of the electronic database (where the product is paper and the patron leaves the library with it forever!) and with CD-ROM products that are expensive and difficult to count as stock items in volumes, the accounting and business definitions of our retail product are undergoing radical changes.

If we accept my definition of our inventory as information that is acquired for, brokered for, or directly utilized by the patron, then a true cost accounting would add to our material costs those information offerings that are outside traditional materials budgets. In calculating the cost of goods sold we should include expenditures associated with inventory control and security, cataloging, equipment needed to access and use information, selection costs (commercial buyers costs) and any other value-added packaging enhanced the raw information.

This theoretical translation into

business terms of our normal strategic question of "how much to spend on materials" is an exercise that can help librarians break away from constraints imposed by current practice and traditional thinking. Here are a few questions librarians might ask themselves:

- If I perceive myself as primarily a retail information store, what mix of value-added services will best serve customer needs?
- Should I reduce processing and cataloging efforts, transferring money to new product acquisition to enhance usage?
- Should I automate more to increase the return on cataloging investment by increasing customer satisfaction and increasing information finding rates?
- Should I offer partial service branch libraries with popular information checkout services to increase materials turnover rates?

These are real question that people are asking—but seldom in standard business terms. Nor are we realizing the full potential of the accounting information that is so industriously collected within our libraries.

Budgeting

In addition to acquisition accounting at the strategic level, we almost all use accounting practices to help us create budgets and plans for information expenditures. Budgets are part of the managerial accounting system. We try to predict and anticipate what resources we need, and what we can get. Most of us are familiar with how resources are divided into logical expenditure categories and adjusted against the basic budget plan. Unfortunately, because few of our institutions allow us to change the resource side of the equation (there is no new money coming into the formula as would be the case in private enterprise), the budget becomes a central, all encompassing, usually "set in cement" vehicle, for regulating expenditures.

Budgeting and accounting systems are usually local in nature. As a result, one very critical part that accounting plays for libraries is defining budget categories for expenditures. The traditional monographs, serials, and microform materials divisions are causing interesting

choices on how to budget for automation, CD-ROMs, video disks and a whole array of new database and subscription services. Some of the budgetary definitional fights revolve around vested interests. (Logically or not, people tend to be loyal to different formats of information.)

The library is constrainted by higher authorities depending on the budget category being increased, decreased, or introduced to the chart of accounts for the first time. How many of us know we need additional equipment, but have absolutely no chance of getting it if we identify it as equipment because the budget and expenditure allocation system precludes adequate equipment? Some are constrained by leasing rules within a municipality. Have you ever tried to move salary funds into computing accounts?

In today's shrinking budgets, getting real live new incremental positions approved is very difficult. Note that few of these constraints have much to do with the strategic plan of the library. They have nothing to do with how to best use a *single amount of total resources* and little to do with efficiencies in acquiring materials. Seldom are they addressed in programmatic budget terms, but all are accounting and budgetary categorical constraints placed on the library by some parent institution or by accounting practices themselves. Whether we like it or not, our ability to maneuver and work within the accounting and budgeting systems at the library and institutional budget level are critical to information acquisitions. Is there any wonder that we spend the amount of time we do in the literature on budgeting!

Operational Acquisitions

After all of this "high falutin'" talk of strategy and budgets, are we ever going to get to the real accounting experts in information acquisitions—the acquisitions staff that has to buy and process all of this stuff? Well, we are finally there. To me, acquisitions staffs have always been the purchasing specialists of the library profession. The acquisitions staff function can overlap many departments outside the formal acquisitions unit, including reference, media, management, interlibrary loan, automation units, etc. Acquisition specialists at any level are in many

ways closer in function to outside purchasing departments, contracts management offices, accounts payable and receivable operations, and shipping and receiving units than they are to reference functions.

Ironically, many speculate that, if these individuals were outside of the library organization and recognized for the specialists they are, they might well be paid better. Of course, they wouldn't be tuned into the needs of the library or have the specialized training and empathy that comes with working in library acquisitions. At Bentley College, our purchasing and business office operations are very glad to have us care for most of our accounting and business issues right here in the library before they have to deal with them.

I know of very few libraries that are part of a larger entity (college, university, city) that don't duplicate the parent organization's bookkeeping system in some way so that more current, accurate information is kept on acquisitions purchases and receipts. The management of the payment system for an approval plan is accounting. With the widespread use of microcomputers in acquisition functions, librarians are working more and more with spreadsheets that can help analyze markup rates, discount rates, order and receipt time analysis. These are all part and parcel of any normal bookkeeping and cost accounting system. Questions that we ask within acquisitions are equally common to other economic entities:

- Are we paying too much for our inventory?
- Can we get a better vendor?
- Can we reduce our cost per order and thus increase materials added?
- Are there special discounts available based on volume of business or time of year purchases?
- Which fiscal year do we charge for materials received at the end of the year?
- Where should we charge postage and handling costs?
- Do we need purchase orders that are part of the central system or can we use our own unique system?
- Does the cash position of the parent institution dictate when we can purchase needed materials?
- Is this an original invoice or the third computer generated notice?

• Do we have a secure cash receipt and deposit system?

To a remarkable degree, almost every library staff member has to think in business terms. This needs to be recognized by library educators and by library management in its efforts in staff development.

Acquisition of information is a critical and major component of library services. We all work at a large or a small business and follow normal business and accounting procedures. Many staff are involved in strategic business planning, budgeting, direct ordering and other accounting functions within the library. All of us should recognize the parallel literature and opportunities available in the business practices of the private and not-for-profit sectors. It does no harm to look at what we do in a practical ac-counting and businesslike way. First and foremost, we are a service industry. For most of us, the profit motive does not dominate our accounting and managerial efforts. We are stewards of many resources, and we need to remember that, particularly in acquisitions, we should count the ways we use and love accounting. ▬

Bibliography

Campbell, Jerry D. "Academic Library Budgets: Changing the Sixty-Forty Split," *Library Administration & Management*, Spring, 1989, pp. 77–79.

Fraley, Ruth A. and Bill Katz. *Finance, Budget, and Management for Reference Services*, Haworth Press, NY, 1988.

Lee, Sul H., Ed. *Acquisitions, Budgets and Material Costs: Issues and Approaches*, Haworth Press, NY, 1988.

Lynden, Frederick C. "Financial Planning for Collection Management," *Journal of Library Administration*, Fall/Winter, 1982, pp. 109–120.

McClure, Charles R. "A View from the Trenches: Costing and Performance Measures for Academic Library Public Services," *College & Research Libraries*, July, 1986, pp. 323–336.

Poole, Jay Martin and Gloriana St. Claire. "Funding Online Services from the Materials Budget" (and reactions), *College and Research Libraries*, May, 1986, pp. 225–237.

Vasi, John. "How Academic Library Budgets are Really Determined," *Proceedings of the ACRL Third National Conference*, Seattle, 1984, pp. 343–345.

Virgo, Julie. "Costing and Pricing Information Services," *Drexel Library Quarterly*, Summer, 1985, pp. 75–98.

Werking, Richard Hume. "Allocating the Academic Library's Book Budget: Historical Perspectives and Current Reflections," *Journal of Academic Librarianship*, Vol. 14, No.3, 1988, pp. 140–144.

ACCOUNTING FOR MARKETING COSTS

Donald Macintyre and Sherman Hayes

Marketing? What marketing? Accounting? Isn't keeping up with the budget a big enough headache? We can almost hear your groans. Marketing is a significant part of most corporate budgets and resource allocations. It is particularly important for service organizations such as libraries, but the terminology hasn't been used until recently. Current library literature shows more librarians addressing the need for marketing in all its facets. However, still missing from most studies for nonprofit institutions are cost accounting models and methods to track all relevant marketing costs.

The following model should help track these costs for your institution. Reviewing your operations from library, marketing, and accounting perspectives will give you a fresh look at the allocation and use of your important resources. Managerial accounting is for management's internal use, to inform financial and planning decisions. The energy put into accounting for marketing costs should return benefits well beyond the cost of the exercise to you and your organization.

The basic components of our marketing accounting analysis are:
- Define your library in the language of a profit-making institution—one belonging to a service industry—and include assumptions on operations marketing cost allocation.
- Identify primary customer groups (market segments).
- Define product mix.
- Identify operations cost components.
- Identify marketing cost components.
- Summarize relative costs of operations and marketing and plan alternative marketing strategies, cost levels and results expected.

Model Definition

Within the industrial model, operations primarily refers to production and related administrative overhead. All other expenditures, including product development, apply to marketing. Typical marketing activities include defining market segments, determining product mix, selecting and creating channels of distribution, promoting the product, offering customer service, and public relations.

Customers of the Library

One of the first steps in a marketing strategy is to define customer groups. The main customer groups for a college library are (a) students, (b) faculty, and (c) staff, collectively called "patrons." A primary goal for any organization is customer satisfaction.

Products of the Library

The next important step is to define your products. The products of a college library are multiple *patron services*:
- services centered around information or tools to access that information;
- instructional support, both physical materials and ideas;
- instruction itself, both specific and general learning experiences;
- study space and environment for meetings;
- goodwill and prestige from association with the library;
- entertainment.

Output Measures for Nonprofits

Most of our "products" or "services" are not as convenient to measure as if we sold waterbeds. Measures of a library's output include actual holdings of all types of materials; use of materials as reflected by internal and external circulation; number of reference questions asked; number of directional questions asked; seating capacity and attendance counts, number of media items delivered, including equipment; database searches performed by staff and patrons; materials photocopied; transparencies and videos produced to support faculty; tutorials and bibliographic instructional classes (number of each and people attending); number of displays and number of people viewing them; and hours of use for patron-accessed databases such as CD-ROM and Dow Jones News Retrieval.

The most common measures of an organization's output in the business world are sales and profits. In principle, a non-profit institution may view patrons' use of its services as analogous to unit sales. Although no money changes hands, a fair valuation may be placed on all "product lines" and considered analogous to dollar sales. Accordingly, the equivalent of a profit measure can be proposed. The excess of the value of the patrons' use of services over the costs of providing them. In our model, costs (a measure of the value of the resources used) are classified as either operations or marketing.

We assume that both management and staff work to maximize profits—that is, to provide the greatest value for patrons relative to the cost of the resources used. Considering the wide variety of products offered by a library, the goal is not merely increased numbers in all areas. Some products have a higher payback to the library, the patron or the parent institution.

Operations Cost Components

Funds are required to make the products for "sale". The following would apply in our model:
Purchasing
Materials acquisition costs, including labor
Materials Management Function
Storage of inventory (shelving)
Staff time to organize the inventory (books, magazines, etc.)
Cost of Inputs
Cost of raw materials, which include collections and related labor, and labor and equipment to produce original products in media and displays
Access costs for information outside the collection, including labor costs
Costs of labor tied to instruction,

particularly bibliographic instruction and reference

Costs of physical facilities required for study, meetings, collections and housing of labor tied to operations

Costs of delivery of media equipment (cable TV, viewing equipment, or in-house lab)

Administrative overhead related to all of these items

Marketing Cost Components

Major marketing costs are classified into six categories:

Customer Service These costs pay for what we do to enhance customers' convenience and respond to their needs. It is a difficult subjective judgment between what is customer service (voluntarily added to enhance the customer's experience) and what is provided as part of the basic product. We might divide some customer service activities into:

Cataloging and Public Catalog Costs: There are many options for the catalog. Is it useful in its existing form? Should it be automated? What aids should be included? What is the speed and accuracy of its maintenance? All these marketing choices affect the patron's ability to find the produce: information.

Circulation: The Circulation Service Desk is an important marketing focal point. Initial relationships between the library and patron are established and maintained by its staff whose efforts help create a satisfied, returning customer.

Directional and Basic Reference Assistance: A basic premise of marketing is that customer relations determine whether or not the patron will use the product effectively and return in the future. Many academic patrons (such as faculty-directed student researchers) are captive customers and we sometimes act as if they need little attention. If the goals of the organization are patron use (sales) and repeat-customer satisfaction, such neglect should be questioned.

Copy Services: This service is also part of marketing costs. Many libraries provide minimal microform reader/printer capacity. Why not make the most of this strategy to enhance marketing the product: information.

Public Relations: Good public relations increases the prestige and recognition of the organization. Most academic libraries, rely on a campus office for formal public relations. A significant part of management's time, particularly the Director's, is spent on PR. This work might include gift negotiations and costs needed to acquire materials or keep potential donors satisfied. Much staff effort for professional development focuses on getting the name of the library and college mentioned in professional associations. Notices in national journals or major collection acquisitions are also part of the public image.

Promotion: Promotional marketing includes advertising, sales promotion, and selling in person and by telephone. We use paid advertising (the student newspaper), direct mail marketing (notices of new books, events and services), printed handouts describing services for visitors and new patrons, and the general "salesmanship" of the staff.

The staff effort to increase use by referring students to proper sources is another difficult area to label operations or marketing. It is subjective whether the primary interaction is marketing (customer convenience and sales assistance) or educational instruction (a product itself). Because academia regularly mixes the two, it is best to state assumptions when dividing reference labor costs between operations and marketing.

Product Development: As is often the case in industry, it is difficult to determine the part of product development which is marketing and that which is operations. We assume that any broad strategy related to product design and development is a marketing cost such as the planning (design) phase of adding a new collection category to the library and catalog or the Table of Contents Periodical Alert System that repackages existing journal information and

BUDGET AND EXPENSE REPORT
FOR PERIOD ENDING JUNE 30, 1988

ACCOUNT	DESCRIPTION	BUDGET	EXPEND	BALANCE
84001	SALARIES/MONTHLY			
84002	SALARIES/WEEKLY			
84003	SALARIES/STUDENT			
85001	BENEFITS			
87001	OPERATING SUP			
87002	POSTAGE			
87003	PRINTING			
88001	UTILITIES			
88002	CUSTODIAL SERV			
88003	R AND M			
88004	SERVICE CONTR			
88005	TELEPHONE			
89001	COMPUTING SERV			
89002	TECH COMPUT			
89003	DATABASE SEARCH			
90001	MONOGRAPHS			
90002	JOURNALS			
90003	SERIALS/CONTIN			
90004	MICROFORM			
90005	CD-ROM			
90006	FILM/VIDEO			
91001	MISC.			
	TOTAL:			

EXPENSE REPORT

ACCOUNT	DESCRIPTION				DEPARTMENTS AMOUNT				
		REFERENCE	CATALOGING	MEDIA	ACQ/SERIALS	COLLECTIONS	ARCHIVES	GEN ADMIN	CIRCULATION
84001	SALARIES/MONTHLY								
84002	SALARIES/WEEKLY								
84003	SALARIES/STUDENT								
85001	BENEFITS								
87001	OPERATING SUP								
87002	POSTAGE								
87003	PRINTING								
88001	UTILITIES								
88002	CUSTODIAL SERV								
88003	R AND M								
88004	SERVICE CONTR								
88005	TELEPHONE								
89001	COMPUTING SERV								
89002	TECH COMPUTING								
89003	DATABASE SEARCH								
90001	MONOGRAPHS								
90002	JOURNALS								
90003	SERIALS/CONT								
90004	MICROFORM								
90005	CD-ROM								
90006	FILM/VIDEO								
91001	MISC.								
	TOTAL:								

increases patron convenience. In most cases, introducing CD-ROM technology would include a marketing effort, as would the design and monitoring of the collection development strategy. The time involved in selecting individual titles would be operations. Much of the actual selection of materials today is done automatically through approval plans, journals, services and other serials (all part of operations).

Channels of Distribution: This area of marketing provides access to the library's products outside of the library itself. While the internal physical layout of the library may be placed in this category, we consider it to be more appropriately part of customer service. Costs related to where you locate outside access points and the space you make available make a difference in use patterns. Examples of "channels issues" might include branch locations, hours of service, availability of remote access via computer into service components (online public access catalog to a faculty office or delivery of video tapes via a cable TV network).

Pricing: Pricing issues for a nonprofit organization not charging its customers directly for most of its services are very different from those in the profit making entity. However, there are still choices whether and how much to charge for selected services and the impact on business. Charging for database searching is being hotly debated. Pricing is usually perceived as a funding question but is equally important as a marketing question in determining the extent to which people will use a specific service.

Integrating the Analysis

The challenge for any cost allocation system is to divide resources and summarize the data in meaningful ways. The traditional budget is divided by object code (some type of numeric summary system) and descriptors. Many libraries might divide it into a programmatic format with standard accounts tied to structure. Our model can be experimented with and used in several different ways to produce both a budget and an expense analysis. A general line-item budget could be analyzed against the operation and marketing subdivision discussed earlier to obtain gross operations and gross marketing costs (Table 1). A departmental or programmatic budget could be subdivided for marketing analysis as well. We judged that nearly 30 percent of our expenses were marketing items.

Another possible arrangement for analyzing marketing costs and also the most difficult is to allocate marketing functional costs to the corresponding patron services, which requires the selection and estimation of appropriate output activity measures that relate the two.

Using the Results

By now, you are probably asking the logical question: Is it worth the effort? We think so and feel that the exercise will demonstrate just how much of your resources go to marketing rather than operations.

The constant resource allocation battle between collection building and access expenses on the one hand and customer and related service expenses on the other is highlighted by such an analysis. Should collections be expanded to increase use or would a larger direct mail budget encourage increased use of existing collections? Are the right marketing people in the right positions? Are you training for 1) customer service, 2) handling problem customers, 3) increasing reference use per transaction, and 4) skills that are very different from traditional bibliographic skill sets? Does the director understand the critical marketing role that he or she plays for your institution? Is there conflict within the organization between marketing and the operations activities?

We encourage you to use our example or comparable cost analysis to examine your efforts from a new perspective. We should all be striving to maximize "profit". Modeling your marketing efforts and analyzing them from a management accounting perspective will help you recognize the right questions to ask about your marketing efforts. ═══

HARNESSING ACCOUNTING THEORY

Scrupulous Coding Can Revitalize University Library Systems

Brinley R. Franklin   **Gary J. Egan**

Library accounts in the university financial accounting system should give administrators information for sound management decision. In light of the extensive body of literature published recently on library accounting and cost analysis, 12 university libraries were reviewed to determine whether their accounting practices were keeping up with theory.

Among the most widely cited monographs on library financial accounting and cost analysis are G. Stevenson Smith's *Accounting for Librarians*;[1] Philip Rosenberg's *Cost Finding for Public Libraries*;[2]

Stephen A. Roberts's *Cost Management for Library and Information Services*;[3] and Betty Jo Mitchell, Norman E. Tanis, and Jack Jaffe's *Cost Analysis of Library Functions*.[4] Recent journal articles and papers on university library financial accounting and cost analysis include Paul M. Gherman and Lynn Scott Cochrane's "Developing and Using Unit Costs: The Virginia Tech Experience";[5] Sherman Hayes's "Management Accounting for Interdependence";[6] Michael Vinson's "Cost Finding: A Step-by-Step Guide";[7] Robert T. Begg's "Internal Control Systems in the Library Environment";[8] and Paul B. Kantor's "The Relation between Costs and Services at Academic Libraries."[9]

To determine the current status of academic library financial accounting, six public and six private universities were reviewed. Direct library expenditures at these 12 libraries range from approximately $3 million to $15 million annually, exclusive of indirect library costs such as university administration, operations and maintenance expenses, and building and equipment depreciation. The 12 are geographically diversified and represent small, medium, and large public and private institutions. Since much of the recent literature has been devoted to cost studies and cost analysis, a secondary objective of the review was to determine whether current financial accounting practices support subsequent cost analysis, which benefits library administrators and university financial administrators in pricing decisions, indirect cost studies, and budget decisions.

Current Accounting Practices

All 12 universities have multiple library systems. Nine universities use commercial financial accounting systems from major vendors and three schools have developed their own accounting systems. Each university uses a fund accounting approach, as recommended by the National Association of College and University Business Officers (NACUBO) and the American Institute of Certified Public Accountants (AICPA).

Fund accounting generally requires that assets, liabilities, and fund balances make up a university's balance sheet. Revenues, expenditures, and transfers are assigned to specific fund groups. These may include cur-

Framingham State College
Framingham, Massachusetts

rent funds (restricted and unrestricted), loan funds, endowment and similar funds, annuity and life income funds, plant funds, agency funds, and other fund groups deemed appropriate for a university, such as a hospital fund. Figure 1 shows a commonly used account code structure under the fund accounting concept.

Within specific funds, the library account identifiers (or their equivalents) developed at the 12 universities for budgeting, accounting, and financial reporting purpose reflect quite different approaches, as do the object codes employed. Although in some accounting systems object codes associated with subsidiary ledger accounts are called subcodes an object codes associated with general ledger accounts are referred to as account controls, in practice, both are almost always referred to as object codes. For this reason, account controls and subcodes will be generally referred to as object codes here. To analyze how library account identifiers and object codes are currently being utilized, three specific questions were asked:

- Is each significant library organizational unit (e.g., reference services) assigned an account identifier? In other words, is a cost center approach employed, or are different library departments (or even multiple libraries) grouped under the same account identifier?
- If the cost center approach is employed, are all object codes assigned to each account identifier?

For example, if a cost center is established for each library and department, are materials, supplies and other object codes assigned to each cost center, or are they combined in a central account such as library administration?

- Are detailed acquisitions object codes developed, or are acquisitions object codes limited to general designations such as books and periodicals or library materials?

Figure 2 is an overview of the findings. Entries reflect the percentage of schools employing the cost center approach, object code assignments to each cost center, and detailed acquisitions object codes. While 50 percent used the cost center approach and 33 percent developed detailed acquisitions codes, only 16.6 percent assigned object codes to each cost center.

The Cost Center Approach

As Peacock pointed out more than ten years ago, a financial system that does not distribute expenditures such as compensation to library activities "conceals almost as much as it reveals."[10] Therein lies the main objection to the cost center approach—many librarians are unwilling to reveal detailed information, fearing negative budgetary repercussions or undue scrutiny of spending patterns.

This fear is often unfounded, since budget decisions are usually made after combining sets of related accounts by home department. In some accounting systems, a pyramid structure permits related accounts

to be grouped at a summary level for analysis. In other words, the budget office is concerned with appropriations and subsequent accounting for home departments such as the main library (and its branches), the law library, or the medical library. The flexibility to reallocate original appropriations among cost centers to offset unexpected expenses is acceptable, and some discretionary funds are usually set aside as well.

The advantages of accounting at the cost center level are fairly obvious. Management information for decision making is more forthcoming and detailed expenditure patterns emerge monthly, annually, and historically. Subsequent cost analyses, such as unit cost calculations, cost/benefit analyses, and indirect cost studies, are simplified. As Virgo points out, once cost centers are identified and the unit of measurement is determined, library cost accounting is a matter of refining cost centers to reflect library activities and tasks.[11]

Organization charts are useful for designing library cost centers; on an ongoing basis, account identifiers reflecting new cost centers are also developed as library operations change.

Half the universities reviewed currently employ a comprehensive cost center approach. The other six are generally aware of the cost center concept, since account identifiers are typically constructed for each restricted fund account. In other words, account identifiers usually exist for each restricted book fund, regardless of size, owing to restrictions on the account. It is not encouraging that these six universities combine main and branch libraries into one account identifier without developing cost centers for the main library's departments or each branch library. It is equally discouraging that only one-third of the six universities employing the cost center approach take the next logical step and assign all appropriate object codes to each cost center.

Object Code Assignments

Of the six universities that account for library operations by cost center, only two private schools assign all relevant object codes to each cost center for items such as salaries and wages, acquisitions, and other operating expenditures. All six allo-

FIGURE 1

Example of an Account Code Structure

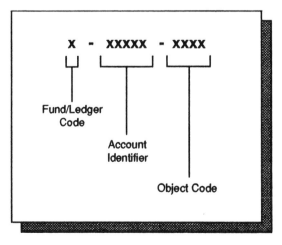

FIGURE 2

Current Library Accounting Practices at Twelve Universities

Type of Institution	Cost Center Approach Utilized in Account Identifiers	Object Codes Assigned to Each Cost Center	Detailed Acquisitions Object Codes Developed
Public (n=6)	33.3 %	0.0 %	33.0 %
Private (n=6)	66.7 %	33.3 %	33.0 %
Total, Public and Private (n=12)	50.0 %	16.6 %	33.0 %

FIGURE 3

Example of an Alternative Account Code Structure

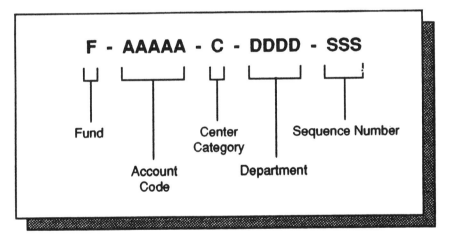

cate salaries and wages to each cost center, but only two distribute acquisitions and other operating expenditures.

Serials and monograph price increases and expanded library spending for automation and equipment are changing traditional library expenditure patterns. As library expenditures shift from the traditional 60-30-10 split among salaries and wages, acquisitions, and other expenditures to a 45-35-20 model,[12] or even a 33-50-17 ratio,[13] accounting for non-salary and wage expenditures becomes increasingly important. Accumulating acquisitions or other operating expenditures object codes under one account identifier, such as library administration, for a main library and six branch libraries gives managers little information

about actual expenditure patterns.

Librarians can work with financial administrators to develop meaningful object codes that also provide useful summary data for statistical compilations. For example, recurring publications such as *ARL Statistics* and *ACRL University Library Statistics* require librarians to report expenditures at summarized object code levels that are not always easily compiled by existing financial accounting systems.

Some librarians will argue that accounting by account identifier at the object code level is time-consuming, reveals too much information, or unnecessarily restricts flexibility among budgetary funds. But the budget office is more likely to review object code detail using a cost pool concept and is not usually con-

cerned with specific object codes. Under this approach, amounts are budgeted for major library cost pools such as salaries and wages, benefits, equipment, travel, acquisitions, and supplies and other miscellaneous expenses. Although specific object codes exist within each pool, financial control is intended at the cost pool level, while the accounting system gives managers more detailed information at the object code level.

Acquisitions Object Codes

Assuming that general university object codes for cost pools such as salaries and wages, benefits, equipment, travel, supplies, and miscellaneous expenses are also relevant to libraries, the unique area of university library accounting at the object code level is for acquisitions.

Of the 12 universities reviewed, only two public and two private institutions use the capabilities of their financial accounting systems to construct detailed acquisitions object codes. Acquisitions librarians often develop their own detailed subsystems to account for library acquisitions independent of their universities' accounting systems. When the acquisitions subsystem approach is employed, it is not unusual to find that the detailed amounts recorded by acquisitions librarians do not reconcile with the acquisitions expenses in their universities' accounting systems. These acquisitions subsystems can usually be incorporated into a university's accounting system at the object code level to eliminate this needless and expensive duplication of effort.

Currently a university accounting system may provide only three detailed object codes for acquisitions: books, periodicals and subscriptions, and other library acquisitions. In a subsystem, the acquisitions librarian may be tracking monograph expenditures for university presses, approval plans, and faculty/staff requests; serials expenditures for periodicals, new periodicals, serials, and new serials; and other library acquisitions by audiovisuals, microforms, and software. To compound this, the acquisitions librarian may also record acquisitions by subject, discipline, or classification code.

If a sufficient number of object codes are reserved for library acquisitions, the acquisition types — by subject, discipline, or classification code — can be accommodated with discrete object codes by most university financial accounting systems. In the account code structure presented in Figure 1, four digits are provided for object codes. The first digit is usually predetermined to reflect a class, such as a cost pool, leaving 999 object code combinations. If the second digit is used to identify a specific type of acquisition, such as an approval plan monograph, there are still ninety-nine object codes available to account for subject, discipline, or classification code.

Under an alternate account code structure, shown in Figure 3, there are five digits dedicated to object codes (referred to as account codes in this case) and a three-digit sequence number for use as an identifier.

A library could assign a five-digit account code unique to each type of acquisition and still have three digits available as a subject or discipline identifier. Sequence numbers, for example, could accommodate 999 subjects, disciplines, or summary Library of Congress classifications.

An example of codes and sequence numbers designed to account for library acquisitions using this alternate account code structure is shown in Figure 4.

Using Accounts Effectively

University library accounts should reflect the library's organization and operations. Structuring accounts around cost centers facilitates cost accounting for library activities and other related cost analyses.

FIGURE 4

Examples of Account Codes and Sequence Numbers for Acquisitions Using the Alternative Account Code Structure

Account Codes	Sequence Numbers
76200 Monographs	010 Biological Sciences
76201 Faculty/Staff Requests	011 Biology
76202 University Presses	012 Medicine
76203 Approvals	020 Physical Sciences
76204 Reserve Books	021 Astronomy
76205 Miscellaneous	022 Chemistry
76300 Serials	023 Computer Science
76301 Periodicals	024 Geophysics
76302 New Periodicals	025 Mathematics
76303 Serials	026 Physics
76304 New Serials	027 General Sciences
76400 CD-ROM Reference Services	028 Statistics
76500 Audiovisuals	029 Technology
76600 Microforms	
76700 Software	

To effectively use library accounts and benefit from the capabilities of university financial accounting systems, librarians must understand account code structures, employ a cost center approach, and fully utilize account identifiers and object codes. Account identifiers should be developed for each library and for each department or operation at larger libraries. Relevant object codes under such general cost pools as salaries and wages, benefits, equipment, travel, acquisitions, and supplies and other miscellaneous expenses should be assigned to each cost center, and detailed acquisitions object codes are also needed.

The capability of combining detailed object code expenditures for recurring external reports results from careful design of object codes or cost pools. Librarians can work with financial officers to learn the structures inherent in their universities' financial accounting systems and to guarantee an adequate range of object codes for acquisitions so that duplicative acquisitions accounting subsystems can be eliminated.

By following these basic guidelines, library practice can benefit from accounting theories in the literature, and library accounts in university financial accounting systems can yield the financial information on which sound management decisions can be made. ═══

References

1. G. Stevenson Smith, *Accounting for Librarians and Other Not-for-Profit Managers* (Chicago: American Library Association, 1983).
2. Philip Rosenberg, *Cost Finding for Public Libraries: A Manager's Handbook* (Chicago: American Library Association, 1985).
3. Stephen A. Roberts, *Cost Management for Library and Information Services* (London: Butterworths, 1985).
4. Betty Jo Mitchell, Norman E. Tanis, and Jack Jaffe, *Cost Analysis of Library Functions: A Total System Approach* (Greenwich, Conn.: JAI Press, 1978).
5. Paul M. Gherman and Lynn Scott Cochrane, "Developing and Using Unit Costs: The Virginia Tech Experience" *Library Administration and Management* 3 (Spring 1989): 93–96.
6. Sherman Hayes, "Management Accounting for Interdependence" *The Bottom Line* 1(2): 30–31.
7. Michael Vinson, "Cost Finding: A Step-by-Step Guide" *The Bottom Line* 2(3): 15–19.
8. Robert T. Begg, "Internal Control Systems in The Library Environment" *The Journal of Academic Librarianship* 10 (January 1985): 337–42.
9. Paul B. Kantor, "The Relation between Costs and Services at Academic Libraries" in *Financing Information Services*, Peter Spyers-Duran and Thomas W. Mann, Jr., eds. (Westport, Conn.): Greenwood Press, 1985): 69–78.
10. P. G. Peacock, "The Presentation of Library Accounts" *Aslib Proceedings* 30 (December 1978):426.
11. Julie A. C. Virgo, "Costing and Pricing Information Services" *Drexel Library Quarterly* 21 (Summer 1985):80–82.
12. Association of Research Libraries, *ARL Statistics 1987–88* (Washington, D.C.: Association of Research Libraries, 1989): 8.
13. Jerry D. Campbell, "Academic Library Budgets: Changing 'The Sixty-Forty Split'" *Library Administration and Management* 3 (Spring 1989):78.

THE BALANCE SHEET
How to Read It and How to Use It

Erica Steinberger

Librarians and corporate information center managers operate in worlds where speaking the language of finance is one of the requisites for the key to the executive washroom. But too few of us know how the basic documents of financial decision making are assembled or how to interpret them to determine the operating health of our organizations. This is not a failure we alone experience; most managers begin in nonfinancial positions. Much of the bewilderment of the world of fiscal nuances can be dispensed with when we understand some fiscal basics, like how to read a balance sheet.

The balance sheet provides a snapshot of the financial health of an organization on a specific date and answers the question: How did we stand at that point in time? As a financial inventory, the balance sheet presents fiscal information in an orderly manner. It offers a comparison of the status of assets and liabilities at the end of an accounting period. The length of time is arbitrary, but usually it is a year or less. According to H.B. Maynard, the balance sheet "provides a continous check on the conservation of assets."[1]

Since the balance sheet of the nonprofit organization is divided into separate accounts or funds, containing more categories of fiscal data than that of the for-profit corporation, it tends to be more complex to read and analyze. Because of this complexity, the examples presented here are for a nonprofit organization. However, the rules for balance sheet construction and interpretation are generalizeable and, therefore, those presented are as applicable to profit-making enterprises as to nonprofit.

Assests and Liabilities

Regardless of whether the balance sheet is constructed for a profit or a nonprofit organization, it always has two main sections, assets and liabilities. These are related to show net worth. Quite simply, assets are what the organization owns; liabilities are what the organization owes. Net worth is the surplus of assets over liabilities.

Assets and liabilities are presented in one of two ways on a balance sheet. When assets appear at the top half of the balance sheet, liabilities appear at the bottom half, as shown in Figure 1. Or they may be presented side by side. Then assets appear on the left and liabilities on the right. The fund balance—the organization's net worth—appears at the bottom of the statement or on the right. The total assets always equal the combined total of the liabilities and the fund balance. That is why this is called a balance sheet.

Relating Assets and Liabilities to Equity

Assets are listed on the balance sheet in order of their liquidity, that is, in order of the rapidity with which they can be converted to cash. There are two classes of assets, current and fixed. As shown in Figure 1, following cash — the most liquid of assets — are short-term investments, such as Treasury bills and Certificates of Deposit, which can be converted to cash through their sale; inventories, including supplies; and receivables. Fixed assets, acquired for long-term use, are comprised of land, buildings, plant, equipment, furniture, and machinery. Their value, as shown on the balance sheet, is fig-

ured after depreciation allowances (which decrease the value of fixed assets over their useful life) are taken.

Liabilities also are divided into current or fixed status. The former are those due for payment within the fiscal year and the latter represent longer-term debts. Current liabilities, as presented in Figure 1, include accounts payable, payment on loans or notes, current portion of the mortgage, accrued expenses (for ex-

ample, wages which must be recorded whenever the accounting period does not coincide with the last day of the pay period). The one long-term liability listed represents the money owed on the mortgage, minus the current portion of the mortgage figure.

The Fund Balance

The concept of the fund balance is easily understood when ex-

FIGURE 1
LIBRARY BALANCE SHEET

	CURRENT FUNDS		BUILDING & EQUIPMENT FUND	ENDOWMENT FUND	TOTAL
	Unrestricted	*Restricted*			
ASSETS					
Current assets:					
Cash	$12,625	$425	$415	$560	$14,025
Short-term securities	5,000	10,000	3,000	15,300	33,300
Fines receivable	125				125
Grants receivable		120,860	40,200		161,060
Supplies	225		420		645
Total current assets	$17,975	$131,285	$44,035	$15,860	$209,155
Investments		18,140	132,000	38,962	189,102
Land, buildings, and equipment			1,860,000		1,860,200
Total assets	$17,975	$149,425	$2,036,235	$54,822	$2,258,457
LIABILITIES AND FUND BALANCES					
Current liabilities:					
Accounts payable	$8,850	2,000			$10,850
Accrued expense	2,900				2,900
Current mortgage payment			$120,000		120,000
Total current liabilities	$11,750	2,000	$120,000		$133,750
Total mortgage payable			675,000		675,000
Total liabilities	$11,750	$2,000	$795,000		$808,750
Fund balances:					
Unrestricted	$6,625				$6,225
Restricted:					
Literacy		$95,000			95,000
Programming		$23,860			23,860
Purchase of fixed assets			$231,235		231,235
Invested in fixed assets			1,010,000		1,010,000
Endowment funds		28,565		$54,822	83,387
Total fund balances	$6,225	$147,425	$1,241,235	$54,822	$1,449,707
Total liabilities and fund expenses	$17,975	$149,425	$2,036,235	$54,822	$2,258,457

pressed in the equation: FUND BALANCE = ASSETS − LIABILITIES.

The fund balance functions both as a residual between the assets and liabilities and as the account which summarizes the year's difference between the inflows of resources and incurred expenses (see Figure 1). This formula illustrates the fund balance as a residual. If liabilities are larger than the assets, the balance is negative, and the organization is described as being "in the red," or "in the hole." When expenses during the year are higher than resource inflows, a decrease occurs in the fund balance. Conversely, when assets are larger than liabilities, the balance is positive, and the organization is described as being "in the black." When resource inflows are larger than expenses, the fund balance experiences an increase.

Ratio Analysis of the Balance Sheet

In itself the balance sheet is a collection of figures that supplies us with some basic information. But as the assorted financial symbols are interpreted and evaluated they can tell us even more. When a series of balance sheets are regularly interrelated, they begin to let us know where the organization stands and whether its current course is healthy. In addition to ongoing comparisons, ratios can be computed based on the data held in the balance sheet; these help us spot trends in the organization's fiscal performance.

Current Ratio. Although the orientation of the profit-making sector is the return on investment and the orientation of the nonprofit sector is its financial ability to continue meeting program goals and providing services, they share one common measure. The Current Ratio is a measure of liquidity − it indicates the ability of an organization to pay its bills. Measures of liquidity answer questions like, "Do we have enough money to pay our bills?" or "Do we have sufficient cash, plus assets that can be turned into cash, to ensure that we can pay our debts due to fall during the accounting period?"

The Current Ratio is one of the best known measures of financial strength. It is computed from the balance sheet by dividing the current assets by current liabilities. Based upon Figure 1, it would be computed:

$$\frac{\text{Current Assets}}{\text{Current Liabilities}} = \frac{\$209,155}{\$133,750} = 1.56$$

Here the ratio is 1.56 to 1.

Acid-Test Ratio. The acid-test ratio, sometimes called the quick ratio, is one of the best indicators of liquidity. More readily applied to the profit than nonprofit organization, it is computed:

$$\frac{\text{Cash + Government Securities + Receivables}}{\text{Current Liabilities}} = \frac{\$208,510}{\$133,750} = 1.55$$

Using the information in Figure 1, we find a ratio of 1.55 to 1.

The acid test ratio is a much more exacting measure than the current ratio. By not including inventories, it concentrates on the most liquid assets with fairly certain values. In the profit arena it helps to answer the question, "If all sales should disappear, could my business meet its current obligations with the readily convertible quick funds on hand?"

There is little difference in the current and acid test ratios computed here because the inventory of supplies is low—a more common event in the nonprofit than profit sector.

Once the ratios are calculated, we can ask if the results indicate a positive fiscal stance for the organization: "Is this a good ratio?" A general rule of thumb for both the current and acid test ratios is 2 to 1. When ratios are too low a new financial strategy may be introduced, like paying off some debts or converting noncurrent assets into current assets.

For ratios to have meaning they must be compared either over a historical period to determine trends, or between similar-sized organizations at the same period, to determine deviations. Such analysis enables us to determine how ratios have changed and whether improvement or deterioration has occurred.

Most librarians would benefit from a systematic, ongoing review and analysis of the information contained in their balance sheet, including the application of these two easily computed ratios. Not only will you achieve better fiscal control, but also an improved image making it easier to sell programs with fiscal implications to the regulatory bodies that hold the purse strings. ▬▬

References

1. H.B. Maynard, editor, *A Handbook of Business Administration* (New York: McGraw-Hill, 1967), p. 3.80.

HOW TO WRITE AN AWARD-WINNING FINANCIAL REPORT:
One Library's Experience

Deanna K. Suter

More and more, libraries are discovering the benefits of preparing and disseminating annual financial reports that meet the high standards set forth by the accounting profession. The uses are many—for internal management, for patrons and employees, for governing boards, for investors and creditors, bond raters, insurers, and others. This article shares the experiences of one library that made the journey from novice to financial award-winner.

Earlier this year, the Fort Vancouver Regional Library received the Government Finance Officers' Certificate of Achievement for Excellence in Financial Reporting—the first library in the program's 42-year history to be so honored. The library, located in Vancouver, Washington, earned the award—the highest form of recognition in the area of governmental accounting and financial reporting—for its Comprehensive Annual Financial Report (CAFR) for the year ending December 31, 1986.

The Government Finance Officers Association (GFOA) began the award program in 1945 to encourage every governmental entity or component unit to prepare and publish an easily readable, comprehensive accounting of the group's financial activities for the year (CAFR/CUFR). In order to win an award from GFOA, a governmental unit must publish a CAFR/CUFR that clearly and thoroughly presents its current financial picture. The report must also conform to generally accepted accounting principles (GAAP) as applicable to state and local governments and Governmental Accounting Standards Board (GASB) standards of financial accounting and reporting, and must be audited by an independent auditor in accordance with American Institute of Certified Public Accountants (AICPA) audit guides.

Developing a CAFR/CUFR to meet the high standards of the GFOA award program is time-consuming but worthwhile. Although preparing an annual financial report that meets these standards is not required, it is very much in the interest of libraries to do so.

To begin with, the report provides essential financial information for management and for others with a legitimate interest in the financial operations of the library. Financial reporting is not an end in itself; it is a tool that has many uses.

One function of the report is to enhance public confidence in government. Public confidence in your library is sustained by assuring the citizens of the impartiality and honesty of library officials in all transactions and decisions. Full access to information concerning the conduct of the library on every level is one effective way to accomplish this.

Who Needs Your CAFR/CUFR?

Another important purpose of financial reporting is to meet the needs of those users who must rely on public records for information. Once published, the CAFR/CUFR becomes a part of the library's public records. Some typical users of the report might include:

Patrons: Patrons may have an interest in the financial standing of their library in order to evaluate the quality and quantity of current and future library services, and the viability of continued library services in their community.

Taxpayers: The primary financers of library services, taxpayers may be asked to vote on a library levy or bond. The report can provide interested taxpayers with the data necessary to evaluate past performance and future prospects, enabling them to make informed voting decisions.

Governing Boards and Oversight Bodies: The American system legally vests the responsibility for protecting taxpayers' and patrons' rights to acceptable organizational performance and effective management stewardship in governing boards and oversight bodies. They are responsible for complying with various financial, legal and contractual provisions. The report provides information needed by these governing boards and oversight bodies to meet their legal responsibilities.

Creditors and Investors: Creditors and investors are concerned with the library's current financial liquidity and liabilities. Creditors may wish to determine the library's ability to repay amounts owed them. Investors are interested in assessing the relative attractiveness of a library's current or future bond offerings as compared to an alternative investment possibility. The report should provide the information necessary for creditors and investors to make informed decisions.

Bond Raters: Bond raters can affect the interest rate at which the library may borrow money. A favorable rating reduces the interest rate on bonds, resulting in significant savings. Current financial information in a format that is free of ambiguities and potentially misleading inferences helps bonding companies determine a library's bond rating. A CAFR/CUFR fulfills these requirements.

Insurers: Insurance companies are interested in a library's finances and their compliance with legal and contractual requirements. They seek this information prior to issuing or renewing policies that cover errors and omissions, employee dishonesty, or replacement of assets. The report provides this data.

Employees: Today's libraries are faced with a dwindling pool of qualified graduate librarians. In addition, a lower unemployment rate has increased competition for nonprofessional, clerical employees. Employees at all levels are interested in accessing the library's prospects for future payments of reasonable salary/wage amounts and the ability of the library to provide effective services. The report should provide useful information for these purposes.

Intergovernmental Grantor Agencies: As direct tax dollars continue to decline, libraries are forced to seek alternative sources of revenue, such as intergovernmental grants. Since these grantor agencies receive their funds from taxpayers, their interests are also indirectly the interests of the taxpayers. Intergovernmental grantor agencies are concerned with the recipient library's compliance with grant requirements, the economy and efficiency of activities financed with grant monies, and the extent to which the library achieved the results intended by the grant. The report provides information necessary for intergovernmental grantor agencies to make their evaluations.

Other Libraries: Finally, the report provides information that can assist other libraries in comparing and evaluating their past and current financial and service delivery decisions.

Developing a CAFR/CUFR

A CAFR/CUFR is more than a report designed to meet the library's responsibility of public accountability. It is also a valuable internal financial management tool that promotes public confidence in governments, provides information needed by governing boards, and meets the informational needs of many other interested parties external to the library. And finally, it is an excellent public relations vehicle. It can be used as a professional publication for presentation by the library to various business and civic groups.

Getting started is the most difficult aspect of any new endeavor, and overcoming the confusion gener-

ated by all the jargon is probably a good place to begin. The Glossary of Acronyms at the end of this article will help. Read it and refer to it often. Understanding what the acronyms mean will make the development of a comprehensive annual financial report much easier.

After studying the glossary, request copies of reports from governmental units that have received a Certificate of Achievement for Excellence in Financial Reporting. Information on recipients is available from GFOA. Review the documentation to determine how your library's current annual financial report compares. Also request a copy of the "Reviewer's Checklist" from GFOA. It outlines the reporting requirements necessary for a CAFR/CUFR to meet the standards of GFOA.

After comparing your annual financial documents with other reports and the GFOA reviewer's checklist, ask the following questions and determine what will be necessary for your library to upgrade its report to meet GFOA standards.

- Does your report provide all of the required financial information necessary to clearly and thoroughly present your library's financial picture, or will you have to develop procedures to accumulate this information?

- Is your current annual financial report prepared in conformance with GAAP, and, if not, what will your library have to do to convert its financial accounting and reporting system to GAAP?

- Does your current annual financial report include an introductory section containing a letter of transmittal, a list of principal officials, and an organization chart?

- Finally, does the report contain a comprehensive statistical section? Does it give a broader view of the library's financial trends than the financial statements and supporting schedules alone? Does this information cover a period of ten years when more than one year is required?

Enlisting Management Support

The next step after reviewing and evaluating your current report—and a key factor in developing it—is acquiring support and assistance from top management. Development of this report can be a time-consuming process and will require funds and a strong commitment from all involved. One approach is outlining a plan of what is to be accomplished, when, and by whom.

Include estimated development costs in the proposed plan. Indicate that the costs associated with upgrading your current annual financial report may be recovered many times over, particularly if bonded debt is outstanding. Other savings may include the elimination of duplicate research when the library is asked for information from different persons or organizations. In many cases, the required information will be found in the report, and the appropriate pages or the entire document can be made available to the requestor.

Once the project has been authorized, your library should become a member of GFOA. The cost is reasonable (normally about $70–$150) and, for libraries, is based on total number of employees. With membership, the library will receive the GFOA *Newsletter* and *Government Finance Review*. These publications are designed to keep finance officials informed on public finance issues and trends.

GFOA publications are key to the dissemination of information on government finance and reporting requirements; the development of a CAFR/CUFR without these publications would be almost impossible. A required publication is *Governmental Accounting, Auditing, and Financial Report* (GAAFR), known throughout the government finance community as the "blue book." A revised GAAFR incorporating all current GASB pronouncements was published in 1988. The GAAFR provides an illustrated, comprehensive annual financial report.

Another useful GFOA publication is the ten-volume financial reporting series. This set consists of examples of ways in which governments have acceptably presented specific financial reporting information.

Each year GFOA, through its Educational Service Center, sponsors numerous seminars throughout the U.S. and Canada on financial reporting and the GFOA Certificate of Achievement. These give participants step-by-step guidance in preparing the report, detailed analysis of the report's components, effective disclosure formats, and highlights of common recurring reporting deficiencies.

GFOA's annual conference is an excellent opportunity to learn the latest developments in government finance. GFOA's Technical Services Center, available by mail or telephone, assists members on questions of financial reporting techniques.

It is also a good idea to join a state and/or local finance officers chapter. They sponsor training programs, discuss new techniques and technology, and are an excellent source of information. State finance officers associations also hold annual conferences, and some state organizations have review committees that evaluate reports. These committees are good sources for preliminary review and critique of reports prior to submission to GFOA.

So, Where Are the Pitfalls?

Now that you have reviewed and evaluated the reports of other entities and the GFOA reviewer's checklist, developed a plan, received authorization and financial support, joined GFOA and your state and local finance officers associations, meeting GFOA requirements is an achievable goal.

Fort Vancouver Regional Library first prepared a CAFR for the fiscal year ending December 31, 1983. It was 31 pages long and fell far short of meeting GFOA requirements. The 1986 award-winning report was 63 pages long, and the report just completed for 1987 is 83 pages long. It is evident that, in today's complex and everchanging governmental accounting and reporting environment, developing and maintaining a CAFR/CUFR is an ongoing process. The library must stay current with new trends and incorporate new standards as they are issued by GASB.

Some of the major challenges in developing a comprehensive annual financial report include: compiling a listing of all general fixed assets and developing an accounting system for the valuation of these assets; converting from a cash basis of accounting to a GAAP basis of accounting; formulating the notes to the financial statements; and compiling comprehensive statistical data. How did we approach each of these areas?

General Fixed Assets: Under the GAAP principle of "accountability," libraries are required to maintain adequate control over their general fixed assets—long-lived assets including land, buildings, equipment, and library resources. To maintain adequate control over these assets, the library must provide a detailed record of all general fixed assets, an accountable method of controlling those assets on a continuous basis, and a method of valuing them.

In 1983 the only requirement Fort Vancouver Regional Library was fulfilling was the maintenance of a detailed listing of all library resources. This inventory was controlled through the library's shelflist or locator files, that is, check-in files of specific materials and their locations. A detailed listing of other general fixed assets was not being compiled.

What Are Your Assets Worth?

In addition to the need to compile a detailed listing of all general fixed assets other than library resources, the library had to formulate a procedure for their valuation.

We requested a copy of the State of Washington's general fixed asset policy and reviewed it. The policy assigned each asset a useful life ranging from five to 12 years. From this data it was determined that going back 12 years was a good premise to adopt in the establishment of a beginning general fixed asset listing. Next it was decided that all long-lived items with a value of $100 or more were to be considered as general fixed assets and accounted for in the general fixed asset account group. All paid invoices for the past 12 years were researched, and a detailed listing of all long-lived items with a value of $100 or more was compiled. Due to inflation, this amount has since been increased to $300.

Valuation came next. Valuing general fixed assets other than library resources was fairly easy. In accordance with GAAP, these assets were valued at historical cost (or estimated historical cost if actual historical cost was not available). The general fixed asset account group does not report depreciation.

Valuation of library resources was not as straightforward. Although the library had maintained a detailed listing of all library resources, it had not maintained the historical cost of each resource. After much discussion and research it was decided to report library resources as a lot since the time and expense required to account for and report the valuation of individual units within the lot was not justified.

Valuation of the lot was computed on a first-in, first-out basis, using average historical cost to estimate single-unit value within the lot. The lot, as a whole, consisted of annual increments of units, and each unit in the lot was said to be valued at the average unit cost for the year in which it was purchased. Units which contained more than one part (i.e. magazine subscriptions) were treated as a single unit.

Under this first-in, first-out method of valuation, the lot value is said to increase annually by the total amount of library expenditures on library resources. Annual average unit cost is calculated by dividing the total amount expended by the total number of units purchased during the year. Then lot value is decreased annually by the number of units at each historical average cost deleted during the year.

Each year's deletions of library resources are subtracted from the oldest annual group until the number of units in that group is exhausted. When the total number of units acquired during the oldest historical year has been exhausted, subsequent deletions are charged against the next oldest historical year, etc.

Net changes in the lot value of library resources are determined by the difference between annual additions and annual deletions. Thus, the previous year's lot value of library resources, plus or minus the current year's net change, equals the current year's lot value of library resources. This amount is then accounted for in the general fixed asset account group.

Cash vs. Accrual

Conversion from a Cash Basis of Accounting to a GAAP Basis: The basis of accounting is recognizing revenues and expenditures in the library's accounts and reporting them in the library's financial statements.

It relates to the timing of the measurement made, regardless of the measurement focus applied.

Prior to 1985, Fort Vancouver Regional Library budgeted and accounted for its funds on a cash basis. Under cash basis accounting, revenues are not recognized until received in cash, and expenditures are not recognized until the period in which the cash payment is made.

Under a GAAP basis of accounting, all governmental funds are accounted for using the modified accrual basis of accounting. This means that revenues are recognized when they become available as net current assets and expenditures are recognized when the liability is incurred. Because the accrual basis stresses matching revenues and related expenses, it provides a more realistic picture of library operations in the accounting period.

Prior to 1985, revenues and expenditures were accounted for on a non-GAAP cash basis and converted to a GAAP basis when the CAFR was prepared. Because this conversion was time-consuming and subject to error, the library converted its budget process to a modified accrual (GAAP) basis beginning with fiscal year 1985. Because all appropriations of the Fort Vancouver Regional Library lapse at the end of each fiscal year with a reversion to fund balance, a 13th-month accounting period was established to record expenditures incurred prior to the end of the fiscal year.

The Footnote Thicket

Formulating the Notes to the Financial Statements: A library's financial statements cannot, in and of themselves, provide all the information necessary for a fair presentation of the library's current financial standing and results of operations. The notes to the financial statements provide additional information that becomes an integral part of the basic financial statements.

GAAP requires that the notes to the financial statements include all disclosures necessary to prevent the financial statements from being misleading. But where to stop? Disclosure can quickly get out of hand and complicate rather than clarify the financial statements.

After reviewing "notes to the financial statements" in the GAAFR and

others' reports, it became evident that a library's notes were, in many ways, different from other entities. Realizing this we set out to write our notes to the financial statements. In 1983 they took four pages and clearly did not contain the detail necessary to meet GFOA requirements. The 1987 report has 11 pages of notes and clearly provides full disclosure without complicating the financial statements.

How did we get to the completeness of the 1987 notes? For clarification, we sought professional assistance from our State Auditor's Office and from a CPA with a strong government accounting background.

Fort Vancouver Regional Library currently includes the following items in their notes to the financial statements: summary of significant accounting policies, property tax revenues, designated fund balances, changes in general fixed assets, changes in long-term debt, pension plan, and risk management. Each library must exercise professional judgment in determining which disclosures are necessary in order to insure that their financial statements are not misleading. In this area we found the GFOA reviewer's checklist helpful in identifying potential footnote disclosures.

Extracting Statistics

The statistical section is the most time-consuming part of the report and one that we continue to work on. It is intended to give users a broad understanding of the library and its financial trends. Much of the information is compiled from sources outside the formal accounts maintained by the library and is sometimes hard to get. For this reason, it is important to maintain a good working relationship with other political entities which can help in compiling data.

Examples of information your library might need from your county treasurer and/or assessor include:

- real and personal property values
- commercial and residential new construction values
- current and delinquent property tax collections
- a listing of principal taxpayers within your district.

Other political subdivisions within your district can provide your library with information for computation of debt and property tax rates for overlapping governments. Information from various state agencies is necessary to provide library service area demographic data such as: population, per capita income, median age, school enrollment, and unemployment rate.

If the library's service area is a city or county, much of this data can be derived from a single source within the city or county government. If, on the other hand, the library's service area overlaps many jurisdictions, the task becomes more complex. Fort Vancouver Regional Library's taxing district encompasses the unincorporated area of three counties and the incorporated area of six cities. Four incorporated cities contract with the library for services. All other locations within the three-county area must be excluded from statistical data compiled by the library. As you can see, compiling data when some jurisdictions are partially in or out of the library district is tricky.

If compiling ten years of data for statistical tables is not possible, indicate that the information is unavailable and also why it is unavailable. If your library is not currently compiling this data, it should begin today. It should also compile data for the past ten years, whenever possible.

The statistical section also includes "miscellaneous information"—non-financial data intended for use in combination with the report's financial data to facilitate economic and fiscal analysis of management and organizational performance. Under miscellaneous statistics, Fort Vancouver Regional Library includes ten years of data on: service statistics, library resources expenditures, library resources by category, and circulation statistics. Also included are current-year miscellaneous branch statistics. Again, each library must determine what data most clearly depict its management and organizational performance.

It is important to remember that a library is a public agency, created for the public good. The library should be an excellent and unbiased source of information for the people it serves. This means the information in a library must go beyond the

resources maintained in its collection: it must also include the maintenance of accurate information regarding its own operations. This information should be available to the citizens the library serves and others who have a legitimate interest in the operations of the library.

It seems evident that one important component for providing information to the public should be timely, accurate, pertinent, and fairly presented financial statements, one being a comprehensive annual financial report. By preparing and pub-

lishing a CAFR/CUFR, a library is demonstrating its commitment to being a source of excellent and unbiased information in all areas. At the same time, the library is meeting its responsibilities for promoting public confidence, maintaining fiscal accountability, providing responsible stewardship of resources, and fulfilling the statutory requirements of a public entity in a democratic society. This is one way a library effectively demonstrates its commitment to fulfill all of its responsibilities to the public it serves.

GLOSSARY OF ACRONYMS

AICPA: American Institute of Certified Public Accountants
The body responsible for establishing, evaluating, and enforcing generally accepted auditing standards and guidelines for financial audits.

CAFR: Comprehensive Annual Financial Report
Official annual report of a governmental entity which is comprehensive in its depth and breadth. This report covers all funds and account groups and represents the results of all budgeting and accounting activities entered into during the year. It also provides full disclosure beyond applicable legal requirements and the requirements of generally accepted accounting principles (GAAP). It is organized into three major sections: introductory, financial and statistical.

CUFR: Component Unit Financial Report
A comprehensive annual financial report issued for a component unit. A component unit is a separate governmental unit, agency, or nonprofit corporation that is combined with other component units to create the reporting entity.

GAAP: Generally Accepted Accounting Principles
Accounting principles that have received substantial authoritative support and are recognized as the uniform minimum standards for financial accounting and reporting. The primary authoritative statement on the application of GAAP to state and local governments is Statement 1 of the Governmental Accounting Standards

Board (GASB) entitled *Authoritative Status of NCGA Pronouncements and AICPA Audit Guides (July 1984)*.

GASB: Governmental Accounting Standards Board
The body designated by the American Institute of Certified Public Accountants (AICPA) to establish financial accounting principles for state and local governments. GASB issues *Statements of Financial Accounting Standards*, which represent expressions of generally accepted accounting principles and provides the framework for standards of financial reporting for governments.

GFOA: Government Finance Officers Association
An association of finance officers from federal, state, and local governments throughout the United States and Canada. The mission of GFOA is "to enhance and promote the professional management of governmental financial resources by identifying, developing, and advancing fiscal strategies, policies and practices for the public benefit."

GPFS: General Purpose Financial Statements
Basic financial statements that include the minimum acceptable fair presentation in conformance with GAAP. GPFs are designed to be "liftable" from the financial section of the CAFR for widespread distribution, along with the auditor's report, to users requiring less detailed information than is contained in the full CAFR. ▬

UNDERSTANDING COSTS

COSTING AND PRICING
The Difference Matters

M.E.L. Jacob

If you ask most people about cost and price they believe they understand exactly what is meant. Cost is what you pay for an item and price is what the seller asks — and for most buyers the transactions are the same. However, cost and price are different to different players in a transaction. There is the cost of creating, developing, producing, marketing, supporting, distributing, storing, and selling an item. There is the retail or list, wholesale, sale, or discounted price at which the item is sold and which the purchaser pays. It sounds simple, but in reality it is a complex process involving a high degree of subjective judgment.

A good deal depends on the perspective from which the transaction is viewed. A purchaser sees cost as the price paid for the product or service. The seller sees cost not as the price charged, but as the price paid to the creator or agent providing the product or service and any added costs incurred in stocking, handling, advertising, or selling it. The creator sees the cost as encompassing all the materials, supplies, facilities, salaries, inventory, maintenance, or charges paid in producing or providing the product or service.

To the seller, the price is what is received from the purchaser, while to the creator or producer, price is what the seller paid. To understand this process more fully, cost, price, and value need definition and explanation.

What Is Cost?

The confusion between cost and price is not helped by most dictionary definitions. *Webster's Ninth New Collegiate Dictionary* offers price as a synonym for cost before defining cost as "the outlay or expenditure (as of effort or sacrifice) to achieve an object." *The Dictionary of Business and Management* defines cost as "the value given up by an entity in order to receive goods or services.... All expenses are costs, but not all costs are expenses.... Expenses are the total cost of resources used to create revenue." One of the most difficult accounting problems is encountered in determining cost and cost allocations.

Concepts and Application

In examining library cost it is useful to review it with regard to the similarities of common elements and the differences in perspectives of librarians and vendors. Common principles of accounting practices and cost accounting skills help develop accurate, reproducible cost data.

Libraries. Numerous articles and some books have been written on cost studies and costing for libraries. A recent bibliography on costing library operations contains items from as early as the mid-fifties.[1] There was a flurry of studies done in the sixties; many were built on earlier efforts done at Florida Atlantic University and were fueled by the application of Operations Research to library activities.[2] More recently the Public Library Association *Planning Process*[3] has added impetus to costing activities as has the continuing need to provide administrators with hard data to justify library activities. Two of the more library-specific works are Stephen Roberts' *Cost Management for Library and Information Services*[4] and Philip Rosenberg's *Cost Finding for Public Libraries*.[5] Roberts defines cost in a similar fashion to the Webster definition, but distinguishes between economists' use of cost focusing on opportunity cost (the cost of foregoing certain alternatives) and the accountants' use of cost for outlays primarily involving money expenditures or translating cost into equivalent money expenditures. Rosenberg repeats a definition almost identical to Webster.

Some of the difficulties associated with costing are discussed by Elizabeth Richmond in her recent article.[6] She points out the problems encountered in full costing which should include the cost of library collections and cost attribution. She highlights some of the difficulties also faced by networks and library vendors.

Most libraries and vendors can identify and account for direct costs which Philip Rosenberg calls "costs that are readily attributable to a specific service, activity, or function."[8] Indirect costs, which can include space and facilities, management, and utilities, are referred to as indirect precisely because they are difficult to assign to any one or any specific set of products or services.

Whereever possible, accountants try to allocate or assign indirect costs to each product, service, or activity. That is one of the most difficult aspects of accounting. Some basis must be used for the allocation. It may be done on the basis of time, percent of total activity or resource, on revenue, or any other basis that appears rational in light of the activity and the information available.

Basically, however, it is an arbitrary decision; costs can be adjusted up or down depending on how allocations are performed. Overall, indirect costs must be accounted for and offset against revenue or total income.

Networks and Library Vendors. Like librarians, networks and ven-

dors must know how much they spend. Also like librarians, they face significant problems in allocating all costs appropriately and reflecting them equitably in the price of goods and services. Among costs that must be recovered at OCLC, for example, are the costs of market research and product research which may or may

Discussion of value raises many questions, not the least of which are what are our societal values and how they influence the pricing, cost, and value of the services we provide or that we buy. One of the raging issues in librarianship is whether society is dividing into the information rich and the information poor and the degree to which an ability to pay for information affects the quality of life. Questions we will have to face now include: Does society have an obligation to subsidize access? For whom will it provide subsidies? For what types of information and access will it provide subsidies?

not lead to successful products.

Product development and support costs may include maintaining user support personnel; a help desk with an 800 number for extended hours of access; the production, distribution, and updating of manuals, user aids, and other documentations; training staff, materials, and facilities; free or discounted system use for training; support for library schools; leasing or low-interest purchase plans; slow payments by some

agencies; technical support staff and maintenance personnel; manufacturing facilities; materials and supplies; discounts to distributors; salaries and benefits for employees.

Other costs can be added depending on the goods and services provided. Some organizations may provide support to national programs, such as OCLC's support for CONSER and the Linked Systems Project and University Microfilms participation in the Library of Congress' Name Authority Cooperative Project. Such projects must be subsidized by other products and services. For survival, income must ultimately exceed outgo.

What Is Price?

Price is not only defined in most dictionaries as synonymous with cost, but it also carries connotations of value. *Webster's Ninth New Collegiate Dictionary* defines price as "the quantity of one thing that is exchanged for demanded in barter or sale for another." *The Dictionary of Business and Management* defines price as "the amount of money a seller receives for goods or services.... Price is not what the seller asks for the product but what is actually received."

When pricing is discussed, the assumption often is made that cost should be the basis for determining price; the price should include the cost of the item and service and perhaps some margin above that. While most businesses do try to recover costs, some items or services may be sold at less than cost for a variety of business reasons, including to draw other, more profitable business; to reduce the cost of inventory or storage; or simply to get rid of an item quickly.

In other cases, full costs including overhead or development costs are not known, or not included or the payback or total period to recover costs has been incorrectly estimated. Clearly, an unsubsidized business or activity cannot continue operating at a loss indefinitely.

Concepts and Applications

As with cost, librarian and vendors approach pricing with different perceptions and with different objectives. Librarians are generally not concerned with pricing services to survive, but may do so in order to offer a particular service or to modify the behavior of library users. Networks are concerned with survival and future growth. Vendors are concerned with organizational survival, future growth, and with making a profit.

Libraries. Librarians differentiate between cost and price in establishing fees for such services as photocopying, loans or services to nonresidents, overdues, and online searches. Seldom do these fees reflect full-cost recovery. Most represent some contribution toward library costs, particularly where the library is billed for a service, such as in online searching. In the case of fines, librarians are trying to moderate certain behaviors by assigning a price which may have little or nothing to do with the true costs of books returned late.

A growing, and sometimes acrimonious, literature exists on library fees.[8,9] The concern of whether, and when, fees are appropriate is outside the scope of this review. But like it or not, librarians do have an obligation to understand the costs of services they supply. And when they do charge for services, librarians need a reasonable rationale for setting the prices of those services.[10,11] Librarians set prices, not costs. They do have some control over elements of cost including their own efficiency and productivity.

Networks and Library Vendors. While costs may not be the basis for determining price, it is usually expected that the price for a service or product will be sufficient to cover the cost of producing and supplying it. Aspects of those costs and some exceptions to full recovery are deliberated in deciding on price. Competition also is considered, as well as what price users are willing to pay for a product or service, and overall strategic objectives. Unfortunately, with new products or services — where nothing similar exists or where there is nothing being replaced — it is difficult to establish prices. The problems vendors of machine-readable products had in trying to develop reasonable pricing strategies exemplify this, as does the recent rationale for changes in pricing the machine-readable files of Chemical Abstracts, discussed by Jeffrey Pemberton and Mick O'Leary in the March 1988 issue on *Online*. Vendors of videotext services have found this a particularly troubling problem, and except for private videotext systems, most have not solved it.

What Is Value?

Value is defined as "the worth of property, goods, services," in the *Dictionary of Business and Management*. Of all the concepts discussed, perhaps this is the most controversial. While cost and price have subjective and objective elements, value is primarily a subjective judgment of the purchaser.

Normally, a rational person will buy when the price of an item or service equals or is less than its value. Value may be determined by the amount of effort it would take the purchaser to create the item or service, the cost of a similar or substitute item, convenience, lost opportunity costs, available funds, how strongly the purchaser desires the product or service — or, in short, what the purchaser is willing to pay. This would make value synonymous with price which it seldom is, but price is often substituted for value in cost/benefit analysis. Art works or other unique items are excellent examples of the difficulty of determining price and value.

Because value is a subjective judgment it also varies depending on the context and socioeconomic status of the purchaser. In areas where water is readily available, it may be free or low in price. In areas where it is scarce, price may be determined by the higher costs of supplying it or by its scarcity. To a rich person the differences may mean little; to a poor person they may become life threatening.

In today's environment, certain businesses and individuals are willing to pay a premium to have rapid, accurate access to specific types of information, such as stock prices. This information has less or no value to the homeless or to those not investing in the stock market. The homeless may be more interested in information on shelters and soup kitchens — or may have no interest in information services at all.

Discussion of value raises many questions, not the least of which are what are our societal values and how they influence the pricing, cost, and value of the services we provide or that we buy. One of the raging issues in librarianship is whether society is dividing into the information rich and the information poor and the degree to which an ability to pay for information affects the quality of life. Questions we will have to face now include: Does society have an obligation to subsidize access? For whom will it provide subsidies? For what types of information and access will it provide subsidies?

Cost allocation, a complex issue, is often used to achieve objectives other than pricing. Like statistics, costs can be treated in a variety of ways depending on what the objectives are. Both vendors and librarians need to understand their individual cost structures, what modifications to them will do not only to their ability to continue offering services and products, but also to their survival as viable organizations. What you don't know *can* hurt you. Understanding the difference between cost, price, and value can make a difference in more effective decision making. ▬

References

1. Lisa Aren and Susan J. Webreck, with contribution from Mark Patrick, "Costing Library Operations," *Collection Building* 8(3), 1987:23–28.
2. John Wilson, Jr., "Costs, Budgeting, and Economics of Information Processing," in *Annual Review of Information Science and Technology*, Washington, D.C.: ASIS, 1972: 39–72.
3. Vernon Palmour et al., *A Planning Process for Public Libraries*. Chicago: American Library Association, 1980 and Charles McClure et al., *Planning and Role Setting for Public Libraries*. Chicago: American Library Association, 1987.
4. Stephen A. Roberts, *Cost Management for Library and Information Services*. London: Butterworths, 1985: 129–30.
5. Philip Rosenberg, *Cost Finding for Public Libraries: A Manager's Handbook*. Chicago: American Library Association, 1985.
6. Elizabeth Richmond, "Cost Finding: Method and Management," *The Bottom Line* 1(4): 16–20.
7. Rosenberg, 70.
8. NCLIS, *The Role of Fees in Supporting Library and Information Services in Public and Academic Libraries*. Washington, D.C., 1985.
9. John Berry, "Practice and Principles: The Fee Example," *Library Journal* (113)2 (February 1, 1988): 4.
10. John L. Crompton and Sharon Bonk, "Pricing Objectives for Public Library Services," *Public Library Quarterly* 2(1) (Spring 1980): 5–22.
11. Frances H. Barker, "Pricing of Information Products," *Aslib Proceedings* 36(7/8): 289–97.

COST ACCOUNTING BASICS: WHEN (OR) DO THEY APPLY TO LIBRARIES?

Sherman Hayes and Lawrence A. Klein

Should public sector libraries, primarily not-for-profit service agencies, use cost accounting? The answer is an emphatic yes. Frequently, non-librarians with little knowledge of the library world judge our work and make important organizational decisions from an accounting viewpoint.

So, effective communication about accounting issues related to the library's mission means that library managers must understand some of the concepts and issues in cost accounting and how they apply to libraries.

Organizations can be classified in diverse ways. Some produce tangible products while others provide services. Some are primarily sellers or distributors of products at the wholesale or retail level. Some operate for profit and others are considered not-for-profit.

Most libraries are not-for-profit service organizations. While there are many important differences between profit and non-profit organizations, there are some similarities.

All organizations, including libraries, are economic entities. They have objectives, inputs, production functions, and outputs; libraries are no exceptions. And every economic entity uses some aspect of cost accounting — an area of accounting that focuses on recording, tracking, and analyzing costs vital to the production of a good or the furnishing of a service.

The dominant literature and emphasis in the accounting field is based on manufacturing techniques in for-profit firms — and uses terminology that *seems* unapplicable to libraries.

To show you how cost accounting can be applied to your institutions we have constructed a "matrix of influence."

The left side of the matrix relates to the dominant characteristic of the economic entity — whether it is profit or not-for-profit. The column headings for the matrix classify the primary function of the entity. We have divided it into three broad categories: manufacturing, sales (wholesale/retail) and service.

MATRIX OF INFLUENCE

Dominant Characteristic	Primary Function		
	Manufacturing	Sales	Service
For-Profit Entity			
Not-for-Profit Entity			

This matrix may be used to analyze the complete organization or a sub-unit or service within that organization. For example, the traditional library (whether school, college, university, or public) falls into the not-for-profit, service entity designation. However, a subunit could make good use of cost accounting techniques from a for-profit entity.

What if you have a profit-making gift shop in your library? It could use inventory cost accounting methods. Or, your library may support a publications unit. It will have manufacturing and sales components.

Cost accounting can be used for *budgeting, pricing, performance evaluations, costing inventory or services*, and *special decisions*.

Budgeting

Budgeting may be the most common denominator between manufacturing, sales, and service organizations. The operating budget, involving a plan to systematically expend resources, is used extensively (if not universally) in almost all organizations.

Budgetary methods vary from organization to organization. Those in the service sector, particularly not-for-profit services, have used such innovative approaches as zero-based budgeting and programmatic budgeting. The most used however is line-item budgeting.

Budgeting can help management development, communication, and coordination across programs. Budgets are what you expect to happen in a cost environment. They are neither pie in the sky or a means to cut costs. Budgets are tools for control — no matter the type of organization.

Manufacturing budgets stress the cost of raw materials, labor, and overhead. Budgets for sales organizations are primarily concerned with labor and overhead in the resale of inventory. Budgets for a service organization usually focus on labor. Libraries spend most of their budgetary energy on labor and materials (books, journals, and other forms of information). These materials could be viewed as a fixed asset.

In profit-making entities receipts (sales and such) can fluctuate greatly. The connection between expenditure patterns and revenue budgets is close. In organizations like libraries, the budget is similarly tied to revenues, but there is less variability over time.

The budgetary process is annual for most libraries. And because we are primarily steady-state organizations, the budget is relatively the same from year to year.

Pricing

Pricing in for-profits is based on the cost of the goods to be sold as well as market forces. The profit motive encourages a constant connection between the price and the internal cost tracking system against that price.

Cost accounting literature covers techniques such as cost-volume-profit analysis, breakeven point pricing, contribution margin approach, and margin of safety approach. Almost all of these pricing theories evolved out of manufacturing approaches. Pricing becomes critical to meet competition, market share, and profit goals.

In most instances, the cost for library services is paid indirectly or picked up by an entity other than the customer. Even if the customer pays a direct cost with, for example, a property tax, seldom does the individual pay for the product at the point of use. An individual transaction is perceived to be free although the public pays through taxes and the college student pays through tuition.

A more systematic use of cost accounting for services has been adopted when libraries are able or forced to put a price on a product or service, such as database searching, interlibrary loan, and the use of facilities by outside groups. Recent studies on pricing of public photocopying in libraries have used the concepts of cost accounting. Since libraries provide a perceived free good, then pricing as a cost accounting element is infrequently appropriate. But an interesting exercise for any librarian would be to determine what you would charge for a particular service in the open market place.

Performance Evaluation

In a for-profit organization with a consistent focus on the bottom line of profit, cost accounting can and does assist in determining the manager's contribution to the overall profitability of the entity. All efforts are tied to improving this ultimate goal—profit.

For instance, a cost-variance analysis can indicate the extent to which actual costs conform to or deviate from those costs the firm would expect to incur given the level of production and sales achieved. The performance of some managers is often evaluated through this analysis. In libraries, the ability to provide maximum services for the budgeted dollars is a critical component of evaluation. The orientation has and probably will continue to be judgment on spending and doing more with resources than on cost savings. Much of the reason that cost savings in libraries has received less emphasis is the nature of the major cost components: after materials and labor there is very little left to analyze and save on. While materials can be purchased or handled at more efficient levels, few librarians are without a long list of "desirable" materials to purchase with any cost savings. The budgeted expenditure then remains the same.

Personnel is a large component in non-profits that seldom changes as frequently and quickly as in the for-profit sector. There seems to be room here for study to determine if measurable cost reductions in a service unit in the library can be tied to merit raises and the like.

Costing Inventory or Services

Inventory costing is central to a manufacturer's cost of goods sold and is typically the largest expense item in any manufacturer's income statement. Cost-accounting terms used in discussing the manufacturing of inventory include fixed and variable costs, work-in-process, finished goods, costs of goods manufactured, incremental costs, cost allocation systems (e.g., labor, materials, overhead) engineered costs, job order cost systems, process cost systems, discretionary costs, standard quantities, and standard prices.

The goal is to identify and allocate costs to the product. The sales industry uses inventory costing extensively to determine costs of goods sold. The costs are not derived from a manufacturing process but are the result of purchased goods.

The service industry has tried to use the manufacturing cost concepts (in order to track the costs of services through the system) and has devised special practices. A typical approach is to define a "service unit" as opposed to a physical product. However, libraries have not been able to use many parts of manufacturing cost concepts. We model ourselves more closely on the service industry. There is extensive literature on reference transaction costs, cost to circulate a book, interlibrary loan costs, cataloging costs per item, and database searching. The technique is to pre-define the product (such as a service) then track the cost through the system using library-measured units.

There are major areas of cost analysis not yet applied to areas of library service, mainly because it is difficult to track costs without a product. Allocation of fixed costs (high in most libraries) also is difficult.

Another major drawback in the service field is the difficulty in measuring outputs. Our counting methods do not measure a real product, rather they measure an activity. In manufacturing it is a high art to count the pieces produced and measure the applicable costs. In sales the items shipped from inventory are known. In libraries it is difficult to classify—or to count—what exactly is a reference question.

Special Decisions

Special decisions in manufacturing might concern replacing equipment, new plant construction, changes in the product line, special orders, and mergers. This activity is similar in sales and service organizations. When an unusual item outside the library's normal operating budget is needed, such as a new building, an automation project, expanding a new service, or using costly new technology, librarians usually have to provide separate cost reports and justifications.

Library managers are like all managers—whether working in a profit or nonprofit organization. They are always under pressure to understand their costs and monitor and manage them in the provision of library services. Cost accounting provides the systematic approach necessary to assess how your library is doing and to decide where it should be going. ═══

COST FINDING:
A Step-by-Step Guide

Michael Vinson

How much does it actually cost to order a book? What impact, if any, would a vendor plan have on library expenses? And what difference would it make to budget planning to have specific figures instead of the guesstimates on which many libraries rely?

At the DeGolyer Library we recently conducted a study to answer these questions. Although we are a research collection of Western American and railroad history, the 11-step cost-analysis system we developed will work for other types of libraries as well.

Our technique is easy to learn—even for those of us afflicted with "number phobia." You don't have to be an accountant to use cost analysis as an effective management tool. To answer questions that arose while we were developing our system, we referred to several textbooks in this area.[1] The result is the following step-by-step guide.

Step 1

The first thing you must do is *identify your cost centers* and their activities. At DeGolyer we used the selection and order process in acquisitions as our cost center since it met the criteria as a "service or responsibility area for which costs can be reasonably accumulated and related to output."[2] Eight activities, outlined in Worksheet 1, were isolated by dividing the process into major work components performed by different staff members. After these activities are completed—four by the secretary, three by the librarian, and one by students—the order department mails the purchase order.

Step 2

Next, *identify each of the tasks* within an activity, as illustrated in Worksheet 2. It helps to have a separate worksheet for each activity with a number of blank spaces added to record other tasks. For example, "searching selections in the card catalog" includes finding the card entry; comparing selected items against the entry, if an entry is found; marking the selection as either "have" or "don't have"; and, when necessary, adding the appropriate edition. Similarly, for the activity labeled "distribution of catalogs," the tasks are: to open announcements and catalogs and to distribute catalogs to book selectors.

Step 3

Identify a proposed cost unit. This is the common element that binds together all of the activities in the cost center—and is the basis for determining and comparing costs. For our study, the individual order stood out as the most easily identifiable unit against which to measure costs. In another area of the library, such as bibliographic control, the proposed unit might be materials cataloged; in public services it might be patron contacts or assistance rendered.

Step 4

Compile a daily log summary for each activity, as shown in Worksheet 3, by tallying the number of items completed in the task along with the amount of time taken to complete them. For example, in the activity "selection form catalogs" the librarian selected books from publishers' catalogs to be searched by students in the library's card catalog. There were 2,172 items read from a variety of catalogs in one hour and 35 minutes and 39 items selected for searching. In dividing the number of minutes by the number of items selected, we found that it took 2.7 minutes to finish this task.

"Searching selected items in the card catalog by students" provides a more complex example of how the daily log summary is put together. Two students assist in searching. The first took 19 minutes to search 25 items in the card catalog; the second took 40 minutes to search the same number. The time per item searched for the first student was 45 seconds; for the second, 96 seconds. Since each one searched an equal number of items, we averaged the results to obtain one figure for the cost study. The numbers can only be averaged if the students do an equal amount of searching.

One word of caution about compiling daily log summaries: whether the figures are kept by persons actually doing the work or are obtained by observation, the time should include normal interruptions and work habits, not expedited procedures.

Step 5

Calculate employees' cost per productive hour to derive the labor costs attributed to each activity. The information needed about all employees involved in any activity of the cost center includes: annual salary; retirement contributions from the institution; number of holidays, vacation days, and sick days; amount of institutional contribution to medical and dental insurance plans; and other benefits.

Computing cost per productive hour begins with determining the number of productive hours worked. This is easier to figure for student employees, since they receive neither paid holidays nor sick days, al-

---

WORKSHEET 1

Activities Within a Cost Center

Cost Center: Selection and Order Process in Acquisitions

Activities:

1) distribution of catalogs by secretary
2) selection of books by librarian
3) searching selected items by students
4) review of search on OCLC by librarian
5) preparation of selected items for ordering
6) typing order cards by secretary
7) recording emcumberances by librarian
8) filing order slips in the card catalog by secretary

WORKSHEET 2

Tasks Within An Activity

Activity: Searching selected items in the card catalog by students

Tasks:

1) find the card entry, if any
2) compare the selected item against the card
3) mark the selected item as "have" or "don't have"
4) other

_____
_____
_____
_____

WORKSHEET 3

Daily Log Summary

Employee: librarian   *Date: October 15*

Activity: selection of books

(1) Task	(2) Time	(3) Count
1) select items	90 mins.	39 of 2,172

Time used per item: 2 minutes 19 seconds

though those who work four hours do take a 15-minute break. The number of productive hours for the students is calculated as the number of hours worked at a time minus the time allowed for breaks. For a four-hour shift, the number of student productive hours is three hours and 45 minutes.

It is more complicated to figure the number of productive hours for a full-time employee, such as the secretary, as Worksheet 4 illustrates. In this case, the total possible days that can be worked during the year is 260 — 52 weeks multiplied by five days per week. Then holidays (including Christmas), vacation (15 annually), and sick days (12 annually) are subtracted. This leaves a total of 221 days. DeGolyer does not compensate for unused sick days. The working day is 7.5 hours, since lunches are not paid. There are two paid 15-minute breaks each day, leaving a total of 7.0 productive hours each day. The total number of annual productive hours is 1,547.

Next, compute the annual cost of the employee to the library. In the case of the secretary, we added the hypothetical annual salary of $16,500 to the retirement contribution of $1,237 and the medical and dental contributions of $1,428, for a total annual cost to the library of $19,165.

To obtain the cost per productive hour, divide the total annual employee costs by the number of annual productive hours — $19,165.50 divided by $11,547 hours — for a cost of $12.39 per hour. Repeat this procedure for all staff involved in the activities of the cost center, including student workers.

Step 6

Summarize the output by bringing together all the direct personnel costs for each activity in the cost center. Fill out one sheet for each activity. In this case there are eight sheets. Place the employee's name on the sheet, along with the amount of time used in the activity, taken from the daily log summary; the cost per productive hour, which should also be divided by 60 to obtain the cost per productive minute; and the number of items processed — in this case the items selected for searching and ordering. Multiply the amount of time used in the activity by the cost per productive minute to ob-

tain the total personnel costs. Then divide this cost by the number of items completed, as indicated on the daily log sheet, in order to obtain the total direct personnel cost per item.

For example, in activity #6, shown

in Worksheet 5, "typing order cards by the secretary," the daily log summary showed that it took 90 minutes to type 46 cards. The total cost of the time used was $18.54 (20.6 cents × 90 minutes), and the cost per item was 40.3 cents.

WORKSHEET 4

Calculating Cost Per Productive Hour

Employee: secretary

Annual Cost to Institution

Annual salary	$16,500
Retirement contribution	$ 1,237
Medical/dental contribution	$ 1,428
Total	$19,165

Total Productive Hours

Total possible working days (52 weeks × 5 days)		260
Holidays	12	
Vacation days	15	
Sick days	12	
Subtotal		−39
Total working days		221
Hours in work day	7.5	
Less paid breaks	.5	
Total hours		× 7.0

Total Productive Hours
(multiply total hours by total days)   1,547

Cost per Productive Hour $12.39
(Divide annual cost to institution
by total productive hours)

WORKSHEET 5

Direct Personnel Cost and Output Summary

Employee: secretary

Activity: typing order cards

(1) Time used   90 minutes
(2) Hourly cost $12.39 (20.6 cents per minute)
(3) Total cost $18.54
(4) Items done   46
(5) Direct personnel cost per item   40.3 cents

Step 7

After compiling the output summary for each activity in the cost center, *prepare a materials and supplies use report*, as demonstrated in Worksheet 6. List each activity in the cost center and then show what supplies, if any, are used in completing that activity. Our report documented that red pencils, self-sticking note pads, order cards, printer paper, and paper clips were the supply items needed. After reviewing how many were used per activity and multiplying that by the number of orders filled per month, we arrived at a figure of $6.85 per month for supplies for the cost center.

Step 8

Figure the depreciation of major equipment, as illustrated in Worksheet 7. The initial, or acquisition, cost of the equipment plus any improvements, minus the salvage value placed upon the equipment by the institution, leaves the net cost, which is divided by the useful life of the item to obtain the cost per year. The figures on the salvage value and the useful life are usually supplied by the parent organization—the college, university, or municipality.

For example, in the selection and order process, DeGolyer used two typewriters and one computer, for which our institution did not assign a salvage value. The useful life of typewriters was figured at 12 months and of computers at 96 months. One of the typewriters is more than 10 years old, so it is already fully depreciated. Another typewriter is only two years old. Its initial cost was $1,005, which, since no salvage value was provided, is also the net cost. Dividing that figure by 10 years gives a cost per year of $100.50. Dividing again by 260 working days gives a total of 38.7 center per day, or 5.2 cents per hour. The same thing was done for the computer, which in our case is an OCLC terminal M3200 with a cost of 29.6 cents per hour.

Step 9

Compute other direct costs, as described in Worksheet 8. At DeGolyer that included determining the cost per OCLC search and the cost for membership in the bibliographic utility. The first cost came to 7.0 cents per search; the second—annual

---

WORKSHEET 6

Materials and Supplies Use Report

Start Date: October 1   *Finish Date: October 31*
[All costs figured in cents unless shown otherwise]

Activity	Items	Quantity	Costs	Total
1) distribution	-0-			
2) selection	pencils	3	14.0	$ .52
	note pads	300	4.0	1.20
3) searching	pencils	2	14.0	.28
4) review	printer paper	113	1.2	1.36
5) preparation	-0-			
6) typing	order cards	113	3.0	3.39
	paper clips	50	2.0	.10
7) recording	-0-			
8) filing	-0-			

Total Expense for Period: $6.85

WORKSHEET 7

Depreciation of Major Equipment

Activity: typing order cards

Equipment: typewriter

Initial cost	$1,005
Less salvage value	-0-
Total net cost	$1,005
Useful life	120 months (10 yrs.)
Cost per year (Net cost divided by 12 months)	$100.50 year
Cost per work day (Yearly cost divided number of work days	38.7 cents
Cost per hour (Daily cost divided number of work hours	5.2 cents
Cost per minute	.087 cents

membership, maintenance, and telecommunications fees—came to 4.7 cents per minute.

To relate the cost per minute to the cost per item, refer to the daily log summary for the amount of time used for each item in the activity. Then multiply the cost per minute by the amount of time used. The result will be the cost per item.

Step 10

After all the direct costs have been compiled—including direct personnel costs, materials and supplies, and equipment depreciation—*combine the figures for each activity* in the cost center, as shown in Worksheet 9. For example, for activity #3, "searching selected items in the card catalog," the direct labor costs were 6.5 cents. Since there were no other direct costs, the cost per unit was 6.5 cents.

Another example is activity #4, "review of the search selection by the librarian on OCLC. The direct labor costs were 33 cents; the cost for materials and supplies, 1.2 cents; the cost of depreciation, 2.7 cents; and other direct costs, related to the use of the bibliographic utility, 8.8 cents, for a total of 45.7 cents per item for that activity.

Step 11

Conclude the cost analysis. Since the unit of cost is the order, costs are calculated on a per-unit bases for each activity in the order process. In other words, the object is to find out how much it costs to execute each activity for one order. The final step is to add up the direct cost summaries for each of the activities to compute the cost per unit. In our library, the actual cost of selection and ordering came to $1.83 for each order.

We did not compute indirect costs, such as administrative overhead, utilities, and janitorial aid, since they would remain constant with or without the vendor approval plan. If desired, these costs can be prorated and included in the final computation of the unit costs.

Backing Decisions with Fiscal Facts

How did the cost analysis help us? Because we had to figure out the cost of each of the 11 steps in the process, it became much easier to make a valid comparison of current costs with costs under the projected vendor approval plan. And we were able to tie financial resources to operational outputs and interpret cost behavior. The full benefits arising from the fiscal control of the order and selection process are still being realized as we apply our new skill at cost finding to other cost centers in the library. ▬

WORKSHEET 8

Other Direct Costs

Activity: review of search on OCLC
Start date: October 1   Finish date: October 31

Fee per search	7.0 cents	
Number of searches	113	
Total cost		$7.91
Other fees		
Membership	$500 (year)	
Terminal		
maintance	$504 (year)	
Telecomm.		
fee	$4,488 (year)	
		$5,492.00
Other fees total cost		(year)
Daily cost		
(yearly divided by 260)		$21.12
Hourly cost		$2.82
(daily divided by 7.5)		
Cost per minute		
(divided by 60)		4.7¢

WORKSHEET 9

Direct Cost Summary

Activity: review of search on OCLC

Direct labor	33.0 cents
Material/supplies	1.2 cents
Depreciation	2.7 cents
Other direct costs	8.8 cents
Total direct cost per item	45.7 cents

References

1. See Elizabeth Richmond, "Cost Finding: Method and Management," *The Bottom Line* Vol. 1, No. 4, p. 16–20; Julie Virgo, "Costing and Pricing Information Services, *Drexel Library Quarterly*, Summer 1985, p. 75–98; G. Stevenson Smith, *Accounting for Librarians and Other Not-for-Profit Managers* (American Library Assn., 1983); and Philip Rosenberg, *Cost Finding for Public Libraries: A Manager's Handbook* (American Library Assn., 1985)

2. Rosenberg, "Cost Finding," p. 13.

COST FINDING:
Method and Management

Elizabeth Richmond

Costing is more than just a buzz word for librarians working in either the public or private sector. We are all concerned with program efficiency, cost containment, and financial management. But, cost studies are a lot of work and not universally popular. In fact, actual cost studies are not common. Those produced are frequently uneven in method and quality and often focus on specific areas such as acquisitions or circulation. As a result, the methodology for arriving at the cost conclusions is at best unique to the specific case; at worst it is incomplete or only implied.

Common reactions when cost studies are suggested or unit cost information is referred to are:

- We already know this
- We don't need to know this
- We don't want anyone to know this

And they are sometimes all from the same source.

Traditional library costing methods can provide unit cost figures and benchmarks for planning. But do they best reflect actual operating costs? For example, when the following two typical formulas are applied, the cost of interlibrary loan transactions is arrived at by dividing the total interlibrary loan expenditures by the total number of transactions, and perhaps, adding an overhead rate equal to 50 percent of the direct salary costs.

$$\text{Cost/Transaction} = \frac{\text{Total Expenditures} + \text{Overhead}}{\text{Total Transactions}}$$

or

$$\text{Cost/Transaction} = \frac{\text{Supplies} + \text{Materials} + (\text{Salaries} \times 1.5)}{\text{Total Transactions}}$$

Traditional models don't convert expenditure into actual expense or use information, define or collect specific cost elements, or examine these cost elements in relation to total service or unit cost. Unlike standard methods, cost finding provides a practical management tool for determining a library's financial resources, allocating resources to outputs or operations, and interpreting cost behavior.

Using the cost-finding model, elements to consider include:

- tasks related to the activity
- labor costs
- materials and supplies costs
- depreciation
- indirect costs and unit cost

The manager can examine the data and determine not just the unit or service cost, but also

- what the cost factors are in expanding or reducing services and what the variable costs are
- what the effect would be of contracting for all or part of the service and what the fixed costs are

- what costs are related to specific tasks
- what the effects are of indirect costs

An analysis of these and other factors can provide obvious cost cutting recommendations or an affirmation of current procedures. The data also provide documentation for management decisions.

Cost Finding/Cost Accounting

The effective use of full-cost accounting in libraries – the traditional method of converting expenditure data to expense data to show when resources are used – has been limited. Full-cost accounting is an ongoing process which collects, classifies, records, and summarizes total cost data within a formal accounting system.[1] It provides for assembling and recording all the elements of actual cost incurred to accomplish a purpose, to carry on an activity or operation, or to complete a unit of work or a specific job.

By focusing on unit cost – the financial resources necessary to provide one unit of service – cost finding offers a compromise method. While it does not follow formal accounting practices, it does allocate indirect as well as direct costs to specific units of service. Cost finding relates the use of financial, personnel, and material resources to the product by converting expenditures, or budget figures, to reflect actual expenses or costs.

By comparison, cost finding is less complicated. In cost finding a less formal estimation is done on an irregular basis. In fact, costs incurred in specific accounts may not be recorded through formal accounting entries in specific cost accounts during the year. Instead, cost finding usually takes available fund financial accounting and recasts and adjusts it to derive the cost data or estimate needed.[2]

In other words, for determining indirect costs, the cost-finding process utilizes available financial data such as budgets, payroll records, invoices, and other reports. These figures are manipulated to ascertain the actual use or expense – as opposed to budget expenditure – of resources and to allocate these resources to services and units of service. This conversion step is essential

if use rather than budgeted figures is the basis of unit cost.

In the past, when models that analyzed and evaluated services were selected, cost components and methodologies might have been discussed to illustrate the usefulness of unit cost information and provide a framework for interpretation. But such models did not provide a costing methodology for full-cost allocation nor steps for costing. Cost finding fills this gap and enables library managers to acquire reliable cost data.

A Cost-Finding Model

When the Public Library Association (PLA), a division of the American Library Association (ALA), published Rosenberg's *Cost Finding for Public Libraries* in 1985,[3] it was the first time a major professional effort was mounted to introduce costing and simplified cost accounting procedures to libraries. Although intended for the public sector, it is a useful model for obtaining unit cost information for all types of libraries. It provides a standard framework for collecting cost data and includes private sector applications. The information gathered may be used for evaluating operational efficiency and effectiveness as well as for evaluating the real costs libraries incur in cooperating with outside agencies and with their parent organizations.

The model includes costing concepts and methodology, a glossary of costing terms, blank worksheets, and sample rules. It provides directions for calculating full productive hourly labor costs, as opposed to salary, determining and allocating depreciation for major equipment or structures, and converting expenditures or budget information into cost or use data.

The steps in cost finding are straightforward:

1. Identify the cost center or responsibility area for which costs are to be calculated – circulation is a cost center, for example.
2. Define the activities and tasks within the cost center.
3. Select units of measure, such as cost per item.
4. Gather information for direct and indirect costs. For direct costs this

includes recording actual time staff spends on an activity or task, preparing other direct expenses, and determining total direct costs for the activity.

For indirect costs this includes determining such indirect operating expenses as utilities and insurance and such indirect support expenses as purchasing, personnel, and administration, and then allocating these costs to the activity to determine total costs.
5. Compile activity and task unit cost information.
6. Analyze cost finding results.

Managing a Cost-Finding Study

Cost data can bring an understanding of unit costs and cost behavior in relation to overall library operations and organization, long-range planning, and setting priorities. Cost finding provides data for making models and projecting costs. But, there are pitfalls in using cost information. The cost finding process as presented in PLA's model requires time and thought — from data collection to interpretation. It is not a quick fix and not without caveats.

Three critical issues must be considered before embarking on a cost study: purpose of the study, rules of the game, and project coordination and training. Resolving them will affect the type and quality of data collected, staff attitudes, and the project's long term usefulness.

The purpose of the cost study should be defined and related to overall planning, goals, and objectives. It will affect the definitions, rules, and selected units of measure. The study purpose should be established and understood before other study rules are written.

For example, the use of voluntary contributions and volunteer time may be counted in various ways, depending on the cost study purpose. It may be defined as zero, or as the cost it would have if performed by paid staff – all depending upon the context and need.

If the purpose of a cost study is to show the real cost of the voluntary contributions made by paid library staff to interlibrary cooperation activities, the time directors and others may be contributing to provide multitype library workshops, newsletters, and other services must be counted as part of the cost.

When the cost of currently donated staff time is computed, it could prove to be more expensive than future paid staff. The more highly paid staff are often the volunteers who plan and provide cooperative activities when cooperation is informal. If cooperation tasks are formalized and funded, service provision on a more routine basis might be implemented by less costly personnel.

Rules of the Game. The purpose of the study affects the rules – in this case how volunteer time is calculated. Clarity and comparability of results are key motives for establishing rules for any cost study. The library staff must understand the rules in order to complete the study. Cost comparisons among institutions may be difficult even when uniform rules are attempted; without rules such comparisons become impossible. Some suggested general rules for costing are in the box.

Just as important are common definitions. Areas to consider are:

Interlibrary Loan: Interlibrary loan is a transaction in which library materials or photocopies of the original material are loaned by one library or information service to another, autonomous library upon request for use by a patron. A subject request is a transaction in which an answer to a question from a library patron is found upon request, the answer being verbal or in the form of material or photocopy.

Delivery: Delivery is a formal method of transporting pieces of resource material or equipment or printed information among members of a set population on a regular basis.

Consulting: Consulting is the provision of advice and/or assistance with professional information or is an aid to in-depth problem solving to libraries and their boards, and to their governmental bodies, upon specific request for assistance.

Continuing Education: Continuing education/inservice is the provision of workshops or conferences to groups; one-to-one training, for the purpose of this study, is considered to be consulting.

Project Coordination and Training. Cost study purpose, rules, and procedures should be formulated

---

Sample General Costing Rules

Rule 1: The value of the building will be based on its replacement cost per square foot, divided by the useful life of the building. The rent will be the cost if the building is rented.

Rule 2: The value of volunteer time will be calculated on the basis of reasonable pay and fringe benefits for a full-time employee, on an equivalency basis.

Rule 3: The value of the library collection will be based on its insured replacement value, divided by the useful life of the collection. The useful life of the collection can be determined by using the weeding schedule or by using ten (10) years.

A second method is the average materials expenditure for the last three (3) years.

Rule 4: The value of the collection will be allocated on the basis of the percentage of the collection that is related to a specific cost center, i.e., if 10 percent of the circulation is for interlibrary loan, allocate 10 percent of the collection cost to this cost center.

Rule 5: In depreciation of fixed assets to determine the annual cost:
   a. Use the auditor's established schedules to calculate depreciation; or
   b. Use the Internal Revenue Service depreciation schedules; or
   c. Use the purchase price minus the salvage value divided by the useful life; or
   d. Divide the original cost by the age of the item.
   e. Groups of similar items, as office furniture, may be grouped for one total.

Rule 6: For fully depreciated items which are still in use:
   a. Use the intrinsic value; or
   b. If the intrinsic value is higher than the annual depreciation rate, use a straight two percent (2%) of the cost per year.

---

with library staff participation. There also should be specific assignments for project coordination and, preferably, one project coordinator.

The project coordinator has authority and responsibility to direct the process, and the time to work with library staff throughout the process. The person who fills the role needs training skills, an understanding of library financial reports, and an ability to be flexible. Coordinator responsibilities might include: developing and publicizing the project objectives, procedures, rules and definitions with staff input; establishing the study schedule, including a data-collection test period and the actual data collection period; training staff; copying and adapting, as necessary, the cost finding data collection forms; collecting indirect cost data from available financial records; troubleshooting; encouraging participants; summarizing data; coordinating data analysis and developing preliminary recommendations; and

writing the final report of findings with optional recommendations. Alternatively, the recommendations may be written separately by the library director or by a library team, based on the findings.

The importance of adequate communication and staff training in the cost-finding process cannot be overestimated. If current staff cannot devote adequate attention to these tasks, it may be worthwhile — or necessary — to obtain consultation or training from someone who has done cost finding. A side benefit of adequate training will be an increased understanding of the library's resources, resource allocation, mission, and management.

Issues in Cost Finding

If PLA's cost finding method brings forth much needed financial information for library managers, it also draws forth debate on its process, use, and usefulness. Issues that deserve attention include full costing versus the PLA model, the value of library materials as an indirect cost to library services; cost attribution; contracts between publicly funded libraries and the private sector, and costing, pricing, and policy.

Full Costing Versus the PLA Model. The total cost of a library service or activity consists of direct and indirect costs. The process of "full costing" or determining fully loaded costs – direct and indirect – involves three levels: Level 1 is direct library costs to the service; Level 2 is indirect library costs to the service; and Level 3 is indirect government, municipal or agency costs to the service.

The PLA model focuses on Levels 1 and 2. Any library found within a larger entity, whether it is in a corporation, school, university or prison, should include Level 3 costs in order to analyze library costs in the context of institutional goals.

A public library manager might determine that Level 3 data are essential in some cost studies. An obvious example might be library use of a municipal automation system. In some cases, using the municipal computer might not only affect library costs through chargebacks, but also the effectiveness of library operations. A cost study comparing the municipal computer and a library turnkey system could provide concrete evidence on the utility of a separate library computer.

The Value of Library Materials as an Indirect Cost to Library Services. The library's collection is an indirect cost to a number of library operations or services – from film showing, circulation, reference and story hours to interlibrary loan. Use, or expense, of the collection can be allocated to services on the basis of the percent of the collection which is used by that service. If 5 percent of the total circulation is for interlibrary loan, then 5 percent of the collection expense would be allocated as an indirect cost to interloan. The problem area is not in determining proxy methods to allocate use of materials, although this may be more difficult in some services such as reference. The difficulty is in determining the value or expense of the collection itself.

One problem is the issue of whether the library collection is a capital item or a fixed asset. For capital expenditures, such as buildings or bookmobiles which provide benefits over a number of years, depreciation methods can be used to calculate the capital expenses for a given period. The PLA cost-finding model provides methods for determining the part of the cost of capital items or fixed assets to be considered an expense in a given time, and allocated as an indirect cost of service.

There are general rules used in defining a fixed asset. The item must be tangible in nature, have a useful

━━━━━━━━━━━━━━━━━━━━━━
━━━━━━━━━━━━━━━━━━━━━━

What is the relationship between determining library costs and establishing library fees? Costing library service is, to some, too close to pricing or setting fees for those services. It is essential to remember that cost finding is a tool, a data-collection procedure not tied to any one policy or to the use of the data. Ascertaining full-unit cost information is not, and should not be, directly linked to any policy on chargebacks or fees.

━━━━━━━━━━━━━━━━━━━━━━
━━━━━━━━━━━━━━━━━━━━━━

life longer than one year, and have significant value.

Library materials, considered singly, do not meet the test of significant value. The collection in total could be defined as a fixed asset, although this is debatable. Even if the definition of fixed asset is assumed, the expense ascribable to the collection is not obvious. Upon what factors or elements should this amount be based? Does the collection depreciate or appreciate over time? This may depend on the collection. Should acquisitions, cataloging, binding, shelf maintenance, and other factors be included in cost?

In addition, if the depreciation method is applied, the useful life of the collection is hard to define. One suggestion is to use the weeding schedule to determine useful life: if 5 percent of the collection is weeded annually, use 20 years as the useful life. Weeding timetables applied differentially to the classification schedule is another option if this much detail is required.

The issue of collection expense is not resolved in the PLA model. Since collection costs are estimated at 15 percent to 20 percent of a library's budget,[4] then this may be an area which library directors and cost study coordinators should consider carefully in determining cost study rules for collection value.

Some possible ways of valuing collections include using: fair market value; insured replacement value; insured replacement valued divided by the useful life of the collection, in which the useful life is determined by applying the weeding schedule or, alternatively, using ten years; annual materials expenditure; and average materials expenditure for the last three years.

Obviously, since the method will affect the value assigned to the library's collection, and ultimately the service and unit costs for services which use the collection, it should be selected carefully. More importantly, the rule or policy followed in ascertaining collection expense should be documented carefully for future comparability of data.

Cost Attribution: Cost to Whom? The cost finding method results are per unit costs for a service within a specific library. Cost finding examines institutional costs. If another library provides a supplementary or reciprocal contribution to the service, this is an external cost. These external costs usually are not included in the library's cost study results.

It may be reasonable to consider the effects of external costs – costs attributable to other agencies or to individuals, including users – in cost analysis, decisions and program changes. Recognizing external costs is especially crucial to benefit studies. If equipment or service costs are shared or provided on a reciprocal basis among institutions, costs savings may be realized to each institution. The library manager should note any unilateral decisions to recover costs. For example, to initiate charges for photocopying previously provided on a reciprocal basis may instigate reciprocal charges.

Some external costs are not always obvious, especially when the focus is an internal cost study. If a filled interlibrary loan request costs $5.42 per unit to the requesting library, this does not reflect the total cost for filling the request. The request accrues some cost at the filling library and, if it was referred or re-referred, there is a cost involved at each step. The request could ultimately reach multiples of the $5.42. Even if the costs of referrals are not absorbed by the originating library, these do reflect system-wide costs. If the libraries are in the public sector, this is a public cost. While these costs do not appear on the library's own ledger sheet, it is important and fiscally responsible to consider the entire system in planning, and to attempt to balance system-wide costs in meeting user needs, or distinguishing user needs from user demands.

Publicly Funded Libraries and Private Sector Contracts. The purpose of a cost study is to collect data, establish unit costs, analyze cost components, and determine changes resulting in cost savings. Cost studies are a tool in achieving program cost efficiency. A possible conclusion in the costing of public sector libraries is that some services may be more efficiently and cheaply provided through contracts with the private sector. Examples might be plant maintenance, database searching, delivery, cataloging services, or other leasing arrangements.

The judicious use of public-private contracts may be beneficial to users of public sector services, including libraries. Contracting is a popular concept in public service delivery in these times of retrenchment. Public capital projects like bridges, roads, buildings, and sewers are often completed through private sector contracts. Recently, other private sector initiatives have created competition in snow removal, maintenance of parks, bridges and roads, and prisons. Some public service planners believe that using volunteers or private providers will save money and that there is nothing inherently good or bad about the public or private sector.

This may, indeed, be true in most arenas. However, public-private contracts in the information sector may contribute to a dangerous trend: the privatization of information.

Access to information, efficiently and effectively provided to their users, is a goal of public sector libraries. Cooperation and contracts with the private sector, including libraries, may help improve access. Nevertheless, in a democratic society, librarians and others must protect the concept of information as a public good, not a private commodity sold only to the highest bidder.

Costing, Pricing and Policy. What is the relationship between determining library costs and establishing library fees? Costing library service is, to some, too close to pricing or setting fees for those services. It is essential to remember that cost finding is a tool, a data-collection procedure not tied to any one policy or to the use of the data. Ascertaining full-unit cost information is not, and should not be, directly linked to any policy on chargebacks or fees.

There are other issues in cost-finding methods and their application to libraries: How can the model be used successfully during, not before, a growth in library services? What is the best format in which to report complicated results? How can cost terminology be used effectively? What cost components can be built into automated system design? If it is more an art than a science, how can results be considered legitimate?

It is well to remember in the sometimes agonizing process of cost finding that establishing quantifiable measures in a service industry is arduous. There are no easy answers, but reasoned conclusions are possible. Cost analysis has deeper roots in the private sector than in the public sector, but should be nurtured carefully in public services if those services are to remain public. ═

References

1. *Governmental Accounting, Auditing and Financial Reporting* (Chicago : Municipal Finance Officers Association of the United States and Canada, 1980), p.59.

2. William W. Holder, Robert J. Freeman and Harold H. Hensold, Jr., "Cost Accounting and Analysis in State and Local Government," *Cost and Managerial Accountant's Handbook* (New York: Dow Jones-Irwin, 1979), p. 97.

3. Philip Rosenberg, *Cost Finding for Public Libraries: A Manager's Handbook* (Chicago : American Library Association, 1985).

4. Bruce E. Roby, "Library Cost Accounting," [1983] paper, University of Wisconsin-Madison, [School of Library and Information Studies], p.32. (In press, *Wisconsin Library Journal.*)

COST-FINDING
The Wisconsin Experience

Elizabeth Richmond

Few library administrators actually determine direct and indirect costs when projecting current service costs. In fact, the most common approach is to apply an inflationary factor to the previous year's budget lines. This makes it difficult, if not impossible, for officials who make decisions about library funding to determine the cost of a unit of service. No one has any idea about whether or not the library is efficiently run.

From 1984 through 1985 seven Wisconsin public library systems took part in a study to develop a model for estimating costs and apportioning them to specific services. The project was sponsored by the Library Services and Construction Act, Title III and the Department of Public Instruction. I was statewide director and Philip Rosenberg was consultant.

Rosenberg's *Cost Finding for Public Libraries: A Managers Handbook*[1] appeared following completion of the study, but it differs from it in significant ways. Some of those differences are explored here and some recommendations for cost finding are made.

Full Costing

The Wisconsin study was set up to develop full costs by focusing on three levels:

Level 1: Direct library costs to the service

Level 2: Indirect library costs to the service

Level 3: Indirect government, municipal, or agency costs to the service

By including Level 3 costs, such as data processing, motor pool, telephone charges, and building rent, we accounted for all costs, including these chargebacks from the municipal government.

Knowing the impact of Level 3 costs puts the library director at an advantage in planning, budgeting, and proposing alternatives. The worksheet shown in Figure 1 was used to document Level 3 costs by assigning them to the library, to the library departments supporting the service, and finally allocating them as indirect costs to units of service.

The Wisconsin study focused on incremental costs, costs that change as a result of a decision. The decision under consideration was expanding such services as continuing education, interlibrary loan, and delivery to special, academic, or school libraries through multitype network participation. Project coordinators wished to estimate the increase in volume and its effect on cost: What will be the additional costs if interlibrary loan services increase by 20 percent? How much more will a workshop cost if participation is increased by 50 percent? To answer these questions project coordinators examined the resources—or cost input, determined unit costs, delineated add-on costs, and estimated

FIGURE 1
INDIRECT SUPPORT
MUNICIPAL DEPARTMENTS SUPPORTING THE LIBRARY:
ASSIGNING DEPARTMENTAL COSTS TO THE LIBRARY

Service _____   Time Period _____

(1) Municipal Department	(2) Total Municipal Department Period Expense ($)	(3) Allocation Percentage (%)	(4) Period Allocation Amount to the Library ($)
Ex. Purchasing	$30,000	6%	$1,800.00
1. Personnel			
2. Purchasing			
3. Bookkeeping			
4. Data Proc.			
5.			
6.			
7.			
8.			
9.			
10.			
11.			
(5) Total			

costs for future multitype library systems.

The use of the term add-on costs is significant. The purpose of the study was not only to estimate costs but also to examine expanding library services and to determine additional required moneys. The rules and assumptions used in interpreting the data and assigning costs reflected this purpose.

Figure 2 is a simplified example of this approach. It shows a system's annual direct costs for a workshop and models for future, expanded services. The current budget A reflects $100 for presenter costs and $400 to reimburse travel expenses for the attending librarians.

Future budget B, the add-on cost model, assumes no cost increase for the presenter; this is a fixed cost of $100, and does not change. But it does include an increase in the number of attending librarians. The "Librarian Travel" category represents a variable cost which will increase, as the attendees do, by 50 percent. In budget B, the option proposed in Wisconsin, the purpose is to estimate the variable or add-on costs for expanded services, not to distribute total, fixed, or sunk costs. A second purpose is to demonstrate possible economies of scale in expanding public library systems to more members. In this example, the speaker's cost is constant and only the variable cost of travel increases. This would be true until the margin was reached and a second presenter was necessary.

In a cost study with another purpose, for example fee setting or recovery of past invested—or sunk— costs, the fixed presenter cost might be allocated proportionately to new consumers of the service. Future budget C represents this cost allocation method. Here the total speaker cost remains at $100, but it is distributed or allocated to users proportionately: $66 to public library users and $33 to the new, nonpublic library users.

Cost finding can focus on service unit costs or on costs associated with tasks within the service. To enhance the clarity in data collection an attempt was made to differentiate between task and service level costs, using the worksheet in Figure 3. It details the direct personnel time spent on tasks or components of ser-

**FIGURE 2
DIRECT COSTS MODEL**

Current Budget (A)

Budget Item	Public	Nonpublic	Total
Presenter Cost	$100	NA	$100
Librarian Travel			
Public	400	NA	400
Total Costs	$500	$0	$500
Percentage	100	0	100

Future Budget B: Add-On Cost Model

Budget Item	Public	Nonpublic	Total
Presenter Cost	$100	$0	$100
Librarian Travel			
Public	400	NA	400
Nonpublic	NA	200	200
Total Costs	$500	$200	$700
Percentage	71	29	100

Future Budget C: Distributed Cost Model

Budget Item	Public	Nonpublic	Total
Presenter Cost	$67	$33	$100
Librarian Travel			
Public	400	NA	400
Nonpublic	NA	200	200
Total Costs	$467	$233	$700
Percentage	67	33	100

NA = not applicable.

vice. It is more detailed than the analogous PLA worksheet. While the PLA model includes task-level costs, the worksheet designed to summarize task or total-service costs does not differentiate between the two.

The PLA model develops an indirect cost rate for the library and applies this rate to the cost centers. While this rate is more accurate than using an arbitrary indirect cost rate, the model does not present a method for ascribing a specific indirect cost rate to a specific service, or for analyzing the effects of these costs. The PLA model also presents a more streamlined approach which appears less formidable; however, steps which some library managers may want are omitted.

Rules and Definitions

The project coordinators devised a set of definitions and common rules to facilitate cost data comparisons.[2] In the first year project coordinators agreed to follow the same general rules and methods, use the same definitions of cost centers to be stud-

ied, and analyze the same tasks or steps within cost centers in the seven participating libraries.

But by the project's second year, coordinators decided that the rules and definitions written as a compromise were of little value to the individual systems. Although many were uniform, in the second year each library system's rules reflected its own situation.

Although the definition of cost centers and tasks within a cost center did not create many problems in uniformity, the general rules proved more difficult to apply to all the libraries. For example, coordinators had to establish a value for each library's material collection as an indirect cost to be allocated to many of the library's services. Collection expense was allocated on the basis of the percentage of the collection used in a specific cost center. For example, if 10 percent of the circulation was for interlibrary loan, 10 percent of the collection cost was allocated to the interlibrary loan cost center.

FIGURE 3
DIRECT COSTS
PERSONNEL/TASK COST SUMMARY

Service: _____   Period Ending: _____

(1) Employe	(2) Hourly Rate Adjusted Employe Cost per Hour	(3) Components of Service or Task															(4) Total Hours and Cost Per Employee	
		CODE:		CODE:		CODE:		CODE:		CODE:		CODE:		CODE:			
		Hours	Cost	Hours	Cost	Hours	Cost	Hours	Cost	Hours	Cost	Hours	Cost	Hours	Cost	Hours	Cost

(5) TOTAL HOURS AND COST per component

1) For adjusted hourly cost see Worksheet 3, column 12.
2) Enter code for components of services or tasks, Worksheet 2, after "CODE:" of column 3.
3) Enter hours summarized from time recorded on Worksheet 4, column 2, for the test period; then calculate cost under each task code.

The collection cost itself was more difficult to define. If materials acquisition accounts for 15 to 20 percent of the library's budget, the defined value of the collection will have an effect on final unit costs for services using the collection. The cost study coordinators could not agree on the best method for determining the collection's value. In addition, not all cost study managers could obtain reliable figures for some of the suggested values for example, insured replacement value.

Finally, library systems and consortia had a more complicated situation than individual libraries. While individual libraries have a collection of materials, this is not always true for library systems. In systems and consortia, materials used for services such as interlibrary loan may not be in a single location, materials may be found in member libraries' collections. The cost of using these materials may be a contractual fee or a reciprocal arrangement involving no fee. Since the arrangements affect cost they should be documented in cost study rules and taken into consideration in interpreting cost results.

Fear of Full Costs

Many librarians assume that finding full costs will result in affixing higher costs to library services. In the Wisconsin study we found that this was not the case. After completing a study of interlibrary loan costs in three of the seven libraries, we compared the costs to those reported on in four other studies. The fully loaded cost allocated to interlibrary loan was comparable to the figures achieved by other costing methods.

The costs per interlibrary loan for three Wisconsin library systems completing studies were $3.50, $5.96, and $4.29. The latter two figures included author/title and subject requests, while the former included only author/title requests. In a 1984 Pennsylvania interlibrary loan study using a survey methodology, the average cost for filled loans was calculated at $6.52 for monographs, $6.93 for serials, and $6.87 for other items.[3] In a 1983 interlibrary loan study Roby used a cost-accounting method in which costs were set at $8.05 per receipt of an item.[4]

Palmour's landmark 1972 interlibrary loan study includes direct costs and a 50 percent overhead rate.[5] Cost data were obtained from a subsample of 12 large main libraries; these costs were projected for 113 academic libraries based on distribution of labor tasks. Herstad adapted Palmour's work.[6] Her methodology

---

Many librarians assume that finding full costs will result in affixing higher costs to library services. We found that was not the case. After completing a study of ILL costs in three libraries, we compared the costs to those reported on in four other studies. The fully loaded cost was comparable to the figures achieved by other costing methods.

---

also included direct costs and an overhead rate of 50 percent plus fringe benefit cost. In applying these figures in 1988 both studies should be adjusted for inflation.

Unit Costs and Output Measures

Unit costs and output measures are used in cost finding depending on the very practical requirements of the data collection. Relating resource costs to product output is a practical and psychological tool. Unit cost information provides the link between the two. For instance, library board members and other governing authorities understand the cost of van delivery service more concretely when alternative delivery methods are compared on the basis of cost-per-item-delivered rather than total program cost. The board can support a program costing, $7,000 a year with the knowledge that the per unit cost is $.21 rather than an alternative delivery method which costs $.40 per unit.

Although they share some characteristics, unit costs are not identical to output measures as defined in *Output Measures for Public Libraries*.[7] Output measures are indicators of the library's service to its community rather than of the resources which the library uses to provide these services. Output measures do not focus on funding level or inputs, but on the measurement of the resultant service. Examples from *Output Measures* include the number of items circulated and the reference transactions per capita.

Delivery Service: Outputs and Unit Costs

Delivery services were included in some of the Wisconsin library system cost studies. We pinpointed several possible delivery unit costs: cost per item delivered, cost per mile, and cost per stop. In selecting units of measure, Rosenberg suggests that the unit should: relate to the activity

---

Rubberstamp Your Thanks!

Successful library fundraisers looking for a novel way to express thanks might use the donor's own check. A rubber stamp saying "Thanks so much" is effective when stamped in red on the face of a check. Donors will notice the message when going through their cancelled checks and may appreciate the reminder to single out that check for their files.

or task; support management informational requirements; be result oriented; and lend itself to accurate data collection.[8]

All three of our possible units of measure met two of Rosenberg's criteria: they related to delivery and they could be counted accurately. The cost per item delivered is the obvious library output measure, delivery of library material is a library goal. This cost could be valuable in comparing alternative delivery methods. A library-operated vehicle, a shared vehicle, contractual services, and mail delivery are possible alternatives.

Cost per stop data might be useful if services were to be curtailed to save money. Fixed and variable costs in service reduction could be examined to determine the effect of eliminating stops. Cost per mile data might be useful in examining the efficiency of van delivery versus mail service for deliveries beyond a certain area or radius. Again, the data collected relates to the purpose of the study.

Process and Job-Order Costing Methods

Unit costs and output measures are related on the very practical level of data collection requirements, that is the analysis or use of data is dependent on the sufficiency and type of data collected. Interlibrary loan provides an example of data collection options and the resultant interpretation or use of per unit costs.

In an interlibrary loan study, the per-unit lending cost could be defined as the cost per request handled (filled, referred or unfilled) or the cost per filled request. The first measure is the measure of a total process or service of interlibrary loan, it is not a measure of individual job success, outputs, or service success.

The second unit of measure can be equated with output measures or the successful outcomes, or jobs, of the interlibrary loan service. There are several ways to obtain the cost per filled request. If an accurate cost of the filled requests is the goal, then each interlibrary loan request, or an adequate sample, must be tracked individually and treated as a job-order cost. This decision must be made before the study starts and it involves significantly more work, including task-level data collection and tracking.

Job-order costing provides an accurate cost of each library service output (filled request) or an average of these actual costs. It should be used when there is a high expectation that the cost or time required in providing individual units of service will vary. That's why interlibrary loan is a good candidate for

A successful cost-finding study requires that hard decisions be made on desired project goals, units of measure, and tasks to be counted, based on management's needs and the resources available for the study. Examining units to be costed and their relationship to real library outputs, the cost finding process increases the focus on the real nature of library outputs.

job-order costing and tracking. The equations for individual and average job-order costs are:

$$\text{Cost of Filled Request} = \frac{\text{Time} + \text{Material} + \text{Overhead}}{1}$$

$$\text{Average Cost per Fill} = \frac{\text{Cost of Filled Requests}}{\text{\# of Filled Requests}}$$

Process costs, obtaining unit costs for operational activities that are more uniform or even in cost or time, may not require tracking. Process costing might be used for overdues, circulation transactions, or periodical check-in. Obtaining a process cost of a unit of service is accomplished by dividing the total service cost by the number of units completed.

In circulation, the equation for process cost of a unit of service is:

$$\frac{\text{Cost per circulation}} = \frac{\text{Total Service Cost}}{\text{\# of Transactions}}$$

With circulation or other relatively uniform and consistent tasks, a unit cost based on total service costs can be used as the output measure cost.

Cost finding provides a method for obtaining full service costs, but decisions about the level and type of unit cost information to obtain may be difficult for coordinators to make. A successful cost-finding study requires that hard decisions made on desired project goals, units of measure, and tasks to be counted, based on management's needs and the resources available for the study. Examining units to be costed and their relationship to real library outputs, the cost finding process does increase the focus on the real nature of library outputs. As a result, library expense is related more closely to the library's real purposes and to the activities which support those purposes.

References

1. Philip Rosenberg, *Cost Finding for Public Libraries: A Manager's Handbook* (Chicago: American Library Association, 1985).
2. These rules and definitions are described in Elizabeth Richmond, "Cost Finding: Method and Management," *The Bottom Line* 1(4):18.
3. *Interlibrary Loan Compensation Plan for the Commonwealth of Pennsylvania, Final Report*, March 15, 1985 (Rockville, Md.: King Research, 1985), p. 11.
4. Bruce Roby, "Library Cost Accounting," in *Wisconsin Library Journal* (p. 34, in print).
5. Vernon E. Palmour et al., comps., *A Study on the Characteristics, Costs and Magnitude of Interlibrary Loans in Academic Libraries* (Westport, Conn.: Greenwood, 1972), pp. 3,23–24.
6. JoEllen Herstad, "Interlibrary Loan Cost Study and Comparisons," *RQ* 20(Spring):249.
7. Nancy Van House et al., *Output Measures for Public Libraries A Manual of Standardized Procedures*, 2nd. ed. (Chicago: American Library Association, 1987).
8. Rosenberg, p. xi, 16.
9. Ibid., p. 12017.

A CIRCULATION SYSTEM COST PROFILE

Christine M. Murchio

The first question a library manager should ask when deciding whether or not to automate the library's circulation function is: Will an automated system help the library meet its priorities better than a manual system? The next consideration is library staff. Personnel play a critical part in determining the success of any library service. And, of course, they are the library's most costly expenditure. Some questions to ask are, will an automated circulation system:

- decrease staff flexibility by requiring more sophisticated skills and more rigid minimum staff levels?
- result in more staff flexibility by enabling the library to divert staff freed from manual activities to those tasks that are still labor-intensive?
- enable the library to provide better service with the same level of resources?
- accommodate growth in direct circulation, interlibrary loan/inter-branch loan (ILL/IBL), reserves, inventory, and other aspects of circulation services without a parallel growth in staff?

Of course, there are no hard and fast answers to many of these questions. The professional judgment of the library manager often determines what is "right" in many cases. It is difficult to calculate some of these "costs." One that *can* be calculated with some precision is the *financial* cost. Here, too, there are a series of issues to consider. Will an automated circulation system:

- decrease budget flexibility by increasing the proportion of mandated expenditures and, if so, how will that impact other library services?
- increase costs more in the long run than a manual system?
- have sufficient longevity so that it will pay for itself, or at least be cost-effective within its life span?

These and other issues were addressed in developing a cost profile for a medium-sized library in New Jersey that has a main library and eight branches. It serves a local population of approximately 100,000 people and has an annual circulation of about 750,000 items. The library was only interested in computing ballpark figures with a minimum of work disruption. What was wanted was a model which the library could use in the future for additional analyses and which would prove helpful to other busy librarians.

The focus of the 13-week study was on personnel costs—the amount of staff time spent on circulation tasks, and circulation supply costs—the amounts of materials and supplies necessary to provide the service.

The study began with an activity and task analysis of circulation services. Mitchell's *Cost Analysis of Li-*

brary Functions[1] and Rosenberg's *Cost Finding for Public Libraries,*[2] can provide conceptual guidance for this. Since the library was considering several automated systems, circulation was broadly defined as all tasks related to lending library materials, including:

- Registration and charge desk duties
- Overdues
- Special messenger responsibilities
- IBL/ILL service
- Book selection and acquisition
- Checking in new books
- Shelf list and catalog maintenance
- Discarding and withdrawing materials
- Inventory
- Shelving materials
- Reading shelves

This breadth allowed the library to compare automated systems to its manual system and so help identify where the most significant costs for circulation lay and assess where savings were likely to occur in the conversion to computer power.

Personnel Costs

Task Analysis. The focus of the task analysis was on both direct circulation—charging out materials to library users, and indirect circulation—the functions that support this service. The library procedure manual and information obtained from the circulation staff became the basis for the analysis. As an example, a portion of the task analysis covering registration and charge desk activities appears in the box. It is for these tasks along with others that staff members kept records of time spent. The task analysis was developed from the staff time logs, shown in Figure 1 on page 22.

The tasks and logs were explained to, and discussed with, 11 line supervisors who were responsible for identifying and training all relevant subordinates for their participation in the data collection and for seeing that completed logs were submitted.

Time Analysis. The staff time logs were analyzed using simple formulas to provide data on the following aspects of the tasks involved in circulation.

Time reported. Figures were derived representing the total actual time to the nearest quarter hour reported by staff in hours for any given task.

Projected annual time. The 13 weeks of project data were applied to a 52-week period. Time was not weighed for seasonal fluctuation, nor were holidays subtracted from the 52-week period:

Projctd annual hrs = Actual time reported (13 weeks) × 4

Circulation time distribution. These figures showed what percent of the time spent on circulation was spent on specific tasks:

$$\text{Circ time dist} = \frac{\text{Time spent on task}}{\text{Total time spent on circ}}$$

Projected annual cost of time. These figures were derived by multiplying the percent of time spent on a particular task by the FTE (full-time equivalent) cost:

Projctd annual cost = % of time on task × FTE cost

Cost distribution. These figures showed what percent of all personnel costs for circulation services were incurred for specific tasks:

$$\text{Cost dist} = \frac{\$ \text{ spent on task}}{\text{Total } \$ \text{ spent on circ}}$$

FTEs. Full-time equivalent figures were obtained by taking the total projected annual hours spent on circulation and dividing them by the annual number of hours for which full-time staff members are paid:

$$\text{FTEs} = \frac{\text{Total projctd annual hrs}}{1820}$$

FTE cost. This cost was derived by multiplying the number of FTEs necessary to perform work (as reported

---

CIRCULATION SERVICE TASK ANALYSIS

Registration Tasks

New Borrower
1. Interview borrower.
2. Check alphabetical registration file for patron who claims not to have a card.
3. Have patron fill out application.
4. Type borrower's card.
5. Type patron's card number and name on numerical file card.
6. File patron's application in alphabetical registration file.

Lost Card
1. Pull registration from alphabetical file.
2. Mark registration with date and "lost card."
3. Type new card with same number, expiration date, and A, B, etc. after number.
4. Refile registration.

Expired Card
1. Have patron fill out new application.
2. Check alphabetical registration file for duplication or risk borrower status.
3. Continue, using the procedure for new applicants.

Charge Desk—Photocharge Agencies

Setting Up Desk
1. Gather and record circulation statistics from previous day.
2. Change all daters, fine counters, etc.
3. Pre-stamp transaction slips, or cards, where necessary.
4. Set up day's money and record files.

Charging Books
1. Photocharge books, records, pamphlets, periodicals.
2. Hand charge art reproductions, rental books, vacation loans, teacher loans as outlined in procedure manual.

Discharging Returns (Owning Agency)
1. Pull transaction slip and compute fine if necessary.
2. Place material on cart.

Discharging Returns (Other Agency)
1. Compute fines if necessary.
2. Route book, with transaction slip, to owning agency.

FIGURE 1
CIRCULATION TIME LOG

Name:_____

Position/Rank:_____

Agency:_____

Dept:_____

Date:_____

Circulation Tasks	Day of Week							
	SUN	MON	TUES	WED	THURS	FRI	SAT	TOTAL HOURS
Registration and charge desk								
Overdues: Preparation								
Typing								
Searching								
Contacting Patron								
Special Messenger								
Reserves: Taking								
Verifying								
Filing								
Processing								
IBL/ILL								
Select/Acquis: BEC								
Agency orders								
Checking in new materials								
Shelf list/catalog maintenance								
Discards/withdrawals								
Inventory								
Shelving materials								
Reading shelves								
Total:								

Total hours worked in week:

FIGURE 2
PERSONNEL COSTS FOR MANUAL CIRC SYSTEM

Circulation Tasks	TIME REPORTED (HRS)	PROJECTED ANNUAL TIME (HRS)	TIME DISTRIB. (%)	PROJECTED ANNUAL COST OF TIME	COST DISTRIB. (%)
Registration and charge desk	$	$	40.3	$	39.3
Overdues: Preparation	$	$	5.3	$	4.8
Typing	$	$	2.6	$	2.5
Searching	$	$	1.1	$	1.1
Contacting Patron	$	$	0.6	$	0.6
Special Messenger	$	$	0.6	$	0.6
Reserves: Taking	$	$	1.5	$	2.2
Verifying	$	$	1.6	$	1.9
Filing	$	$	0.9	$	0.9
Processing	$	$	2.1	$	2.0
IBL/ILL	$	$	4.1	$	4.3
Select/Acquis: BEC	$	$	4.8	$	6.8
Agency orders	$	$	3.1	$	4.8
Checking in new materials	$	$	3.7	$	3.9
Shelf list/catalog maintenance	$	$	5.5	$	5.8
Discards/withdrawals	$	$	4.2	$	4.3
Inventory	$	$	4.6	$	4.1
Shelving materials	$	$	9.4	$	7.1
Reading shelves	$	$	3.9	$	3.1
TOTAL			100%		100%

TOTAL FTE's   = ____(#)____

TOTAL FTE COST = ____($)____

in the logs) by the appropriate median salary for a given position:

FTE cost = FTE × median salary

A sample of the data analysis format appears in Figure 2. Separate analyses were performed for each type of staff—professional, nonprofessional, and pages—according to type of agency—small branch, large branch, and main. For the main library, there was differentiation among departments as well. Separate analyses were made to reflect the differences in staff composition and work emphases in the different agencies and departments.

Cost Estimate

The figures calculated for personnel costs using this model are estimates. Several assumptions were made about the data from the time logs. The first was that all staff who should have kept logs did so; the second was that logs were completed according to the directions given; the third was that times were reported accurately to the nearest quarter hour; and the last was that log tallies were accurate. In addition, costs for employees were calculated on the basis of logs submitted. No estimates were developed for missing information.

Because of the wide range in salaries and hourly wages paid to staff, and the constraint of time, all calculations for the cost of staff time were based on median salaries. Median salaries for professionals, nonprofessionals, and pages were determined for those employees working in large branches, small branches, and main, and these medians were then applied to the calculations for all members as a group regardless of actual individual salary earned. The median was selected rather than the mean because of wide salary ranges.

The estimates of personnel costs were somewhat low because holidays, vacation time, personal days, and sick time were not taken into account. In reality, the library would need more full-time employees than indicated by the study in order to offer service at the current level. In cases where an hourly wage was earned, it was converted to a yearly salary by multiplying the hourly rate by 1820—the number of hours in a year for which a full-time employee is paid.

The costs of staff benefits were not calculated because information about benefit rates was not readily available, and because benefit rates received by staff were varied.

Implications of the Personnel Cost Profile

The personnel cost figures reported do not necessarily mean that the staff resources expended on a given task were those necessary to perform that task adequately. For example, the 4 percent of staff time spent reading shelves does not mean that the shelves were in good order for users, it simply means that 4 percent of the staff time reported was directed toward that effort. This is particularly important because reallocation of staff resources must be considered in analyzing the potential impact of automation.

It is difficult to judge the tradeoffs between a manual circulation system and an automated one without concrete information about the specific functions and costs for individual systems. From this study, it seemed doubtful that an automated system would be less costly than the manual one, but it also seemed likely that an automated system would provide better circulation service than the manual one.

Based on the definition of circulation used for the cost study, it is possible to look at the tasks performed in the manual system and note where shifts in personnel costs could occur with an automated system. The largest amount (40%) of staff time reported was spent on the staffing the circulation desk. Since an automated system would require the same level of staffing throughout the day that the manual system does, it is unlikely that any significant savings in staff time or cost would be realized for this task.

Almost one-tenth (9%) of staff time reported was spent on overdues. Since an automated system would prepare, type, and address overdue notices—and also reduce search time for items—much of the staff time spent on these activities could be eliminated.

An automated system could not perform the tasks of the library's special messenger (an employee who contacted delinquent borrowers and retrieved library materials).

Reserve activities accounted for 6 percent of staff time spent on circulation. For items owned, an automated system could be much more efficient. An automated system would also reduce the amount of time spent (4%) on IBL/ILL paperwork, but, of course, it would not reduce the amount of time spent on physically handling the materials.

Materials' selection/acquisition required 8 percent of reported staff time. An automated circulation system would not have an impact on the selection practices used at the time of the study and so would not result in saving staff time spent on the task. However, an automated system could result in a reduction of time spent in actually placing orders for materials.

Physically processing—labelling, stamping, taping, etc.—new materials could take place on a more extensive level with an automated system, but it is not known to what extent recordkeeping for new materials, which accounted for 4 percent of the time, would change.

Automation could perform shelf list/catalog maintenance much more efficiently. Since a clean database of library holdings is crucial for an effective automated system, however, the amount of time (5.5%) spent on this task, at least initially, would be likely to increase with automation.

Discarding and withdrawing existing records can be done more efficiently with an automated system than with a manual one. The amount of any savings realized in this cost (4%) would be affected by the extent to which physical handling of items is necessary, since those activities are manual in nature.

Shelving materials and reading shelves will remain manual operations. Time spent (13%) on these activities might increase with automation if staff can be shifted from other activities to these.

Circulation Supplies Costs

Costs for circulation supplies were grouped according to the tasks that defined circulation services—registration, charging, overdues, reserves, the special messenger, interlibrary loan, book ordering, acquisitions, checking in new books,

---

CIRCULATION SUPPLIES

Registration
Registration forms
Library cards
Numerical list strips

Charging
Circulation books
Band daters
Fines counters
Transaction cards (Main)
Transaction slips (Branches)
Transaction rolls (Branches)
Microfilmer's service contracts
Kodak microfilm
Regiscope microfilm
Fines reports forms
Nonresident borrower forms

Overdues
Demco sheets
Keysort equipment
Microfilm readers service
  contract
Overdue notices
Envelopes
Postage
Risk borrower forms

Overdue form letters
Postage for letters

Reserves
Card stock (no postage)
Orange reserve cards
Branch reserve slips

Special Messenger Forms

Interlibrary Loan
IBL forms
ILL forms
ILL book cards
Renewal cards

Book Ordering
Order slips
Color banded catalog cards

New Books
Color tape

Shelf List and Card Catalog
Red flags

Book Processing
Book pockets
Book cards
Date due slips

shelf list and catalog maintenance, and book processing. No supply costs were identified for shelving materials or reading shelves.

The library procedure manual served as a starting point again, this time for identifying any circulation activity that required the use of some type of supply. (the circulation supplies that were identified as necessary for both photocharge and handcharge manual systems are presented in the box on page 89.)

Cost Estimate

The overall cost of circulation supplies that was calculated was an *estimate* because some of the supply costs were based on the amounts of supplies ordered during the year, rather than the amounts used during the year; some figures were based on replacement cost; no costs were calculated for items for which it was not possible to determine annual quantities used by the system (the cost of such items was not significant); the costs of some items, such as daters, were not included because they were infrequently purchased; and no amortized costs for equipment were calculated.

Implications of the Supply Cost Profile

The estimated costs of circulation supplies were about 5 percent of the total costs of circulation estimated in this study. It is likely that supplies for registration, charging, overdues, reserves, and IBL/ILL activities will be most affected by the switch to an automated system. While the individual forms, or types of forms, for an automated system might be more costly in price, they would probably take less staff time to process.

Implications of the Circulation Cost Profile

The main objective of automating circulation in the library studied was to improve service to library users at a cost comparable to, or cheaper than, the manual circulation system. Improved service would result from an automated system's ability to provide:

Management information. An automated system could provide reports on such things as collection demand, utilization, and users. This information would aid staff in col-

lection development, inventory, weeding, and registration file maintenance.

Better control of the collection. An automated system could enable the library to more effectively and efficiently account for the location of materials throughout the system and those in use; to monitor re-

> *If the library manager formulates a clear and comprehensive conceptualization of circulation—what is done and with what resources—then she or he should be able to develop a valid, reliable, and useful estimate of circulation costs. While the cost of automating circulation services is only* one *factor affecting the decision of whether or not to automate, it is a* significant *factor in the decision.*

serves; to increase collection use through off-site, online access to information about holdings; to produce overdue notices on a more regular basis; and to maintain up-to-date borrower files.

Materials acquisition and processing information. An automated system could improve procedures for materials acquisition and processing by centralizing information about items ordered, cataloging data available, and items owned. An automated system could also greatly reduce the amount of time necessary to revise and maintain the catalog.

Collection information for users.

An automated system could improve library service to users by providing very current information about holdings; by making complete information about holdings for the entire system available to all users, regardless of which individual agency they use; and by speeding up delivery of materials to users by tapping the system as a whole to fill user requests.

If the library manager formulates a clear and comprehensive conceptualization of circulation—what is done and with what resources—then she or he should be able to develop a valid, reliable, and useful estimate of circulation costs. While the cost of automating circulation services is only *one* factor affecting the decision of whether or not to automate, it is a *significant* factor in the decision.

Having a sound estimate of the cost of whatever circulation system is in place, including a profile of how cost is distributed among circulation tasks, will strengthen the decision-making process about automating circulation services in a number of ways. The library manager will have flexibility in assessing the financial implications of the different options of various systems; will know where the major costs of "circulation" are and so be better able to judge vendor claims of system impact and savings; and will be able to determine how the circulation tasks performed by the system in place and the systems offered by vendors differ in fact and in price. =

References

1. Betty Jo Mitchell, Norman E. Tannis, and Jack Jaffe, *Cost Analysis of Library Functions, A Total System Approach* (Greenwich, Conn.: JAI Press, Inc., 1978).
2. Philip Rosenberg, *Cost Finding for Public Libraries, A Manager's Handbook* (Chicago: American Library Association, 1985).

PRODUCTIVITY MEASUREMENT FOR FISCAL CONTROL

Catherine R. Reilly

Productivity is not merely a new buzz word, it is a national concern being discussed in the highest circles of government and business. Historically, productivity measurement has been most heavily used in the manufacturing sector, mainly on blue collar jobs. That is no longer true. Today, more and more service-sector managers are looking for and identifying ways to measure the productivity of staff at all levels.

For the industrial engineer, the goal behind any productivity measurement system is to increase the amount of output produced per unit of input and, consequently, reduce the unit cost. The system, as implemented at the Chase Manhattan Information Center, started with a time and motion study and has resulted in a measurement system that gives management standards by which they can gauge the effort of their staff.

These standards were created by industrial engineers who spent from six weeks to three months surveying the center, talking to the staff, collecting data, checking results with management and, finally, issuing a report. The report presented the measurement standards with their definitions and suggested new methods of work-flow, elimination of some parts of functions, and/or redistribution of work. In today's economy, productivity holds promise for documenting efficiency and effectiveness in all types of libraries and information centers when qualitative as well as quantitative inputs are made part of the measurements.

The Need for Productivity Measurement

In library and information center management it is not uncommon to be confronted with decision-makers who do not understand what it takes to produce a certain service, and who are not about to learn any more than the basics — budget dollars, functions, staff numbers, services offered. Productivity measurement systems' results offer the manager numbers — a universally respected and understood language. These numbers come about through using an established mathematical formula coupled with fact gathering. Data are collected and computed by an objective third party, a key ingredient to their successful implementation.

With a productivity management system, the upward communication problem is somewhat simplified for managers. They can discuss not only what processes must be performed to provide a service, but also how long and how many people they need to provide it. With this system managers have at their fingertips measurement standards that they can use to

- increase or defend staffing levels.
- measure employee performance.
- justify equipment purchases.
- justify the cost to automate a function.

A productivity measurement system sounds like the manager's nirvana, but it can also be the manager's nemesis. Measurements are only worthwhile when

- they are true reflections of the work.
- they have been done with the

cooperation and understanding of the staff.

- the processes included in the functional measurement do not change.
- the measured functions reflect the majority of the staff's time spent performing the principal services.

A poor standard will reflect either a consistently low or high level of productivity, which is meaningless for rational decision-making. As a result, the manager loses the benefits of the standard and ends up either defending it or having to redo the entire study. The major drawback of productivity standards in the service sector is that they assume the quality of the product at the time of the study is the norm and that the norm is acceptable.

Creating the Productivity Standard

Historically, the Chase Manhattan Bank has used productivity measurement in its operations area. In 1973, this practice was expanded into previously unmeasured areas, including the Information Center. New management felt it was an objective method of identifying the Center's major functions, verifying staffing levels, and better understanding how the functions were performed.

Prior to actual data collection or discussions with the staff, the industrial engineers and the Center management dedicated a large block of time to decide what functions should be measured — in essence identifying the functions that were the most representative of the dollar investment in the area. Some of the functions earmarked for measurement in the Center were cataloging, research inquiry, routing, circulation, orders processed, and subscription renewed.

Then the staff was introduced to the industrial engineers so they could feel they could be open in describing what their functions are and how they perform them. It was important that the industrial engineer, with members of the staff, be able to identify all the processes that must be performed within the major functions to produce the service or product that was being measured. As an example, some of the processes in the Chase standard for cataloging were

Weeding	Per Book
Checking in Books	Per Book
Tracing Selection	Per Trace
Selecting Cutter Numbers	Per Book
Typing	Per Item
Serials Preparation	Per Book
Recataloging	Per Book
Adding Shelf List	Per Book
Headings for Filing	Per Piece
Binding	Per Book
* Cataloging	Per Book

Processes are combined to define an overall function. The item in the list preceded by the asterisk (*) — cataloging — is referred to as the Key Volume Indicator (KVI). The KVI is the culmination of all the processes; this count is considered the most representative of the function.

Every time one of the processes is performed, it is recorded. The volume of activity is calculated for each process and then multiplied by a standard time factor to produce the total time it should take to perform the recorded volume. An industrial engineer, after deciding with management what the area's KVIs are, observes the staff performing each function. It is vital that staff understand how and what to report; they *must* know how to count the KVIs. If the count is performed dissimilarly, the standard is worthless.

Discussion with the staff was also required to allay any fears that might arise. They had to realize their jobs were not in jeopardy. Above all, they had to take the exercise seriously. In effect, the staff provides the principal ingredients for the standard.

To provide a valid measurement, both the time spent in completing the KVI and the KVI volume were calculated by staff members on two charts. For research inquiries, as an example, they recorded six processes daily: how many calls they took, how many places they looked for the information, how many items they typed, copies they made, memos they wrote, and, finally, the total number of questions they answered. On a corresponding sheet, called a time ladder, shown in Figure 1, they recorded how they spent their time each day.

Every activity is given a code, which is reported along with the number of times the activity is executed. This is an extremely detailed process, which may be considered annoying by some staff members. Management plays a role when the daily time ladders are reviewed with the industrial engineers. Where any noticeable swings from the norm appear on an individual's ladder, the person is asked to describe why the variation occurred. Data are collected in this fashion for more than twenty days.

A study should not be undertaken at a time when the volume is above or below the norm; or when new, untrained, staff are working on measured functions; or when a large number of hours will be spent on special projects. If the time is wrong, tell the industrial engineer that it is, since managers will have to live with the standards set for years to come.

Figure 1—The Time Ladder

Dept.	Section	Employee	Starting Time	Date	Subj. No.	Proj. No.
			A.M. ☐ P.M. ☐			

Time	Code	Units	Time	Code	Units	Time	Code	Units	Time	Code	Units	Time	Code	Units	Time	Code	Units	Time	Code	Units
8:00			9:30			11:00			12:30			2:00			3:30			5:00			
01			31			01			31			01			31			01			
02			32			02			32			02			32			02			
03			33			03			33			03			33			03			
04			34			04			34			04			34			04			
05			35			05			35			05			35			05			
06			36			06			36			06			36			06			
07			37			07			37			07			37			07			

Figure 2—Research Services Reporting Form

ADMINISTRATION SERVICES
INFORMATION CENTER
RESEARCH SERVICES

Week of: _____

Task Description	Decimal Hours	Unit of Count	Task Code |18|19|20|21|	Activities |22|23|24|25|26|27|28|29|	Total Hours (Do Not Punch)
Microfiche Req. Proc.	08322	Req. Proc.	0 0 0 1		
New Fiche Filed	08816	Fiche Filed	0 0 0 2		
DPL Inquiry	17196	Inquiry	0 0 0 3		
			0 0 0 4		
			0 0 0 5		
			0 0 0 6		
			0 0 0 7		
			0 0 0 0		
			0 0 0 1		
			0 0 0 2		
			0 0 0 3		
			0 0 0 4		
			0 0 0 5		
			0 0 0 6		
			0 0 0 7		
			0 0 0 8		
			0 0 0 9		
			0 0 0 0		

Total Hours

	F ILE |TX| BATCH NO |11|12|13|14|15|16|	FMISNO. |17|18|19|10|11|	DATE YR |12|13| MO |14|15| DA |16|17|
All Cards	A 2	0 0 0 1	0 2 0 3 5	

	2 OF TOTAL ACTIVITIES |22|23|24|25|26|27|28|29|	NO. TX'S |30|31|
BATCH CARDS		

Figure 3—Research Services Reporting Form

		MONDAY EMPL / HOURS	TUESDAY EMPL / HOURS	WED EMPL	TIME CODE |18|19|20|21|	TOTAL HOURS |22|23|24|25|26|27|28|29|
A	Full Time Employment	No of Employees assigned to shift Including Vacation, Absent, etc.				1 1 1	
B	Borrowed	No of Employees borrowed from other Areas.				1 1 2	
C	Overtime	Hours worked beyond 7 hour day				1 1 3	
D	Part Time Employees	Includes Per diem, Part Timers, Outside contractors, etc.				1 1 4	
E	A+B+C+D+E	Sub-Total				X	
F	Loaned	Number of Employees Loaned to other Areas				2 1 1	
G	Support	Include all Employees identfified as Support				2 1 2	
H	E F G H	Sub-Total				X	
I	Vacation	Number of Employees on Vacation				3 1 1	
J	Absence	Number of Employees absent (Sick - Excused etc.)				3 1 2	
K	Lateness	Actual Hours of late arrivals early departures				3 1 3	
J	I+J+K+L	Non Productive Hours				X	
M	H L	Total Available Hours for Production					

	F ILE |TM| BATCH NO. |1|2|3|4|5|6|	IF MIS NO. |7|8|9|10|11|	DATE YR |12|13| MO |14|15| DA |16|17|
ALL CARDS	B 2	0 0 0 2		

	OF TOTAL HOURS |18|19|20|21|22|23|24|25|26|27|28|29|30|31|	NO TX'S
BATCH CARDS		

The study should be done when conditions are as close to the norm as possible. It is not wise to accept a bad standard, nor to subject the staff to another period of data collection.

When the study is completed, and the supervisor has been informed of the results, they must be tested and proved prior to acceptance. With the final results of the study, supervisors should be given the average KVI volume for each function. This provides a benchmark that will immediately tell supervisors whether or not their group's work is currently within the standards' ball park.

Once the standards have been tested and found acceptable, supervisors can begin to report their activity to upper level management. Figures 2 and 3 show Chase's form for one section of the Information Center's Research Services. The first page, on Figure 2, tallies the weekly volume and the total standard hours these tasks should take to complete. The verso, shown in Figure 3, tabulates the actual time available for these tasks.

Using the data gathered on the forms, the standard time is divided into the available time to arrive at the section's productivity percentage for that week. There are rules that are used to interpret these figures:

- Acceptable productivity is 75 to 85 percent in many work envi-

ronments.
- Consistently low productivity will highlight excess staff.
- Consistently high productivity will make the standard questionable.

Managers should be aware of these rules and be ready to explain any divergence. They should also reinforce two things to the staff: that the ongoing counting process must be the same as it was during the study, and that staff must report any time they spend on any task that was not included in the study, called nonstandard time.

If the standard starts to become problematic, a new study is not sought immediately. Instead, the count is examined. Has the volume decreased? Has the function been drastically altered? Review the time. Have staff members reported their time in more detail? Only when all else fails, or when the function has undergone drastic change, is a recommendation for a new study made.

Using the Standard

Each year, management at Chase has to estimate volume, staff, and productivity levels for each measured task with totals for the areas they supervise. Later reporting compares actual work effort against the projection. As Figure 4 depicts, volume is estimated and multiplied by

the standard to forecast the number of hours necessary to complete the volume. Then, as Figure 5 shows, the hours needed are converted to projected productivity and costs.

The final base for computing the costs is the Center's complete budget, including overhead. The end result is a mechanism which demonstrates that, if productivity can be increased, unit cost can be reduced at no additional expense.

Outside of reporting statistics, how are these standards used in the Chase Information Center? They played a major part in the following project proposals:

- justification for automation of the routing and cataloging functions.
- justification for new equipment in Microfiche Services.
- justification for automating the subscription/purchasing function.
- justification for automating the monthly abstracting service production function.

When automated routing and cataloging were proposed, as an example, the productivity standards were used as the basis for much of the justification along with the following facts:

- There was a constant backlog in the routing function; this caused overtime since routing slips were

Figure 4—Volume Projection Sheet

```
ADMINISTRATION GROUP
DIVISION: _____                          1982 Budget
                                                      Standard Hours Worksheet
DEPARTMENT/COST CENTER: _____
```

Task Identification	Standard Time	JULY Volume	JULY Standard Hours	AUGUST Volume	AUGUST Standard Hours
1. DPL Inquiry	.17196	1533	263.6	1606	276.1
2. MF Request	.08322	441	36.7	462	38.4
3. MF Filing	.00816	9681	78.9	10142	82.7
4.					
5.					
6.					
7.					
8.					
9.					
Total Std. Hrs.			379.2		397.2

Figure 5—Area Productivity Projection Sheet

1982 BUDGET
MONTHLY ALLOWED HOURS
RECAP

ADMINISTRATION GROUP   DIVISION: General Services   COST CENTER: 02035

Month	Std. Hrs.	% Perf.	Avail. Hrs. Budgeted	Support & Non-Std. Hours	Vac. Hrs.	Abs. Hrs.	Total Allowed Hrs.	Avail. Hrs. for Month	FTES	Total IFMIS Cont. Exp.	Unit Cost
Jan.	4822	79	609	6580	210	140	1302	140	9.3	34900	72.37
Feb.	4340	83	516.8	5990	280	280	1171.8	126	9.3	34900	80.41
Mar.	5497	82	666.3	8170	70	70	1497.3	161	9.3	34900	63.48

typed and changes made manually.
- All cataloging was original, taking an average 40 minutes per title.
- Processing involved manually typing card sets, pockets and labels.
- Access to a Wang mini-computer was available for the cost of a work station ($5,000).
- The Information Center had access to an area with programmers and systems analysts who could design a routing/check-in system.
- OCLC had opened its services to for-profit institutions in New York State.

The proposal made to upper-level management showed that with an investment of approximately $35,000 for equipment and conversion of the collection to the LC classification the area could:

- eliminate the routing overtime, saving $1,000.
- increase routing productivity so the function could be performed in 80 percent of the available time.
- reduce processing time in the cataloging function by 80 percent.
- reduce cataloging time by 65 percent, allowing the absorption of a greater volume and the ability to catalog other areas previously uncataloged with no increase in staff, for a cost avoidance of $12,000.

In the cost study defending this proposal, Information Center managers showed a payback in year three, a productivity increase, a staffing decrease, and a better quality of service for users.

Productivity standards were used to calculate how much time would be saved between the old and new methods. When a study shows, as this one did, that a function has been eliminated, a recommendation to transfer staff may be in order. If a large backlog exists in another function, the position may be switched and a better quality of service proposed, which includes a cost avoidance for the additional staff that would have been required to eliminate the backlog. The productivity standard is not a magic number that provides all the improvements a supervisor may want, but it does make it easier to deal with upper level management in explaining what is needed and what changes will occur.

Addressing Quality Through Productivity Standards

A major factor in any task performed in a library or information center is quality; but quantitative productivity standards make little provision for it. Productivity standards of 80 to 95 percent may appear impressive, but if the quality of the service is unacceptable to the users then that standard is worthless.

In 1982, Chase's industrial engineers created a system that measures quality of service in conjunction with the productivity measurement system.

To create the quality measures, each area in the Information Center was asked to define its products — products that were meaningful to users. In this case, since previously established productivity standards had no user-judged quality counterpart, new quality measurements were introduced.

What is being measured in quality? The Information Center's six products and their definitions for quality measurement are:

Information on Demand (Research): Research requests made to the professional staff, via phone, mail, or in-person from the user community. These requests are measured from the time of receipt of the request to the response to the user. This product includes database searching and manual research.

Biz-dex Requests: Requests for free reprints generated by the monthly *Biz-dex* issue. This product is measured from the time of receipt of the order to the mailing of the requested items to the user.

Orders: Requests for one-time book purchases from any publisher. This is measured from the time of the receipt of the order to the receipt of the purchase order "receiving copy" from the user confirming delivery.

Figure 6—Quality of Service Parameters

QMC = Quality Measurement Criteria
T = Timeliness
C = Completeness
A = Accuracy

I/E = Internal/External
I = Internal
E = External
Q/I = Quality Indicator
$ = In Thousands

GENERAL SERVICES DIVISION
QUALITY OF SERVICE INDICATORS
PRODUCT COST & STANDARD INTEGRATION PROGRAM

Product	Prod. #	QMC	Q/I	I/E	Method of Tracking	Samp. Dur./ Samp. Vol./ Rep. Freq.	Parameters of Performance Measurement
Info on Demand	A1	T	3 Hrs.	I	Time recorded re-search request	Daily 87(100%) Monthly	User request received–user response provided
Biz-dex	A2	T	3 days	I	Time recorded reprint request	Daily 15(100%) Monthly	User request received. User response provided.(Internally reproduced material)
Orders	B1	T	20 days	I	Time recorded purchase order request	Daily 12(100%) Monthly	User request received. Receiving copy dated and returned.
Credit Agencies	B2	T	2 days	I	Time recorded credit report request	Daily 15(100%) Monthly	User request received. User response provided.
Circulation	C1	T	2 days	I	Time recorded items overdue	Daily Monthly	Time from overdue until returned (for waiting list)
Routing	C2	T	1 day	I	Time recorded item received until sent out.	Daily 41(100%) Monthly	Time of subscription issue receipt until initial distribution.

Figure 7—The Information Center, Quality of Service Questionnaire

The Information Center will be periodically surveying users to monitor your experience with our ability to respond quickly and thoroughly to your requests. Please take a moment to answer the following questions so we can determine the adequacy of these services:

1. The Information Center has set the following <u>goals</u> of average response time to user requests:

    (1) research   3 hours
    (2) biz-dex requests (Section B)   3 days
    (3) orders (one-time purchases)   20 days
    (4) credit agency reports   2 days
    (5) circulation (reserve/waiting list)   2 days (from time item is
                                                             due from prior indiv.)

    (6) routing (1st on list)   1 day

Based on your need for the product requested (please use the product number(s) 1 through 6 when answering), do you feel our service is:

    ____ a) faster than you require

    ____ b) acceptable as is

    ____ c) slower than you require

If you answered a or c, please indicate what your usual requirements are and briefly explain your reason for setting that priority.

_____

_____

2. To determine how well we are meeting our goal, please indicate your actual average experience by product.

PRODUCT	Less than 3 hrs.	3 hrs.	Same day	1 day	2 days	3 days	4 days	Other (specify)
Research								
Orders								
Credit Agency Reports								
Circulation								
Routing								

3. In your opinion, is the quality of service supplied:

    ____ a) better than expected
    ____ b) about what you expected
    ____ c) less than expected

If you answered c, please briefly describe where the service is lacking and indicate whether you feel your request required more than the average length of time.

_____

_____

_____

Credit Agency Reports: Requests for Dun & Bradstreet reports providing credit information on companies. This is measured from the time of receipt of the order to the time the response is provided to the user.

Circulation: Reserve requests for Information Center material currently in circulation to be sent to a user upon its return. This is measured from the date the item is due to be returned from its original borrower to the time it is received back in the Information Center and sent to the person who is first on the reserve list.

Routing: Provides copies of current periodicals to a number of users. A maximum of 15 users share a copy and are placed on the list by seniority and then location. This is measured from the time of receipt of the item in the Information Center to the time it is sent to the first person on the list.

Figure 6 illustrates the quality parameters set and how the standards are to be tracked.

Quality of service indicators are reported monthly and cumulated quarterly. Chase also tracks the quality of service through the quarterly questionnaire represented in Figure 7, which is distributed to users and returned to personnel at the division level. In the case of quality measures,

costs are not quantified at the unit level; they are figured for each of the six products, and costed out for the year.

Faced with the costs, the results of the user quality survey, and the productivity performance standards, a manager should have a new understanding of the value of the library and information center and where adjustments are needed. If a product creates a large expense, gets little use, and has high productivity, its continuation should be questioned. If another product exists with a large user base, high expense, mediocre quality, and acceptable productivity, an additional investment might be recommended to improve it.

Chase has been using an objective, disciplined measurement technique in its Information Center for the past eight years. As each technique is tested or improved, Chase managers gain in understanding the value and capabilities of their areas. When measurement is proposed, the resistance of both staff and management is usually high. Job loss, function change, staff decrease are all envisioned. In fact, all are possible. While Chase's use of productivity measurement in its Information Cen-

ter may currently be unique, more and more corporations are moving in this direction.

Managers must work honestly and closely with the industrial engineer and upper-level management, making sure they are fully aware of the strengths and weaknesses in their areas, involving staff in the process, and making sure they fully understand the process of productivity measurement. They must set objectives for productivity increases and implement any changes needed to reach those objectives.

Measurement systems can be beneficial. They provide a means of communication and evaluation. They assist managers in making sure there is a real value in what is produced, that it is produced efficiently, and that it is reflective of the investment. The facts cannot be ignored. Productivity is a concern of the present and the future. Measurement techniques based on productivity are a reality in the corporate information center, but their usefulness is more generally applicable for managers interested in tracking and improving service as a means to document the case for fiscal support in all types of library and information centers.

COST-BENEFIT ANALYSIS
More Than Just Dollars and Cents
Thompson R. Cummins

In our era of scarcity, there is renewed interest in weighing benefits against costs. Today, library managers must do more than set goals; they must also consider the cost of attaining the goals. The methodology for this kind of assessment has been around for decades. Most depend on certain common elements: how to analyze and measure costs, benefits, and discount factors, and how to apply decision rules.

Assume that your library is considering a new book detection system. To capture all effects, the library director must systematically break down costs and benefits into major categories. Real benefits are those enjoyed by the user of materials that the library protects from theft. The real benefits are balanced against the real costs of resources withdrawn from other users and other uses. The cost of the system is considered against alternate ways the money could have been spent in order to determine the course that offers the most benefit to the library and the community it serves.

Since the single most important function of a library director is to develop and maintain an organization that performs its mission effectively, efficiently, and dependably, cost-benefit analysis has high priority. But directors must beware of the illusion of efficiency. Anyone knows that spending less will lead to cutting costs. It is quite another thing to pinpoint the real costs and benefits of such reductions. For example, spending $100,000 for the cheapest automated system available, instead of $250,000 for a better system, does not necessarily represent a real saving of $150,000. In fact, if the $100,000 system performs so poorly that it must be replaced by an effective one, the loss could exceed $100,000 when lost time, staff frustration, and service interruptions are factored in.

An effective cost-benefit analysis will consider many points, the first of which is whether or not the automation project fits into the mission statement of the library. Analysis requires several steps: Identify the current resources needed by the staff if they are to remain effective in their fight for future resources. Make sure that the conditions are right for automating human work. Create strategies for using the human and fiscal resources available in the library. And develop necessary resources that do not yet exist.

Cost-benefit analysis is not just cutting costs; it is making the best use of the resources the library commands. One good application of cost-benefit analysis in automation projects, for example, is to insist on functionality in the contract. Without it, when the carton of equipment arrives at your door, the vendor has fulfilled the agreement. If you specify functionality, however, the vendor is responsible for the quality of the equipment delivered, including acceptance and benchmark tests.

Obviously, if the sum of gains and losses is positive for gains, then that is a benefit. However, the *total* change in benefits must be measured for all affected users, not for a particular individual. Costs and benefits are ordinarily measured as the sum of individual recipient's valuations. Thus a dollar of benefits enters the equation with the same weight regardless of who derives the benefits. In order to evaluate the distribution of costs and benefits among the patron population or community in general, weights are attached to the gains and losses of each individual.

Benefit Analysis

Since the administration of library resources involves important decisions about the allocation of funds, scrutiny of these decisions continues to grow as public demands for accountability of scarce funds increases. Important questions are asked about the return-on-investment of funds and changes in the value of outputs and outcomes expected from management options.

For example, with a proposal to construct a new library facility, the important issue may be the relative value of the facility against the cost of alternate opportunities for spending those same funds. Cost-benefit analysis can be a useful way to evaluate these and other questions concerning the desirability of reallocating scarce public resources. Changes in the value of goods and services can be assessed in light of improvements expected from one option or the other. So, it is important to quantify both sides of the equation. The additional value of goods and services that could be produced is measured against the increase in expenditure of resources. The difference is net benefits.

The concept of cost-benefit analysis is best appreciated if its motivation is understood. The key is whether reallocation of resources results in being better off—and certainly not being worse off. The simplest way is to ask those who will be affected; for example, library patrons might be polled on whether they would be willing to pay for a new program and, if so, how much.

Cost-benefit analysis is not an attempt to convert decision making into a formula, but it does provide a framework for decision making—a method of listing and quantifying the pros and cons of a problem or opportunity in order to weigh the importance of each. As a tool for better fiscal control, it supplements but does not replace judgment or political acumen.

The concept of cost-benefit analysis is best appreciated if its motivation is understood. The key is whether reallocation of resources results in being better off—and certainly not worse off

It is important to determine what you hope to accomplish through your analysis. Are you undertaking an efficiency study? Are certain costs and benefits weighted? Are only the gains and losses of patrons considered, or are the figures computed for staff and all taxpayers? How will you measure the costs and benefits?

Usually, the measurement of costs is the most straightforward part of the analysis. Frequently, social or other weights (to which it is difficult to assign a dollar figure) are added to the benefit side of the analysis.

Perhaps the most difficult part of the analysis is deciding what the report will say when the analytical work is finished, especially the interpretation of the results and their use. Nevertheless, simply having a report is a big asset for the library manager when it comes time to discuss appropriations and budgets with the administration or governing board.

Constraints

Even though a project has tremendous benefits, the library still may not be able to afford it. Few librarians are in the happy position of deciding both the size and allocation of their budgets. But they are free to set individual service goals. In fact, there are many worthwhile projects competing for limited dollars in every library. Those selected for funding and implementation must be not only beneficial, but of maximum net benefit compared to all the other alternatives.

The same high criteria should be applied to existing programs as to new ones. The natural impulse is to look at an existing program and assume that its benefits will remain the same as when it began. That assumption may not always hold true. Many programs and services yield diminishing returns as the years pass.

How To Do It

There are five basic steps in conducting a cost benefit analysis:

- establishing objectives;
- estimating the program's impact on those objectives;
- determining costs;
- discounting costs and weighing or establishing benefits;
- summarizing the findings.

The first step lays the groundwork for the benefits that the program or service will produce. The relationship between the program and the objective must be traceable in order to establish a sound foundation for analysis. For example, a literacy program should produce individuals who are able to read at a basic level, enabling them to contribute more to the community and society, while at the same time reducing social program costs that require more taxes. A new library branch might reduce operating costs, increase the community's educational level, and lower patron's gasoline costs if it is more centrally located. A computer might optimize productive work while cutting down on material costs and filing expenses.

Cost-benefit logic is not limited to complex facility projects or major programs. It can be just as useful in decisions about day-to-day tasks: whether to buy or lease, whether to repair or replace, to streamline operations, or to update technology. It helps achieve the maximum benefit for the minimum cost.

After you estimate a program's impact, you must calculate the dollar worth of that impact. Such valuation permits comparison of cost-to-returns to establish whether the undertaking increases the net worth or well-being of the community. The worth is generally expressed in terms of money values because exchange values provide a standard to compare that worth with the monetary value of the resources used by the program. Benefit calculation will depend on whether the analyst decides to use a narrow efficiency approach or prefers to try to place patron-determined values on services, which are difficult to quantify. For example, a $50,000 security system may prevent the theft of 3,000 books worth $30,000: resources of one type are used to save resources of another. (In a sample efficiency approach, the costs incurred in the loss are compared to the costs incurred to prevent that loss. But deciding whether the community will be better off requires a more complex analysis. The books may have cost $30,000 to buy but may be difficult or impossible to replace at any price.)

For programs like recreational reading, outputs are not linked to dollar value directly. When that is the case, you apply a different cost-benefit approach–the estimate of surplus. Surplus is the calculated difference between the maximum price patrons would willingly pay for given amounts of a service and the price that the market demands for the service ($0 in the library's case, as library service is generally free).

The underlying logic of the surplus approach is represented by points along a demand curve for a service that shows the value the patron places on particular amounts of the service in question. The individual would voluntarily exchange any amount up to the top dollar on the demand curve rather than not have the service – the curve represents the patron's valuation of the service. Suppose a patron were willing to pay $25 to have ten reference questions answered. If the charge is $15, the patron would have maximum use of the service. If the price goes above $25, the patron would seldom, if ever, visit the library. Any time the price is below $25, the patron receives a surplus – the service costs less than he or she is willing to pay. Surplus equals the difference between the maximum price the patron would have paid and the price actually paid, multiplied by the number of units used or visits made.

If the price is $0 (the library is free), the total surplus would equal $450. That figure is computed:

$$(\$30 \times 5) + (\$25 \times 5) + (\$20 \times 5) + (\$15 \times 5)$$

This represents the entire area under the demand curve for that particular service.

The demand curve is one of the few feasible techniques available for valuing public services. It is used to show that most free library services carry implicit prices. Patrons must pay travel costs to the library, and this amount can also be included in cost determinations. Utilization is usually greatest by those who live closest to the library, indicating that both travel cost and convenience are factors.

Even if cost-benefit analysis is not used in decision-making efforts, it can still serve the valuable purpose of focusing public attention on what a library is all about and why it should be supported.

It is much harder to deal with benefits than costs because they are so much more diverse and difficult to quantify. In a wide range of cases, the benefits involve patron surplus gains of one sort or another. For example, the library makes services and materials available more cheaply to patrons and the community, and saves on materials needed to satisfy patron demands. The benefits are simply the patrons' surplus gains, as shown on a relevant demand curve. The benefits reflect the fact that patrons or individuals are more productive or more valuable in society as a result of their use of the library. Developing more valuable human resources within the community justifies the cost of investing community tax-dollars in libraries.

Cost Estimates

An estimate of the total cost of a program includes any and all capital costs as well as operating costs for the life of the program. As the total amount cannot always be definitively determined, the important cost becomes the opportunity cost of the program, which is the cost loss of alternative programs not pursued.

Discount Rates

The costs and benefits of most programs and services do not occur within one fiscal year. More often than not, after the initial expenditure, the operating costs and program expenses persist and accrue over the life of the program. It is difficult to compute returns or benefits in the future since, according to economic theory, a return in the future has less value than an equal return available immediately. Comparing the two impacts is called discounting, a process of converting a flow of returns or costs incurred over a number of years to a single present value. The present value takes ac-

Price (Value)

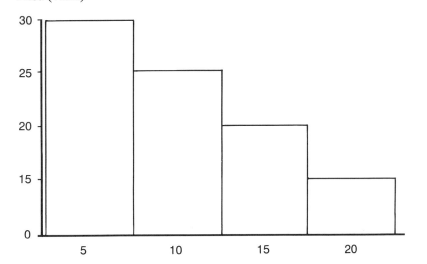

(Number of Reference Questions Asked)

count of both the absolute size and the timing of impacts generated by the proposed program.

Discounting means that a payment of $100 to be received at the end of the year is not equivalent to $100 received now, due to inflation and interest rates. If the money is received today, not only will it be worth more because of rising costs but, if invested, it will earn interest over the year. Money acquired now has greater value than money received at the end of the year, as it can become money-plus-interest at the end of the year.

Since many programs and services involve multiple-year decisions, the returns are compounded over several years. Discounting simply adjusts sums expected in the future to their present value equivalent: the amount that would accumulate if the sum were invested at prevailing interest rates. Even though the library does not have the choice between investing its budget or spending it— it must be spent—discounting, as part of the cost-benefit analysis, helps make adequate comparisons of actual program costs.

Decision Criteria

The decision stage in cost-benefit analysis applies the decision criterion to the discounted cost and benefits to summarize the economic case for the service. The summarization will either identify whether a program is economically justifiable or establish rankings among programs competing for limited dollars. Two criteria basic to decision making are the benefit-to-cost ratio and the net present value of the program. The benefit-to-cost ratio gives the present value of benefits less the present value of costs. If the ratio exceeds 1, or if the net present value is positive, the program passes the economic efficiency test. It is said that resources used for the project will increase economic well-being, be-

Project	Cost	Benefit	Net Present Value	Benefit Cost
A	$500	$600	$100	1.20
B	$150	$200	$50	1.33

cause alternative use of the same resources will produce a lower return or value for the community.

Frequently, program analysis requires not just evaluating the economics of a number of program alternatives but also selecting particular programs from several alternatives. Here the programs are ranked by ratios of benefit-to-cost or by net present value. Program rankings generally are the same with either approach unless the program sizes are substantially different. A typical comparison is shown at the top of the page.

Equalizing Fiscal Distribution

Cost-benefit analysis without weighting gives primary emphasis to the economic impact of programs and services. In libraries, however, economic impact is only part of the story. Librarians are equally concerned with the distribution or redistribution of information in the community. With such an underpinning, benefits received by the information-poor are weighted more heavily than benefits received by the information-rich. Benefit values need explicit adjustments to encompass redistribution concerns. Normal analysis accepts all portions of the community as equal. Gaining and losing groups or individuals are not considered.

It is possible to allow for distribution effects by weighting benefits by a measure of the societal importance of the recipient. Values received by some groups count more than values received by others, making selection of weights a possible problem. How much weight should

be given to programs and services designed for unwed mothers, inner-city children, the illiterate, poor readers, etc.? As another example, should weight be added to the classics in book selection and taken away from romance novels? Or should all patron demands for books be treated equally?

One approach would supplement general cost and benefit totals with a tabulation of how they are divided among the population. Weight could be given to income, age, race, sex, geographic location, education, reading level, or any other important category. By providing such an array, it is possible to avoid weighting on the social importance of groups in the community. Librarians provide the weights to each recipient group as reflected by the level of need identified.

Most simply put, cost-benefit analysis determines whether the benefits of a service outweigh the costs. The process is similar to the logic used in problem-solving or decision-making. Benefits in a library are defined in terms of the community rather than in terms of dollars and cents. Of course, any community has the moral responsibility to look beyond the bottom line — the simple monetary gains and losses of library services and programs. It must consider whether library services lead to non-monetary gains and losses; changes in people's lives, their businesses, and their use of spare time. Changes in any of these accounts are as much a benefit or cost of library service as a monetary gain or loss. ■

VALUING INFORMATION SERVICES

The economics of information has received a great deal of attention in the literature of information science over the past 20 years. Of particular interest has been the evaluation of library and information services through the measurement of cost efficiency, cost effectiveness, and cost benefit.

In practice, some evaluative models have concentrated on efficiency. By comparing units of service supplied with the resources required to produce them, they provide a relative idea of how well the library avoids waste. But most models focus on effectiveness–is the library fulfilling its purpose?–by comparing goals with results. This emphasis has stemmed from the general agreement that when effectiveness is not considered in evaluation the resulting analysis–although it may tell us how busy the library is–won't tell us how well the library is serving its various publics.

The analysis of benefit–or, the impact of information services–although widely discussed, has generated little activity. No less an illuminary than Fritz Machlup, in his seminal *Knowledge: Its Creation, Distribution and Economic Significance* (1980), declared futile attempts at developing measures to determine the influence of information on users or on society.

In any case, whether looking at efficiency, effectiveness, or benefit, librarians have shied away from analyzing them from the perspective of costs. Models such as *Objective Performance Measures for Academic and Research Libraries*, produced by the Association of Research Libraries, and the first and second editions of *Output Measures for Public Libraries*, produced by the American Library Association, have shown little or no relationship between library performance and costs. And costing models such as those produced by Philip Rosenberg have arisen separate from our expenditure-barren analyses of effectiveness and efficiency.

The economics of information service will never be understood thoroughly without incorporating facts about users, their uses of information, and the effects of that use. And what is most striking about all of these evaluative models is that they were designed from the point of view of the professional librarian. They don't require–or ask for–any input from users about what they think constitutes efficient or effective service, or what they perceive as the benefits of that service.

It's only within the last six years that we are beginning to see models for cost benefit analysis that brings dollars and users into the performance evaluation equation. Referred to as techniques for determining the value of information services, these models are based on the significance of information as measured from the users' point of view–whether that user is an individual, organization, or community.

Here the definition of cost is the first task in determining information value; it is no longer a forgotten element. Then, value is defined and weighted by users' answers to such questions as: How much time or money does the library save you or your organization? How long would it take you to acquire this information without the aid of the library? How does the information you get from the library affect your work? The life of your organization? Your quality of life? How much is the information worth to you? What are you willing to pay for it? How much could you pay? In a series of studies using these dimensions King Research Associates equated the ultimate value of library service with amount of use, benefits derived from use in time and money, and benefits lost if service was not available. In a study of 12 companies and government agencies in 1982 they concluded that the availability of information services resulted in a ten-to-one return on investment.

Soon after, Robert S. Taylor added to the concept of information benefit by borrowing the value-added approach from business. Adapting it to library and information centers, his investigations have turned up 23 values placed on services by users. High on the list are precision in the amount of information provided vis-a-vis the amount of information needed; ease of use of the information supplied; coverage; cost savings; and physical availability.

In late 1987, the Special Library Association issued its final report from the President's Task Force on the Value of the Information Professional and Information Service. It includes a model, conceptualized by Miriam Drake, that allows us to distinguish the worth of library services at four levels of cost, depending upon the comprehensiveness of the service provided.

What's missing that would make this value-added approach useful for librarians in presenting their case for support is a universal methodology that measures cost differentials at each level and a test of that methodology in all types of libraries to determine its general applicability.

With models based on the value of information and value-added service, librarians can begin to integrate the mosaic of cost efficiency, effectiveness, and benefit in our struggle for greater fiscal vitality. To do this, however, requires the concerted effort of librarians from all types of libraries and information scientists. The emphasis has to be less on the scientific quality of research and more on practical benefits. Then interest in the economics of information can finally produce tangible results for libraries.

Universities that house programs of library and information studies are the natural catalysts to get this effort off the ground. Let's get on with it.

FINANCING
PROGRAMS
AND
SERVICES

FINANCING LIBRARY AUTOMATION
Selling the Benefits and the Budget

Murray S. Martin

Libraries are costly, labor-intensive institutions. Moreover, their costs tend to rise rapidly.[1] The suggestion that automation should be superimposed on rising operating budgets is likely to meet with considerable resistance. Plans for automation need to be presented as an expression of the library's concern for cost containment, increased productivity, fiscal responsibility, and resource management.

Automation, as discussed in this article, refers to the purchase and installation of a "turnkey" system, rather than the inhouse development of a system or the adoption of various automated service contracts. While this article will follow the form of a case study loosely based on the experience of Tufts University in seeking such a system, the concepts and guidelines presented are useful for academic libraries in general. As background, Tufts University has about 7,200 students (4,500 of them undergraduates) on three campuses, a decentralized library system with eight locations, a collection of about 650,000 volumes and about 500,000 transactions annually.

Groundwork and Stage Setting for Automation

In preparing for automation there are two products to sell — first the idea of automation itself, second the actual automation proposal. The first requires setting a suitable climate before the second can even be contemplated. Preparing statements of goals and their benefits for different audiences is a time-consuming and frequently frustrating task. Library service benefits are dispersed and notoriously difficult to quantify. Most of those who have to be convinced are not regular library users and may not even have much idea of how libraries operate. One must also have in mind the ultimate sources of funds — tuition, capital reserves, grants, loans — each of which requires a different strategy to bring them into the project.

Not everyone is convinced by the same kind of argument. For example, competing with other colleges can be a strong incentive for those concerned with future admissions of students, but the financial people want to be convinced that any added cost is going to bring in adequate returns. Some will argue that improving the library's productivity is well and good, but what does that do for the students. Others will want to know what the visible differences will be and how they can be sold to potential donors. Some are fascinated by the technology and see it as a way of meeting their private goals. Finally, nearly everyone has some other more important priority; some will support the project to further their own ends, while others will oppose the diversion of funds. Given this background of conflict, any march towards automation must be a mix of strategy and tactics. It is seldom a straight line and, indeed, may more closely resemble a cross-country steeplechase.

Automation and Reduced Costs

No automation project yet has resulted in decreased total cost of library operation. This must be made clear. There will be shifts in staff and expenditures and there will be efficiencies. Over time there will be reductions in what would otherwise be unavoidable cost increases. The principal benefits, however, arise from the increased flexibility which allows shifting resources to activities more in need of them, and from the added productivity of staff members.

Smaller institutions seldom have much to spare in their library budgets and to deliver major offsetting savings requires some fantastic legerdemain. There will indeed be costs avoided such as OCLC charges for catalog cards, but these are relatively small in relation to the total added cost. Arguments based on such savings will have very little impact. They are, however, useful as ways of indicating the impact of automation on library operation.

Instead of promising savings, it is better to attempt two things. First, separate capital and operating costs. Capital costs, though substantial, can be found more readily because they are clearly identifiable and separable. Strange as it may seem in view of the totals involved, continuing operating costs loom larger in financial planners' thinking because these are usually paid for by tuition increases. Second, emphasize ongoing benefits to the principal library users — faculty and students. All benefits, of course, have associated costs and the goal should be to show that the costs are outweighed by the benefits.

Depending on the sophistication of the audience it is also possible to point out the ways in which automation can hold down the otherwise inevitable cost-increases associated with library growth. Here is where the shift of personnel from maintenance to service activities can be used for telling effect. Instead of filing cards, both in the public catalog and the various circulation files, staff can be used to add services. Even quicker reshelving is a benefit that can easily be understood. Better control of overdues and loss can be stressed, since these losses represent real money. Further, any increases in income or decreases in costs can be seen as reducing the added overhead caused by automation.

Benefits and Budgets

The principal public benefit — enhanced bibliographic access — is little understood and will not be evident until the system is in operation.

Nevertheless, particularly in a decentralized library setting, i.e., where services emanate from a number of sites, this improvement is very real and can be related directly to improved support for study and research. The reduction in travel time represented by such a change is substantial. When accompanied by an increased level of satisfaction in retrieval because of prior knowledge of whether specific books are on reserve or otherwise in use, the improvement in library-user activities is dramatic.

Care must be taken to avoid the implication that the actual contents of the library will be available online. Much current writing about electronic publishing has led partially knowledgeable faculty and administrators to confuse access to the bibliographic record with access to the information they represent. While online access to full text is becoming an economic possibility for libraries, it is not yet feasible on any large scale. Existing library automation systems do not provide such a linkage. They do provide the first step, particularly if the necessary wiring is undertaken with that development in mind. So this venture can be presented as offering a double return on the investment, first enabling the library to install an automated system and then allowing access to a larger electronic communications network.

The principal library benefits will be understood most by those who have had to deal over the years with library budget requests. Increases in services and activities most frequently require increases in staff. The relationship between size and cost has been amply demonstrated by several ARL studies[2] though it is not yet entirely clear whether such relationships are true for all sizes of libraries. Automation can address only some of these factors. Added books still require added shelving. Increased circulation results in increased reshelving. So far these continue to be human activities. Reference continues to be a one-on-one activity, though even here automation can increase the speed of finding pertinent information. Online access to dictionaries, encyclopedias, even the library's own database, eliminates the need to leave the desk to find information.

It is mostly in the "back room"

activities that automation can increase productivity. Acquisitions, serial check-in, cataloging, and processing can all be speeded up and the personnel resources dedicated to filing can be redirected. Libraries have seldom calculated the actual cost of maintaining all the files they must have in a manual setting. Because it is mostly a part-time activity all costs cannot be eliminated directly, only redirected to more productive activities in service terms. Speed in turnaround for circulated materials and more accurate records will influence a library's finding rate which, while it does not guarantee dollar savings, certainly reduces user frustration.

Expenditure Alternatives

The question will always be raised as to whether the money might not be spent more wisely on added acquisitions or more space. These are complex arguments to counter because all libraries require both — in addition to automation. Most faculty and administrators have difficulty in understanding the ramifications of additions to the book budget — added processing costs and added collection space. These facts can be used to demonstrate that automation helps librarians utilize book funds better and plan more adequately for meeting actual, rather than perceived, needs. In fact, the money spent on automation would buy very little space at $100 or more per square foot. Rather, the proper use of the managerial data retrieved via computer can assist in the better use of space in collection management. Space for study is not an issue that should be linked with automation, but it is the principal issue for students, and the need is to demonstrate that automation can actually assist them by improving basic services like reserve reading and circulation.

Diverse Perceptions and Funding

How then do these diverse perceptions affect the financing of automation? Mostly they affect the ways in which it must be presented in order to show the link between cost and benefit. Automation costs big money and the results must be worth it. The financial presentation must show this clearly.

From a set of requirements developed by the librarians, an RFI (Request for Information) can be generated both to determine if prospective vendors can meet the requirements and to obtain a preliminary fix on costs. The first determination helps to set the limits on any proposed system, based on feasibility. In this case the search is for an integrated (i.e., all-purpose) turnkey system with minimal university systems involvement. The second enables the development of a generalized cost statement which can be used to determine whether the system is financially feasible.

Several elements are required:

Capital cost — central installation, terminals, printers, etc.; communications, which is particularly important for a dispersed institution; installation.

Maintenance — hardware and software costs, staff.

Preparation — cost of record conversion, item preparation, labelling.

It is important to note that, if it is necessary to borrow money for the capital purchase, there will also be interest charges.

The distribution of library sites requires a higher number of terminals than would be the case in a more centralized university, in this case 100 to 125 terminals. This also affects the size of the central computer installation.

The result is a system with the following preliminary financial profile:

Capital cost: $750,000 – 800,000
Maintenance: $100,000 – 125,000
(annually)
Preparation: $600,000 – 700,000

Once these figures are established with some credibility, they must be presented in a cost-benefit package to those who will have to pay for it. When library budgets are decentralized, it requires a wide variety of approaches; to the central administration as a general benefit to the university's image; to those with the biggest direct interest as a long-term investment in improvement; to those with more modest commitments as not being an unmanageable burden; to all of them as a shared project none of them could afford independently. Potential sources of funding need to be identified, which means a lot of work with the development staff. The computer staff should be involved, particularly since they are going to be asked to look after the installed system. Likely faculty supporters need to be rallied. And all of

this must be approached with the knowledge that most outsiders have little specific knowledge of library use or library management.

Establishing the Financial Context

Libraries are seldom seen as capital investments, largely because their collections are paid for from current income. Yet over the years the capital investment represented by the library can be vast. For academic libraries, it is often greater than for any other segment within the university. The annual library budget at Tufts is approximately $4,000,000. This expenditure is distributed thus:

Collections	$1,500,000
Processing	800,000
Administration	200,000
Services	1,500,000

The accumulated value of the collection is $70,000,000 at replacement cost. Library buildings represent a further $16,000,000 in capital investment.

In this context, the added capital value of automation at $1,500,000 represents the addition of less than 2 percent to the existing capital investment. The operating costs of $125,000 represent only a 5 percent increase which can be diminished by generated savings.

The point to be made is that the added value of automation, represented by time-savings and added productivity, represents a highly desirable return. Via automation the libraries can double their capacity for such operations as circulation and cataloging, without added staff. The return to users comes in quicker access to information, faster turnaround in circulation, and better use of collections. All this can be achieved without having to promise to reduce current personnel costs.

An even greater return results from better record control. The added value of online catalogs is not readily understood. In most libraries, because the collections are scattered through several physical locations, it is impossible to provide copies of the entire card catalog. The cost of duplicating the card catalog, which is the equivalent of installing terminals with access to the online catalog, is so great as to be out of reach of any library system. From this flows not only the difficulty of ensuring that users find what they need, but the necessity of duplicating both books and serials. No one can pretend that all such duplications can be foregone, but they can certainly be reduced, especially older runs of serials, saving money for their purchase, housing, and maintenance.

Financial Impact

The result of this process is a kind of impact study. Its tentative nature must be stressed, and care must be taken not to overestimate savings. In view of the continuing importance of operating costs, a period of five years is recommended. This represents the likely period during which the system is expected to be stable. Table 1 illustrates this. Transferable, direct costs represent expenditures for all items, such as catalog cards, which are no longer required. Reassignable savings occur through tasks replaced such as filing.

A listing of ways in which the system can help improve and simplify library operations emphasizes the added nonmonetary value of automation:

- Total catalog record access at all locations simplifies library activities in support of study or research. Particularly important for branches and separated campuses.
- Simplified circulation and better

TABLE 1
FISCAL IMPACT OF AN INTEGRATED LIBRARY SYSTEM
(Preliminary Figures)

	Year One	Year Two	Year Three	Year Four	Year Five
Capital	$ 750,000	$ 50,000	—	—	—
Quasi-Capital	450,000	250,000	—	—	—
Operating	75,000	100,000	$125,000	$125,000	$125,000
Total	$1,275,000	$400,000	$125,000	$125,000	$125,000
Transferable Direct Costs	6,000	15,000	25,000	30,000	30,000
Net Impact	$1,269,000	$385,000	$100,000	$ 95,000	$ 95,000
Reassignable Savings	$ 10,000	$ 30,000	$ 35,000	$ 40,000	$ 40,000

control over losses and overdues.

- Simplified and improved communications between libraries, easier borrowing of materials, consultation on new purchases, actual savings on OCLC costs for interlibrary loan.
- Internal simplification of acquisition and cataloging procedures to ensure faster processing.

Acquiring the Funds

At this stage a number of questions are sure to be asked: Where will we get the money? Does the university have capital reserves? Are there funds set aside for automation? What is the current state of fund raising? Is a library building planned or contemplated? What is the university's attitude to bond issues? Is an issue planned? Are there interested donors? What is the university's track-record with known major donors, such as the Pew Trusts or Kresge Foundation? Are there local or regional foundations with a known interest in libraries? Does the university possess collections that might be of national importance that would qualify for grant sources such as Title IIc?

At Tufts, the final purchase cost was about $900,000. Associated costs of about $200,000 were for site preparation and electronic networks. The initial impetus came from a federal building grant for a new health sciences learning center, which included money for library automation. To this $400,000, as the proposal developed, were added $500,000 from the Pew Trusts, smaller foundation grants of about $40,000, and, finally, agreement to provide $400,000 from capital reserves. Actual site preparation was met from loan funds. The Pew Trusts Grant included $300,000 for data preparation to which was added about $200,000 from library operating budgets. Cobbled together as it may seem, the total represents commitments from across the university. The range of possible direct annual savings is from $10,000 to $50,000; the reassignable operating costs exceed $60,000 per year.

The fact that this was the first university-wide venture into electronic communications on such a scale made some of the initial cost estimates soft, to say the least. It did, however, require the university to come to grips with the subject and

more parts of the broader communication network are now under active consideration. The library has gained from this the recognition that it is an integral part of the university's information system.

The answers to most questions are likely to be ambiguous. A library considering automation needs to jockey for position with other known fund-attracting activities, like athletics or scholarships. The best situation to be in is to have a portion of the funding assured via a building project, or in association with some other goal, such as curriculum improvement.

Given this background of conflict, any march toward automation must be a mix of strategy and tactics.

Sad to admit, libraries are not, in the words of one fund raiser, "sexy." They are simply necessary and frequently taken for granted. The object of the activities outlined earlier in this article has been consciousness raising. With any luck, some of the pace-setters within the university will have been convinced that library modernization is an important measure of the university's commitment to a better future.

The Catch-22 in financing automation is that fund seeking cannot effectively precede agreement to automate, but that commitment frequently depends on having the finances in hand. Breaking from this cycle is usually dependent on having convinced one or more of the prospective financial supporters that the project is worthwhile. This is as much a matter of political skill as practical skill. Sounding out the ambitions and goals of the leadership can pay dividends.

If approval is given to go ahead with a full bidding process, guarded by the proviso that final approval will be given only if funding can be assured, it is possible to seek external funding even though it must proceed in parallel with the actual bid process. The first product, the RFP (Request for Proposal) weeds out actual

contenders from prospective suppliers and derives firmer cost figures with which to approach possible donors. It also provides a firmer base for internal cost calculations.

Fund Raising

Armed with these figures (for the purpose of this discussion we'll use $850,000 for hardware and software and a direct annual cost of $100,000), and a fairly clear idea of the probable vendors, requests for funding can be sent out. Multiple approaches to foundations for system purchase are unwise; select a major target and subordinate requests to other donors. Target foundations may well differ from region to region, particularly where there are local foundations with a long history of institutional support. Strategy sessions with financial and development officers pay off here.

Institutional Support

All fund raising should be undertaken with a healthy dash of realism; donors are not usually falling over themselves to give money. They need to be assured that any project has full institutional support and will result in substantial benefits. Moreover, libraries are seen as activities the institution itself should support. It is, therefore, highly beneficial to be able to demonstrate institutional commitment. Since foundations and corporations are seldom willing to provide all the funds, and are more willing to support a joint venture, the goal should be to present a project with multiple financial sources, so that each donor can feel he or she is providing a distinct part of the whole. It has also to be remembered that some donors require a visible product for their money and others are willing to fill in the gaps or support data conversion.

Fall-back Position

A lengthy funding campaign can be fatal. Major foundations usually take some months to decide, and do not always give prior indication of interest. They also wish to be assured that the rest of the cost is covered. A fall-back position is necessary. In most cases this turns out to be postponement. A better position is to gain consent to include library automation in a bond issue. This incurs interest costs, spread over several years, but enables fund raising to be pursued aggressively rather than diffidently, because any funds so raised will reduce potential debt, always attractive to the financial administrators. In Tufts' case, funding success was assured when The Pew Trusts made a major grant towards capital and quasi-capital costs.

Simpler goals are equally useful. A Friends Group can make it part of their program to fund specific items. It is possible to seek from alumni and parents small sums to be identified with individual terminals, thus allowing public recognition. Interest in the project can be generated by news releases on retrospective conversion, where students are involved. The object of such an approach is to place the project in a positive context — even if one has private nightmares. Nevertheless, the work involved is substantial. Only one approach in five is likely to result in a real accession of funds. But the first major donation leads to others. People more naturally support something that others believe in.

Rallying Internal Support

When a university is decentrally organized — a frequent arrangement in private universities — it is important to bring all the constituencies on board. This requires the development of a kind of cost-benefit statement for each unit. What do they get from the system, what must they contribute to it? Do they participate in any savings? Will they benefit from fund raising? Unless the system has been poorly conceived, all these questions can be answered, *and* positively. Don't understate costs nor overestimate savings. The latter should only be those resulting from direct cost transfers, e:g., OCLC costs. Stress the benefits to study and research of having direct access to all library records. Use-statistics can be valuable here. There is always more interlibrary use than the separate constituencies realize. For the largest library in the system the principal benefit is increased efficiency, and, therefore, improved service. For smaller libraries it is as if their collections were quadrupled. Sharing is not a much-touted virtue in a decentralized system, but it is possible to point out the costs of independence as against the fruits of coordination.

The Cost Projection

When a system has been selected a

TABLE 2
LONG-TERM SYSTEM COSTS

	System 1	System 2	System 3
Capital Cost			
Hardware	605,000	700,000	760,000
Software	95,000	65,000	80,000
Installation	50,000	60,000	60,000
Sub-total	750,000	825,000	900,000
Direct Maintenance Costs (5 years)	600,000	500,000	500,000
Direct Savings (5 years)	−40,000	−150,000	−50,000
Deficiency costs (variable periods)	50,000	10,000	10,000
Sub-total	610,000	360,000	460,000
TOTAL (5 years)	$1,360,000	$1,185,000	$1,360,000
Functional preference	3	1	2
Cost preference	2=	1	2=
Timing to installation	9-12 months	4-6 months	4-6 months
General order of preference	3	1	2
Recommendation	System 2.		

Sources of Funding:		
Foundation Grant	200,000
Smaller donations	100,000
Capital Reserve	400,000
Bond issue (prospective)	125,000

Setting up costs are covered by a combination of grant and operating funds. Effects of direct annual operating costs on student tuition (7,500 students)

System 1 $15 per year per student
System 2 $10 per year per student
System 3 $12 per year per student

five-year cost projection should be prepared, and not only for the system chosen but for the runnersup, so that the total costs can be compared.[3] This is the point at which the benefits of lower maintenance or specific savings become obvious. The choice should, of course, be based primarily on functionality, but there is frequently little to choose functionally between systems and the bottom line will make the difference. It may be necessary to point out problems associated with cheapness. In the old adage, good may be cheap, cheap is never good.

If an entire subsystem is lacking, alternatives will have to be paid for; perhaps by the maintenance of files that would otherwise have been closed. Some advantages or disadvantages are difficult to put a price on, partly because there is no easy way, for example, of making up for the absence of cross-linked subjects, but the attempt must be made. Tables can show clearly how the long-term advantages of less costly maintenance or directly attributable

savings offsets higher capital expenditure. As Table 2 shows, the greater savings from System 2 arise from the substitution of access to LC tapes for OCLC cataloging. Deficiency costs represent funds that would be expended for missing elements until they are available, for example, costs of maintaining the union catalog until the bibliographic data is online.

Cost Allocations

Distribution of cost by college can be made with accuracy only following system selection. Presuming that the System 2 recommendation is approved, a tentative allocation can be made. There are no ground rules for such an allocation since these will be affected by existing precedents. Student numbers are frequently used, though it must be pointed out that faculty use the library, individually, more than undergraduate students. The capital cost should reflect the numbers of terminals, which can be costed directly to each unit, since these relate directly to the size of

TABLE 3
SYSTEM COST DISTRIBUTION

	School A	School B	School C	School D	School E
Library					
Collections	400,000	100,000	80,000	(see A)	20,000
Students	5,000	250	1,800	200	250
Faculty	400	40	500	10	50
Terminals	63	10	40	2	5
Capital Cost	52.5%	8.3%	33.3%	1.7%	4.2%
(based on # of terminals)					
Operating cost:	(Equal Weighting to All Factors)				
Terminals	52.5	8.3	33.3	1.7	4.2
Students	66.7	3.3	24.0	2.7	3.3
Faculty	40.0	4.0	50.0	1.0	5.0
Collections	66.7	16.7	13.3	—	3.3
Average (div. by 4)	56.5%	8.1%	30.2%	1.3%	4.0%

CPU needed. Arguments will be made that smaller libraries should contribute in proportion to their holdings. In fact, the benefits are in inverse proportion to input. In the long run, therefore, capital costs can best be distributed by number of terminals.

Operating costs are much more difficult to allocate in advance. Since projections of use have already been computed to estimate the size of system needed, some proportional allocations can be made, but it is just as likely that an existing formula for the allocation of central costs can be used. A good argument can be made for a mixed distribution, directly allocating terminal maintenance costs and sharing the remaining costs according to a formula. Transaction-based cost allocation is complex, un-certain and, in any case, cannot be contemplated until a complete year's transactions are accumulated. Table 3 illustrates a more useful method. Schools B, C, D, and E are all professional schools with significant research, hence the different faculty ratios.

Continued Fund Raising

Fund raising should not stop. In fact it can be redoubled because there is a real product to offer. Further, actual contract negotiations may change or reduce some of the costs — not all terminals need be installed immediately, for example. Small though it may seem, there are real savings in substituting a general terminal for a circulation terminal plus light pen, where the number of circulation transactions does not jus-tify a dedicated terminal, and vendors, when making actual site inspections prior to installation, are willing to make recommendations resulting in greater efficiency. The goal here would be to eliminate the funding gap represented by the prospective bond issue.

A process as complex as this takes a great deal of time. Selling the need for a system within the institution can take at least one year. The process of selection and negotiation will also take a year. Fund raising will probably take more than a year — for example, foundations frequently take six to eight months to respond — and should, therefore, be proceeding parallel to the other aspects of the project. Then, of course, it is time to start planning for the next stage. Since at least four years are likely to elapse between initiation and realization of automation, it is extremely important to think in terms of the the future to avoid having to re-estimate goals and costs to meet changed conditions.

References

1. D. Kent Halstead, *Higher Education Prices and Price Indexes* (Washington, D.C.: G.P.O., 1975).
2. William J. Baumol and Marcus Matityahu. *The Economics of Academic Libraries* (Washington, D.C.: A.C.E., 1973) and Kendon Stubbs. *The ARL Library Index and Quantitative Relationships in the ARL* (Washington, D.C.: ARL, 1980).
3. Joseph R. Matthews, *Choosing an Automated Library System* (Chicago: ALA, 1980), pp. 50-51.

ADULT PROGRAMMING ON A SHOESTRING

Sandra Bokamba Lockett

You want to create a series of programs for adult — ongoing programs that increase library visibility in your community as well as adult circulation and usage. You have no money earmarked for this endeavor. As the adult services librarian, you *know* your community. You are aware of adult patron tastes and reading preferences. While developing a well-rounded collection, you are ordering books that reflect your community and, when funds permit, you are recommending innovative services. You plan programs at least six months in advance.

Your preparation includes encourag-

ing staff input; producing flyers to be distributed throughout the community; preparing press releases that request registration by a specific deadline. You have done your homework, and you are certain that this is only the beginning of successful adult programs at your library. You are enthusiastic, inspired, and *ready*. Or are you?

When I presented this topic at the Third Annual Public Library Association Conference, I felt that I was. I had planned relevant and timely programs. The majority were spin-offs from programs funded by grants and so were cost-effective for the library. But at that time, although the Milwaukee Public Library System (MPLS) had a five-year long-range plan, the library role as defined in the Public Library Association's *Planning and Role Setting*[1] had not been developed for the system or for specific neighborhood libraries. Since then, roles have been set, and in retrospect I can look back at my programming plans for the Center Street Library and see the missing pieces.

Long Range Planning

When your library system has no long-range plan (including the library's role in the community), you are working without direction in planning programming, services, and collection development. This is the perfect opportunity to develop the library's mission statement and to plan for future library services, studies, and funding in order to maximize your library's service to the community.

Planning for the future enables libraries to know where they are going and how they intend to achieve their goals. It also helps ensure that decision making about programs will be effective and enhance the ability to foresee staffing and resource needs. Developing a library profile is an essential part of determining library roles. Similar to a community profile, the library profile is more statistically oriented. Using Census data, you can develop a primary official document that can be used as the basis for grant proposals and funding requests. If your library is located in a transient community, statistics, although official, will not accurately reflect the current population of the community. Nevertheless, as the best data available, they will provide direction and a basis for projecting and planning to meet community needs.

Milwaukee Public Library Profile

The plan we developed was based on the MPLS Profile. The system services a population of 636,236 people. It consists of the Central Library, 12 neighborhood libraries, two bookmobiles, two community library vans, and the Wisconsin Regional Library for the Blind and Physically Handicapped. Monthly circulation is approximately 260,000, with an additional 17,000 volumes circulated each month by the regional library.

Monthly Young Adult and Adult Program Activities average about 100 programs at the Central Library with over 2,000 in attendance, 200 programs at the neighborhood libraries with over 3,400 in attendance, and 730 programs coordinated by extension services with over 1,200 in attendance. These statistics included program activities utilizing library staff and facilities. Center Street Library is the smallest neighborhood library; it serves about 60,000 people, the majority of whom are African-Americans. Adult illiteracy, unemployment, teen pregnancy, and high school drop-out rank high in the community. The annual circulation is about 32,000. A new building is scheduled to replace the present facility. The collection will double in holdings to 60,000 volumes; the facility will be three times the size of the present outdated building, or 15,000 square feet.

As branch manager, I initiated a variety of adult programs. I was determined to increase adult usage and circulation at a neighborhood library that had served primarily children and young adult patrons since 1928. Within the immediate community, the library is the only space for the children to go when they are not in school.

The Library's Role

Determining Milwaukee's role became a significant part of the planning process. The latest American Library Association planning manual recommends eight roles or service profiles that public libraries may carry out into their communities:

1) *Community Activities Center.* The library is a central focus point for community activities, meetings, and services.

2) *Community Information Center.* The library is a clearinghouse for current information on community organizations, issues, and services.

3) *Formal Education Support Center.* The library assists students of all ages in meeting educational objectives established during their formal courses of study.

4) *Independent Learning Center.* The library supports individuals of all ages pursuing a sustained program of learning independent of any educational provider.

You can use census data to create a library profile — a good basis for grant proposals and funding requests

5) *Popular Materials Center.* The library features current, high-demand, high-interest materials in a variety of formats for persons of all ages.

6) *Preschoolers Door to Learning.* The library encourages young children to develop an interest in reading and learning through services for children, and for parents and children together.

7) *Reference Library.* The library actively provides timely, accurate, and useful information for community residents.

8) *Research Center.* The library assists scholars and researchers to conduct in-depth studies, investigate specific areas of knowledge, and create new knowledge.[1]

In Milwaukee, while developing our long-range plan, we recommended allocating a percentage of our endowment monies to adult programming, thereby creating a continuing source of funding for programming. A committee was appointed to manage these funds.

The Milwaukee Public Library Adult Programming Committee consists of the communications coordinator, one representative from the Central Library, and two representatives from the neighborhood libraries. Together we set the criteria for funding system projects to include demonstration of the need for the program and how the programming relates to the library's long-range plans. Funding is available for large or small programs and cooperative programs among the neighborhood and central libraries. The grants, if approved, pay for honoraria, travel, materials, and refreshments. The committee requires an evaluation following each program. With roles set and a plan for funding in place, grant competitions were created for support, and a series of programs to enhance the roles were initiated.

Timely Programs

When the film *The Color Purple*, based on Alice Walker's 1982 book, was produced by Steven Spielberg, there were nationwide protests against the portrayal of a black man's brutality to his wife and children. In response to these issues, a panel discussed on the pros and cons of the issue was planned for the Center Street Library. An Adult Program Grant was written for $150 to provide honoraria and refreshments for The Color Purple program. A large cake was prepared, decorated with the profile of the main character Celie in her rocking chair. The funding was approved by the Adult Program Grant Committee. Approximately 90 people attended the program. It was stimulating and controversial; it was clear that the library community was hungry for similar programs.

The large turnout was due to several factors. Program participants encouraged their friends to attend. Flyers were distributed throughout the immediate community and city, including schools, organizations, and local businesses. The library publications department mailed press releases to local newspapers. The library staff talked up the program as they checked out library materials. Flyers were placed in patrons' books as they were checked out. Librarians mentioned the program during reference interviews.

During the program a sign-up sheet was given to the audience, requesting their name, address, and phone number. They were also asked what programs they would like to see in the future.

Four months later, the Reflections Book Discussion group was formed as a spinoff from the Color Purple Program. The cost of this ongoing program was minimal, involving for coffee, cookies, and staff time to print/ distribute flyers announcing the formation of Reflections on Writers of African Descent Book Discussion group. The group continues to meet at the library monthly, and its members now wish to pursue funding to develop future programs. The $150 spent two years ago for The Color Purple program was cost-effective.

Funding Service Programs

Of course, we couldn't present viable programs without adequate funding. The approach the MPLS established through endowment funds is one other libraries might try. But grants were sought from outside as well as inside the system, and full-blown program development was instituted. Grants based on competition ensured that the best-planned programs would be supported. For example, the Center Street Library staff knew that 45% of the adult reference questions concerned basic skills. Questions on math, reading, and writing were the most prevalent and were needed by patrons preparing for employment or for the high school equivalency (GED) examinations. Federal monies were solicited through a proposal for a Community Development Block Grant (CDBG) for $35,000, with the monies requested to establish an adult literacy/tutoring program at the Center Street Library.

After nine months of justifying the need for the adult tutoring program at our library before various advisory committees, we were informed that our library had been awarded $30,000. The Center Street Library Project Open Door Adult tutoring program was formally opened in conjunction with the ABC/PBS sponsored Project Plus promoting the event throughout southeastern Wisconsin. With the funds, two part-time coordinators were hired for one year to recruit and train volunteer tutors and to canvass the community for adult learners. Adult literacy mate-

rials including books, videotapes, and educational software were ordered. An Apple IIE computer and Epson FX-286 printer were also purchased.

One-on-one tutoring sessions for a maximum of 40 adults with lower than a sixth grade reading level were offered from four to six hours per week whenever the library was staffed. Enhancing the community was an important aim of the program; students were encouraged to use the skills learned in our program to contribute to their community.

A steering/advisory committee made up of community representatives, students, and tutors planned programs for the year.

The programs were open to the public and cost little or no money since they were staffed by volunteers. Once a month students and tutors attended separate programs on self-worth, interviewing techniques, résumé writing, or test-taking strategies. Tax preparation information and computer skills workshops were also presented.

At the end of the first year an awards ceremony was planned for all students who participated in the program. The positive aspects of networking and contributing to the community were evident in the implementation of Project Open Door. The library became more visible to the community by becoming a part of the Milwaukee human services network.

Center Street Library is located in a central city area, and serves many "at-risk" young adults. Teen pregnancy, substance abuse, and negative peer pressure are quite visible.

A proposal, Teens on Target, was written for a grant under the Library Services Construction Act—Special Needs Category (LSCA) for $14,000. When the funds were awarded, the program was implemented at four neighborhood libraries in the central city.

A Community Educator was hired to work part time at the four libraries. The ambitious goals of the project were 1) to recruit youth who are at risk; 2) to form a young adult advisory council at each library; 3) to enable the library to become part of the youth-serving network and to work closely with agencies who serve at-risk young adults; 4) to develop core collections at each of the libraries in the areas of teen pregnancy, substance abuse, health, and

employment; 5) to plan programs in these areas that would attract young adults to the library and encourage them to read and to share their feelings with their peers; and 6) to increase young adult usage of library materials and resources.

Teens on Target is a prime example of the library networking with community agencies to provide low-cost relevant and entertaining programs for young adults. Planned Parenthood presented teen parents sharing their experience with the young adults. The young adults participated in role playing regarding sensitive situations. For example, how do I say no to sex, particularly sex without protection? Or how do I tell my parents that I am pregnant?

There was no cost to the library except for the community educator's time to coordinate the programs. A local cable company donated an outstanding program of training workshops to teach young adults how to produce a 30-minute video. The workshops are free and available to all Milwaukee residents. Liability policy regarding the equipment and transportation to the studio was a problem. To solve this, the library informed the parents that they must assume responsibility for the video equipment as well as for the young adults' transportation to the studio.

Volunteers

Volunteers are wonderful resources for developing low-cost programs. Recruiting them is most successful during the reference interview. While retrieving books, magazine articles, and audiovisual sources on how to operate a small business at home, the librarian can determine if the patron is interested in presenting a program at the library on this topic either alone, or with other volunteers. If the patron is hesitant but is interested in attending such a program, the librarian began a mailing list to promote the program once it was planned.

The Volunteer Services Coordinator directs all volunteer activities at the Milwaukee Public Library. These include tutoring, maintaining the newspaper clipping files, welcoming visitors to the library, and answering the library literacy hotline. In addition, the coordinator maintains records of volunteer hours contributed. At an annual luncheon the library honors volunteers who have served 100 hours or more annually.

At Center Street a series of programs were provided by volunteers, including: Feeling Good About Yourself—a program on self-esteem and empowerment for survival in society; résumé and interview skills workshop; test-taking strategies; and computer skills workshops. Volunteers were representatives of local organizations.

The self-esteem program was planned for Project Open Door adult learners and received good feedback from participants. While Feeling Good About Yourself did not guarantee that higher self-esteem would lead to a job, the program did emphasize that high self-esteem improves the quality of life.

The résumé and interview workshop was presented by a volunteer who was a career specialist and published poet. When she heard of Project Open Door and the need for a résumé workshop, she volunteered. Participants not only constructively criticized sample résumés, but also held simulated job interviews.

Test-Taking Strategies was less successful. Despite high registration, fewer than ten people attended the session. Ironically, this program was relevant to the library's goals, objectives, and roles. The program cost no money to present and was a co-operative program with the City Service Commission and the local vocational technical school, Milwaukee Area Technical College.

Fundraising

Besides creating an internal grant mechanism and soliciting outside grants, the library undertook other types of fundraising. The library system hired a financial development campaign officer to coordinate a fundraising drive similar to the United

Your vision of the library's role must be supported by a sound plan for program funding

Way. An advisory board consisting of local corporate directors was established. Mailing lists with patrons' names and addresses were also developed. The information was entered into a database. Flyers were mailed to the patrons informing them of local library programs. Another flyer was designed to inform citizens of the major role the Milwaukee Public Library has played in the community since 1878. Service to the many segments of the community was promoted. The collection of 2.5 million books and additional materials were highlighted as the heart of the library.

The fact that a modern, progressive library must have ways to disseminate new information through computerized databases, microfiche and other microforms, compact discs and educational videocassettes was emphasized. The campaign focused on how the library was meeting the challenge posed by the ever-increasing volume of information, its cost, and the growing demand for it, even as the amount of tax money available continued to decrease. The library was soliciting funds from individuals, corporations, and foundations to expand the collection and to provide other services to the community.

Library staff is encouraged to submit program ideas in need of funding to the financial development officer, who is aware of funding sources throughout the community. Program ideas can then be matched with funding sources by the campaign officer.

Friends of the Library

In Milwaukee, the Bookfellows are well established as the Friends of the Milwaukee Public Library. Annually, they contribute $15,000 to fund new services and programs that do not require additional staff and can be continued once the funding period has ended. The Community Library Program, which promotes library service to economically and educationally disadvantages minorities, received monies to acquire materials (mostly paperbacks) to expand a Browsing Center for Native Americans.

Still Moving Ahead

Developing programs that have a positive effect on your community and increase the library's visibility requires long-range planning. Your vision of the library's role within the community will ensure that your library is no longer an invisible institution. It must be supported by a sound plan for program financing. At the MPLS that includes a grant program based on endowment funds, entering external grant competitions, enlisting the help of volunteers, and an overall library fundraising campaign. We found that the secret to successful programs is a first-rate development plan. ≡

Reference

1. Charles R. McClure, et al., *Planning and Role Setting for Public Libraries: A Manual of Options and Procedures.* Chicago: ALA, 1987.

PLANNING PHOTOCOPY SERVICES
A Success Story

Ralze Dorr

Several years ago, the Central Library of the University of Louisville moved into a spacious new building and was immediately innundated by greatly increased demands for photocopy services. The library had four obsolete photocopiers, one broken-down coin dispenser, and a minimal photocopy staff. To make matters worse, the vendor for the photocopiers announced that it would not extend its maintenance contract beyond the next year. There were massive complaints from users about the poor quality of service. Clearly, the library had to act quickly to make improvements.

We took steps immediately to make the old photocopiers as reliable as possible during the time a systematic plan for improved service was developed and implemented. A comprehensive plan for photocopy services entails a great deal of time and effort. It should include: conducting a user survey, translating user needs into service requirements, developing criteria on which to base the selection of a standard photocopier, carrying out a market survey and selecting a photocopier, determining staffing needs for the service and preparing a cost analysis to test the economic viability of the service plan. The planning effort was carried out over a period of six months, after which the plan itself was implemented. The success of the plan in the intervening years has attested to its value.

Before planning started, certain assumptions about the future had to be made. First was that there would be 1,314,000 copies produced annually by users of the central library (a 10% increase over the current number). The second was that the then-current budgetary arrangement would be continued, with revenues from the photocopy service offsetting expenditures for the service and returning a percentage to the University, the amount to be adjusted each year based on projected revenues and expenditures. The third was that a photocopier would have outlived its useful life after five years in service or after 600,000 copies, whichever occurred first.

User Survey

A questionnaire was developed to survey users about several major topics: the extent to which each principal user-group utilized the existing photocopiers; the frequency of use; the volume during various times of the day and week; the average number of copies made each time; the types of materials most often copied; user experience with and evaluation of the existing service; perceptions of improvements needed; users' willingness to pay more than the old price of five cents per copy. We decided to distribute the questionnaire in the photocopy rooms of the central library and at the circulation desks in three other campus libraries. It asked 20 questions and was distributed near the end of the spring semester when research on term papers was highest. Results of the completed questionnaires were entered in the university's computer and tabulated.

The questionnaire return rate was 84%. A large majority (75%) of respondents were undergraduates, with graduate students the next largest group (15%) and faculty, staff, and other users composing only 8%. The largest numbers of subject majors returning questionnaires were in Arts and Social Sciences (44%) and Sciences (38%), with those in Business the next largest group (15%). The majority of the faculty and staff were in the College of Arts and Sciences; the next largest groups were in the Science Departments, the School of Engineering, and School of Business.

Of the total respondents, the majority (60%) used a photocopy machine at least once each week. Nearly 78% answered that they used photocopiers most often during mornings and afternoons, while only 22% indicated their most frequent use in the evenings. By far the greatest number of respondents (89%) said they used photocopiers most often Monday through Friday, while only 11% made most frequent use on weekends.

Of the average number of pages copies each time, a majority (71%) made three to five copies; 11% made more than five copies at a time; and over 7%, one to two copies. Materials copied most often were bound periodicals (180), then reserve materials (113), reference books (108), current periodicals (103), and "other" (101). Users identified "other" as theses, homework, notes, and personal items.

Questions about the existing service showed that a large majority of users frequently waited five or ten minutes just to gain access to a photocopier. An out-of-order machine was the greatest cause for long waits.

Evaluating Services

Evaluation of the existing service ranked cost (.05 cents per page) as what they liked best, with quality of copy and convenience of machine location ranked second and third. What users liked least were bad quality of copy, waiting to use a machine, not enough machines, and machines being out of order.

To improve service, users stressed the need for additional photocopiers. They ranked better quality of copy the second most wanted improvement and availability of change third.

Asked, "Would you be willing to pay more per copy for any of the improvements you have suggested?" nearly 90% said no. That "no" was further reinforced by "additional comments" given at the end of the questionnaire.

The most meaningful (if predictable) correlations were: those who used photocopiers the most (at least once a week) found them out of order most frequently; those who used them most during peak times (Monday through Friday, mornings and afternoons) found them out of order most often; those who copied the most pages at a time did so in the peak times; users at the most popular location (near bound periodicals) had to wait longer. No significant correlations were drawn between experience with the existing service and status or subject major.

Unfortunately, survey results from the three other campus libraries were flawed by inadequate distribution of questionnaires. The resulting samples were too small and had to be deleted, liming the analysis to the central library.

Users expressed very clear priorities for the central library's photocopy services. Of the greatest importance to them were: low cost per copy; good quality copies; fast and reliable photocopiers in greater numbers at convenient locations; prompt access to photocopiers; and ready availability of change for the machines. No strong desire was expressed for any special features such as enlargement, reduction, or collation. The survey data revealed that a substantial volume of photocopying was done every day of the week and during all periods of the day. Photocopiers and change dispensers were used most for bound periodicals, current periodicals, reserve materials, and reference books.

The survey isolated the users' three major needs: quality, speed, and cost. These results were a major component of the plan for new photocopy services.

Choosing the Machine

For speed in making copies, the chosen brand of machine would have to produce a substantial number of copies per minute. Even more important, it would have to produce the first copy in a very few seconds. The latter requirement was particularly significant as the machine would be most used for initial copies. To achieve a low cost per copy, the photocopier selected would have to meet very low maintenance costs for technical repairs, stocking paper, clearing paper jams, adding toner, etc.

The number of photocopiers it

Figure 1. Requirements on which to base the selection of photocopier and explanation of how the requirements would achieve speed in photocopy transactions and low cost per copy.

REQUIREMENT	EXPLANATION
SPEED:	
Simplicity of operation	Reduces user time in learning to operate machine
Production of first copy in 5.5 seconds	Reduces user time in generating initial copy
Simplicity of paper path	Avoids frequent paper jams and consequent down-time for machine
COST:	
Low purchase price	Promotes ability to purchase maximum number of machines from first year's revenue
Designed to produce 30,000 copies per month	Meets use requirements thus avoiding high costs for maintenance and repair
Paper tray capacity of at least 1,500 sheets	Reduces labor costs for refilling paper trays at frequent intervals
Low supplies cost per copy	Ensures low operating costs with resulting low cost per copy to user
Vendor trains and certifies library technician	Reduces costs for technical maintenance and repair resulting in low cost per copy to user
Generates adequate ratio of revenues to expenses	Allows for purchase of maximum number of machines and support for operations from revenues in first year

FIGURE 2. EVALUATION OF SEVEN PHOTOCOPIERS BASED ON CRITERIA OF THE UNIVERSITY OF LOUISVILLE LIBRARY

CRITERIA	Number 1	Number 2	Number 3	Number 4	Number 5	Number 6	Number 7
Price	$4,000	$5,550	$7,358	$4,096	$3,890	$32,000	$4,895
Uses Plain Paper	Yes	Yes	Yes	Yes	Yes	Yes	Yes
Simple to Use (Simple,Intermediate,Complex)	Complex	Simple	Intermediate	Simple	Simple	Simple	Intermediate
Recommended Volume (Copies Per Month)	15,000	30,000	30,000	30,000	40,000	300,000	16,000
Size of Paper Tray (Capacity)	250	250	1,500	500	1,500	2,000	250
Number of Copies Per Minute	25	40	45	30	35	N/A	40
Time to Make First Copy (In Seconds)	5.6	7.8	4.5	4.3	5.1	N/A	7.8
Supplies Cost Per Copy	.02	.01	.01	.01	.01	N/A	N/A
Copies Bound Books	Yes	Yes	Yes	Yes	Yes	Yes	Yes
Provides Training for Repairs and Maintenance	No	No	Yes	Yes	Yes	Yes	Yes
Simple Paper Path (Paper Jam)	No	No	No	Yes	Yes	N/A	N/A
Two Sizes of Paper	Yes	Yes	Yes	Yes	Yes	N/A	Yes
Net Revenue for First Year Based on Cash Purchase (Maintenance Provided by Company)	N/A	N/A	($10,897)	$8,611	$13,147	N/A	N/A

would be feasible to provide related directly to the type of machine selected. It would have to be able to produce its share of the total copies generated annually and still have low operating costs; thus, if two million copies are produced annually the average share for each of seven machines would be 285,714 copies per week. The brand selected would have to produce 285,714 copies without incurring high operating costs. For that reason, even if it were determined that 20 machines were necessary to ensure speedy service, if operating costs exceeded revenues, a higher cost-per-copy would have to be charged to make up the difference. Of the users' two highest priorities: would it be possible to achieve speed and still maintain the desired low cost per copy?

Repair and Maintenance

To have machines always in working order, an in-house technician would be preferable to a maintenance contract with a vendor. By being available for the systematic maintenance of the machines, an in-house technician would be able to keep them in much better operating condition than vendor technicians making sporadic visits.

It remained to be determined whether the lowest cost-per-copy could be achieved using a vendor maintenance contract or an in-house technician. If the latter, then the photocopier selected would depend on the manufacturer's or local vendor's willingness to train and certify the library's technician.

Routine servicing (clearing paper jams, restocking paper trays) would need to be available all hours the library was open for service. In addition, change-dispensing machines would have to be refilled during the same periods. This service could be performed by student assistants, but the costs incurred annually would still be substantial.

At least three change dispensers, placed near clusters of photocopiers, would be necessary to meet user need for easy availability of change. Over a period of a year, additional change dispensers, aside from their initial purchase cost, would require a substantial investment in wages for staff and student assistants for stocking the machines, counting money, and transporting money to and from the Bursar's Office. The question is whether this cost, added to service costs, could be covered by revenues.

Having used the survey to establish general requirements for a photocopier, it was necessary to evaluate photocopiers available in the market. The major determinants would be speed and cost per copy (see Figure 1.)

The Market Survey

The library investigated approximately 20 machines; seven were candidates for a final evaluation. Figure 2 charts evaluation of the seven finalists.

Machine Number 1 did not meet requirements for simplicity of operation, volume of copies per month, paper tray capacity, provision of training for the library's in-house technician, and simple paper path.

The controls, switches, and directions for use were considered too complex for easy operation by the public. In addition, control buttons were fragile, subject to breakage, and easily removed. The recommended volume of only 15,000 copies per month was far below the library's projection of 30,000. The small paper tray would require excessive restocking. The vendor's refusal to train a library technician would incur excessive operating costs. The paper path was complex and susceptible to frequent jams.

Machine Number 2 had some excellent features but fell short in: purchase price; paper tray capacity; time required to produce first copy; lack of training for in-house technician; complex paper path. At $5,550 apiece, six of these photocopiers would cost $33,300 substantially reducing the first year's profit margin and making it harder to replace them in four to five years. The 250-sheet paper tray was too small. The 7.8 seconds for the first copy was a bit too slow. The uncooperative vendor and the complex paper path were further drawbacks.

Machine Number 3 appeared to be exceptionally well-made and met most of the library's requirements, but the cost of six machines ($7,350 × 6 = $44,100) ruled out a purchase from the first year's projected revenues. In addition, the paper path was susceptible to jams, and although controls were fairly tamper-proof, it did not have the simplicity of several other machines.

Machine Number 4 met all of the library's requirements, but its purchase price was $206 more than one other machine and its projected net revenue for the first year was $2,381 less. This photocopier used a "wet process" requiring more frequent cleaning than a dry-process machine to insure good quality of copy. In addition, if left unused for a day, the liquid might adhere to the drum, requiring repair at the vendor's plant, causing more down-time.

Machine Number 5, at $3,890, was the least expensive in the survey. It used plain paper, and its controls were very simple and would be easily understood by users. Its recommended volume of copies per month (40,000) exceeded that of all of the machines in the survey except the ultra-high-volume, high-priced machine. Its paper tray capacity of 1,500 sheets placed it among the top three in that category. It produced 35 copies per minute, considerably less than some of the other machines but well within the library's requirements. Time required for the initial copy was 5.1 seconds, not the best but well within acceptable range. Supplies cost-per-copy was one cent, which was typical for all of the machines in the survey. The vendor was willing to train and certify an in-house technician, free of charge, to perform technical repairs and maintenance (in contrast to vendors for four of the machines surveyed, who refused to do so). This photocopier had the simplest paper path of all of the machines surveyed. Its projected net revenue in the first year of operation exceeded that of the other machines for which figures were available.

Machine Number 6 appeared to be an excellent photocopier, meeting all of our requirements except purchase price. The $32,000 price related to its extremely high capacity (300,000 copies per month), making it a prime candidate for a printing operation or campus copy center, but not for the library.

Machine Number 7 was ruled out by a volume of only 16,000 copies per month, a paper tray capacity of only 250 sheets, a first copy time of seven seconds, and a complex paper path.

Based on this evaluation, Machine Number 5 came closest to the library's requirements, but we needed to prepare a detailed cost assessment of its operation before making a final decision.

```
Figure 3.  Assessment of expenditures and revenues for the University of
Louisville's photocopy services plan in its first year of operation.

====================================================================
FIXED COST:                      UNIT COST      QUANTITY       TOTAL
Cash Purchase - Photocopier      $3,595.00            6    $21,570.00
Cash Purchase - Coin Box            740.00            6      4,440.00
Cost of Training                    900.00            1        900.00

Total Fixed Cost                 $5,235.00                 $26,910.00

VARIABLE COST:                      AMOUNT        COPIES     COST/COPY
Toner                            $   26.00        10,000        0.0026
Developer                            54.00        60,000        0.0009
Silicon Oil                          15.00        20,000        0.0008
Paper                                 2.01           500        0.0040
Drum                                190.00       100,000        0.0019
Maintenance:
   Allowance for Parts            1,800.00     1,314,000        0.0014
   Labor - In-house Tech.         6,440.00     1,314,000        0.0049
   Labor - Student Assts.        $7,176.00     1,314,000        0.0055

Unit Variable Cost                                             0.0219

CONTRIBUTION MARGIN:
Unit Selling Price                                             0.0500
Unit Variable Cost                                            0.0219

Unit Contribution Margin                                       0.0281

BREAK-EVEN ANALYSIS:
        $26,910.00        =      957,651 Copies @ .05    $47,882.60
        ----------
          0.0281

REVENUES:
Average Number of Copies Per Month                            18,250
Number of Machines                                           x    6

Number of Copies Per Month                                  109,500
Number of Months Per Year                                    x   12

Number of Copies Per Year                                  1,314,000
Price Per Copy                                               x  .05

Revenue                                                  $ 65,700.00
Less Variable Cost (1,314,000 @ .0219)                    28,776.60

Contribution Margin                                      $36,923.40
Less Fixed Cost                                           26,910.00

Net Revenue                                             $10,013.40
====================================================================
```

Cost Assessment

Cost assessment of the initial year would include the purchase price, while that for the second year would not. Both would include all components of the service plan: supplies, parts and labor. The end result would determine whether the revenues generated in the first year would cover the purchase of the new photocopiers and the operating expenses of the service and still yield a modest return of net revenues; it would also ascertain whether the revenues in subsequent years would cover the expenditures for the year while also providing a depreciation reserve to replace machines and yield a more substantial return to the university.

Shown in Figures 3 and 4 are the cost analyses, for the first and second years. The analyses are divided into: fixed cost, variable cost, unit contribution margin, break-even analysis and revenues. Fixed costs include the purchase price of the photocopiers and other hardware and the initial training and certification of the in-house technician. Variable costs are expenses that vary with the number of copies made on a machine and include supplies, paper, replacement parts, and labor to repair and service the machines. The unit contribution margin is the profit-per-copy after expenses. The break-even analysis is a calculation showing how many copies, at a certain cost-per-copy, will be needed to meet the expenses of the service. Revenues shows the total monies generated by a certain number of copies at a certain cost-per-copy and the net revenues, which are determined by subtracting expenses from total revenues.

Variable costs are expressed as a cost-per-copy: the amount necessary to expend on an item (once a certain number of copies has been produced by a machine) divided by that number of copies.

The unit contribution margin is calculated by subtracting the unit variable cost (what the service actually costs) from the unit selling price (what is charged to the user). The difference (unit contribution margin) is the profit per copy received by the library.

Reflecting the first year of operation and using the selected photocopier as a model, Figure 3 shows that total fixed costs would be $26,910, including the purchase of six new photocopiers with coin boxes and the cost of having the library's in-house technician trained and certified by the vendor. Total variable costs for the new photocopiers are shown to be 0.0219 cents per copy, with the unit selling price set at 0.0500 cents per copy; the profit per copy to the library would be 0.0281 cents per copy. The break-even analysis shows that the six photocopiers will need to generate 957,651 copies to achieve revenues of $47,882.60 — the amount necessary to cover all costs associated with the first year of operation.

A further analysis (Figure 3) shows that 1,314,000 copies per year will be produced by the six photocopiers at five cents per copy, producing total revenues of $65,700. If $28,776.60 in variable costs is subtracted from the total revenue of $65,700, the total profit over expenses should be $36,923.40. Subtracting fixed costs of $26,910 from the profit of $36,923.40 results in a first-year net revenue of $10,013.40.

Based on the analysis of Figure 3, the first year's projected revenues from the photocopiers would be suf-

ficient to cover not only the operating costs but the costs of the purchase of the six photocopiers as well; in addition, the revenues would be adequate for replacement parts; the technician's salary (calculated as 50% of full-time salary, the remaining half being devoted to other duties); and 40 hours per week of student time devoted to routine servicing of the photocopiers and change dispensers. There would be a net profit of $10,013.40 to the university. In the second year of operation (after the photocopiers had been paid for) the expected net profit would be much higher.

Figure 4, shows total fixed costs of $5,202 for the second year of operation, including $4,314 in depreciation reserves (for ultimate replacement of the machines) and $888 for the six coin boxes. Total variable costs (increased by 8% for inflation) are shown as 0.0235 cents per copy (reflecting 0.0016 cents increase for inflation over the previous year). Note that the per-copy profits for the service may be expected to undergo a progressive decline if the rate charge per copy remains static and variable costs continue to rise with inflation.

The break-even analysis for the

Figure 4. Assessment of expenditures and revenues for the University of Louisville's photocopy services plan in its second year of operation.

FIXED COST:	UNIT COST	QUANTITY	TOTAL
Depreciation - Photocopier	$719.00	6	$4,314.00
Depreciation - Coin Box	148.00	6	888.00
Total Fixed Cost	$867.00		$5,202.00

VARIABLE COST:	AMOUNT	COPIES	COST/COPY
Toner	$ 28.08	10,000	0.0028
Developer	58.32	60,000	0.0010
Silicon Oil	16.20	20,000	0.0008
Paper	2.17	500	0.0043
Drum	190.00	100,000	0.0019
Maintenance:			
Allowance for Parts	1,944.00	1,314,000	0.0015
Labor - In House Tech.	6,955.20	1,314,000	0.0112
Labor - Student Assts.	$,750.08	1,314,000	0.0059
Unit Variable Cost			0.0235

CONTRIBUTION MARGIN:	
Unit Selling Price	0.0500
Unit Variable Cost	0.0235
Unit Contribution Margin	0.0265

BREAK-EVEN ANALYSIS:

$$\frac{\$5,202.00}{0.0265} = 196,302 \text{ Copies at } .05 \qquad \$9,815.12$$

REVENUES:	
Average Number of Copies Per Month	18,250
Number of Machines	x 6
Number of Copies Per Month	109,500
Number of Months Per Year	x 12
Number of Copies Per Year	1,314,000
Price Per Copy	x .05
Revenue	$65,700.00
Less Variable Cost (1,314,000 @ .0235)	30,879.00
Contribution Margin	34,821.00
Less Fixed Cost	5,202.00
Net Revenue	$29,619.00

second year of operation (Figure 4) shows that 196,302 copies must be produced at five cents per copy to cover the total fixed costs for the service of $9,815.12 Because the purchase price is not reflected in the second year, the break-even figure is substantially reduced.

Analysis of revenues shown in Figure 4 for the second year of operation reveals total revenues of $65,700 (the same as for the previous year). When variable costs of $30,879 are subtracted, the total profit is $34,821. When fixed costs are deducted, there remains $29,619 in net revenues.

The analyses of Figures 3 and 4 have tested the previous assumptions made in regard to the selected photocopiers and to other aspects of the photocopy services. The test has confirmed the library's selection of the photocopier, showing that its total variable costs per copy are only around 50% of the price per copy as charged to the user. The test has also shown that the revenues for the service will easily support all expenses, including in-house technical repair and maintenance, leaving the university a first-year net profit of approximately $29,619. Of particular significance was the cost associated with technical repair and maintenance of the photocopiers. As shown in Figure 4, the salary of the in-house technician was $6,440 (@ 50% FTE) and the allowance for replacement parts for the photocopiers was $1,944—a total of $8,384 for technical repair and maintenance. If that is compared to the cost for a maintenance contract with a vendor, shown in Figure 5 as $13,140 (for the six photocopiers), there is a difference of $4,756. Based on that comparison, the library's cost for its in-house technician was $4,756 less than the cost of a maintenance contract with the vendor. Thus, the in-house technician not only contributes to faster repair of machines (resulting in user speed and convenience) but to increased revenues as well.

The cost assessment has also answered in the affirmative questions previously posed: revenues will easily support the six photocopiers being considered at this time; in-house technical repairs and maintenance can be covered from revenues in addition to servicing the change dispensers.

Figure 5. Assessment of expenditures and revenues for the University of Louisville library's photocopy services plan in its first year of operation, illustrating the effect of a vendor maintenance contract for the six photocopiers

==

FIXED COST:	UNIT COST	QUANTITY	TOTAL
Cash Purchase - Ricoh 5050	$3,595.00	6	$21,570.00
Cash Purchase- Coin Box	740.00	6	4,440.00
Total Fixed Cost	$4,335.00	2	$26,010.00

VARIABLE COST:	AMOUNT	COPIES	COST/COPY
Toner	$ 26.00	10,000	0.0026
Developer	54.00	60,000	0.0009
Silicon Oil	15.00	20,000	0.0008
Paper	2.01	500	0.0040
Drum	190.00	100,000	0.0019
Maintenance:			
@ .01 Copy	182.50	18,250	0.0100
Labor - Student Assts.	$7,176.00	1,314,000	0.0055
Unit Variable Cost			0.0256

CONTRIBUTION MARGIN:	
Unit Selling Price	0.0500
Unit Variable Cost	0.0256
Unit Contribution Margin	0.0244

BREAK-EVEN ANALYSIS:
    $26,010   =   1,065,984 Copies at .05 $53,299.22

REVENUES:	
Average Number of Copies Per Month	18,250
Number of Machines	x 6
Number of Copies Per Month	109,500
Number of Months Per Year	x 12
Number of Copies Per Year	1,314,000
Price Per Copy	x .05
Revenue	$65,700.00
Less Variable Cost (1,314,000 @ .0256)	33,638.40
Contribution Margin	32,061.00
Less Fixed Cost	26,010.00
Net Revenue	$ 6,051.60

==

The Outcome

Although undertaking a comprehensive planning project for photocopy services in a relatively short time imposed a great strain on all concerned with the project, the results were found to be well worth the effort. In less than one year, the library's photocopy services were transformed from a source of embarassment to one of great pride.

New and highly reliable photocopiers replaced the old and obsolete machines; an in-house technician maintained the photocopiers in top operating condition and achieved an average repair time of two hours; student assistants stocked the machines with paper, cleared paper jams, and serviced change dispensers within minutes of reported problems. All of this was accomplished with the revenues generated by the service—and without having to raise the cost to the user. This success was particularly gratifying to those of us who had planned the service because we were certain that we had achieved the two-pronged goal of meeting our users' highest priorities and making a prudent investment of resources by the library and the University. ==

TO LEASE OR TO BUY

Malcolm Getz

Library managers are facing numerous capital investment choices as a result of new electronic systems, other technological innovations, and increasing space requirements. While libraries are capital-intensive organizations, their sources of capital are often limited. Every use of capital must be evaluated in terms of investment opportunity; library managers should weigh alternative uses of capital. The concept of the present value of cash flow can be helpful in this evaluation.

For example, suppose that a square foot of space costs $150 to build and will hold about 20 books; that comes to $7.50 per book. Suppose that space lasts 50 years and that capital costs 10 percent. The annual lease value of the space to hold a book is then just about $0.76 (that is, the present value of $0.76 each year for 50 years at 10 percent is $7.50.) Annual maintenance may run just about $5.00 per square foot, implying a per-book charge of $0.25 per year. The annual lease and maintenance cost for keeping a book on a shelf then runs about $1.00 per year per book. (This figure excludes any staff, work, or public space.)

You can arrive at a similar figure by looking at rental rates on space adequate to carry bookshelves. The present value of the storage space (construction, replacement, and maintenance) for holding one book in perpetuity is $10.00 when the cost of capital is 10 percent and storage space runs $1.00 per year per book. (The present value of a constant perpetual flow of X per year is the amount of funds to remain invested to earn the given flow each year, namely, X/interest rate = $1.00/ 0.10 = $10.00.) This figure or a local refinement of it can prove useful in thinking about preservation and weeding, about microforms and electronic document storage, and about interlibrary loans and cooperative collection development. You might want to compare the present values of cash flows including space costs for alternative strategies of supplying information.

Another useful application of present value of cash flow is in deciding whether to lease or to buy. For instance, should a library lease or buy its photocopy equipment? Let's assume that either way the library will get a service contract that yields the same level of vendor support. Assume as well that the library will continue to determine price, collect revenues, and have the same internal costs of operation whether the equipment is owned or leased. If the level of service and on-site costs are the same under either arrangement, then the issue is the comparison of the two cash flows.

Here are two hypothetical comparisons. The first library commits to an annual lease, with payment made at the end of each year; $2,500 per year pays for the lease of the equipment and an added $2,000 pays for service. The cash flow with the lease will continue over the life of the contract. The second library buys the equipment for $9,000. The cash flow with the purchase will involve an initial outlay, and then the library will incur only the annual service cost, $2,000. Let's assume that the equipment will give satisfactory service for four years and then be sold as used equipment for a net of $500. Which cash flow is more advantageous to the library, the lease or the purchase?

Comparing Cash Flows

A first impulse is often to add up the cash flows: the $2,500 per year lease totals $10,000 over the four years. The total for the purchase is the $9,000 purchase less the $500 used equipment price, for a net of $8,500. Is purchase superior? The purchase of equipment involves the expenditure of funds at the outset, an investment with the expectation of lower continuing or operating costs over the life of the equipment. Is purchase superior?

Such a simple comparison of cash flows ignores the fact that funds spent now cost more than funds spent later. If a library borrows funds to make equipment purchases, it must pay interest over the life of the loan. Suppose the loan extends over the four years of the life of the equipment. The cash flow for purchase now should reflect the cumulative interest payments on the loan.

Suppose the library purchases the equipment from an endowment. Endowments earn interest in financial markets. If the library purchases the equipment (leaving other expenditures unchanged), the endowment will be lowered by the amount of the purchase. In later years, the endowment will grow faster because no lease payments are made for the machine. But the evaluation of the equipment purchase should reflect the foregone interest during the period when the endowment was lowered because of the equipment purchase. In effect, the equipment purchase acts as a loan from the endowment with the cost being the rate of interest the endowment funds would have earned had they remained in the endowment.

Suppose a library (or its parent) is supported primarily by taxes. The purchase involves somewhat higher taxes in the year of purchase and lower taxes in subsequent years relative to the cash flow with the lease. If the households are the principal taxpayers, we can think of the interest they could earn on the funds they would have available for a longer period of time if the library leased the equipment.

Suppose the library (or its parent) is in the for-profit sector using funds raised in equity capital markets, that is from the sale of stock to finance the equipment. Buyers of stock have expectations of rates of return on their investments. Firms raising money by selling stock typically have minimum rates of return they expect to earn on an investment before they make it. Such a minimum rate of return before corporate taxes might be in excess of 20 percent. When a firm has investment projects available with rates of return of 20 percent or better, then its library will want to note that purchase of equipment in the library uses funds that could have earned 20 percent or more elsewhere in the firm.

Suppose the library is in the nonprofit sector. Nonprofit firms borrow funds, they have endowments, and they sometimes receive tax dollars. Thus, funds for capital projects do not come at zero cost. Nonprofit firms must choose among available investment opportunities in allocating their scarce capital. They generally have specific missions and aim to focus their limited resources on projects that will fulfill their aims most effectively. An investment in equipment for the library will be made at the expense of other worthwhile investment projects. The nonprofit manager will want assurance that the investment in the library equipment earns returns comparable to or better than other valuable projects the firm has not undertaken. One way of formalizing that idea is to identify a particular rate of return on funds the firm would expect to receive on financial transactions. The rate might reflect the rate at which the nonprofit borrows, or it might reflect the rate of return on its endowment. Ultimately, it will reflect the board of directors' judgment about the value of capital in the organization.

Capital is scarce in all organizations in our society. The use of capital to purchase equipment must be weighed against alternative uses of capital elsewhere in the library and, indeed, elsewhere in our society. Capital should be put to the most productive uses. In comparing cash flows of alternative investments, the interest that could be earned if the funds were used in the next most productive way must be considered.

Comparing Cash Flows in Terms of Present Value

Suppose the library's endowment will earn 12 percent over the next four years. Adding one more dollar to the endowment now will mean the endowment will be larger by $1.12 next year. To have one more dollar in the endowment next year, we need only add $0.893 now (that is $1/1.12). This may be easier to follow in symbols.

To get X next year,
    spend Y now: Y x 1.12 = X
This implies: Y = X/1.12

We call Y the present value of X; that is, Y is the amount that must be invested now at interest to yield an amount X next year. The present value of $2,500 next year is then $2,500/1.12 = $2,232.

When funds are invested over several years, interest will be earned over the several years. For simplicity, assuming that interest is compounded annually, this year's interest will earn interest next year. Investing Y now will yield (Y x 1.12) x 1.12 in

At Interest Rate	Present Value — Lease	Present Value — Purchase
0 %	$10,000	$8,500
5	8,865	8,589
7.5	8,373	8,626
10	7,925	8,658
12	7,593	8,682
15	7,137	8,714
20	6,472	8,759

two years. Therefore, the present value of X dollars in two years is now $X/(1.12 \times 1.12)$ or $X/1.12^2$). The present value of $2,500 in year two is then: $2,500/1.254 = $1993.

To have one dollar three years hence, we need invest $1.00/1.12^3 now. The present value of $2,500 three years from now is $2,500/1.405 = $1,779. To have one dollar four years from now, we need invest $1.00/(1.12^4) now. The present value of $2,500 four years hence is $2,500/1.574 = $1,589.

The present value of the cash flow for the leased equipment is then the sum of the $2,500 for the four years:

$$\frac{\$2,500}{1.12} + \frac{\$2,500}{1.12^2} +$$

$$\frac{\$2,500}{1.12^3} + \frac{\$2,500}{1.12^4} =$$

$2,232 + $1,993 + $1,779 + $1,589 = $7,593.

The present value of the purchase option is the $9,000 to be spent today less the present value of the $500 sales price. Discounting the $500 to present value yields $500/1.12^4 = $318. The present value of the cash flow with purchase is then $9,000 − $318 = $8,682.

When alternative investments yielding 12 percent per year or more are foregone in order to allow the library to purchase rather than lease its photocopy equipment (given the terms in this example), then the purchase option is more expensive in present value than the lease.

The present value of a cash flow is exactly the amount of money that would have to be invested today at a given rate of interest to pay out the cash flow overtime. To observe that the cash flow for the lease is less than the cash flow for purchase is to observe that a smaller amount of money would need to be invested today to cover the cost of the lease overtime than would be needed to cover the cost of the purchase.

The Role of the Cost of Capital

The comparison of the cash flows in terms of present value takes account of the fact that invested funds are costly when capital is scarce.

When capital is very expensive, that is when it bears a high rate of interest, then the lease option will be more attractive. When capital is inexpensive, then the purchase option will be more attractive. To see the significance of the cost of capital or interest rate, let's compare the present values of the two cash flows for different interest rates. (See chart above.)

At zero interest rate, we simply sum up the cash flow. This would be appropriate if capital were not scarce. At a cost of capital near 6.3 percent, the present value of the two streams is equal and the library could choose either option. At higher costs of capital, say 15 or 20 percent, the advantage of the lease is marked.

What cost of capital should a library manager use in evaluating a particular investment project? The answer to this question should depend on the source of the funds to be applied. If the library (or its parent) will borrow funds to make the investment, then the cost of borrowing might be most appropriate. If general funds are used, then the rate of return on the endowment might be most appropriate. When tax support is used, it may be necessary to identify the proportion of tax from households and from businesses. A weighted average of typical rates of return on household financial assets and of typical before tax returns on business assets might then be the appropriate choice of interest rate to use.

For libraries in large organizations, the source of capital might be other foregone projects within the organization. The organization might promulgate a nominal rate of return to be used in evaluating projects as a way of signaling to middle managers the value of capital in the organization. For projects with multiple sources of finance, a weighted average rate of return reflecting the different sources of finance may be appropriate. Because a project represents a new commitment, the relevant cost of capital is the cost of new funds to the organization. Within the federal government, an administrative directive established 10 percent as the default rate to be applied in project evaluation and that rate might be an appropriate default for many other government and non-profit libraries.[1]

Inflation and the Evaluation of Investments

So far, I have ignored the possibility that price levels may change over the period of the investment. For example, suppose that the price of the lease goes up by 5 percent per year with the general cost of living — how will our evaluation change? One commonly hears the observation that it is important to build a road, school, or library now because it will cost much more at higher price levels in the future. This idea is wrong.

Not only will future prices be inflated (when there is inflation) but the dollars needed to pay the future prices will be inflated as well. As a consequence, for most investments inflation has no net effect on our evaluation. The only reason to take explicit account of inflation for a particular project is if one is willing to forecast that the rate of inflation for prices in the specific project will differ from the general change in price level. In formal terms, one could note inflation by adding the inflation factor specific to the project in the numerator of the present value, (include it in the cash flow) and include the rate of inflation (the general price level increase) in the denominator, (the interest rate or cost of capital). The net of inflation on the evaluation of the project may frequently be nil.

References

1. Office of Management and Budget, *Circular #A94,* "Discount Rates to be Used in Evaluating Time-Distributed Costs and Benefits," March 27, 1972.

ARE LIBRARIES HOSTAGE TO RISING SERIALS COSTS?

Richard M. Dougherty

The serials pricing crisis—and its underlying causes—is now being recognized. The alarm was sounded several years ago when librarians discovered that some British publishers were adding hefty differential subscription charges to their North American customers. Almost immediately serials librarians at a few libraries began to analyze the problem. The libraries at the Universities of Michigan and Louisiana State constructed databases from which valuable information could be gleaned.[1] This information was used to explain the full dimensions and implications of a problem that was already well on the way to becoming a full-blown crisis.

Gradually, researchers beyond the library profession began to take notice. Constance Holden, writing in *Science*, alerted the scientific community to the problem libraries were facing.[2] Judith Turner presented an informative picture of the situation to readers of the *Chronicle of Higher Education.*[3]

Recently, publishers have begun to rebut the accusations that they have been charging excessive prices. They retort that it is the weakened dollar, the internationality of science, and the phenomenon of good journals becoming bigger and therefore more expensive that are the causes for the recent price escalations.[4]

Although escalating serials prices should be of concern to the entire academic community, until very recently the brunt of the problem fell on the shoulders of academic librarians charged with the management of serials budgets. A survey of ARL libraries revealed a variety of pragmatic, short-term responses. These included canceling duplicate subscriptions, cutting back on new title purchases, becoming more selective or deferring "big ticket" purchases, and launching new resource arrangements with other libraries. Several libraries reported taking actions to put pressure on publishers identified as pursuing particularly aggressive pricing policies?[5]

An important aspect of the current crisis is whether libraries are allowed to manage their serials budgets free of outside interference in order to minimize damage to collections and maximize the library's ability to provide timely access to cancelled titles. If so, one would expect a library to cancel expensive, little-used titles, with the most likely candidates being titles from the publishers who have contributed most to the current situation. But are librarians *really* free to manage their serials budgets, or have they become hostage to the scientific and technical communication system and captive to the publishers of scientific and technical journals? What prompted the question in the first place were reports revealing that the average price increase of journal titles to which the University of Michigan Library subscribed, from publishers such as Pergamon, Blackwell's Scientific, Francis and Taylor, Elsevier, Springer Verlag, and Gordon and Breach, had increased 30 percent in just one year. Subscription rates of numerous titles from these publishers had risen more than 100 percent in just two years. These were sobering revelations. Regrettably I learned we are not free, we are hostages.

The Counterattack

The changing economics of scholarly communication have forced librarians to ask probing questions about journals to which libraries have subscribed routinely for many year. The intellectual value of the expensive journals may not be in question, as many journals among the most expensive are also the most prestigious. But do all libraries need to subscribe to these expensive journals when copies of articles can be obtained quickly from another library or purchased from a commercial vendor such as ISI or UMI? That was the question my colleagues and I began to ask as we laid plans for a ten percent cutback in serial titles.

If cutbacks were necessary, I wanted to find a dramatic way to draw attention to this serious problem, which had not yet captured the attention of either the typical researcher or academic administrator. Most still viewed the inflation of serials prices as a library problem.

The strategy we devised was novel, but somewhat risky. Staff agreed to identify four publishers whose prices we could document as increasing beyond normal inflationary increases and/or currency fluctuations. The task of identifying the "winners" was not difficult because we had accumulated three years of detailed pricing documentation on our publisher database for a group of major publishers. Staff quickly identified the four targets: Pergamon, Elsevier, Springer Verlag, and Gordon and Breach.

The goal of the targeting project was to reduce our dollar commitment to these four publishers by 20 percent for 1989. The library subscribes to almost 1,000 titles published by these firms, but because so many of their titles are expensive, we soon realized that the 20 percent thresholds could be reached with the cancellation of fewer than 100 titles.

And we learned that most of the thresholds could be attained simply by cancelling duplicate subscriptions. Moreover, since faculty can request that journals be delivered to their offices through the library's campus document delivery system, we assumed that faculty, once they understood the library's plight, would be willing to cooperate with us. Herein lies the tale. What happened when we actually mounted the targeting project?

The principal objective of the project was to draw attention to a serious problem. We were to saying to the publishers, "Enough is enough." We also wanted to convince the faculty that the problem of run-away serials prices was a campus problem. Since the faculty as editors, editorial advisors, referees, and contributors to these journals are part of the problem, we believed that to solve the problem, it was necessary to make this group part of the solution. Right up until the end, some people still believed our objective was to save money, when in fact the potential savings were very modest, at most, $67,000, only 1.5 percent of the total materials budget.

The Dialogue with Faculty

Throughout the spring semester, I met with faculty, individually and in groups. Some of the meetings proved to be fascinating encounters. Many faculty were supportive of our intent; some felt that we should adopt an even more aggressive posture, e.g., let the faculty purchase a title (at an individual's rate) and subsequently turn it over to the library. That suggestion was logistically impractical, if not illegal, but it reflected the anger some faculty felt toward these publishers.

Others who spoke out, however, felt that the absence of even duplicate titles would erect barriers to research and consequently place Michigan's researchers at a disadvantage with peers (translation: competitors) at other institutions. It was never made clear to me why, since the library could so quickly deliver requested journal volumes, issues, or articles. More than one faculty member said I was simply naive to believe that such a tactic would make an impact on publishers. My usual response to such comments was, "Maybe so, but maybe we can

at least get their attention." One distinguished faculty member equated the targeting project to solving a problem by "jumping off a cliff."

Another researcher spoke with conviction that the university should simply pay the higher costs, as they had done when energy prices skyrocketed a decade ago. He reasoned that the journals in question were simply part of the "overhead" of doing research: since the university provided laboratory space, equipment, computers, and graduate student support, why not journals! His logic, though possibly reassuring to some faculty, was flawed. And, as I admitted to myself later, it was particularly galling because both of us knew full well that there is rarely enough laboratory space, equipment frequently is obsolete, computer support often lags behind demand, and student aid never meets actual needs. How, I wondered, could anyone argue with a straight face that library acquisitions should be exempted from the normal programmatic and budgetary reviews?

To get another perspective on the issue, I invited a group of faculty who currently serve as editors for scientific, technical, and scholarly journals to meet with me and the librarians who were managing the targeting project. My hope was to learn how editors might view this issue. Do they view the pricing trends with as much alarm as do librarians? Did they have any alternative solutions or strategies to offer? The invitees represented a diverse group of disciplines, including engineering, chemistry, classics, economics, medicine, history, and literature. Moreover, the publications they edited included titles of not only commercial firms, but of scientific and technical societies, professional associations, and university presses.

The editors expressed concern and even sympathy; however, they were not well informed about the problem. With one or two exceptions, most of the group were concerned almost exclusively with the content and quality of their own journals. The journal pricing problem was not high on their agendas, although several individuals did point out that their journals were very dependent on library subscriptions for economic survival. Although the meeting engendered no solutions, we did learn that the economic stress libraries were feeling was not generally understood or appreciated, at least by this group of editors. I suspect the same observation could have been made about any similar group of scholar/editors. The library, it seemed, was still on its own.

Making Our Case

As the spring wore on and the targeting project received more publicity, more faculty began to take notice. The reactions continued to run the gamut from deep concern and support to outright opposition. As the library's staff made final preparation to implement the cancellation project, a motion urging the library to defer its journal cancellation project until a faculty/librarian committee could study the issues further was introduced at a meeting of the faculty of the College of Literature, Science and Art (LS&A). The motion was tabled to allow time for the dean to invite me and Robert Houbeck, the Head of the Serials Unit, to address the group at its next meeting.

Houbeck explained why journal prices have increased, and I reviewed what steps the library proposed to take and why. I also outlined the likely impact on the library's overall acquisition program if current pricing trends persisted.

Following our presentations, we were subjected to 45 minutes of intense questioning. Most of the comments mirrored previous arguments pro and con, but one new concern did surface. The library had promised intensified interlibrary cooperation to ensure continued timely access to publications. But several faculty objected to the prospect of becoming even more dependent on the collections of the other libraries for access to cancelled titles. We were reminded that historians are not as likely as their colleagues in the sciences, to know exactly what information they are seeking and, as a result, often don't know what items to request from another library. It was also argued—and correctly, I fear—that as more libraries cancel subscriptions, publishers would simply move to recover lost revenues by imposing higher subscription prices on the remaining subscribers. If such is the case, we and the publishers are engaged in a sort of "war

of attrition."

The debate showed no signs of running its course when the dean called time and brought the issue to closure. An amended motion calling for the provost and vice-president of the university to appoint a special committee was agreed to and passed almost unanimously. There the issue rested until the provost, now president, James J. Duderstadt, issued the following statement to deans, directors, and departmental chairs:

We all acknowledge the problems which are resulting from the high cost of library journal subscriptions. It is apparent that we must address this issue, and we intend to do so in an effort to devise a long-range strategy which recognizes the importance of our excellent research collections.

As we begin to address this matter, we will be cooperating with national efforts as well as assessing the situation on our own campus. In the meantime, the proposal to cancel some journal subscriptions from "targeted" publishers is being held in abeyance while we endeavor to develop a broad strategy for dealing with rising costs. I would appreciate it if you would relay this message to your faculty colleagues in order to allay growing concern.

Increased costs are an intractable problem, and we intend to call upon the creativity and experience of our faculty and library administrators in our effort to manage the situation.

The Lesson Learned

With the provost's announcement, the targeting project was put into permanent mothballs. What had we learned? What had we accomplished? We learned that serial cancellations can still be a very volatile issue to some faculty and that they will rise to defend the library's materials budget. We also learned how difficult it is for libraries to cancel "core" journals. Publishers must now realize that libraries have indeed become hostages—at least in the short run. We did accomplish our objective of bringing the problem to the attention of faculty and administrators. But we did not reach the goal of cancelling targeted subscriptions—not a single title was cancelled.

As I noted previously, libraries and a small group of publishers seem to be engaged in a "war of attrition"—a war in which neither side is likely

to be judged the winner. The publishers will lose because eventually universities will reenter the publishing arena. The commercial publishers will not disappear, but they will be faced with competition for the first time. As a colleague from the astronomy department pointed out, researchers themselves, once educated, can exercise their right of choice in selecting journals in which to publish, and if they choose, they can avoid specific publishers. He cited a journal, started recently, which failed after a few issues simply because astronomers did not submit manuscripts to it. He noted that the publisher had brought together an excellent editorial board and plenty of libraries and individuals had subscribed to it, but nobody wrote for it.

Libraries, too, are likely to be losers. In the short term, the coverage of their journal holdings will be reduced and gaps in holdings will grow. This problem will be partly offset by expanded efforts among libraries to share collections. In the long term, the entry of new publishers, some using desktop publishing technology, others exploiting the capacity of central mainframes and distribution networks like NSFNET, will create a new generation of vetted, electronic journals and newsletters. What role will the library play in this changed information environment? That question still remains to be answered. ▀

References

1. Astle, Deana & Charles Hamaker, "Pricing by Geography, British Journal Pricing 1986, Including Developments in Other Countries," *Library Acquisitions Practice and Theory*, 10, 1986, p. 165–81. And Robert Houbeck, "If Present Trends Continue: Forecasting and Responding to Journal Price Increases," *Journal of Academic Librarianship*, September 1987, p. 214–20.
2. Holden, Constance, "Libraries Stunned by Journal Price Increases," *Science*, May 22, 1987, p. 909-10.
3. Turner, Judith A., "U.S. Research Libraries Search for Ways to Combat Spiraling Subscription Costs of Scholarly Journals; Prices Rose 18.2% in 1986-87 Study Finds; A Few Publishers Account for Most of the Increase," *Chronicle of Higher Education*, June 8, 1988, p. A4.
4. Tegler, John, "Counterpoint: A Publisher's Perspective," *American Libraries*, October 1986, p. 767.
5. "Paying the Piper: ARL Libraries Respond to Skyrocketing Journal Subscription Prices," *Journal of Academic Librarianship*, March 1988, p. 607.

MANAGING OVERDUES:
Facts From Four Studies

Paul Little

Historically, librarians have resorted to short-term, charitable, punitive, and legalistic means to resolve the mounting problems associated with overdues — materials unreturned from circulation. In their quest to retrieve overdues we hear and read reports of librarians confronting delinquent borrowers by sending staff to private homes, filing criminal charges or claims in small claims court, engaging credit collection agencies, sending overdue notices as Western Union Mailgrams, conducting "fine free" amnesty days for return of all overdue materials, and offering rewards for returning books. There

is an air of desperation in these moves. Despite that desperation, however, while anecdotal accounts pepper the pages of library literature, there is surprisingly little hard evidence that can guide policy decisions to lessen the probability of unreturned materials.

Hard Facts Added

Two studies of public library systems in 1981 and 1983 by Robert Burgin and Patsy Hansel and one of college and university libraries by Jim Broussard are the exceptions.[1,2,3] Burgin and Hansel collected data first in North Carolina's public library systems and later in systems across the country to determine if any of the tactics used by public library systems in their "wars" against overdues were most effective.[4]

Burgin and Hansel's more substantive conclusions are that:

- Libraries with 28 days or more loan periods have better overdue rates.
- Using a collection agency gets more books back when they are due.
- Sending out overdue notices sooner reduces overdues significantly.
- Libraries that go to court have higher overdue rates.
- Libraries that restrict overdue patrons do significantly better at getting materials returned.
- Libraries that renew books tend to have higher initial overdue rates, but the trend reverses itself after eight weeks.
- Libraries sending two overdue notices tend to have a higher overdue rate than either libraries sending only one notice or libraries sending three or more notices.
- Libraries that don't charge fines tend to get their books back more slowly, but ultimately get more of them back; they have higher overdue rates in the short run, but lower overdue rates in the long run.
- If the final notice is a bill, the library tends to get more books back.
- The higher the daily fine the faster the books come back.[4]

They propose a series of tactics to reduce overdue rates[5] that covers a year's period of time (see box).

Broussard's major conclusion from his survey of 22 circulation librarians in Louisiana encourages libraries to operate on the premise that a portion of the books borrowed will never be returned.

OVERDUES CHRONOLOGY

Last Date (Date Due)
Charge 10 cents per day in fines
Restrict patrons with overdues
Automate circulation
Don't renew books
Use a collection agency
Loan books for at least 28 days
Charge fines per overdue notice

Send the first notice within 15 days

6 Weeks (After Due Date)
Charge fines
Restrict patrons with overdues
Send four or more notices
Send the first notice within 15 days
Make the final notice a bill

8 Weeks (After Due Date)
Restrict patrons with overdues
Make the final notice a bill
Loan books for at least 28 days

6 Months (After Due Date)
Restrict patrons with overdues
Make the final notice a bill
Loan books for at least 28 days or
    loan books for fewer than 15

1 Year (After Due Date)
Restrict patrons with overdues

The Metropolitan Library System Enhances Evidence

Over the past 15 years, the Metropolitan Library System (MLS) in Oklahoma City, which serves a community of approximately 603,000 persons, has analyzed its overdue rate and procedures to see what is successful and what is not. Some of our findings agree with Burgin, Hansel, and Broussard's evidence, some enhance it, and some bring us to different conclusions.

In 1973 MLS revised its maximum fine from the purchase cost of the overdue materials to $1.50 per item regardless of how long the material might be overdue. Almost immediately the library system documented an increase in the dollar value of fines collected and a decrease in the number of overdues.

An analysis of materials borrowed and their borrowers from 1975 to the middle of 1981, depicted in Table 1, led to a determination of the total value of the materials overdue and the relative cost to replace them.

The largest category of overdues fell in the range of materials costing between $1 and $30. That category contained 64 percent of the dollar value of all overdues and 89 percent of all the borrowers who held them. In fact, in all ranges as the value of the materials borrowed increased, the number of overdues decreased, as did the number of borrowers holding the materials.

Collection Agency Tried

Opinions from local attorneys, credit collection and reporting agencies, court and police officials, and library staff led us to decide that the most immediate and possibly effective step was to hire a credit collection agency. We interviewed both local and national organizations. Neither would handle bills older than three years; both preferred to have an account turned over to them as early as possible. Their experience was that newer accounts are easier to collect. All agreed that we must start by officially billing borrowers for the dollar value of the materials they held without returning between six months and two years. None of the agencies interviewed handled small accounts. The national agent would take on nothing less than $40 accounts and the local agent nothing less than $50 accounts.

We engaged a national firm that used only mail collection and guaranteed its results. The initial billing went to 540 borrowers. Each owed a minimum of $40 for materials not yet returned. As a result of this first-time effort, the library system collected a combined total of $2,068.76 in cash payments and returned materials.

TABLE 1
OVERDUE MATERIALS ANALYSIS 1975–1981

	Purchase Price $1–$30			Purchase Price $31–$75		
Year	Patrons	Vols.	$ Value	# Patrons	# Vols.	$ Value
1975	1,023	1,876	$ 11,349.97	4	502	$ 3,528.05
1976	2,822	5,004	31,383.83	258	1,595	11,153.75
1977	3,106	6,380	33,909.81	299	1,766	13,240.60
1978	3,414	6,193	39,225.68	363	2,014	15,682.07
1979	3,591	6,561	42,523.10	427	2,428	18,777.10
1980	4,290	7,333	49,761.64	544	2,933	23,795.20
1981	2,289	3,804	25,613.24	235	1,247	10,100.05
TOTALS	20,445	36,231	$233,786.27	2,210	12,485	$96,284.82

	Purchase Price $76–$110			Purchase Price $111–+ $		
Year	Patrons	Vols.	$ Value	# Patrons	# Vols.	$ Value
1975	7	76	$ 692.56	3	59	$ 544.52
1976	25	285	2,208.95	8	150	1,220.06
1977	29	314	2,595.97	9	191	1,626.81
1978	35	426	3,215.79	13	295	2,330.53
1979	45	427	3,961.69	15	183	2,203.94
1980	49	484	4,406.53	17	316	2,947.05
1981	28	273	2,556.20	15	198	2,064.63
TOTALS	218	2,285	$19,637.77	80	1,392	$12,945.54

TABLE 2
RELATIONSHIP BETWEEN OVERDUES
AND LIBRARY'S PROXIMITY TO USER

Library Number	% of 1983–84 Total Circulation Unreturned After 6 Months	% of Users Who Used Library Because Close to Home	% of Users Who Took 1-5 Minutes to Travel to Library	% of Users Who Used Library Because Close to Job
One	.91	86	39	12
Two	1.12	78	44	12
Three	1.12	81	36	8
Four	1.12	90	49	4
Five	1.14	63	29	17
Six	1.22	72	37	12
Seven	1.23	78	43	15
Eight	1.29	84	39	5
Nine	2.67	62	28	17
Ten	3.86	21	29	44
Eleven	8.23	72	34	22

In October 1983, the library system gave the collection agency over 100 accounts that totalled between $40 and $60 each and 100 accounts of more than $60 each. The agency made two guarantees: The total cost in fees to the library would not exceed $1,875 and the agency would collect 300 percent of that cost in repayments or returned materials.

One year later the agency proved minimally effective. With those accounts owing from $40 to $60 each they had guaranteed to collect $1,875 and had collected a total of $2,075.51. Their success was more limited with persons owing $60 and over, however. There they had guaranteed to collect $3,750 but only collected $1,981.68. In December 1984 the library system cancelled the arrangement.

We were surprised at the collection agency's success with accounts of lower value and their marginal record with those at a higher range, since both local and national agencies had at the outset indicated that overdues of less than $40 were not economically feasible for them to handle.

By observing overdues during this period, we discovered that sending at least one bill for the money owed in lieu of an overdue notice was effective in getting the materials back and the fine paid. Other observations showed that while stiff fines can have a positive effect in causing materials to be returned on time or four weeks or less late, they can also inhibit returning materials that are more than four weeks overdue. Rather than pay as much as the book in fines, we found that borrowers often opt not to return the book.

We also found that the more overdue notices we sent to borrowers, the better was the return rate. However, the effectiveness of these no-

TABLE 3
TRENDS REVEALED
BY MLS OVERDUES

Factors	Higher Non-return Rates	Lower Non-return Rates
Use of library due to convenience of library to user's residence		XX
Use of library due to convenience of library to place of employment	XX	
Users travel 5 minutes or less to reach the library		XX
Users travel 6 minutes or more to reach the library	XX	
Users come from all over city	XX	
Users come from immediate neighborhood		XX

TABLE 4
NET PERCENTAGE OF MATERIALS
LOANED (BY TYPE) UNRETURNED SIX
MONTHS AFTER DUE DATE

Library Number	Total Collection	Adult Nonfiction	Adult Fiction	Juvenile Fiction	Easy & Readers
One	.91	1.23	.26	.56	.26
Two	1.12	2.80	.64	.65	.54
Three	1.12	2.70	.98	1.35	.52
Four	1.12	1.43	.98	.57	.62
Five	1.14	1.60	.68	.34	.46
Six	1.22	2.07	.69	.58	.67
Seven	1.23	1.69	1.01	.64	.28
Eight	1.29	2.11	.96	1.58	.58
Nine	2.67	3.80	2.20	4.30	1.70
Ten	3.86	4.80	1.14	3.17	2.39
Eleven	8.23	8.67	3.21	4.79	7.76
Library System	1.54	2.37	.85	.94	.60

tices appeared to decline sharply within a short time after the due date and with each subsequent notice. (We also had to consider the costs of sending and administering multiple notices.)

We found that restricting borrowing and other library use privileges was one of the most effective tools, in the short- and long-term, in retrieving borrowed materials. We also found that using mass media to draw occasional attention to the problem of overdue materials helps retrieve them. Infrequent publicizing of possible legal action against overdue holders and special events brought the materials in.

Residence Related to Timely Return

Still perplexed by our inability to substantially improve the rate of overdue returns, in 1984 the MLS undertook an analysis of circulation losses based on data from a complete fiscal year and three user surveys conducted in three separate seasons of that year. The loss rate was determined by reports indicating the gross number of materials unreturned six months after due dates less the number of materials returned and reinstated that were due in the time period.

Results are depicted in Table 2, where libraries are organized according to their nonreturn rates, from Library One with the smallest rate to Library Eleven with the largest.

User surveys were searched for positive relationships to the pattern of unreturned materials including demographic patterns, library-use patterns, reasons for using the library, and opinions of librarians. The factor that displayed the most consistent relevancy to the rate of returns was accessibility of the library to the residence of the borrower. Library Eleven, with the highest percentage of its circulation unreturned, drew borrowers from every zip code in the library's service area. Library Ten drew from the next largest number of zip codes, and so on in descending order to Library One, where the users were drawn from the zip codes in which the library was located. Table 3 summarizes the trends identified.

Essentially, the data confirmed that the more the library is used because it is convenient to the borrower's residence, the more likely is the borrower to return the materials. Libraries drawing borrowers from the most scattered distances are more likely to have the highest percentage of materials in all overdue categories.

We discovered that sending at least one bill for the money owed in lieu of an overdue notice was effective in getting the materials back and the fine paid. Other observations showed that while stiff fines can have a positive effect in causing materials to be returned on time or four weeks or less late, they can also inhibit returning materials that are more than four weeks overdue. Rather than pay as much as the book in fines, we found that borrowers often opt not to return the book.

An analysis of the fiscal year's materials lost through circulation by types of materials is shown in Table 4. The percentage of the collection not returned when due is indicated for the total collection and then for subsections, including adult nonfiction, adult fiction, juvenile fiction, easy and juvenile readers. Adult Fiction does not include such categories as mysteries, science fiction, and new books. Juvenile Fiction does not include books written for children under ten years of age.

These data, demonstrating variable rates of return for different categories of materials, suggest that instead of a fixed set of borrowing policies libraries might benefit from variable policies. For example, based on Hansel and Burgin's findings, the categories that are chronically overdue might be accorded longer loans and more generous renewal terms.

Interestingly, an earlier study of borrowing in the MLS, conducted by Martha Hale and Roger Greer, indicated that the libraries with the highest overdue rates—Libraries Nine, Ten, and Eleven—were also visited less frequently by borrowers than the other eight libraries in the system.[6]

It is worth further study to determine if frequency of use is directly related to overdue rate. And, the realities of unreturned materials should be taken into consideration when planning new library facilities.

For the Future

Library policies and procedures on length of loan period, renewals, and timing of notices and bills can be written to lessen the probability of materials remaining overdue based on the data reviewed in this article. In addition, although unreturned materials traditionally have been treated as a loss of capital investment, the next step, as Broussard recommends, must be putting the issue of unreturned materials into the relative terms of acceptable rates of loss incurred rather than viewing zero losses as the only acceptable objective. A maximum anticipated loss rate should be projected and reflected in annual materials budgets, where materials are recognized as short-term, depreciable investments for public libraries. ═

References

1. Robert Burgin and Patsy Hansel, "More Hard Facts on Overdues," *Library and Archival Security* (Summer/Fall, 1984):5–16.
2. Patsy Hansel and Robert Burgin, "Hard Facts About Overdues," *Library Journal* 108 (February 15, 1983):349–352.
3. Broussard, Jim, "To Due or Not to Do," *Louisiana Library Association Bulletin* (Winter 1980):54–57.
4. Hansel and Burgin, pp. 350, 352.
5. Burgin and Hansel, p. 15.
6. Roger Greer and Martha Hale, "Community Analysis: A Tool for Public Relations," *Show Me Libraries* (January 1980):6–10.

FUNDING LIBRARY LITERACY

Carol A. Cameron and Barbara A. Humes

Literacy is a hot topic. One of the top items on the agendas of both First Lady Barbara Bush and Illinois Senator Paul Simon, to name two influential advocates, it is finally getting the national attention it deserves. Under the Library Services and Construction Act (LSCA), there are two mechanisms by which libraries can gather added funds from the United States Department of Education to get into the fight for a literate America. The first is through Title I, where monies are dispensed through the country's State Library Agencies. The second is through Title VI, where funds are granted directly to state and local libraries.

The Library Literacy Program, funded for the first time in fiscal year 1986 at $4,785,000, has supported over 200 literacy projects each year. This article aims to make you aware of the funding opportunities and some of the programs that have developed throughout the United States that may serve as models for your library's efforts.

Administered by the Office of Library Programs' Library Development staff, the Program is authorized to award grants of up to $25,000. State libraries may allocate grant funds to coordinate and plan library literacy programs and to train librarians and volunteers to carry them out.

Local public libraries may spend their grant funds to promote the use of voluntary services—of individuals, agencies, and organizations—to provide literacy programs and facilities, acquire library materials, and train volunteers from local literacy programs. To date, Library Literacy has funded over 900 projects, averaging about 230 projects a year. Small decreases in the federal funding level over the last two years, combined with small increases in the average size of the grants, have resulted in fewer proposals funded at a time when more are needed. There were 245 projects funded, at an average cost of $22,103; that seemingly minor drop had more than a minor influence when only 214 projects could be funded.

The Library Literacy Program reached approximately 45,000 people each year, including about 25,000 students who receive tutoring or other literary services, about 15,000 tutors who are trained to provide literacy instruction, and about 5,000 librarians who receive training to provide library services to adult new readers. Since two of the goals of the Library Literacy Program are 1) to help libraries to be more actively involved in literacy and 2) to encourage cooperation among literacy providers in a community, it is not stretching the truth to point to the program's success. In well over half of the projects funded by LSCA Title VI, the library is the community's primary provider of literacy services with the library playing two key roles: establishing a literacy program where none existed, or serving as the primary contact for seeing that literacy services, information, and referrals were provided to the public.

Collaborative Mobilization

All LSCA Title VI projects involve some type of collaboration with other literacy providers in the community. Comparative mobilization ranges from keeping literacy organizations apprised of the project, soliciting volunteers and students from literacy organizations, to becoming a member of a literacy coalition, to conducting the program as a joint venture with another organization. Over three-fourths of the funded projects have developed formal cooperative relationships with nationally recognized literacy, education, and volunteer organizations. As an example, the Pigeon District Library in Michigan is participating in a cooperative project with HELP (Huron's Efforts for Literacy Progress, a county-wide literacy program) to identify, serve, and support Huron County's adult illiterates. The Library is acquiring a collection of adult basic reading materials and tutor support materials and is increasing community awareness of the collection so it is used by as many people as possible, not just HELP participants. The floating collection will be available for intercounty library loan. HELP is recruiting and training volunteer tutors, recruiting students, developing a student assessment method, evaluting its services, and developing a long-range plan.

Almost half of the LSCA Title VI projects work closely with local adult basic education programs. For example, the Ellinwood School-Community Library in Kansas is combining efforts with the Barton County Community College in a collaborative project that involves area librarians, reading specialists, literacy volunteers, and adult education coordinators. The program goal is to develop and implement a math education program for functionally illiterate adults. Individualized math plans are prepared and a "math partner" who serves as an instructor and mentor is assigned to each adult in the literacy program.

Who Gets Funded?

A wide variety of literacy activities are suppported by LSCA Title VI with tutoring, training, collection development, and public awareness occurring most frequently.

Most of the literacy instruction is one-to-one, using volunteer tutors and almost all programs provide access to, or support, literacy instruction in some way, such as through literacy groups or adult basic education classes offered at a school or college.

While some public libraries are heavily involved in training activities, they are the overwhelming favorite area of activity for state libraries with under 80 percent of the state libraries using federal funds to establish or expand their training programs. Training consists of teaching volunteers or librarians to provide instruction to new adult learners and teaching others to be tutors.

The Massachusetts Board of Library Commissioners, for example, developed a Literacy Training Kit for tutors and teachers which includes material to help tutors better identify adults who have low reading levels or who may be learning disabled and provides guidance on how to work with them. The Colorado State Library is addressing the shortage of certified trainers to teach others to be tutors by developing a group of 10 tutor trainers. Recruited by regions in the state, the recruits will obtain trainer certification so they can conduct tutor training workshops back in their regions. The Washington State Library is training librarians to conduct literacy projects by initiating a statewide needs assessment and using the findings to develop a continuing education curriculum focusing on literacy that will be offered in several areas of the state.

Approximately 70 percent of LSCA Title VI projects develop literacy collections. Here the effort is directed at establishing core collections in libraries, or expanding existing collections by adding more instructional and recreational print and nonprint materials. The Onslow County Public Library in North Carolina, for example, is developing a variety of fiction, nonfiction, and instructional materials, both print and nonprint, for use by ABE and GED students at the local community college. Previously, the students didn't have access to these materials since they were ineligible to use the college library. Some build collections to meet the needs of specific populations. The Fort Berthold Reservation Library in North Dakota is developing, writing, and publishing a collection of essays on three progressive levels of reading skills that are culturally relevant to Native Americans residing on the reservation.

Libraries are also funded to conduct public awareness activities that alert the community to the availability of literacy services; to recruit volunteers, tutors, and students; and to generate support from community agencies and businesses. In its awareness campaign the Cherokee County Library in South Carolina creates a special literacy supplement for the local newspaper, prepares public service announcements, distributes posters and brochures, and produces slide/tape and video shows that promote the library and its literacy services. Some of the brochures are printed in Spanish and Japanese.

Almost all activities necessary to run literacy programs can be funded under LSCA Title VI. Some have focused on general literacy services, English as a second language instruction, coalition building, services for special or targeted populations, technology-assisted projects, special instructional components, intergenerational and family literacy activities, and employment-oriented literacy services.

The State Library of Pennsylvania has initated literacy initiative for rural areas. The Agency trains public library directors in rural areas in coalition building and community leadership so that local literacy coalitions can be established, provides assistance in selecting project sites, and in training library staff and volunteer tutors.

The Brookline Public Library and the Boston Public Library in Massachusetts each have LSCA Title VI programs that focus on student writing. The Brookline Public Library is a cooperative endeavor with the Adult Literacy Resource Institute, together they publish and distribute high quality literacy materials produced by students in their programs. Through a series of workshops, seminars and conferences, the program encourages integrating writing in adult literacy curricula. The Boston Public Library is working with the adult services librarians at three community libraries to select teachers and students from adult basic education and English as a second language classes to participate in their project. The goal is to develop a publication on how each community uses the students' writings to distribute to other community libraries in the Boston area and throughout the state.

The Alabama Public Library Service has joined a coalition that includes the State Departments of Corrections, Mental Health/Mental Retardation, and Youth Services to determine needs among the three populations as a basis for establishing client/inmate literacy programs and identifying high-priority sites in State institutions for establishing these programs.

The Iowa State Library is identifying family literacy programs nationwide so they can develop models and techniques for conducting family literacy programs locally. Special attention is given to identifying services from the small public library. A manual of these programs will be the underpinning for statewide workshops on family literacy for librarians, adult educators, and human service workers.

The New Britain Public Library in Connecticut is using computer-assisted instruction, interactive video and audiocassette programs to expand its literacy programs to serve the many members of the community who do not speak English. A special collection of videodiscs and microcomputer software and the backup hardware has been established at the library's new Learning Center.

The Eugene Public Library in Oregon is working with the local community college to develop a mobile learning lab that will take the county's literacy program to social services agencies and businesses that need on site services.

Some libraries screen potential students for visual and auditory dysfunctions as part of the intake process and refer them to agency that can offer special help. Other projects de-

The Library Literacy Program, funded for the first time in FY 1986 at $4,785,000, has supported over 200 literacy projects each year

velop programs designed to meet the literacy needs of the handicapped. For example, the Hawaii State Library System has started a program to improve the literacy of adult deaf persons who have no written English language skills. These adults are tutored in reading, writing, and communicating in English. The tutor is reinforced by field trips, interactive games, and computer and video programs.

Most of the money in LSCA Title VI projects goes to pay salaries and fringe benefits or to purchase library literacy materials. Over one-third of the funds are expended for salaries and fringe benefits to hire competent personnel to manage literacy projects. Over one-fourth of the funds are expended for the acquisition of library materials to support instructional efforts. The other major categories of funding are: travel, equipment, supplies, and contractual services.

Evaluating the Programs

Program evaluation is becoming a more critical component of literacy projects as more agencies and institutions want to know the effectiveness of literacy programs. There is no way to evaluate a program and there is some disagreement in the literacy field on how to measure a program's success. Among LSCA Title VI projects, most libraries depend on quantitative measures, such as number of students, tutors, instructional hours, and books acquired or circulated. However, many projects are beginning to measure the progress of their students. This usually involves pre-tests when a student enters the literacy program and post-tests after a designated number of hours of tutoring have

been completed. The testing maybe supplemented by collecting data on other factors, such as the number of hours each student is tutored, employment, and demographic information. Some libraries, such as the Camden County Library in New Jersey, conduct followup interviews with students to determine if their individual goals have been reached, if their self-esteem has been improved. They also attempt to discover why students no longer in the literacy program leave it and their feelings about he tutoring they received.

How You Can Get a Grant

To obtain a grant under the Library Literacy Program, a state or local public library must submit an application to the U. S. Department of Education, Office of Educational Research and Improvement. Application packages, usually available in September, may be requested from the Office of Library Programs. Only one grant competition for the Library Literacy Program is conducted each year. The deadline for submitting applications is announced each year in the *Federal Register*. For the past two years, this announcement has been published in June or July as part of a joint notice for all the direct grant programs administered by the Office of Library Programs.

Applications are normally due in November. Decisions on awards are usually made by the next May and announced in June. Projects operate for 12 months, generally from October of one year to September of the next.

Currently, LSCA Title VI funds approximately 40 percent of the applications its receives. In FY 1989, the program received 535 applications and awarded 214 grants.

For More Information

To obtain an application package or for more information, contact Carol Cameron or Barbara Humes, the Program Officers for the Library Literacy Program at: Library Programs; U.S. Department of Education; 555 New Jersey Avenue, NW; Washington, D.C. 20208-5571; telephone: (202) 357-6315. Join libraries and librarians who have made commitments to create a more literate America. ▬

FEES: A HOT POTATO

As the implementation of technology in providing information services continues to grow and budgets continue to decline, the pages of our professional literature remain full with the opinions of library pundits on fee vs. free services.

While early debate was heated, recently it has changed in character. Now it centers on *when* and *how* to price services, rather than on *whether* to charge for them. Francis Wood's article and Malcolm Getz's column in this issue are a reflection of this.

Many people have decided that there is nothing left of interest to say about the philosophical issues and have moved to the practical. But a number of important questions about the relationship between technology and cost per use remain.

Our interest in the fee vs. free issue is normally high. But it has been further piqued by the recent report from ALA's ASCLA (Association of Specialized and Cooperative Agencies) – which is reviewed in this issue by Jeanne Isacco.

Despite the pro fee bias that has crept into this study – as well as that in the 1985 NCLIS study – investigators for both reports agree that to make reasoned decisions about whether libraries and fees are compatible we need *further* studies.

As our reference tools are increasingly packaged in mag tapes and microchips instead of print, we are being told first by one study and then by another that we are ignorant of the issues surrounding fees for service.

Frankly, we are unconvinced. We do suspect, however, that no amount of data will stop the profession's increasing bent towards charging fees.

And this is in spite of the evidence that access to information is reduced for those who can't afford the substantial charges for online searches, that such charges discriminate against the young, for example. We also know that even doctors reduce their requests for information when fees are imposed. So, fees limit access for persons unable to pay for the service as well as for those who

can pay but are unwilling to do so.

We don't need expensive research to convince us that many users cannot afford the high cost of electronic reference. Many of us who work in an academic environment know that the quality of our work is directly related to the quantity and quality of information that is available. But even those of us familiar with searching online databases find that the process can end with a bill for $40+$ – and nothing of substance to show for it.

Before online reference, little thought was given to fees. Few questions were raised about expenditures for the high cost of minimally used print reference works. And no one was moved to charge users in order to recover or even subsidize their purchase.

Now it seems the profession has adopted a new nomenclature to gain distance from the pangs of conscience that ensue from our deliberate adoption of tactics that limit access to information. Instead of referring to the process as electronic reference, we call it online searching. This implies a service class that stands alone, with no obvious ties to a longstanding tradition.

The fact is that electronic reference makes it easier to do cost accounting. Those costs that were completely shared and paid for as part of the reference materials budget are now broken out and charged for per use. The result is that when we charge users, we are charging the same people who already have paid once for library service through their taxes or tuition.

How have we gotten to this point? Perhaps it's due to our misinterpretation of the new emphasis in the private sector on the special library as a profit center in the corporation. Librarians have worked hard to lose their designation as a costly service center. Now their work is charged back to the departments for which they do searches as a part of the cost of product development. The difference is that this charge is made to corporate profits – *not* to the individuals who make the requests!

When information comes from books there is no question that the point of use is not the point of payment. Why has technology changed our thinking? Librarians justify and budget enormous sums regularly for backroom technology. But we show a mystifying reluctance to foot the bill when it comes to direct public provision of electronic information. The problem becomes even more crucial when information is *only* available electronically.

Logic seems to be thrown to the wind when librarians are confronted with "the cost of providing service." There's no question that the electronic tab is high. But we react as if we've been thrown a hot potato. There is an overwhelming need to get rid of the bill as soon as possible – and before us stands the person with the information need who caused us all this angst in the first place. Our phobic response to electronic reference is to toss the charge right back to the public!

Many in the library profession, in order to side step any question on access to information – a hallmark of our profession – suggest that there is a real distinction between essential services, which should remain free, and special services, which will come with a fee. Some have actually recommended vouchers for free service, tied to a means test. Still others have chosen not to offer electronic reference at all in order to avoid making a decision. All of these responses are short-sighted.

Mooer's Law reminds us that information seekers will choose their source of information in an inverse ratio to the time and effort it takes to use them. If we logically examine fee vs. free on the basis of our own self-interest, we could use the rapidity and convenience of electronic reference to attract more users by providing free access to it, rather than reduce their number through fees.

Information has always had a cost – no matter what the format. The question is: Who should pay?

We believe charging fees will ultimately lead to less support for libraries. And, a democracy without free access to any and all information cannot survive.

Betty J Turock

USER FEES: PROS AND CONS

by Pete Giacoma

User fees are charges levied against individual consumers of publicly produced services and commodities and publicly granted privileges on a cost-per-unit basis. In the broadest definition, user fees include charges for specialized database searches performed by public libraries, for electricity produced by a city-owned utility, and for liquor licenses. In each of these cases, an individual can avoid the charge by consuming zero amount of the service, commodity, or privilege. By comparison, an individual cannot avoid the general taxes assessed for support of the library or other government services

Reprinted from The Fee or Free Decision: Legal, Economic, Political, and Ethical Perspectives for Public Libraries, *published by Neal-Schuman.*

even if his or her direct consumption of a given service is zero.

However, publicly owned utilities and the regulatory and licensing activities of government constitute economically and politically distinct categories of public service provision. The criteria that can be best used to analyze fees related to these services are of limited value in analyzing fees associated with libraries, parks, roads, and garbage collection. Consequently, the focus here is on that class of fees frequently referred to as "user fees" or current charges— "those amounts that a government receives from the public for its performance of specific services benefiting the person charged and from the sales of commodities and services."[1]

This category of fees is recognized by the Bureau of the Census for statistical purposes. In its summary of municipal finances, the Bureau identifies the following classes of current charges: education (school lunch sales and "other"), hospitals, highways, airports, parking facilities, water and transport terminals, parks and recreation, housing and community development, sewerage, sanitation other than sewerage, miscellaneous and commercial activities, and "other."[2] Charges related to these services and types of activities are distinguished from other revenue categories such as utilities, motor vehicle licenses, and liquor store revenue.

Although user fees have increased dramatically as an element of local own-source revenue (revenue exclusive of transfers from state and federal governments) since the onset of the property tax revolt in 1978, the trend toward user fees has been underway since at least the mid-1970s. There are several ways of looking at the figures that support this assertion. First, the rate at which fees have grown in absolute terms is in itself impressive. In billions of dollars, *not* adjusted for inflation, the course of this growth has run as shown in the table at the top of the following page.

In a single decade, revenue from fees rose by more than 166 percent. By contrast, property tax revenue rose by approximately 78 percent, from $60.2 billion to $107.3 billion. Over the same period of time, total local government own-source reve-

Year	Local Revenue from Fees (in billions)
1976-77	$18.9
1980-81	31.4
1981-82	34.9
1982-83	39.4
1983-84	43.2
1984-85	46.9
1985-86	50.4

nue rose 96 percent, from $119.3 to $233.4 billion. In short, the rate at which user fees grew exceeded the rate of growth for total local revenue, while property taxes grew at a somewhat slower rate than total user-fee revenue. The logical conclusion is that fees have come to bear a larger portion of the costs of local government while property taxes bear less.

Additional data confirm this deduction. From 1975–76 to 1985–86, fees and property taxes accounted for the percentages of total local own-source revenue:

Year	Property Taxes	Fees
1976-77	50.5%	15.9%
1980-81	49.4	21.6
1981-82	48.3	21.4
1982-83	48.0	22.0
1983-84	47.1	21.7
1984-85	46.2	21.7
1985-86	45.9	21.6

A clear plateau seems to have been reached, at least temporarily, by fees at approximately 22 percent of own-source revenue, while property taxes are steadily becoming less important to local governments. A final way of confirming this shift in the relative contribution of each revenue source to local government is to compare them directly by determining what percentage of property taxes user fees constitute. It is reasonable to assume from what has already been presented that over the 10-year period, fees should have increased as a percentage of property taxes. The data validate this assumption:

Year	Current Charges/ Property Taxes
1976-77	31.5%
1980-81	43.6
1981-82	44.2
1982-83	45.8
1983-84	46.7
1984-85	47.0
1985-86	46.9

Given these various perspectives, it is more than safe to conclude that the property tax, the traditional main source of local government own-source revenue and the primary source of funding for most public libraries, is of diminishing importance in the arsenal of revenue tools. While fees may never overtake property taxes in raw dollar figures, it is evident that fees are generating revenue to replace that which has been lost to the lowered productivity of the property tax.

And it is widely expected that these trends will continue on their current courses, although economic principles, politics, and sound public financial planning suggest that there is a limit to the amount of revenue burden that user fees can carry. Anthony T. Logalbo, finance director for Concord, Massachusetts, believes that user fees "can sustain perhaps as much as one-quarter of local government activities under the most favorable conditions." But he goes on to warn that user fees

will not supplant the need for tax diversification nor for the continuing effort to find cost-cutting alternatives. Injudicious use of fees and charges can undermine basic public support for the full range of local government activities while permitting the maintenance of services susceptible to pricing. It would be ironic if the move toward user charges resulted ultimately in the withering of services that remained to be financed from taxes.[4]

A sharper picture of which services are being charged for in the public sector—and the variations among local governments—emerges from the work of political scientists James H. Ammons and Thomas R. Dye. Ammons and Dye have compiled figures gleaned from a variety of sources, including a 1982 study published by the International City Managers Association, which covered more than 1,200 cities of all sizes and economic types. The cities assess user fees for specific services as follows: residential refuse collection, 55 percent; residential sewage services, 91 percent; off-street lots and garages, 66 percent; swimming, 85 percent; golf, 98 percent; ball fields, 31 percent; museums and zoos, 29 percent; concerts and galleries,

38 percent; non-emergency ambulance, 58 percent; and emergency ambulance, 45 percent.[5]

Local governments are finding more and more uses for fees in their search for additional sources of revenue to support services that were once supported almost exclusively by the property tax. Although the most obvious, this is not the sole application of fees. Fees are also employed as a decision-making aid when some services must be cut in a retrenchment effort. Rather than guessing at which services the public would prefer to see reduced and which survive, public administrators employ fees as a device for measuring public preferences through citizen willingness to pay. In this case, fees may well be viewed and termed as "public prices," for they serve the same function as prices in the private sector. They signal management as to the level of demand for a product so that production of those goods in high demand can be maintained or increased, and those in low demand reduced. Prices are a means toward efficient production in the private sector and serve a similar purpose in the public sector when introduced in the form of user fees.

Fees as a Management Tool

Free services attract users, but when administrators have to choose which free services to reduce or eliminate during a fiscal crisis the politics of budgeting are as likely to determine the outcome as is any objective decision-making criterion. Client groups and department heads will argue for the survival of those programs that benefit them or are under their jurisdiction. So long as services are provided free, "we can expect that excess demand will develop, with 'cries of alarm' suggesting that more production is needed."[6] Even in the absence of a fiscal crisis, influence, tradition, and bureaucratic pressure may encourage spending on free services that citizens use heavily. As economists Selma Mushkin and Richard Bird have written, "Under present public resource allocation practices, within the public sector itself the wrong product is sometimes produced, in the wrong quantity, and with no (or inappropriate) quality differentiation."[7]

Many proponents of fees believe that fees can improve the allocation of resources by assisting administrators in identifying those services that the public truly prefers. This faith is revealed in the nine advantages of user fees listed by the Colorado Municipal League, which include the following:

- Even nominal or token fees for services motivate citizens to give some thought to the value of the service they received. Fees set at a fraction of costs, rather than a flat amount, motivate citizens to be concerned about the quantity of service they consume.
- Services with no charge attached to them may lead to overuse, overcrowding, and waste of the service, ultimately resulting in public pressure to expand the service facilities.
- Demand for services for which there is a fee reflecting full cost can serve as a guide for public decision makers in determining which services citizens want and are willing to pay for. Also, full-cost accounting can aid decision makers in comparing alternative methods of providing the service.
- Fees or penalties for excessive use or abuse of public services, such as fees for false fire or burglar alarm responses over a certain minimum, can encourage citizens to reduce the number of these incidents and can offset the costs of providing the service.[8]

In other words, fees are seen as a mechanism to force citizens to make more thoughtful choices about uses of services and can help administrators reacting to altered citizen behavior adapt service and expenditure patterns to better and more efficiently satisfy citizen preferences. Ideally, "as citizens become customers rather than clients, managers must become more directly responsive to their needs,"[9] as failure to do so will cause a service to fall into disuse, and perhaps the fortunes of an agency to decline, just as a private business suffers if the needs of its customers are not central to its operations. In the words of Robert W. Burchell, et al., as user fees have become more prevalent, "business acumen has been instituted to guide municipal agencies; no such feedback/restraints exist under the current taxation method of financing municipal services."[10]

When the promise of improved efficiency is added to the revenue potential of fees, they become a doubly attractive revenue option. Fees only provide at least a portion of the money needed to fund a service, but they can also function as a safety valve to assure that the service will not be used at wastefully high levels. As Mushkin and Bird write, "Asking consumers to pay for public services through the price mechanism gives them a chance to record their desire to have the priced service in at least that quantity for which the priced demand is registered."[11]

The property tax — is of diminishing importance in the arsenal of revenue tools

Stated this way, fees take on an almost democratic character, functioning in the same way as a vote. Indeed, Burchell and his colleagues make this very claim. After noting the frustration that many citizens feel in trying to voice their preferences and complaints about services to city hall, they observe that when fees and privatization programs are implemented, "consumers directly 'vote' support through their willingness to pay for services offered."[12] With fees, a hybrid is created: the citizen-consumer, who may express satisfaction or dissatisfaction with public services not only in the voting booth but also in the economic sphere, through his or her willingness to pay fees.

Disadvantages of Fees

User fees have disadvantages, which can diminish their value as a revenue source, as a management device, and, in the broad context of social justice, as a determinant of who has access to public services. Ironically, in terms of revenue — perhaps the area of their greatest appeal — fees are an unstable source. When the use of a service dependent on fees is voluntary, the many variables that affect use rates also directly in-

fluence outcome. Like consumer purchasing behavior in the private market, fee activity is sensitive to changes in taste and to the state of the economy. Consequently, in the short run it is difficult to budget and to plan expenditures. But long-range planning is especially difficult since income from fees for a particular service is liable to fluctuate, both within a given budget year and from one year to another. In order to compensate for this erratic revenue flow, Neels and Caggiano observed in a report prepared for the Rand Corporation, "a city department that is heavily dependent on user charge income therefore must maintain much larger working capital reserves and must be able to respond much more quickly to changing circumstances. The job of departmental management becomes more demanding."[13]

From a management perspective, the logic of using fees as a decision-making aid may force basic services to be curtailed as more attention is paid and resources devoted to those services that are revenue-productive. This is the concern underlying Anthony Logalbo's earlier statement that fees might lead to "the withering of services that remained to be financed from taxes."

Clearly, it is politically advantageous in budget battles to demonstrate high patronage and high use — circulation — as a means of winning tax dollars. Similarly, once fees are adopted, patron demand for a service is demonstrated by the revenue generated by the service. Soon, services that generate little or no revenue are endangered as they cannot compete with successful fee-based services, and they become of minimal use to administrators fighting for an agency budget. Money chases money; tax dollars tend to flow to those services that are income-producing.

Finally, the use of services by the economically disadvantaged is likely to be extremely sensitive to price, and so fees can exclude low-income citizens from use of fee-based services. Even those who support user fees recognize this hazard. For example, Neels and Caggiano recognize that when a fee is charged, "poorer households may forgo use of the service rather than strain their already limited budgets."[14]

Beyond this obvious effect of fees, political and equity questions arise as well. As economist Paul B. Downing acknowledges, "User charges in any form allow high-income people to purchase more and better services than provided to the general populace. This could result in a politically difficult situation—low service levels for low-income people, and high service levels for high-income people."[15]

Of course, a major purpose for funding services from taxes is to make them available on an equal, no-charge basis. When full tax support of a service is abandoned, careful thought must be given to the impact on the poor. Given that the policy objective of many public services is to redistribute the wealth of society to the poor in the form of services, ways of mitigating the adverse impact of fees must be designed. For the most part, those who favor fees are confident that any negative effects can be avoided through the conscientious selection of those services for which fees will be levied and through the implementation of policies that recognize the differing abilities of citizens to pay. However, whether or not this ideal is accomplished can only be judged on a case-by-case basis.

Often, practical considerations obstruct the best intentions of policy makers. How are we to know the poor from the wealthy when charging fees for using a tennis court in a public park, or for weekly garbage pickup, or for performing a database search? Conducting tests of a person's means in many service situations challenges administrative ingenuity, adds to the cost of providing a service, and threatens the right to privacy. Many citizens will not disclose their income in order to receive a nonessential public service at no charge. Rather, they will forego using the service. Thus, either the fee itself or the procedure for avoiding the fee will effectively deny the poor access to the service.

The Dilemma of Fees

The growth of fees as a factor in local government finances has been sustained for over a decade and is likely to continue. Fees are attractive to elected officials who do not want to raise taxes, to administrators who wish to implement new

services and to better secure the funding of existing services, and to citizens who desire improved services but not tax increases. So, despite their disadvantages, fees are becoming too attractive to be ignored. In addition, the most striking disadvantage of fees—their adverse impact on the poor—affects that segment of our society least able to speak for and advance its own interests, and most dependent on the judgment and actions of others. It is therefore incumbent on public officials to place the interests of the socially and economically disadvantaged at or very near the cen-

---

Fees can exclude low-income citizens from use of fee-based services

---

ter of their deliberations on fees.

After the theoretical advantages and disadvantages of fees are considered, practical decisions remain to be made. Services must be singled out for full or partial fee-based financing. If fees are deemed inappropriate, some services must either be given new infusions of tax support or curtailed. Among agency staffs and between agencies, elected officials, and citizens, questions about fees are resolved as one piece in a larger puzzle of government finances and services. For the puzzle to fit together properly, decision makers must face the full range of questions about fees and understand well the long-term implications of fees for the blend of services their agencies will provide, the clienteles they will serve, the characters their agencies will take on, and the role their agencies will play in society.

Fees do not merely perpetuate the status quo; nor are they merely an alternative source of funds. Rather, fees have the potential to dramatically change the operations of an agency. Agencies considering fees should realize that fees are more than revenue; they are catalysts for change. A complete process of deliberation on fees therefore requires decision

makers to ask not only what the agency was in the past and is now, but also what it will and should be. In terms of the public library, the question becomes: Is the fee-based library, understood to be fundamentally different from the free library, the library that a given community wants for its future? As the professionals entrusted with the operation of the public library, librarians have a primary role to play in helping to answer this question. =

References

1. Selma J. Mushkin and Charles L. Vehorn, "User Fees and Charges," in *Managing Fiscal Stress: The Crisis in the Public Sector*, ed. Charles H. Levine (Chatham, N.J.: Chatham House Publishers, 1980), 222.

2. These specific categories of current charges are listed in U.S. Department of Commerce, Bureau of the Census, *1982 Census of Government*, 4, *Government Finance*, no. 4, "Finances of Municipal and Township Governments," Table 4, pp. 8–9.

3. All of the following figures regarding fees and property taxes are computations based on data found in the respective yearly editions of U.S. Department of Commerce, Bureau of the Census, *Governmental Finances*, which is volume 5 in the yearly *Governmental Finances* series. Tables and page numbers drawn on for the respective years are as follows: 1976–77, Table 5, p. 19; 1980–81, Table 5, p. 18; 1981–82, Table 5, p. 20; 1982–83, Table 5, p. 6; 1983–84, Table 5, p. 6; 1984–85, Table 29, p. 46; and 1985–86, Table 6, p. 7.

4. Anthony T. Logalbo, "Responding to Tax Limitation: Finding Alternative Revenues," *Governmental Finance* (March 1982): 19.

5. James H. Ammons and Thomas R. Dye, "Marketing Public Services: Test of Costs and Needs," *National Civic Review* (October 1983): Table 1, p. 500.

6. Jerome W. Milliman, "Beneficiary Charges—Toward a Unified Theory," in *Public Prices for Public Products*, ed. Selma J. Mushkin (Washington, D.C.: Urban Institute, 1972), 29.

7. Selma J. Mushkin and Richard M. Bird, "Public Prices: An Overview," in *Public Prices for Public Products*, ed. Selma J. Mushkin (Washington, D.C.: Urban Institute, 1972), 21.

8. "How User Fees Can Help a Municipality," *Colorado Municipalities* (July-August 1983): 32–33.

9. Kevin Neels and Michael Caggiano, *The Entrepreneurial City: Innovations in Finance and Management for Saint Paul* (Santa Monica, Calif.: Rand, 1984), 9.

10. Robert W. Burchell, et al., *The New Reality of Municipal Finance: The Rise and Fall of the Intergovernmental City* (New Brunswick, N.J.: Center for Urban Policy Research, 1984), 305.

11. Mushkin and Bird, 22.

12. Burchell, 320–321.

13. Neels and Caggiano, 10.

14. Ibid.

15. Paul B. Downing. "User Charges and Service Fees," in *Crisis and Constraint in Municipal Finance* (New Brunswick, N.J.: Center for Urban Policy Research, 1984), 177.

HOW TO TURN A LIBRARY INTO A PROFIT CENTER:
The Law Library Example

Walter E. Doherty

Can a library sell a bibliography the way Ivory sells soap? The answer used to be no, but today the answer is somewhere between maybe and yes and involves marketing the library, along with any products the library may wish to sell.

But can the library be considered a profit center? The answer lies in the definition: a profit center is any department, section, or part of a company, institution, or firm that brings in more money than must be paid to run it—or, at least, that brings in an amount large enough to reduce operating costs significantly.

So, how can a library be turned into a profit center? By setting up a business plan; changing the library's image, if necessary, to make the idea acceptable; and determining what can be billed and how much to charge.

Note that, although this article is about turning a private law firm library into a profit center, the principles can be applied to any type of library. Dealing with a board of trustees or an academic dean is not all that different from dealing with a firm's library committee or managing partner.

The first step is to treat the library as a business. Independent law librarians offer their services and deliver products—i.e., running a business—and do it successfully. There is no reason why a library can't use some of their techniques, the first of which is developing a business plan.

Assess the need: What is your situation? Are the partners complaining that the library costs too much? Would selling services and/or products help your situation? Do a market analysis to see if the idea would be useful.

Determine your goals: What are you trying to accomplish? How long do you expect it to take?

Describe products and services: That is, know what you want to do. What can be sold or charged to a firm's clients?

Cost analysis: To assess economic feasibility, you need to know how much it will cost to provide these products and services.

Determine benefits: What will be the monetary return? Will there be any non-monetary benefits? Will it improve staff morale or increase tensions? Try to anticipate the drawbacks as well as the advantages.

Develop a presentation: Sell the idea to management because, in turn, management will have to explain new or additional charges to clients.

The business plan is a guide for successfully turning the library into a profit center. A similar business plan should be drawn up for each product or service the library wants to offer.

Preparation

You may need to change the image of both the library and the librarian to make them integral parts of the firm in order to encourage support for the library's new approach to service. The first step is for the librarian to make him/herself a visible and valuable partner in all phases of the firm's work. If the firm offers new associates brown-bag lunches to introduce them to specific legal topics, contact the people giving the sessions and provide them with a current bibliography of locally available materials. Attend the session and be prepared to offer assistance and handle questions. Establish credibility and be someone worth listening to.

Start a library newsletter. This will help keep the attorneys aware of the library and can be used for publicity. Include things like the recent acquisitions list, notices of online training sessions, new items available at the local county law library, new online services. Some hints: make it short; magazine-length newsletters won't be read. Make it one (or, at the most, two) legal-sized pages. Also, print it on colored paper so it won't get lost on the sea of white paper on most attorneys' desks. Include awards that the staff members have been given. Let people know that you and the library are highly regarded.

What Can Be Billed?

Billable services are limitless. The first and main item to bill is your time. Attorneys, paralegals, and litigation assistants already bill their time; in some cases, legal secretaries are billing their time. There is no reason why the librarian and his or her staff can't do this as well. The most obvious place to start is with online legal bibliographic services such as Westlaw or Lexis. The costs are more than likely billed to clients even now, and the attorneys who do their own research are certainly including their time.

From this, it's a small step to start billing for research done offline. After all, if your time spent sitting at a computer terminal is valuable enough to bill, isn't your time spent going through the *Index to Legal Periodicals* or the *Congressional Record* just as valuable?

Furthermore, not only is the librarian's time billable, but the library staff's as well. The only difference is in the rates charged.

It is appropriate to add incidental costs to billings. Just as lawyers currently charge clients for their inter-

nal photocopying and messenger services, costs involved in getting information should also be charged. The cost of long-distance telephone calls made to obtain interlibrary loans should *not* be absorbed by the library, nor should copying charges or the cost of messengers.

Billing for specific products is trickier. The actual costs for putting together a legislative history, bibliography, or report of business statistics can be determined (online connect charges, personnel time, typing and photocopying, etc.) and then charged to the client. But should there be an additional mark-up—say, $50 for a bibliography, $35 for a census/market report? This is a policy matter and should be determined beforehand.

There is also the question of how much to charge if another client requests the same information. You can update any item given to additional clients and bill the costs of updating. Also, even though you haven't spent the same amount of time in preparing the report, time spent is part of the original value of the report and should also be included. The original online costs (if any) have already been paid and probably should not be included.

It may be simpler to charge a flat fee for additional copies based on the original cost of creating the report. Just what the fee should be is another policy question. Several freelance services charge costs plus $50 an hour, and the original cost is applied each time.

Watch services can also be charged. Lexis provides Eclipse service, which runs a search on a regular, predetermined basis. If the library checks the newspapers daily for stories on specific topics, or keeps track of legislation or a specific bill's progress in the legislature, why not bill for this service?

Making the Profit Concept Work

There are other hints that will help make the switch a success. Involve yourself and the library in the billing process. If your firm offers a billing orientation, take it and have the library staff take it. For example, law librarians can find out just how attorneys do their time-keeping, and proceed accordingly. Keep reference logs. These will help you to track what you're doing and to com-

pile statistics you need. Include the date, attorney, client, and log number, short descriptions of the request and the results, the amount of time spent, and incidental costs. Keep track of your own and the staff's time.

Don't be afraid to ask attorneys for clients' names and numbers. That they are to give you this information should be established as a matter of policy. If the attorneys do *not* give you this information, the costs should be billed back to their business accounts; that provides a remarkable incentive for cooperation. Contact local library services, independent librarians, etc. to determine the going rates for various services. Also, contact your neighboring law firm librarians to check on what they are doing. They will certainly have helpful suggestions or comments.

Years ago, the library and its services were considered overhead. If this is still your firm's philosophy, you will need to change management's mind and get their backing and support. Today, it may be easier. Firm administrators and managing partners are keenly aware of rising costs and will probably welcome your initiative in offering some relief.

Bibliographic Notes.

Strain, Laura, "Billing for a Librarian's Services: Pro and Con," in *The Private Law Library: 1980's and Beyond*, New York: PLI, 1979, pp. 213–5 (PLI Course Handbook No. 108).

Sloane, Richard. "Turning the Office Library into a Profit Center," in *Legal Research and Law Library Management*, 1985 Supplement, New York: Law Journal Seminars Press, 1985, pp. 113–7.

Sloane, Richard. "Librarians as Entrepreneurs," *New York Law Journal*, May 5, 1988, p. 4.

Newman, Mark. "Why a Law Firm Needs a Librarian," *Legal Reference Services Quarterly*, Winter '85/'86, pp. 57–64.

Sloane, Richard and Julius Marke. *Legal Research and Law Library Management*, see above. Chapters 32–34: "Law-Office Librarians Pave Way for Lawyers," "Librarian's Participation in Research Activities," and "A Guide to Hiring a Law Firm's First Librarian."

Wallace, Marie and Julius Pomerantz, eds. *The Private Law Firm Library: An Integral Tool of the Law Firm.* New York: PLI, 19. (PLI Course Handbook No. 85). ▬▬

WHEN DO DOLLARS FOR INFORMATION SERVICE MAKE SENSE?
The Wisconsin ISD Experience

Frances K. Wood

If you were asked to envision some information services in your library that could feasibly be offered for a fee, what would you choose? A list of such services probably would include many that are currently being offered for free and others that could be offered under the right circumstances.

Fee-based information services are widely used today by the business and industrial community and are generally accepted—or at least tolerated—by the library community. A considerable number of established libraries and information centers have found it acceptable,

feasible, and profitable to offer information for a fee.

Reasons for having a fee-based information service vary, but the decision is usually based on at least one of four factors: the service can bring in additional, needed revenue; overwhelmed by outside user requests for information, the library or information center staff needs to have some of the pressure removed (charging fees may cut down on the number of requests and/or generate money for additional staffing); the service can be a good public relations/outreach vehicle; and since everyone else is selling information, the administration wants to get into the act.

When an established library or information center is considering the possibility of operating and managing a fee-based information service, seven key issues must be addressed so that the staff knows what is expected of the operation:

1. Is the service to be a cost-recovery service or should it be expected to make a profit?
2. What expenses are the fees to cover?
3. What kinds of support can be expected from the parent library or information center?
4. What funding will be made available to the new service and for what period of time? For what can—and can't—the funds be used?
5. Are there provisions for adding new services, updating services already in place, updating equipment, adding additional staff, and bringing in new clients?
6. When a profit is made, who will decide how the money is to be used? And how will the money be used?
7. What does the administration expect from the service this year, two years from now, and five years from now?

How these issues are resolved depends on a number of factors, both internal and external. These will no doubt change over the life of the operation. External factors that can affect decisions are type of clientele and the changing needs of clientele. Internal factors can include the parent administration's policies and a physical relocation.

Another consideration is whether

or not to conduct a marketing survey. Although this *should* be undertaken, I'm not aware of any established fee-based information service that has actually done one. If such a survey has been done it would be useful to find out how it was constructed, what area was surveyed, how the results were used by the administration underwriting the survey, and whether or not the people in charge felt the end results were worthwhile.

Setting Policy

Once the administration has determined that the library or information center should and can start a fee-based information service and decisions have been reached regarding the seven key issues — and before advertising and promotion can begin — there are a number of policy decisions to be made. These can affect the cost of providing services and are as follows:

- Who will be your clientele? Will there be a different fee structure for members and nonmembers, clients with deposit accounts, residents or nonresidents, etc? Remember, price breaks are nice gestures but price variations for the same service will increase record-keeping time.
- Will the service be limited to information that is available only on site?
- Will the service have unrestricted access to its customary information sources and be able to do any necessary processing on its own or will it encounter delays as a result of being dependent on other library staff for check-out, photocopying, and the like?
- How will the service be staffed? An ideal information service using on-site library material requires a staff that knows the collection, outside resources, understands and speaks "libraryese," and can relate to a public that is not conversant in library and/or academic terminology.
- If document delivery is one of the services, what is the time frame for delivery? What is considered rush service? How much additional staff will be involved in processing a rush request? What level of staff personnel will be involved?

- If there is a state sales tax, will any or all of the services offered require the tax to be added?
- What records have to be kept — and for how long? What or who will determine this? What formats are available and acceptable? Will the storage area be reasonably accessible?
- What statistics will be produced and for what purpose?
- What format should be used for

Reasons for having a fee-based information service vary, but the decision is usually based on at least one of four factors: the service can bring in additional, needed revenue; overwhelmed by outside user requests for information, the library or information center staff needs to have some of the pressure removed; the service can be a good public relations/ outreach vehicle; and since everyone else is selling information, the administration wants to get into the act.

accepting information requests? Which require the least amount of time? How will this affect the pricing policy?
- How much space will be allotted for the information service? Will there be provision for walk-in clients? Will there be space set aside for working with on-site clients? Will the service have its own telephone number?

Operating Within

Capitalizing on organizational strengths and offering services accordingly is good business procedure. Most information services are highly dependent on their parent library's collection and the good will and cooperation of the staff. In fact, there are numerous benefits to be gained from operating within an established organization.

The Information Services Division (ISD) at the Kurt F. Wendt Engineering Library at the University of Wisconsin, Madison, was founded 23 years ago by the director of the Wendt Library. It is a cost-recovery, fee-based information service primarily serving the business and industrial community of Wisconsin and the surrounding states.

In addition to the expertise on the Wendt Library staff, ISD has access to the support and expertise of some 120 campus librarians in 42 other libraries and information centers. There's excellent rapport between ISD and campus librarians.

The University of Wisconsin's central business office also is very helpful in explaining how to follow their and the state's rules and regulations regarding invoicing and payments. The office receives all payments made to ISD, deposits checks, and sends ISD a monthly statement reflecting invoices paid.

When we were setting up operations 23 years ago, the central business office provided us with information about University regulations, Wisconsin sales tax, record retention, invoice formatting, and collection procedures. If a collection agency is needed, the business office handles it for us.

A Labor-Intensive Service

Operating an information service costs money. Like any other business, an information service requires staff, equipment, and supplies. Substantial sums are paid out before clients are invoiced or invoices paid.

An information service is also a labor-intensive operation. To fulfill an information request, someone has to identify it, "pull it," organize it, prepare it for delivery, and record the details necessary for determining costs and invoicing. It may cost five or ten cents to photocopy a page of information, but the labor — the time involved in logging in the request, locating the material, copying, closing the log, and arranging for delivery of that page — add to the cost.

At ISD we often take a specific service and follow it through in an attempt to simplify and combine procedures. In this way we can determine whether the procedures are performed at the proper level and how much time they involve. We can also see whether or not charges for the service recover costs.

Consider photocopying that one page of information. Assume the request is accurately cited on a correctly filled out and separated ALA form. Our ISD flowchart shows 22 procedures that need a clerk's and student's intervention before it is ready for mailing!

Approximately 41 percent of our budget is used for classified and unclassified salaries and student wages. University policy requires that 29 percent of this be targeted to defray costs for such fringe benefits as vacations and medical insurance. The staff is made up of one full-time librarian, a three-quarter time reference librarian, a full-time clerk, a one-third time fiscal clerk, and the equivalent of 80 hours per week in student help. The reference librarian and the fiscal clerk are full-time positions shared with the Wendt Library.

ISD also has an arrangement with Computerized Bibliographic Services (CBS) located within the Wendt Library. We are charged by CBS for staff and search time on a cost-recovery basis, which also includes the recordkeeping involved in doing searches. ISD receives the searches ready for delivery to the clientele. ISD and CBS staff collaborate on determining the databases to be searched and the terms to be used, but ISD is responsible for the searches. ISD also uses CBS staff expertise to write simple computer programs for runs of mailing labels, dialing into outside sources, etc.

Approximately 55 percent of ISD's budget is spent on supplies and services. This is a broad category that includes a spectrum of supplies necessary for operating an efficient labor-intensive office. ISD's requisitions for all supplies and such services as online searching, foreign patents, and other materials not available on campus are processed through the Wendt Library business office. The office processes the requisitions, keeps records, and follows through to be certain that ISD's accounts are accurately posted by the University's business office. The remaining four percent of ISD's budget is set aside for new capital equipment, replacement, or repairs.

If CBS's services and the recordkeeping by the Wendt business office had to be performed by ISD, an additional 40 to 60 hours of staff time would be needed.

There is little doubt that if a fee-based information service is to be successful, its goals, objectives, and clientele must be clearly defined at the outset. Cost controls must be established and firmly adhered to. Realistic criteria for creating fee structures and services offered must be established, and the latter continually reviewed in the light of these criteria. Finally, a competent, service-oriented staff must be recruited and trained so that the all-important client base can be retained and expanded. ▬

This article was adapted from a chapter in the proceedings of the Second Conference on Fee-Based Research in College and University Libraries, *which was published in fall 1987 by the Michigan Information Transfer Source, University of Michigan Libraries.*

FUNDRAISING
STRATEGIES

FUND RAISING BY STRATEGIC DESIGN

Edwin S. Clay, III

In a scene from *Alice in Wonderland*, the White Rabbit waits nervously to testify before the Red Queen. Explaining that he has never given testimony before, the Rabbit asks for help in how to proceed. "It's simple," replies the Red Queen. "Begin at the beginning. Go to the middle. Come to the end. Then stop!" The same kind of logic applies to library fund raising from the private sector.

Why and when should a library turn to the private sector for support? How should a library make that determination? Strategic planning is an essential tool in this decision-making process.

Fund-raising campaigns can be grouped into two types: capital and annual appeals. Each has a specific purpose. A capital campaign seeks to raise money for a new building or to remodel an existing one. It may attempt to acquire land or establish an endowment. Pledges in a capital campaign are sought primarily from individuals. Large gifts are targeted and the donors are allowed the option of paying their pledges over several years.

Capital campaigns have substantial goals and are held only once or twice in a decade, if the institution or group is smart. Funds raised in this manner are seldom or never used for maintenance, salaries and/or programs. If so, they only are used for start up endeavors.

Annual appeals are quite different. They raise funds for current operations and the appeal will be repeated every 12 months. Small gifts from many individuals is the annual appeal strategy. Pledges are sought in cash as opposed to property, stock, etc., and are payable upon agreeing to participate. Annual campaigns do not attempt to build endowments nor do they attempt to underwrite major building programs.

Issues to Address

Each of these campaign types has its advantages. Each can aid the other. Some fundraisers contend that the annual appeal paves the way for the capital drive. Then, the capital campaign strengthens the annual drive. Obviously, these two categories of campaigns are not the only sources of donations for libraries; there also is the bequest and the occasional large gift coming from an individual or corporation. But the capital and annual campaigns are the two major avenues to private sector funding.

Libraries supported primarily with public funds and that are involved in or thinking about launching annual or capital campaigns must consider the financial and political implications of going to the private sector. These issues have the potential to act as time bombs and the ability to negate all of the positive benefits of a successful fund drive. Look before you leap has never been a more appropriate aphorism.

Your first step is to determine the mix of the library's revenues by asking the following questions:

- What percent is derived from public sources? From earned income? From private gifts?
- Is this amount sufficient for current operations?
- Will it be enough in five years?
- What is the history of the library's funding mix?
- Has the percentage of public funds increased, or has it decreased with a concommitant increase in earned income?
- Examined over a 10-year period, what patterns emerge?

In short, you have to thoroughly review the revenue history of your institution. Interesting trends may appear and areas of need that can be addressed by the campaign could come into focus.

If this examination of the funding mix reveals that the percentage of public funds has been steadily declining, other questions must be asked: What factors have led to the decline? Has the state's economy changed? The political atmosphere? Can the decline be reversed? Are there methods and/or strategies available that deflect the trend?

It is crucial that you know without a doubt—and can clearly demonstrate—that a fund-raising campaign is absolutely necessary. This financial mix review will help you determine this. I suspect that most librarians will decide that an annual campaign is unnecessary, but that budget adjustments are in order. The few who learn that a campaign is definitely required will have the documentation to prove it.

Political Implications

To no one's surprise, public institutions exist in the context of politics. It is axiomatic, then, that political leaders at the local level establish local funding priorities. It can be argued that these individuals determine whether or not a library has to turn to a capital campaign, or the more drastic annual campaign.

Let's take a library in need of a new expanded, or renovated building. A capital campaign is suggested for raising the funds. Before proceeding, though, a second review is in order. How has the library—the locality—provided for capital costs in the past? What has the role of gov-

ernment been with regard to providing for public buildings? What is its capital improvement program? If there is a history of directing public funds to construction, pursue that route. If not can the policy be established or the existing one which disallows this expenditure be changed? If a portion of the financial support is forthcoming, what is the government's fair share? These answers are

To no one's surprise, public institutions exist in the context of politics. It is axiomatic, then, that political leaders at the local level establish local funding priorities. It can be argued that these individuals determine whether or not a library has to turn to a capital campaign, or the more drastic annual campaign.

necessary before any further steps are taken.

Just as important as political leaders are the local government's chief executive officers—the city manager, the county manager, the county executive, etc. They also establish spending patterns and priorities. Does your city manager have a library card? Does he or she use it?

Before beating a path to the private sector, you are urged to consider how your efforts will be viewed within the political/administrative environment. For example, if you choose to undertake a capital campaign for a new building, what prec-

edent are you establishing or breaking? What expectations are you raising for the future? If you turn to the private sector for funding this building, where will you turn for its expansion or for the new branch? What position is the library board placing itself in when a capital campaign is authorized?

A Fund-Raising Policy

The financial and political terrain has been studied. You have decided to proceed. Now, the answers gleaned from your investigation must be translated into a library board policy on fund raising. This policy should state specifically:

- Why your library is fund raising
- the type of campaign that is to be undertaken
- the role of the Library Board in fund raising
- the role of the staff and Friends of the Library in fund raising.

Once the Policy on Fund Raising is adopted, all individuals (e.g., members of the board, staff) with full or partial fundraising responsibilities must understand the policy so they can support it and be prepared to implement it. With a fund-raising policy in place, you also have to appoint a person or persons who will be responsible for conducting the campaign. Then you are ready to begin—planning, not fund raising.

Strategic Planning

Planning for library fund raising should be based on two givens: that the library has clear goals and objectives based on its response to community needs and that fund raising is simply one means of realizing the library's goals. Strategic planning is the key ingredient to successful fund raising; you should not embark on a campaign without employing it.[1] Strategic planning is a process that uses data from the environment to determine directions for the future; it places emphasis on implementation.

Step one is to seek commitment: support and participation from the Library Board, the Friends of the Library, community leaders, and staff. All need to be totally involved in—and committed to—the library and its fund-raising campaign.

Campaign staffing is the next

priority. Roles and responsibilities have to be assigned and volunteers recruited. A campaign budget must be established, indicating costs for salaries, office expenses, printing, postage, art work, travel, lodging, meals, etc. It ought to be realistic and adhered to as the campaign progresses.

Leadership is also key to strategic planning, and so leadership selection is an important undertaking. Who serves as chair of the campaign will depend on such factors as the particular locale and its political environment.

Setting the campaign's chronology is another step. How long should it last? When should it take place? What other campaigns are being planned for the community? Who usually raises funds and when? Create a reasonable schedule.

Finally, the campaign strategy is composed. Will direct mail be used? How about personal visits? Should a kick-off dinner be arranged? How will the campaign be conducted?[2]

The Case Statement

Planning also includes composing the case statement, which is the campaign's major resource document. This is the vehicle by which the library presents itself to the public.[3] The case statement speaks to donors' needs, not library needs. You are not asking the donors to give money to build a library for the library board or the staff. Rather you are providing donors with the opportunity to participate in the creation of a community institution that will benefit all—themselves included.

The case statement becomes, in effect, an investment prospectus. It should demonstrate a sound return for the donor's gift. It places the library in the context of its importance to the community, and so should show that the project has been endorsed and that community leaders are committed to the project.

Make statements that are both supportable and defensible. Each and every statement must be backed up by facts. The case statement can be rational and emotional—these terms are not mutually exclusive. Giving springs from feelings; then it is rationalized. Structure your case accordingly. Be optimistic—it projects success—and be brief. Make your case easy to remember. Its central theme should be presented in a straightforward manner, responding to such questions as: What is the library about? Why give to the library and not to...? What is the lasting benefit of this campaign? Who else is participating?

The case statement should make a plea for action. It is designed to engage the public, present an opportunity, and convince a potential donor to contribute. Its urgency should compel commitment.

The Iceberg's Tip

Planning is only the tip of the fundraising iceberg, but it is important to determining why and when a library decides to turn to the private sector for support. It is somewhat ironic that many public libraries are facing this question if you consider the early history of public libraries. Initially, they were financed by individuals through dues paid to an association. Little by little, public funds began to flow, better yet—trickle, to libraries. States adopted state aid formulas to assist libraries, and then local governments began making significant contributions. The federal government joined in channeling millions of dollars into libraries for construction, services, and co-operative endeavors.

It appears now that we have come back to where we began—to the private sector. Certainly public libraries are still dependent on public funds for operation. But, as these amounts diminish and decrease, many are looking elsewhere for money.

However, before turning to the private sector, each library's particular history and role in the community must be thoroughly examined. Library managers and boards must know exactly why they think they have to turn to new sources, and they have to be aware of the consequences of such a move. Only then can the courtroom full of potential donors be convinced to vote "yea" on the library's fundraising campaign. ▬

References

1. James Gregory Lord, *Philanthropy and Marketing: New Strategies for Fund Raising* (Cleveland: Third Sector Press, 1982).
2. From materials presented at the workshop, "Raising Funds for Libraries: Paths to the Private Sector," sponsored by the American Library Association and developed by Brooke Sheldon during her year as President of the American Library Association, 1983–84.
3. Lord, pp. 4–13.

From The Library Dollar Stretcher

Millions of dollars each year are spent replacing burned-out motors and broken belts and fans in one of the most important, though most neglected, pieces of library equipment—the vacuum cleaner. The cause of many of these problems is the common paper clip or stray staple dropped from desks or tables or just simply casually discarded. The Library Dollar Stretcher recommends purchasing a new magnetic bar available to fit almost any size upright vacuum at a cost of between $15 and $25. The magnetic strip fastened to the front of the vacuum picks up, in advance of the vacuum brush, staples and paper clips, significantly prolonging the life of the equipment.

SEVEN STRATEGIES FOR EFFECTIVE FUND RAISING

Daniel J. Bradbury

A FABLE: Once upon a time, a library decided to launch a direct-mail campaign at Christmastime for a new endowment fund. The library had made meager attempts at fund raising for several years. A mock Christmas card was developed, inviting the recipient to "celebrate with a gift that lasts forever," i.e., a gift to the library's new Book Endowment Fund. Design help was engaged, copy was written, a slick brochure was developed, and 20,000 pieces were prepared and readied for mailing between Thanksgiving and December 1. As visions of dollar signs danced in their heads, the library administrators settled down to await the returns. Responses began trickling in, along with legitimate Christmas cards, publisher's catalogs, bills for books, and seasonal solicitations from other organizations.

On January 6th a letter arrived from a far-away law firm informing the library administrators that a former library patron had died nine months earlier and the library was the beneficiary of his estate—some $1.3 million. The library administrators were delirious. The total for the Christmastime library endowment development campaign now stood at $1,306,527. Prior to this last bit of good news, there was some unfounded speculation as to whether the endowment campaign would even pay for itself—speculation, in fact, that you can't build an endowment by direct mail and that the campaign would fail.

The moral of the story is clear. To raise $1,306,527 in endowment for your library, all you need do is design a solicitation that looks like a Christmas card, mail about 20,000 of them out before Christmas, and wait for the results. You too can be successful!

While the above story is fictitious and the formula for success a classic "*non-sequitur,*" like all good fables it does contain elements of truth. Direct mail can be a good tool for library fund raising, libraries do receive bequests from patrons out of the blue and, most important, those libraries that plan and then take action, usually wind up with more money.

The fictitious library might not be able to legitimately claim the $1.3 million gift as part of their endowment campaign, but the existence of an organized fund-raising program identifies the public library as an appropriate place to give and may have been a catalyst for the bequest.

Fund raising or development consists of a planned program of activities. Fund raising can and should be embedded in the library's planning process. It should emanate from the library's mission, goals, and objectives. Developing alternative financial resources—like automating the catalog, providing adequate delivery service, or performing other support functions—is an important support activity in maintaining a quality program of library services.

Fund Raising Made Simple.

First things first. The library must decide what it needs. Not a general idea of what it needs for the organization, but exactly what it needs to provide better service to its public. If, listed among these needs, are monetary resources to buy books, offer programming, fund staff positions, erect buildings, etc., then fund raising is one appropriate solution to satisfying these needs. The rationale for this should be worked out, preferably on paper, and is often referred to as the "Case Statement". Case statements may be developed for overall fund raising programs, or for individual projects.

Deciding what the library is going to do with the funds when it gets them answers the question "Who do I make the check out to?" To avoid answering this question with a "Gee, I'm not sure," forethought and advance work are required. Typically, one of three approaches is used: 1) the library (or its parent institution) will receive and manage the money itself; 2) the library will have set up a foundation or other non-profit, tax-exempt entity to receive and manage the money on behalf of the library; or 3) an existing support group, (i.e. Friends of the Library, Community Foundtion, etc.) will receive and manage the funds.

Once the library has fund-raising targets and has decided what it is going to do with the funds when it gets them, the next step is developing strategies to produce or contribute to the results desired. Philanthropy is the act of giving, fund raising is the art of getting.

Give a library some money, and it either spends it or saves it. "Spending it" means fund raising aimed at annual operations or a specific project. "Saving it" means fund raising aimed at endowment development. Of course, it is also possible to do some combination of the two, allowing portions of funds raised to flow to annual operations or special projects, while earmarking other portions for endowment or trust development. In a given campaign, however, this approach can breed confusion.

The Plan

Most libraries successful at raising funds have an overall fund-raising/

financial development plan. In addition to bringing dollars to the library, a multi-faceted approach to fund raising or financial development accomplishes these three objectives for the organization: it positions and promotes the organization as "an appropriate place to give"; it establishes multiple programs or channels through which a

Developing alternative financial resources. . . is an important support activity in maintaining a quality program of library services.

donor can give; and it builds the donor/potential donor base. Achieving these objectives is critical to the goal of raising funds.

Here are seven (plus two) types of programs or components that a financial development plan might contain: the seven are rather conventional fund-raising approaches; the two others are not, strictly speaking, fund raising, but are ideas worth considering in special circumstances. The seven are:
1. Tribute and memorial-type programs
2. General gift programs
3. Grant programs
4. Membership-type programs
5. Special events
6. Deferred giving programs
7. Major campaigns
   The "plus two" are:
1. Asset liquidation
2. Entrepreneurial activities

Depending on how a library structures its financial development/fund-raising plan, it may engage in all or a mix of these programs: it may manage some itself and assign others to Friends or support groups; or it may seek outside fund-raising help for certain turnkey components. The programs or activities the library decides to undertake become the strategies for achieving its financial development plan.

Tribute and memorial programs are basic fund-raising tools as both a source of ongoing operating income and a method of identifying donors.

The library positions itself as an appropriate place to contribute to satisfy a social obligation either in memorial or as a tribute. Frequently, the library associates the gift with a particular title and affixes a book plate, or arranges some other appropriate form of donor recognition. Examples of brochures promoting Tribute and Memorial programs abound, and several samples can usually be picked up from the "swap and shop" offerings at the American Library Association's Annual Conference. Many libraries, such as San Diego Public Library, have adjusted this approach to encourage larger gifts—for a $300 contribution, the donor can buy the library a book a year in perpetuity, and the $300 can be paid in four installments.

Gift programs are less specific and may include tribute and memorial gifts, among others. Such a program would also include things like a $200 gift from a service club, gratuities given in appreciation for outstanding service, funds for the purchase of specific equipment, etc.

A more organized approach to focus and encourage general contributions is found in the gift catalogs produced by a number of libraries. Typically a gift catalog will offer a rationale for giving, list organizational wants to satisfy patron needs, and offer a wide variety of suggestions. The gift catalog of the Janesville, Wisconsin, Public Library, produced in 1984, suggests possible gifts ranging from a $25 magazine subscription to $900,000 for a mini-branch. An earlier example of this approach was the gift catalog issued by the Boulder, Colorado, Public Library in the late '70s. Examples of this approach can also be found at local Parks and Recreation departments. In September 1978, the U.S. Department of the Interior, Heritage Conservation and Recreation Service produced a *Gifts Catalog Handbook*, which is an excellent crib sheet for libraries contemplating this approach.

General gift programs are also effective when they focus on a particular aspect of library operations. Equipping a new branch, outfitting a new department, or simply focusing on funds for acquisitions are some approaches. The Las Vegas-Clark County "Bucks for Books" program is an example of a focus on acquisitions. In 1986 the Clark County program raised $67,000 for materials acquisitions, primarily through direct-mail solicitation.

Membership programs are another component of an overall development plan. Many libraries reserve this type of solicitation for their Friends of the Library organization. Others successfully use this approach in the absence of a Friends group or in addition to a Friends membership campaign. The library must specify what the donor is becoming a member of (a member of the XYZ Public Library's Angel Club) and what benefits, if any, membership brings. In-house distribution and direct mail are the typical methods for publicizing membership programs, but the San Antonio Public Library was successful in piggybacking its solicitation onto the utility bills received by the 450,000 customers of the San Antonio Public Services Commission. The first year's mailing netted over $50,000.

Grant programs are a staple of any financial development plan. Although time-consuming, they are targeted to funding for special projects, ongoing operations, endowment development, or capital campaigns. Targets for grant proposals include government grant programs, corporations, foundations, or individuals.

Special events are considered the fund raisers' bane because they are labor intensive and frequently prompt the question "Was it really worth the effort?" Yet they are valuable for identifying potential donors and lending a social/cultural air to library happenings.

Gala events proved popular throughout the '80's with New York Public Library's "Night of 100 Dinners," Plano, Texas, Public Library's $60,000 extravaganza, Lexington, Kentucky, Public Library's "Celebrity Dinner," and Enoch Pratt's "Mid-Summer Night's Dream."

Less spectacular, but often effective, are events such as bake sales, book sales, read-a-thons, walk-a-thons, benefits, sporting events, etc.

Aside from raising funds for special projects, operations, or endowment development, all of these activities serve to develop a prospect list for *Deferred giving*. Deferred, or planned giving can elicit the "big gift," even from donors of modest means. Options that enable a donor to give now and/or later include: wills, life insurance, gift annuities, charitable remainder annuity trusts, charitable remainder uni-trust, charitable income trusts, pooled income funds, and revokable living trusts. Each of these approaches has significant advantages for both the donor and the library, but may well require considerable legal and investment expertise to execute an appropriate instrument.

Major campaigns might include any or all of the above strategies, but this is where eyeball-to-eyeball asking comes into play. Whether for a construction project or endowment development, characteristic components of a major campaign are a substantial dollar goal and a short timeline (usually two to five years). Frequently, the fund-raising pot can be sweetened by the addition of matching money from a local or national foundation, or a particularly interested donor. The National Endowment for the Humanities has a

> *Opportunities abound for both fund raising and profit-making ventures. The programs selected. . . should support the library's mission. . .*

development grant program that offers a three to one match on major campaigns. In early 1987, New York, Boston, Los Angeles, San Francisco, St. Louis, Denver, and Enoch Pratt Public Libraries all had major campaigns underway. These libraries had combined campaign goals of close to $435 million, with proceeds to be used for a variety of construction, materials and endowment development needs. In smaller communities, the same concepts can be applied for equally beneficial results.

The seven program strategies listed above are conventional approaches to fund raising, but don't overlook the less obvious "plus two" possibilities: asset liquidation and entrepreneurial projects. Local practice and state law may limit a library's option to follow these two approaches, but they are certainly worth investigating. First, the administrators or board should ensure that the funds derived will accrue for the purposes intended—either to offset specific operations, contribute to or establish a given account, or build an endowment.

Asset liquidation is an activity most libraries pursue to some extent. Sale of gift books or items weeded from the collection is usually considered merely miscellaneous income, or sometimes channeled to the Friends of the Library organization. But it is potentially a source of significant one-time fund raising.

In addition to the routine flow of discarded and duplicate or unwanted gift books, many libraries possess discrete collections of rare or valuable books peripheral to the library's mission. If such a collection exists, and is not necessary to fulfilling the library's role within the community, it may be converted to cash through book sale or auction. If the collection is large enough, it might interest one of the larger book auction houses.

Unwanted book collections are only one of the assets a library might consider liquidating to build its endowment or gift fund. Accumulations of old furniture and equipment can yield small earnings; donated works of art, gathering dust in storage or an inconspicuous corner, have the potential for high yield in the collectors market. In 1985, the Kansas City Public Library sold, through a New York broker, a Bouguereau painting for $110,000. Surplus land can be converted to a cash asset to benefit the library's financial development.

Libraries have typically charged and collected a wide variety of miscellaneous fines and fees in return for service or extended use, but only recently have they begun to explore avenues for *entrepreneurial activity*. These activities, or profit centers, have been introduced into a number of libraries over the past decade. While many other non-profit organizations have begun setting up subsidiaries to manufacture and/or distribute goods or provide services, few libraries, if any, have taken this route. More typically, libraries have left this type of activity to their Friends or other support groups, or the enterprise has been embedded in their operating budget with the revenue flowing to the general operating fund.

One of the most common projects established by libraries are used book shops to sell unwanted gifts and/or discards from the library collection. Operated on a self-service basis, or staffed by Friends or other volunteers, these operations contribute a small revenue stream to library operations. More ambitious enterprises have been undertaken by libraries such as Dallas Public Library, where the concept has been expanded to that of a book/gift shop with inventory including posters, note paper, new books of special interest, greeting cards, t-shirts, coffee mugs, etc. In 1987 the Dallas Public Library generated more than $60,000 from this activity.

Libraries as landlords is another avenue for entrepreneurial activity.

Anything from leasing the air rights for high-rise development over a prime site main library or branch to renting office space to other non-profits or governmental units have at least been considered. The Kansas City Public Library leases space to the U.S. Post Office for a postal station in one of its branches. In 1987 the Milwaukee Public Library entered into negotiations with McDonalds Corporation, which proposed spending $730,000 to open a restaurant on the ground level of the central library. If and when the deal is consummated, Milwaukee will follow the lead of Broward County and Sacramento in providing public library patrons with a convenient place to eat, while generating additional income for the library.

Other entrepreneurial activities under discussion, if not yet implemented, include: developing a research bureau to provide contract services to small and medium-size business firms; selling photographic reproductions of maps, prints, old photos, etc. of items of historical significance; establishing a graphic cen-ter and table top publishing unit for preparation and printing of governmental and non-profit organization newsletters and publications; conducting fee-based workshops for community organizations or the general public; brokering database services through library computers to other users; and maintaining city or county archives and historic records on a fee basis.

Extensive planning and a firm legal foundation for the activity is essential in setting up a successful profit center; however, such entrepreneurial activities can be a significant component of an overall financial development plan.

Opportunities abound for both fund raising and profit-making ventures. The strategies or programs selected for a library's development plan should be consistent with and support the library's mission, goals and objectives. To achieve success, the library administration and Board must *decide* and *do* only three basic things: decide what they want; decide what they are going to do with it when they get it; and go get it! ▬

THE JOY OF STAGING SPECIAL EVENTS

Mark Reidell

For those of us who have served on the special events front line to raise money for our libraries; for those of us who have shown the willingness to battle and overcome frustration, rejection, and last-minute crises; for those of us who remain undaunted and resilient, even when our net take from an event is $37.50 — the belief that we are supporting a vital institution keeps us from retreating.

For those of you who haven't served on the special events front-line, my advice is: Be wary of anyone who claims raising money at special events is a piece of cake. Think twice about someone who tells you a "Jack and The Beanstalk" story, claiming that you can start with a handful of beans, and — after a few phone calls to the caterer, a newspaper editor, and some volunteers, and a brief but pleasant chat with the president of the local megacorporation — you'll magically end up with a goose the lays golden eggs.

Most of what you read and hear about special events could leave the uninitiated thinking that nearly all of them are sure-fire, never-miss moneymakers for libraries. After scanning the library literature on the subject and recalling the many speakers I've heard at American Library Association conferences and elsewhere, it seems that everybody concludes that their special event was a smashing success.

There are at least two ways to look at these interpretations of reality: Nobody needs to read another article on how to stage a special event, or a lot of people have taken to downsizing the meaning of the word success.

Much of my experience with special events fund raising stems from my involvement in planning and implementing Saint Paul Public Library's 100th Anniversary Celebration and Fund Drive.[1] At that time our library worked with its Friends organization to eventually raise over $2 million dollars through corporate and foundation appeals, direct mail, and a multitude of special events including author receptions, a gala kickoff night party, luncheons and banquets, and a birthday in the park festival which served as the backdrop for a mammoth used-book sale.

Mistakes Are Inevitable

Most of our success resulted from the learn-as-you-go method. We suffered a lot. Some of our problems were the result of klutziness — like dropping our anniversary cake just as the birthday gala was about to begin. Some fall under the heading of "who would of guessed it" — like the morning five days before the kickoff night party when I received a phone call informing me that our Emcee, Garrison Keillor, had to go to Washington D.C., to accept a Peabody Award. This was the one event that many dignitaries, including our Mayor, had planned to attend, and for which refreshments for 400 were ordered, musicians were scheduled to perform, and invitations and media releases had advertised as the "Big Day." It became the day for which everything had to be rescheduled. When the event was finally held, the electricity died just after I turned on our fund-raising slide/tape program for our 400 dignitaries.

Other problems were simply labeled, "The bad luck continues." The graphic designer we hired to make anniversary banners for each of our 11 libraries was about halfway through the project when a medical problem sidelined him for almost two months. Numerous typos and gliches mysteriously popped up on our promotional brochures, news releases, and invitations. It was nothing serious, just enough to turn a few more hairs gray.

Most of our special events showed a profit, but some of the events raised only enough money to treat our volunteers to lunch at McDonald's. Nevertheless, we made every effort to view these experiences in a positive light. We contended that we had made great strides in heightening awareness or improving the chance for donations at the next event. We blamed a low turnout on the weather, competition from other events, or excessive sun spots. In figuring out the net profit, we did the typical maneuver of not putting a dollar figure in the expense column for staff time (If this is not an expense, why not have a staff person work full-time on fund raising?). We did everything we could to avoid self-criticism: Why cut our own throats?

Yet, self-criticism coupled with a hard-nosed view of costs is essential for an honest appraisal of whether or not an event was successful. One good measure of success I picked up in hindsight: Was last years's event scheduled again for this year?

It's difficult—if not impossible—to find the right words to tell a group of people (especially volunteers) who have just spent many hours (days, weeks) working on a special event that it was a bust. But evaluation shouldn't be avoided just because it's painful. Consider approaching it from the angle: What did we learn that we can do better the next time around? or Even though most of what we did was right, here's one or two things that need more

work. Be tactful, but be honest.

One useful form of evaluation is to corral a small group of attendees following an event to get their reactions. Encourage them to be frank. Remember that special events—especially first-time events—are risky ventures. Few are done without mistakes.

The Importance of PR

Many events planners begin thinking about public relations when it is too late—after most of the work is done. No matter how great the idea is for a special event, how well it's organized or staffed, if not enough of your target audience knows about it, or shows interest or feels enthusiastic, you effort is wasted.

Above all, your public relations effort must answer one question for your audience, "What's in it for me?" Your communications need to be compatible with audience motives and needs, not the library staff's needs.

Check your promotional brochures, news releases, and public service announcements against these four principles:[2]

Identification: Is your message related to the interests of your audience?
Action: Have you provided an easy means by which supporters can make a contribution?
Familiarity and trust: Will your audience have confidence in the speaker or source of your communications?
Clarity: Are the words and symbols that you employ comprehensible?

Once again let me recommend that you don't rely exclusively on your own answers to these questions, but instead try them out on unbiased members of the target public.

What Is a Special Event?[3]

Special events defy simple definitions. There are a multitude of activities—from used-book sales and author receptions to phone-a-thons and auctions—that can become special events. They can last a few hours, a day, a week—or, when they are not going well, an eternity. They can be an isolated project or part of a larger ongoing fund-raising campaign.

Special events can be geared for residents of a neighborhood or a city,

college students, a group of legislators, regular library users, yuppies, supporters of the arts, or anyone within shouting distance. The bottom line, however, is that they are organized for the purpose of raising a net profit of more than $37.50 for your library.

It's important that people enter into the world of special events planning with as few illusions as possible. It is *not* the cleverness of an idea that makes a special event produce dollars for your library, but the willingness of enough people to wrestle with the planning and managing of a myriad of minor and major headaches while remaining enthused. If you set a goal of $10,000 and you don't reach it, try to figure out why.

Some things to consider so that your next special event is a "10" follow.

10 Questions to Answer Before Deciding to Hold a Special Event

1. Do you have a realistic picture of the staff time and seed money necessary to pursue the endeavor?

2. Is there sufficient lead time for planning?

3. Is your fund-raising need one that the community will support? Why?

4. Will the person in charge have total authority to marshall the necessary workers and resources?

5. How much money are you shooting for? Think big—if you only ask for a pittance, your need may not be perceived as important.

6. Do you have money for start-up costs or does that have to be donated as well?

7. Has anyone ever done this before? How did it go?

8. Will the project create an undue burden on library staff? How heavily can you rely on volunteers?

9. Is the project novel enough to capture the public's attention?

10. Will you run the risk of having your traditional funding sources reduced if you're too successful with special events and other development strategies?

10 Preferred Special Events

1. The library classic is the used book sale. You can sell books by weight, thickness, or quantity. My recommendation is that whatever

you've planned to sell them for, charge at least 25 percent more. If your library has a line of trinkets (book bags, T-shirts, posters, stationery, buttons, or coffee mugs), sell them at this and all other special events. Other items, like old films, furniture, phonograph records, and framed pictures, also attract people to used book sales.

2. Author receptions. Have the author give a short talk or reading followed by the selling and autographing of his or her new book. Acquire the books from your local wholesaler. If the author is amenable, ask the audience for a donation or charge a minimal admission. November and December are the best times to arrange a reception since signed books make wonderful holiday gifts. Bringing several authors together for one event may increase your sales dramatically if the event is well publicized.

3. Grand opening of a new or remodeled library. There are several ways to make this into a successful fund-raising event. Hold a dinner/dance, dinner/author, dinner/concert program to commemorate the opening. Charge somewhere between $15 to $100 a plate. Seek out supporters who will donate the cost of a catering service. Print classy invitations. Ask your Friends group or board of trustees to invite personally the dignitaries and celebrities.

Contact your local retail merchants. Ask them to offer a discount (10%-30%) to anyone using the new library during its opening week. Bookmarks can double as the discount coupon. If a retailer's sales improve, you've created a good friend for future special events. If a new store opens near an existing library, consider the same tactic. Establish a relationship between library users and the new business. This concept has been given the label of "caused-based marketing strategy."

4. The library anniversary. Any combination of book sales, food affairs, author receptions, and benefit concerts is appropriate. Just be sure you have enough staff and volunteers committed to organizing and promoting each separate activity. The general publicity about the rich history and tradition of your library makes it easier to promote specific fund-raising events.

5. Thons. Read-a, Walk-a, Dance-a, Jog-a, Eat-a. Charge a participant fee when appropriate. Make it easy for the participant to obtain pledges for each book read or mile walked.

Award library T-shirts or buttons to participants. Ask local retailers to donate prizes, funds for printing promotional materials, and refreshments. Whatever you do, make sure it's fun for both your workers and participants.

Special events defy simple definitions. There are a multitude of activities—from used-book sales and author receptions to phone-a-thons and auctions—that can become special events. They can last a few hours, a day, a week—or, when they are not going well, an eternity. They can be an isolated project or part of a larger ongoing fund-raising campaign.

6. For the liberal states, hold a Casino or Bingo night. If charity gambling is legal in your state, this is a good choice. People can gamble for cash or accumulate credits that allow them to bid on prizes or gift certificates donated by local merchants. If a cash bar is permissible, have one. The more enjoyable the event, the more money you will raise.

7. Raffles or auctions. Get your prizes donated by local merchants. The Salt Lake County Library mailed requests to over a thousand hotels and resorts asking for the donation of a free vacation for two. Twenty-four responded affirmatively. These packages were auctioned off at about 25-30 percent of their retail value.[4]

8. More thons. Telethons, Radiothons. Lots of volunteers are needed for dialing or answering phones and other behind-the-scenes work. You need guidance from entertainment professionals. The Altoona, Pennsylvania, Public Library used this format to win the first Gale Research Company Financial Development Award in 1983.[5] Ask a local fast food czar to provide burgers or pizza for your volunteers. Have a party when the day is over.

9. Celebrity sporting events or tournaments. Give people the opportunity to play golf or tennis with a local celebrity. Or have the library softball, volleyball, and basketball teams challenge a local TV or radio station to a game. Sell tickets to the game, handling the concessions yourself.

10. The bizarre or unique. Try off-the-wall ideas, usually frowned upon by staid board of trustees—they can work. One of the best I discovered was called "Faculty Foot Fetish."[6] Photographs of the feet of college faculty were displayed in the college cafeteria. Students cast votes by making a donation to the library on behalf of their favorite feet. The winning pair was crowned and connected to a face. The contest allowed the college library to purchase several expensive reference books.

Another unique event was called "The Fantasy Ball," sponsored by the Association for Family Living in Chicago.[7] This organization sent invitations to potential contributors announcing the following:

A white tie (and tight collar) affair featuring continuous (and crowded) dancing and a delicious (high calorie) buffet. BUT—you don't have to attend. No need to wear that tight tie...battle the crowded dance floor...regret those high calorie delicacies...

"Contribute to the organization instead," requested the invitation, adding that "the Fantasy Ball is only a fantasy—a wonderful way to escape a gala evening without escaping responsibility."

10 Ways to Increase Your Odds of Winning

1. Pretest your ideas with six or seven members of the public you will be trying to reach. Marketing experts call this a focus group. Run your plans by them, get their reactions. It is far easier for people who are not part of your organization to evaluate your ideas objectively. According to marketing experts, 24 out of 25 new products (e.g., underarm deodorants, lipstick, breakfast cereal, etc.) die in the pretest stage.

2. Write down your action plan. Make a detailed to-do list of tasks and the people who will undertake them. Don't assume everyone understands or is committed to their assignments—ask for feedback and suggestions *before* you proceed.

3. When you select a date and place for your special event, make sure there are no conflicts. It's very tough for people to come to your used-book sale if a big football game is on TV or a rock music concert has traffic tied up for 12 blocks in every direction. Also, nature's whims put a higher risk on most outdoor events.

4. Seek volunteer expertise from the community. Ask an ad agency about the appropriateness of your theme or graphic design. Have your local newspaper's food editor suggest the menu for your gala banquet. Consult a local bookseller about pricing any rare books you are selling. People are more committed to a project if they have a say in its development. If volunteers and staff are excited and committed to a project, their positive feelings will be passed on to the public you're trying to persuade to make a donation.

5. Depending on the magnitude of your special event, form an honorary committee and/or appoint an honorary chairperson, preferably using people with contacts in the community. Don't ask or expect them to make a major time commitment, but put their names on your stationery and ask for their ideas on reaching your financial targets. You'll be amazed how much easier it is to obtain donations and commitments when you have well-connected people saying a few words on your behalf.

6. Learn as much as you can about the psychology of giving. Know how to make people feel good about giving.

7. If you're going to ask local businesses to underwrite the cost of your special event, make sure you give them credit. Acknowledge their support as much as possible. Be ready to offer them something tangible in return, preferably something that may eventually help increase their sales.

Most of our special events showed a profit, but some of the events raised only enough money to treat our volunteers to lunch at McDonald's. Nevertheless, we made every effort to view these experiences in a positive light. In figuring out the net profit, we did the typical maneuver of not putting a dollar figure in the expense column for staff time. We did everything we could to avoid self-criticism: Why cut our own throats?

---

8. Select a clever but pertinent theme that is short enough to fit on a poster, be used in a ten-second public service announcement, and be remembered by library staff and volunteers.

9. Keep things moving. Tight schedules get people's adrenalin flowing. It's harder for people to duck an assignment if they know they'll be held accountable at your next meeting or if time is running short. Frequent discussions can also prevent minor headaches from becoming major obstacles.

10. Even if you have organized the biggest and best special event ever, it won't mean a thing unless you've mapped out a public relations plan to persuade and excite your audience. It's amazing how often people put off publicity and promotion until the other work is done. By then, it's too late!

10 Reasons Why People Give to the Library[8]

1. They are convinced there is an immediate and pressing need that affects them personally.

2. They helped in the past.

3. They have good childhood memories of the library and don't want their children to be deprived.

4. They succumb to peer pressure: "I gave, so should you."

5. They feel it's part of the responsibility that comes with being a good citizen.

6. They believe your event will be fun.

7. They get something in return, e.g., a library poster, a bronze miniature of the library, a book bag, a gold-plated bookmark, tickets to a benefit concert, a gift plate bearing their name in a library book.

8. They get personal satisfaction from contributing to a favorite service or collection.

9. They can deduct their contribution from their income taxes.

10. They receive public acknowledgment for their gift. ═

References

1. *SUCCESS STORIES, How 15 libraries raised money and awareness* (Chicago: American Library Association, 1983), p.22–25.

2. Scott M. Cutlip and Allen H. Center, "Persuasion & Public Opinion," in *effective PUBLIC RELATIONS* (Englewood Cliffs, N.J.: Prentice-Hall, Inc., 1978), p.134–135.

3. Harold N. Weiner, *Making the Most of Special Events* (New York: National Communication Council for Human Services, 1977), p.4–5.

4. "Northern Virginia Community College foot fetish contest raises funds," *Library Journal* (July, 1983):1304.

5. *SUCCESS STORIES*, pp.13–15.

6. "Salt Lake County fundraiser auctions off vacation for two," *Library Journal* (August, 1983):1412.

7. Harold N. Wiener, p.18–19.

8. Marian S. Edsall, *Library Promotion Handbook* (Phoenix: Oryx Press, 1980), p.17.

HOLDING A SUCCESSFUL REFERENDUM

Jane Morgan
Elizabeth Mueller

When a library referendum appears on a ballot, it is because a library board wants to "let the voters decide." There are several different kinds of library referenda, but the most common bond issues seek approval either to finance the purchase or construction of a library building or addition, or to increase a tax rate.

Typically, the idea for a referendum starts out as one of many options considered by the library board in planning future library services. Not until all of the alternatives are investigated and eliminated will the referendum become the "way to go."

This article was adapted from the series Trustee Facts File, *a project of the Illinois State Library.*

In the Richton Park Library District, dollars were needed as soon as possible to maintain our current level of service. We were in the midst of a building program which was going to add approximately 50 percent to our space *and* almost wipe out our interest-producing capital fund which had been accumulating for about 11 years.

The history of the public's acceptance of referenda was not a positive one. Twice since the creation of our library district in 1974 we had gone to the voters with a proposal for a bond issue to build a new facility, and twice we were defeated. When the village government moved to a new village hall in 1981, cooperative work between the library and village boards had made it possible to use village revenue-sharing funds, matched by library funds, to renovate the old village hall into a new library. However, after only three-and-a-half years in that facility, we had outgrown the space.

Since wise money management had made it possible for us to set aside a small amount each year, the library board approached the village board once again to ask for revenue-sharing money to pay for the new addition. For a second time the answer was yes. So an architect was hired, bids were let, old walls came down, and new ones began going up.

When Is a Good Time to Hold a Referendum?

Our need for more operating funds became acutely apparent when the addition was nearing completion. Although we had known a referendum was in our near future, the urgency of the need took us unawares.

The discussion was heated at the January board meeting. For the first time in our almost 11 years of existence we needed to ask for an increase in our authorized levy rate. We could all agree that we had reached a crossroads, but there was a difference of opinion on the timing. By the meeting's close we had come close to unanimity, and the motion for a referendum on April 2 carried. We all left the meeting with a common goal—to work as hard as we could to pass this much needed referendum to nearly double our currently authorized tax rate.

Typically, communities have specific times for elections. Technically, city, village, and township libraries must have their corporate bodies place their question on the ballot. In order to foster mutual respect and an amicable relationship with the library's taxing body, any serious discussion of a referendum by the library board should be reported immediately to the mayor, village president, or township supervisor. Of course, this extra step necessitates a longer time line for planning.

The ideal is to have the library issue by itself on a ballot, but the election schedule may offer only limited opportunities when that can be accommodated. Since there is nothing to prevent other taxing bodies from placing issues on the same date the library's corporate authority chooses, it is a good idea to check with those other bodies before the county certifies the ballot.

Times to avoid are election dates for voting for municipal and library boards, especially if they are hotly contested races. Otherwise, the referendum may prompt the candidates to take a stand for or against the library question. If at all possible, the initiators of a library referendum—normally the library board—want their issue to be nonpartisan or bipartisan. Nevertheless, if delaying a referendum from spring to fall means foregoing an entire year in tax dollars, the decision might be to move ahead, regardless of what else is on the ballot.

National elections in November of even-numbered years tend to overshadow efforts by any local taxing bodies. Yet, if a concerted effort is made by the library to buck all the partisan publicity and get the word out, November library referenda do pass. However, if there is a choice, November in the odd-numbered years is best.

Generally speaking, if the library board has to choose between a referendum date less than four months away and one eight or ten months away, it is advantageous to pick the later date. This gives the workers as well as the public more time to absorb the information. Sometimes a hasty decision gives the public the impression it is not carefully thought out. Still, local conditions may force a short timetable.

In Richton Park, we knew time was short. We knew that our already funded building program would confuse the issue. We didn't know the high school district would place three referenda on the same April ballot. We didn't know that Matteson, our next-door-neighbor village which shares a local newspaper edition with Richton Park, would place

Dollars were needed as soon as possible to maintain our current level of service. We were in the midst of a building program which was going to add approximately 50 percent to our space and almost wipe out our interest-producing capital fund which had been accumulating for about 11 years.

a village library building bond referendum on their ballot, putting them into competition with us for front-page space. Hindsight tells us we were rushing in where angels fear to tread—but *then* all we knew was that we had only 10 short weeks to organize, get our story told, and get the referendum passed on April 2.

Timetable

The campaign timetable is constructed in reverse chronology, working backwards from the referendum date. If letters or brochures are part of the strategy, both the mailing date and the approximate date of receipt are placed on the calendar. Even though the library board and staff will feel the information is old hat two or three weeks before the referendum, that is just about the time the general public really awakens to local issues. The board must take this into consideration when setting the schedule.

The Campaign Strategy

Most importantly, library board members must be aware of the laws governing referendum voting. In Illinois, for example, "No public funds shall be used to wage any electorate to vote for or against any candidate or proposition." This means the board cannot use tax money to urge people to vote for referenda propositions. How then can the public be made aware of the pros in a legal fashion?

The Richton Park library board distributed a one-page "Facts Concerning the Upcoming Referendum," which clearly explained the issues without using subjective phrases, such as "only $.05 a week," and without urging the reader to vote for the increase. At the same time the Friends of the Library, as the publicity arm of the campaign, paid for the printing and the distribution of literature that urged a "yes" vote.

If the campaign is going to be costly, it is best that the group bearing the costs be chartered as a not-for-profit public organization. This way donations made to them will be tax-deductible. Established Friends groups are a natural for the campaign. If, however, the Friends of the Library only are able to pay for bills and cannot participate in any other way, a concerned citizens group can be formed to run the campaign, prepare the copy, write press releases, and make door-to-door visits and telephone calls, etc.

Every well-run campaign has a campaign chair. This can be a board member, a concerned citizen, or someone from the Friends of the Library—*not* a paid staff member. The chair meets regularly with the board and library administrator to maintain communications. The public role of the library director throughout the campaign is that of a resource person, even though he or she may be the real organizer.

Every household eligible for the vote has to receive information about the referendum. In Illinois, it used to be permissible to use the list of library card-holders for referendum mailings, but the *Illinois Revised Statutes*, 1983, changed that. Library registration records now are considered confidential and cannot be used for campaign purposes. Most campaigns use voter registration records for a mailing list.

Once every household has received information on the upcoming referendum, the campaign workers concentrate on contacting the voters to determine whether or not they are "yes" voters. The objective is to have a list of "yes" voters completed one week before the referendum so that they can be called and reminded to vote the day before and from 4:00 p.m. to 6:00 p.m. on the day of the referendum.

The first action the Richton Park Library District Board took after agreeing to try to get a referendum passed was to inform the Friends of the Library of the decision, ask for their support, and request $200 to $500 from them. The second public action was the appearance of the library director at the village board. Since Richton Park is a library district, this was purely a courtesy call. However, by telling the village officials about the referendum ourselves, instead of the news coming via the grapevine or newspaper release, we took the lead. We tried to maintain that attitude throughout the campaign.

One week after our decision-making meeting, the library board sat down to brainstorm as a referendum committee-of-the-whole. The board president served as referendum chair and one of our number volunteered to act as vice-chair. We created a calendar of all anticipated pre-election activities.

Other important decisions were made at that first meeting. We would run an up-front, open campaign, getting as much information as possible to the voters. We would reach active library users; our target group of voters was current users of the library with cards no more than two years old. Since the public would probably only remember one major reason for our need, the main emphasis would be on maintaining and improving our level of service.

Our general plan was to get out the positive vote by making presentations at as many meetings as

possible, sending releases to local organizations' newsletters and the twice-weekly local newspaper, contacting local radio and cable TV stations, and hanging posters in the library and in local businesses. Our target group of voters would receive a mailing from the Friends of the Library and at least one follow-up telephone call.

If the library board has to choose between a referendum date less than four months away and one eight or ten months away, it is advantageous to pick the later date. This gives the workers as well as the public more time to absorb the information. Sometimes a hasty decision gives the public the impression it is not carefully thought out. Still, local conditions may force a short timetable.

A library newsletter sent irregularly to all Richton Park households would be delivered to each household in the village; it would highlight the construction program and the need for the money to improve services. We would make up packets of information for all phone volunteers, all current village trustees, and all library trustees. One trustee would make presentations at meetings with the library director available as a resource person. As many trustees as possible would also attend to validate the urgency of the need.

We made a list of former library board members to tap as a source to expand the referendum work force.

Then the following specific tasks were developed:

1. Construct a list of possible meetings at which presentations can be made—PTA's, homeowners' organizations, churches, service clubs, candidates' coffees, and senior groups. See if a list of organizations is available from the village hall.
2. Develop a presentation for the meetings.
3. Produce visuals to use at presentations.
4. Decide the contents of the information packet. Assign a member to research some figures on assessed home valuations to develop cost-per-home data.
5. Write a library board letter for Friends; a Friends letter for patrons; the library newsletter, newspaper releases, and a library letter for current patrons. Prepare the packet of materials for distribution.
6. Determine the best way to deliver written materials to voters—U.S. Mail, paid teenagers, volunteers. (As it turned out, in this comparatively small village of 10,000 it was more dependable and no more expensive to hand deliver most promotional material.)
7. Investigate radio and cable TV possibilities.
8. Locate statistics of the last comparable election in Richton Park to help determine the number of votes needed to pass the referendum. (The county clerk's office proved to be the proper place.)
9. Produce posters for display in the library and at local businesses. (Since taxes were involved, many local businessmen didn't want to display a large poster, but many agreed to put in their windows the 8 1/2 x 11 inch yellow VOTE YES flyer from the Friends of the Library.)
10. Develop a 1/2 hour training session for telephone volunteers.

Posters went up in the library and the volunteers' sign-up sheets went out on the desk weeks earlier than anticipated. The library staff encouraged regular users to sign up for one of the three training sessions scheduled two weeks before the referendum. We scheduled one in the morning, one in the evening, and one on a Saturday.

Our first presentation at a large PTA meeting was a learning experience. We were on the program along with the high school district making its pitch for its three referendum proposals. They had a slick 15-minute sound-slide program, a polished business administrator to make their appeal, and almost all department heads from their three sites there as visible support. In contrast, only our library director and two board members attended. Our unrehearsed presentation was given with a half-dozen overhead transparencies to illustrate various statistics. We died!

We went back to the drawing board. We realized we weren't using our biggest asset—the director. In this village he *is* the library. His sense of humor is widely known and his love for children is obvious even to the casual observer. The director became our main speaker, introduced by a board member with a few pertinent facts. A one-line graph which contrasted our income of the past three years with our soaring circulation figures for the same years was put on large poster board and displayed on the wall behind the director.

The high school agreed to let us present first at the three other meetings when we shared the program. It made a difference. The local cable company recorded our last presentation and showed it several times during the last five days before the referendum. By that time we were even pleasing ourselves.

Another idea came from the Friends group. They decided it would be good timing to hold their semiannual used-book sale in our almost completed meeting room on the Saturday before the election. It was a great success. Good will was generated, many tours of the new facility were given, and a lot of flyers were passed out.

The first newspaper article which covered the proposed referendum carried an interview with the library director who emphasized what the maximum increase in the levy rate might be. We took care after that to make prominent our promise to budget only one-third of the requested 1.4 million increase in our

next fiscal year. We determined as accurately as possible the per-household cost for homes of various market values and published these costs.

The real backbone of campaign strategy is identifying the hard-core "yes" voters before the referendum.

Once every household has received information on the upcoming referendum, the campaign workers concentrate on contacting the voters to determine whether or not they are "yes" voters. The objective is to have a list of "yes" votes completed one week before the referendum so that they can be called and reminded to vote the day before and on the day of the referendum.

All other activities are embellishments to the procedure. Snappy slogans are catchy; coordinated logos are attractive and appealing; slide-tape shows are helpful; but none of these can bring out the "yes" vote as well as the personal contact.

The number of registered library borrowers is very significant in referendum planning. A library serving under 50,000 people should attempt to have at least one-third of its residents using the library before holding a referendum. Sometimes this isn't possible, but waiting an extra year to increase usage before a referendum is announced may insure a successful vote.

Recent Referenda

If the recent record in Illinois is any indicator, referenda have a good chance of success. From July 1, 1982 to July 1, 1985 there were 20 public library referenda in Illinois pertaining to tax increases or bond issues. Of these, 13—65%—passed; 7—35%—failed. An increasing number of li-

brary issues are being placed on the ballot and this trend will probably continue because some of the perks that public libraries have enjoyed, such as revenue sharing, have disappeared.

As a result of improved library long-range planning, with master plans being developed in five- to ten-year segments, referenda fear is decreasing among board members. Then, too, the informed voter is able to follow the planning and can readily accept its logic. Naturally this places an increasing burden on the library administrators and board members to keep the voters informed.

The Voters Say Yes

On the Sunday prior to the election, the Friends of Richton Park placed a 10 x 3 inch column ad to "VOTE YES" in the local paper. It served as a reminder that the issue would be on the following Tuesday's ballot. The telephone volunteers did their work over that weekend, too, still encountering an amazing number of patrons unaware of the referendum activity. However, when urged to vote, they were happy to do so.

The vote was fairly heavy on Ballot Tuesday. At about 10:30p.m. we learned that the referendum had passed, carrying by a 798 to 506 margin. Only one of the high school referenda passed, and Matteson's building bond issue failed. Apparently we had done our homework.

Thank-you letters were sent to each volunteer within a week after the vote. Thank-you letters were also sent to the local newspapers as "letters to the editor." In this way the entire community was made aware of the number of people who actually volunteered their services to the library.

Would we do it again in the same way? Probably not. The time element is the real key. The rush of doing it all in a 10-week period was too much. Knowing a year ahead and organizing at least six months before election time would have provided the real advantage of time to plan and complete the tedious behind-the-scene preparations at a slower-than-breakneck pace.

At any rate, we would still advise others, "Make no small plans, organize, and go for it!" ═══

ALTERNATE FUNDING SOURCES
DIRECT MAIL CAMPAIGNS
Gail McGovern

Over one-third of philanthropic giving in the United States comes as a result of direct mail, which is why direct mail campaigns are such an important funding source for libraries of all types.

Direct mail is an intimate, person-to-person communication which commands attention by taking advantage of an individual's habit of reading and responding to mail. Direct mail is a proven way to reach people; it increases public awareness of services, attracts volunteers, and identifies and cultivates future givers.

The major disadvantages of a direct mail campaign are that it requires a sizeable investment of time and funds, it is complex to design, and it is a long-term process. The return rate is small and the cost of a mailing could exceed the amount raised.

Although the disadvantages may daunt the spirit at first, the benefits of a well-planned and executed direct mail campaign can make it worth the effort — 80 percent of all direct mail gets opened and one out of every three dollars raised by charities is the result of direct mail campaigns. And, the first year is just the beginning: the real financial success of a direct mail campaign are the repeat contributions made year after year.

Planning for the campaign is essential. Why do you want people to give? How will you use what they give? If you target your mailing and the language is clear and direct, your audience is likely to do as you ask. Typical campaign goals include: to increase the number of people who give; to increase the amount donors give; to raise funds for a specific project as opposed to operating funds; to increase the library's visibility in the community; to increase awareness of an issue or project; and to stimulate action, such as letter writing to legislators or attendance at a function.

Since a direct mail campaign asks people to give to your library, there are two important factors to consider before you design your mailing: why people give and what is impressive about your library.

Since people give based on the benefits they receive, design your mailing with these reasons in mind:

Commitment to the library — the library is an important part of the donor's life since the individual makes use of the services.

Support for the work the library does — the donor values what the library gives to the community, for example, a real estate broker uses library services as a selling point to clients.

To get something — the library may give pins or certificates or special privileges.

To win approval — the donor's friends will know the donor has done a good deed.

To belong — the donor wants to be part of a group such as Friends of the Library.

To share — the donor wants to give to those less fortunate.

Guilt — the donor wants to get rid of feelings of not doing enough or of having too much.

Use what you know about your potential donors in designing your mailing. To tailor the mailing, match the donor needs and interests with information about the library by choosing facts which will most interest and impress your potential donors. Think about how you can answer the following questions about the library and translate the information into your sales pitch. Include the library's strong points in terms of *benefits to donors*; stress any unique services.

Why does the library exist?
What services does it provide?
Which service is the most important?
What types of people does it serve?
What types of people volunteer?
Why do people use the library?
What is unique about the library?
What are the library's major weaknesses?
What issues are important to the library?
What could affect the library's future?
How has the library changed in the last five years?
How should the library change in the next five years?
What should the library's main sources of income be in the next five years?

Compiling the Potential Donor List

Your objective is to develop as large a house list as possible. A house list includes those who have already responded positively to the library. They may have given funds, volunteered time, or supported the library in other ways. You build the house list by using prospect lists — lists containing potential donors based on demographic or special interest lists.

To develop your first prospect list, ask staff, board members, Friends, and current donors to give you at least ten names of people they think would give to the library, excluding businesses or corporations. Add these names to the Friends of the Library list. Include names from other library data such as library card holders, attendees at book sales, film showings, story hours, etc.

Next, create your donor profile. The profile helps you identify prospective donors by categorizing the types of people who would be most likely to give to the library. You might include love of reading or books, occupation, education level, etc. You use your donor profile categories to identify other mailing lists to add to your prospects. You can swap lists with other libraries or community groups, or buy them based on donor profile categories.

Information about lists is available in *Standard Rate & Data Service-Direct Mail List Rates & Data*, which includes over 50,000 mailing lists. Entries contain title of list, name, address, phone of owner or broker, name of contact, description and arrangement of list, maintenance, quantity, price, specific identification of source of list, addressing selections, method of delivery, mailing services offered, and restrictions on use. Also included are brokers who can help you find the most productive lists for your purpose. Brokers play a similar role as travel agents; you do not pay them a fee. They provide information on renting and exchanging lists. The list rentals are expensive so your ability to recognize which lists will produce new donors is important.

Maintaining Your List

The system for maintaining your list will vary depending on its size, arrangement, and frequency of use. The list is only as valuable as it is accurate. You must update any changes of name and address as well as keep records of donation level — 20 percent of the people on your list are likely to move within a year. Keep a tally of the times of the year that address changes usually happen so that you can plan when you might need additional volunteer help. Think about assigning volunteers to locate lost donors. Decide on codes for Board members, special donors, those who do not want their names rented or exchanged, and other special groups. Also keep track of those who are interested in the library, but can not donate funds at this time. The rule of thumb for maintenance systems is manual (e.g., photocopy labels) for 1,000 names or less; plate (e.g., addressograph) for 10,000 names or less, and computerized for 10,000 names or more.

Designing Your Direct Mail Package

The elements of your package are an outside envelope, a letter, a reply device, and a reply envelope. If your budget permits, include a brochure. Your package is in competition with the barrage of appeals we all find in our mailboxes. The outside envelope must be eye-catching and enticing to convince the recipient it is worth opening.

In fact, the outside envelope is such a crucial element that most designers spend 40 percent of the package design time on it. If the reader doesn't open the envelope, it doesn't matter how appealing the letter is. Don't over-economize on envelope stock or color; you don't want your package to look like junk mail. Use a logo or symbol relating to the library.

The letter must seem like a personal communication. It should look personally typed and be easy to read. The first sentence must be so compelling that the reader will want to read the rest. Present a community need and describe how the library could help. Give examples of how

individuals in the community have been helped by the library. Explain how the donor will be involved, that is, what a contribution will do. Explain how to use the reply device and how much to send. Stress the need to respond promptly. Be sure to add a thank you. Have the letter signed by a well-known person — the president of the Friends or Library Board, a celebrity involved with the library, etc. Whenever possible include a "P.S." to emphasize a special point. Make sure the letter and all other materials are proofread carefully. Good proofreading will save you from costly — and embarrassing — errors.

The reply device and envelope can be combined into one — forming a wallet flap envelope. Although more expensive than a separate envelope, it eliminates the need for two separate items. The reply device should be easy to fill out and fit neatly into its return package. If your budget permits, use postage-paid envelopes.

A brochure briefly describing the library is a good supplement to your letter if your budget will permit it. Its style should be descriptive rather than the personal approach of your letter. Try to provide the reader with more information about the benefits the library adds to the community.

One way to save money in producing your direct mail package is to use volunteer help. Fund-raising consultants, graphic designers, community college or high-school students, printers, small businesses, and corporations may be willing to help. But no matter who is involved, be sure to work closely with them.

Keeping records of costs and tasks will help you control the entire process. Prepare a timetable like the one below and follow it closely:

Time Before Mail Date	Task
6 months	Define goals and set budget
4 months	Send copy ideas for price quotes
3 months	Work with list broker and order lists
2 months	Decide on final copy
	Get printing quotes and decide on printer
1 month	Send envelopes to be labelled

Have package mailed

Acknowledging Donations

Thank donors promptly. A simple card will mean a lot to a donor, but donors giving large contributions should be acknowledged with personally typed letters. Explore the possibility of having certificates, pins, or other recognition devices for large contributions.

Testing

Repeatedly try new approaches with small numbers of names. Some types of changes you can test are package format, paper quality, copy length or content, the benefits of library service that are highlighted, dollar amount requested, first class vs. bulk rate postage, and what time of year mailing is done. Compare your mailing to other libraries and community organizations.

Direct Mail As A Continuing Funding Process

Once you have captured donors there are ways to maintain or even increase their gifts in the succeeding campaigns: ask the donor to increase last year's amount by a specified percentage; allow the donor to spread payment of the increased gift over a number of months; inform the donor about how to move into a different category of giving by increasing last year's gift; establish a challenge match (where a wealthy individual, business or corporation pledges a certain amount provided it is matched by the total of other donor contributions).

For More Information

Direct Mail Fund Raising (San Francisco: Public Management Institute, 1980).

Sexton, Marie. *Direct Mail* (Chicago: American Library Association, 1984).

Standard Rate & Data Service-Direct Mail List Rates & Data (Chicago: Standard Rate & Data Service, 1985).

Tenbrunsel, Thomas W. *The Fund Raising Resource Manual* (Englewood Cliffs, N.J. : Prentice-Hall, 1982).

GATHERING GRANTS
Financial Boon or Bust?

Alice Gertzog

Some librarians have found the sweet experience of winning a grant soured by an unexpected cut of a comparable amount in the next year's funding allocation. These librarians warn that "grants may be hazardous to your library's health." In voicing their concern, they caution that a variant of Gresham's Law can occur in which bad money (in this case grants) chases out good (regular municipal funding support). How does this peculiar phenomenon work? What causes it? Can it be avoided completely? Or, if not, can its harsh results be softened?

To begin, let me pose a hypothetical situation. The Daedelus Public Library has identified the need for a collection of 1,000 new large-print books to place in ten senior citizen centers throughout the county. These new acquisitions will form the core of a rotating collection which will, after the grant

year, be integrated into the library's normal operation. The library submits a grant request to the Thanatopsis Foundation and receives $20,000 in support of the project. Proudly, Daedulus issues a press release to the local newspaper heralding the grant. The newspaper, in turn, gives the announcement prominent play on page three. At the next week's budget hearing, one Councilmember says: "I see by the paper that you have received a grant of $20,000 to buy books. Now we can save the town money; we'll reduce your budget by that amount." Quickly the other members of Council concur. "But . . . " you sputter, of course to no avail. Down comes the figurative gavel and you're out-of-pocket a sum commensurate with the amount you must, according to the terms of the grant, spend on large-print books. And your operating budget now sports a healthy deficit of $20,000.

Punishment or Reward in Exchange and Transfer

From the outset, I want to be clear about the fact that punishment at the fiscal trough is by no means a universal or automatic result of winning grant support. To the contrary, many librarians maintain that they are rewarded for securing outside sources of support, that their success in the private sector is mirrored by appropriation success within their community's funding stream. Some economists talk about the possible outcomes in "epidemiological" terms — that grants beget grants. Others refer to the "multiplier" effects. Grantsmanship books and seminars stress the importance of producing a track record in order to insure credibility. The question "What other grants have you been awarded?" often appears on grant applications. The ability to provide a respectable list of past awards enhances the chances of being awarded the one in prospect.

Noted economist Kenneth Boulding estimates that somewhere between 20 percent and 50 percent of the United States economy is centered around grants[1] and most students of the human services sector would support Roger Lohmann's assessment that "the realities of financing human services today mean that only a handful of agencies — the smallest, the most securely funded, and the least successful — can steer away entirely from the realities of grant financing . . . for all the rest, grants are an integral part of the capitalization process."[2]

Elliot Shelkrot, State Librarian of Pennsylvania, agrees: "We have to go where the funds are," he believes. "We cannot afford to be 'niche pickers,' to just find a safe, comfortable place to perch. As a matter of fact, we cannot afford *not* to apply for certain grants."[3]

When economists talk about grants, they define the term to mean a one-way *transfer* of economic goods. They contrast this with a two-way *exchange* — the kind of activity which happens when, for instance, you buy a product. More formally, they say "an exchange is a re-arrangement of assets of equal values among owners, but where the total net worths of the parties are not changed."[4] A grant, then, represents a gift which transfers net worth from the donor to the recipient. Boulding points out that while the exchange-transfer dichotomy is a useful model for looking at the problem, in reality there is probably a continuum in operation. A grant may resemble a budget allocation if the donor — for instance a municipality — regards the assets of the recipient — the library — as part of its own asset structure. The grant then may be more a rearrangement of assets among parts of a single organization than a true transfer.[5]

Grants to libraries and other human service agencies are generally program/project-oriented, rather than in support of an institution's operation. There is a substantial literature which describes how grants reallocate resources in a direction which a grantor finds desirable. Indeed, Boulding asserts that grants from foundations are usually devised to push recipients into activities they might not have otherwise preferred.[6] More subtly, procedural strategy often has important policy consequences for the recipient. Because programs supported by outside funding can be pursued at less financial sacrifice than unaided ones, policy choices must be carefully scrutinized. Grants may distort the expenditure patterns of agencies in unwanted ways, or they may pull funds away from programs because of matching requirements.

Although we have spoken of grants as part of a transfer, rather than an exchange, economy, we must be aware that exchange is always present — at least in the form of psychological and social demands made by the grantor and the agreement to meet these obligations by the grantee.

Legitimate Purposes for Grants

Shelkrot identifies what he sees as four legitimate purposes for allocating LSCA grants, and places them under the following shorthand rubrics: accelerator, capital venture, visibility, and development. All are project-oriented and of short-term duration. All serve to further the Pennsylvania State Library's objectives for quality library service in the Commonwealth.

An *accelerator* grant provides an opportunity for a library to try a program, to see whether it is useful, and to work out the kinks. This type of innovation is generally integrated into the library's main program if the results are found to be positive.

Capital venture grants give libraries a chance to build, buy, install, and promote seed money for an endeavor which would otherwise be impossible. Grants for *visibility* make it possible to undertake a project which will put the library in the limelight, giving it a more favorable position down the road. *Development* grants help a library get ahead; for instance, to plan a program to educate trustees, influentials, and community leaders to the library's goals and needs.[7]

A typology for viewing grant effects rather than uses is offered by political scientist Deil Wright, who employs the terms stimulative, additive, and substitutive to describe different financial outcomes of outside funding.

A *stimulative* grant is one which has the effect of raising for its recipient unit more financial support than a required matching amount. For instance, a matching grant to set up a literacy program within a library may be so favorably viewed within a community that it attracts a number of generous donations, or, alternately, increased municipal funding.

An *additive* grant is one which increases expenditure by the amount of the grant or the required match, if there is one. The *substitutive* grant is one which Wright calls interchangeable. Substitutive grants should be feared by librarians. Wright illustrates substitutive grants by describing how federal funds intended to create new jobs and ease unemployment were used to hire temporary laborers while at the same time permanent state-paid laborers were terminated.[8] Revenue sharing has been accused of being "substitutive" and of producing similar results. Many communities which have transferred essential services — fire, police, libraries — to revenue-sharing budgets fear the termination of the program since they will be hard-pressed to find local funding to cover the deficit that will be created. As of this writing, the Reagan Administration, with Congress concurring, has slated Revenue Sharing for termination in 1987.

Why do some grants culminate in substitutive outcomes rather than in stimulative, or at least additive ones? Michelle Ridge, Executive Director of the Erie County Library System, comments pointedly. "They (the funding bodies) understandably look for any possibility of shifting the financial burden to someone else's shoulders and will seize any opportunity if it is offered."[9] David Wendtland, City Manager of Meadville, Pennsylvania, puts the burden on municipal agency grant-seekers rather than on funding bodies. He feels that grant applications should focus on ways to reduce operating expenses while improving service. He finds least productive the grant which expands service and which may mean additional future operating costs. According to Wendtland, if a new service is introduced through grants which subsequently must be municipally funded, the agency (library) will have then to decide which services it must provide and which it can do without.[10]

A Fair Share May Not Include Grants

Wendtland's argument rests on an assumption which may help to explain why some libraries experience difficulty with grants. Aaron Wildavsky, whose 1974 study of the national budgetary process is still considered by many to be the definitive work on the subject, looks at how the fair-share concept works among federal agencies. Agencies, he says, work on a base — those funds which are relatively secure or taken for granted as belonging to an agency on the basis of past practice. Fair-share, however, relates not only to the base an agency has established, "but also the expectation that it will receive some proportion of funds, if any, which are to be increased over or decreased below the base of the various governmental agencies. *Fair share, then, reflects a convergence of expectations on roughly how much the agency is to receive in comparison to others."* [11]

In other words, the community's notion of fair share is made manifest during the budget process. An agency which appears to be the recipient of more than its share of material wealth — a "fat cat" — will be squeezed back into its proper shape in the next fiscal cycle. Shares of the community pie can be increased or, alternately, decreased. But this has to do with tradition, long-standing relationships, and incremental change. Budgets are not only plans of action for communities; they are a reflection of its norms and culture. Unfortunately, there is still much about community dynamics which is both subtle and little understood.

At this point some examples may serve to illuminate the problem. For obvious reasons, and to protect the innocent, the communities and libraries shall remain nameless.

A county library system found itself the recipient of the state's largesse in the form of a supplemental, unexpected (read unbudgeted) state-aid check. The commissioners in this county were not in the habit of revising an agency's budget once adopted. Both the revenue and expenditure bottom lines were considered inviolate. The additional state aid was, therefore, substituted for county funds on the revenue side of that year's library budget. Not suprisingly, the County found other uses for its own money. State aid in this locality, as it is in many others, is based on LFE (Local Financial Effort) for the previous fiscal year. Since the county's contribution during the period in question was less than it would have been if the supplemental state aid had not surfaced, the library/county lost many thousands of dollars from the state during the following aid period.

When four different library agencies were awarded a cooperative federal grant to catalog newspapers, the grant included funds to hire eight new people — two for each agency — to carry out the project. One

agency's funding body had instituted a freeze on hiring, making it necessary for the agency to request an exemption in order to employ the two workers, despite the fact that with the outside funding for salaries it would cost neither the agency nor the funding body any new money. The exemption was allowed. But the head of the agency is convinced that the Exemption Board thinks it has given his agency a *real* exemption from the freeze and permitted it additional manpower. They don't understand, he believes, that special project personnel (as opposed to permanent operating employees) should not count.

━━━━━━━━━━━━━━━━
━━━━━━━━━━━━━━━━

Many communities which have transferred essential services—fire, police, libraries—to revenue-sharing budgets fear the termination of the program since they will be hard-pressed to find local funding to cover the deficit that will be created.

━━━━━━━━━━━━━━━━
━━━━━━━━━━━━━━━━

Perhaps the most blatant example and saddest story emerges from one middle-size community library. Enterprise, skill, and a certain amount of good luck combined to make available funds to build an addition, enlarge and totally renovate the children's room, and install a much-needed elevator. When the project was completed most observers agreed that the library was a jewel in an otherwise down-at-the-heels community. The region was suffering severe economic dislocation, including high unemployment and failing businesses.

Anticipating words of acclaim from this triumph and for the library's contribution to the community's well-being, the librarian sud-

denly found herself with a $25,000 budget shortfall in the City Council's allocation and she was repeatedly admonished by Council members to seek funding elsewhere. Boon had turned to bust and she was being punished for her success.

Guidelines for Avoiding the Hazards

What is to be done? It is probably inevitable that outside funding will have some unanticipated consequences, at least from time to time. After all, as Herbert Simon says, we live in a world of bounded rationality, and we cannot know what will result from our actions. But some of the potential negative impacts can be contained. Here are three guidelines:

Try to anticipate the economic effects of each grant, from the smallest to the largest. Since a grant is essentially a redistribution of net worth, it is likely to set in motion all kinds of behavior and reverberations that will involve further change.

Boulding says "grants increase the net worth of the recipients by far more than the grant . . . A single grant echoes and reechoes through the system as it changes people's behavior, and it is often hard to predict what the total effect will be." [12] Certain outcomes may be suggested initially, but when the total impact is considered, the exact opposite may prove to be true. It is often assumed that all grants viewed as investments will have positive economic ramifications. As we have seen, positive impact may not always occur. In some instances, grants may indeed produce a negative impact.

Be aware of the cost of grants. Michelle Ridge warns that there is *no* grant which does not involve expenditure of local operating funds. Some grants (LSCA, for instance) do not permit the inclusion of indirect costs in the request. Typical overhead costs, including supplies, furniture, equipment, and insurance must be considered. If these costs are not allowable, the requester must decide whether the administrative costs in time, energy, and accounting make the grant worth pursuing. Remember that a funding agency can take funds away; that grants must be renegotiated periodically; that guidelines may be revised; and that demonstration projects generally have set limits on the number of years for which funding may be received.

It is almost axiomatic that grant funds should not be sought for general operations. Foundations and other granting agencies do not find these requests exciting. More importantly, the temporary life of grants renders requests for general operating funds short-sighted if not downright fool hardy.

Keep funding bodies informed. The word co-optation may have some negative connotations, but the process of co-opting — which includes planning, accountability, and to a lesser extent marketing — describes the best defense against the potential hazards of grants. Although it is useful to take advantage of grants when they appear, an application should emerge primarily from an *identified* and anticipated need and should be consistent with the goals and objectives of the library. If a library has shared its short-term and long-range plans with its funding agency, and if it can point to an objective or objectives which the grant will help to achieve, its position is strengthened.

Assuming an available grant has met the criteria of addressing an objective or an identified need, and the library decides to seek it, the next step is to gain the approval of its funding body or bodies — before making the formal application. The request for approval should be accompanied by careful and complete documentation.

Wildavsky admonishes agency representatives to establish credibility and community confidence in two ways. First, by "being what they think *they* are." What he means is that funding bodies think of themselves as efficient, effective, devoted to their work, and careful with taxpayer's money. They think of themselves as aboveboard, fair, square-shooters, and frank persons. Libraries should communicate that they too share these traits. Secondly, by "playing it straight." Wildavsky considers lies, misstatements, and deceptions as poor strategy. Playing it straight with funding sources should, over time, produce a relationship of mutual trust between grantor and grantee, one that will substantially enhance the bargaining position of the agency and simplify the negotiating process for everyone.[13]

If the grant application is successful, and the grant awarded, the library should request the funding body to *endorse* acceptance of the grant. Approval is no longer sufficient. This is a crucial step in the prevention of a grant becoming substitutive rather than additive or stimulative. Leave no room for the claim of ignorance or misunderstanding of the nature of the award. Endorsement means that the funding body, at least tacitly, accepts the terms and obligations of the grant. In effect it says: "We agree to accept the responsibilities which this grant carries for our agency." To try to exchange grant money for local money now represents a betrayal of its word. Needless to add, the funding body should be routinely made

---

"Warning: If taken in incorrect doses, and without proper safeguards, grants may be deleterious to the health of your library."

---

aware of the grant's progress.

On receipt and acceptance of the grant, the public must be informed. Accountability as well as marketing of the project demand this step. Since the media are the prime transmitters of the information, it is important that reporters, editors, et al., understand what the grant is for — as well as what it is not for. Here, language is crucial. Avoid jargon, assume public ignorance, and eliminate unnecessary detail. Always affirm the additive nature of the project. Constantly play up the separation between the grant and the general operation of the library.

Facts Needed

In preparing this article, the lack of substantive research on the subject of grant impacts became clear. There is an ample supply of documentation on available grants, as well as on the grantsmanship process (the "how to" and "where to"), but little has been written about the financial impact (short-term and long-range) of grants, and what there is focuses on the effect on local communities or target audiences, rather than on agency budgets. Research is needed. It would be relatively easy to document changes in budgets following receipt of grants. An investigation into the relationship between the nature of a community — the extent of its cosmopolitan orientation, its history, size, socio-economic condition — and its response to grants might provide interesting results.

A consideration of whether private funding diminishes traditional public funding could lead to a larger, perhaps more significant, question: Does a library which is predominantly privately funded fare better or worse over time than one which receives the bulk of its funding from public coffers?

These are important matters which should be addressed. Perhaps if we had more facts at hand, library grants would not need to have a familiar admonition attached: "Warning: If taken in incorrect doses, and without proper safeguards, grants may be deleterious to the health of your library."

References

1. Kenneth Boulding, *A Preface to Grants Economics* (New York: Praeger, 1981), p. 2.
2. Roger Lohmann, *Breaking Even* (Philadelphia: Temple University Press, 1980), p. 64.
3. Elliot Shelkrot. Interview. July 11, 1985.
4. Boulding, p. 1.
5. Ibid., p. 4.
6. Ibid., p. 10.
7. Shelkrot.
8. Deil Wright, *Understanding Intergovernmental Relations* (North Scituate, Mass., Duxbury Press, 1978), pp. 141-143.
9. Michelle Ridge. Interview. June 19, 1985.
10. David Wendtland. Interview. June 20, 1985.
11. Aaron Wildavsky, *The Politics of the Budgetary Process* Second edition. (Boston: Little, Brown, 1974), pp. 16-17.
12. Boulding, p. 10.
13. Wildavsky, pp. 74-77.

Did you know that since 1983, one out of every four government publications has been eliminated?

WRITING A WINNING GRANT PROPOSAL

Irene E. Moran

Awarding funds is the reason grant-making programs exist, and their administrators are anxious to receive proposals that meet their program's interests—your library's success is their success. A well-written proposal may increase your prospects of winning a grant, but success depends on a variety of elements. Above all, you must design a carefully conceived program to meet a clearly defined goal. And you must present that program to the right funding source at the ideal time.

Over $4.5 billion in foundation grants and $3.4 billion in corporate grants were awarded last year.[1] That is no small amount of money, and libraries have a good chance of getting at least some of it. The New York Foundation gets 500 requests a year, but makes only 80 grants, of which only 20 — or four percent—are to new projects. Other New York City foundation executives have placed the figure at anywhere from six percent to 10 percent.

In fact, there is no guarantee that you will win a grant even if you fulfill the grantmaker's requirements; the one you target may have committed all available funds, or may be currently supporting a similar program, or may have decided to switch to another field of interest. Still want to try it? Welcome to the world of grantseeking.

Identify and Document

Working with the overall set of goals or objectives that guide your library's activities, you should have no difficulty identifying important areas that have funding potential. You know the community you serve—whether it is a student body or an urban population. You know the community's needs and how the library could address them with the proper funding. You have anticipated future roles for your library as well.

Since grants are usually made for specific programs or projects rather than for ongoing support, this is your opportunity to take a chance, to experiment, to be creative and innovative. Libraries receive grant dollars for buildings and equipment, acquisition of library materials, computerization, cataloging, circulation and reference services, microfilm, bibliographic projects, special exhibitions, unique programs, and more. On the basis of your particular situation, determine which possibility should be given priority. Then document the need, establish the objectives the proposal will address, determine how the projected effort will reach those objectives, and begin to ask questions:

What kind of personnel will be required?
What will they do?
What money will be required?
How will it be allocated?
Is our library the best organization to handle the proposed project?

Do we have the expertise to make it successful?

Can we—should we—work with another institution?

Will this project duplicate what another agency is already doing?

If several library staff members are working on the same proposal, have them put their ideas in writing and then discuss and analyze them. Ask the hard questions that a potential funder will ask and keep a record of the answers. A review of this background material is vital when the time comes to write the proposal, especially if the writer has not been involved in designing the program. No matter who writes the proposal, a project can change its shape as it is being developed, and it is a good idea to refer to these changes in order to clarify the proposal's final configuration.

Find a Source

Only when you have defined the project can you begin looking for a foundation, corporation, or government program that shares the same interest. It cannot be repeated too often that a big part of the secret to writing a winning grant proposal is finding the funding source that is right for your project. Foundations, corporations, and government programs have very specific goals and objectives. Be sure to expend your efforts so that your proposal will pass this initial hurdle: estimates show that the number of grants rejected because of inappropriateness for the funding source ranges from 50 percent to 80 percent.

Librarians have a head start in researching these vital connections because of their ready access to research tools and their knowledge of where to get them. In addition to the obvious sources (*The Foundation Directory*, the *Foundation Grants Index*, The Foundation Center's COMSEARCH printout on Libraries, *Marquis' Annual Register of Grant Support*), many state foundation directories are also available.

If you have access to one of the Foundation Center's regional libraries, you can do additional research on targeted foundations. Their 990-PF forms which list the names and addresses of officers, their assets and investments, and every grant made during the year covered by the re-

port are available for examination on microfiche. Many foundations issue annual reports and/or guidelines. A growing number of corporations are using application forms as well, which provide additional details on their goals, as well as specifics on how to proceed.

Since 90 percent of corporate philanthropy is dispensed at the local level, do not overlook local or community foundations, utilities, businesses, or financial institutions. One of a growing number of corporate-giving directories, *The Corporate Fund Raising Directory*, reports that the top 500 corporate givers have over 12,000 operating locations (headquarters, subsidiaries, affiliates, plants) around the country.

Grantmakers' major restrictions are usually based on geographic location and field of interest. It would make as little sense for a college library in Iowa to approach a corporation which only gives to causes in Georgia as it would for a library to seek support for a continuing education program for older adults from a foundation which is only interested in medical research.

The size of grants foundations fund varies. If your program requires a $25,000 grant, don't count on a funder with a range of $1,000 to $5,000 unless you plan to put together a consortium in which each member will receive the maximum allocation.

Timing is another critical factor. For instance, if a grantmaking board meets once a year—and it met last month—you may have to wait for the next funding cycle. Or, if your

---

RESOURCES FOR FUNDRAISING

The Foundation Center
79 Fifth Ave.
New York, NY 10003

Public Management Institute
358 Brannan St.
San Francisco, CA 94107

Public Service Materials Center
111 N. Central Ave.
Hartsdale, NY 10530

The Taft Group
5125 MacArthur Blvd., N.W.
Washington, DC 20016

Whole Nonprofit Catalog
The Grantsmanship Center
1031 S. Grand Ave.
Los Angeles, CA 90015

---

project has to start in September, and a decision on funding will not be possible until November, you will have to look elsewhere.

Don't limit your research to grantmakers that give or have given to libraries. Search the subject indexes, and if anything sounds remotely promising, dig deeper! Weed out those foundations or corporations that seem unlikely targets and gather as much information as you can on those that seem to have potential. Keep records on all funding sources you locate—a funder that is completely wrong for your current project may be precisely the one you will need in the future.

Writing the Proposal

Some of the basics of grant writing can be learned through the many books and periodicals on your library's shelves and by attending seminars and workshops on proposal writing, but personal experience is the best teacher. Proposals are not easy to write: they have to be concise, precise, detailed, and exciting. Requirements vary. A large foundation may specify a page limitation, while a small foundation may want only a long letter.

Ideally, the individual who has designed the program will also write the proposal. If someone else is assigned the writing, make sure he or she has access to all the background materials mentioned earlier, as well as input from the originator. Most important is to assign a person who can write well.

The writing must be clear, sincere, enthusiastic, fresh, eager. Tell the story of your project with brevity and simplicity and avoid library jargon. Foundation executives like proposals that use positive, expressive, action-oriented words in short sentences and paragraphs. Detail what the program will do for its intended audience—not for your library—and how it will meet the goals of the grantmaker. Write the proposal so that it appeals to specific funders. According to Madeline Lee, Executive Director of The New York Foundation, there is always room for creativity and maneuvering, but she cautions that you should never lose sight of your objectives just to get a grant.

The guidelines provided by grantmakers themselves are probably the best source for writing a good proposal. Typical are the requirements detailed by The Coca-Cola Foundation in their guidelines:

- a description of the project, the sponsoring organization and its mission;
- a description of the need, target group and timetable;
- an explanation of why funding from The Coca-Cola Foundation would solve a problem, as well as meet a need;
- a current, itemized budget of the project and sponsoring organization;
- the total project costs, other sources of funding, and the amount requested of the Foundation;
- a list of current directors and paid staff;
- a method of evaluation should the organization receive funding;
- evidence of your library's current tax-exempt status.

Whether you use guidelines or create your own, you must include several critical ingredients. These are the letter of inquiry, cover letter, title page, table of contents, program summary, introduction, problem/need statement, program objectives and methods, timetable, future funding details, evaluation, budget plan, and appendix.

Letter of Inquiry. Some foundations request a full proposal; others only want a letter of inquiry first. The letter of inquiry should clearly establish the relationship between the goals of your proposal and the grantmaker's objectives and show how your interests mesh. The letter should briefly describe your library, the project, and the amount of funding requested. Be sure to indicate whether you are asking the foundation for the maximum amount or only a part and if you are seeking funds elsewhere as well. Ask if you may submit a full proposal. (The response will vary—from a form letter saying no, to a postcard saying your letter is under consideration, to a call asking for more information or the encouraging, "Yes, we'd like to see your proposal.") The signature on the letter should be the library's top manager—not the director of the project or the development officer.

Cover Letter. This is your letter of transmittal. If the proposal is being forwarded in response to a funder's positive answer to a letter of inquiry, be sure to mention it. If this is your first contact, include all the information you would have put into the letter of inquiry and attach the proposal. If an official application is required, affix it to the cover letter unless otherwise advised.

It cannot be repeated too often that a big part of the secret to writing a winning grant proposal is finding the funding source that is right for your project. Foundations, corporations, and government programs have very specific goals and objectives. Estimates show that the number of grants rejected because of inappropriateness for the funding source ranges from 50 percent to 80 percent.

Your earlier research should have revealed whether you or a staff person or board member knows any officers of the organization. If you can personalize the cover letter in this way, do so. But never abuse a relationship by assuming that if you have a contact, you will get a grant—and that you don't have to prepare a solid proposal.

Title Page. Supply the name of the project—making it descriptive of the program—the name of the institution, the name of the foundation, the date of submission, and the name, address, and telephone number of the library's contact person.

Table of Contents. Unless you have a brief proposal of four or five pages, you should provide a table of contents for the reader's convenience. Check the final document and make sure that the page numbers agree with the contents and that the appendix items are correctly identified in the text.

Program Summary. This is the re-

fined, carefully honed description of what your library intends to do with the requested funds. It should contain a brief description of your institution and its role in the community; explain the problem you have identified and how you propose to solve it; specify the cost and the time frame. As you work to give a clear, concise description of your program, you may find the summary needs reworking and refinement. There may be an aspect you overlooked which strengthens your proposal or a segment you want to deemphasize, or your goal may shift slightly, especially if you find that by stressing certain factors you will appeal more to the grantmaker's goals. Don't consider the program summary finished until the proposal is ready to be mailed.

Introduction. This is where you establish identity and credibility. Tell your institution's story: its history, goals, mission statement, resources, services, and role in the community. If your library is part of a university, a consortium, or a network, explain the relationship. Include current statistics; describe your program of overall service and the community you serve; detail your priorities and objectives; identify your key personnel. Keep in mind all the stereotyped images of libraries that appear in the media—if yours is a library where quiet and silence are found only in the dictionary, make sure you convey that picture. Supporting data—charts, letters of support, printed materials—should be included in the appendix. When you describe your funding needs give assurances that if you are given money you will supervise its expenditure. Your balance sheet and other financial reports should be referred to and also included in the appendix.

All of this material can be reused as a boilerplate for future proposals, so keep it current by periodically revising the statistics and any salient points. The one variable added to the boilerplate will be an explanation of how the funding you propose fits into the library's overall operation. Whether it's an outgrowth of historical service or a new direction—show its relationship to the total program.

Problem/Need Statement. What you identified when the program was first conceived is covered here: the need on which you based your decision to move ahead with a grant request. Detail, substantiate, and clearly define the problem, citing appropriate statistics. If the problem is national in scope, show how it affects your individual community. If it is a local situation, document that.

Include facts and figures, but also humanize the need; bring the situation to life for the reader. One foundation director said that "real experiences and concrete statements are so rare you want to fund them regardless." If you can, append letters of appreciation as well as letters of support.

Show how your library is ideally suited to move into the situation and change it. You may improve access to information or increase the hours when all students can use the resources of your institution. But show that there is a situation which needs attention. If something is already being done, show that you know about it, and explain how your plan is different, or innovative, or handling a different aspect.

Program Objectives and Methods. The majority of authors of books on grant writing advise readers to present the objectives and methods separately. I prefer a joint section that details what you intend to achieve and how you mean to do it. Objectives cover the specific, measurable results of your program; methods describe how you will achieve each of the objectives. It is more impressive and comprehensive when these subjects are addressed as a unit— showing cause and effect. And so you should describe the program or project you want the grantmaker to support, incorporating the objectives and methods, and show that the program or project is timely, practical, and unique, and that it complements the grantmaker's goals.

When you enumerate the objectives, be specific and show a definite action. Many library programs don't readily lend themselves to measurable results. For example, you can't really measure how much a particular program will increase awareness or promote interest in some important topic, but you can design a project that will reach 500 people. Numbers are important, but they must be realistic. Don't promise more than you can deliver just to make the proposal sound impressive. If you do get the grant, you have a commitment to realize the objectives.

Detail the methods by which the library plans to reach its objectives and satisfy the need. If there are a variety of possible approaches, explain why you selected the one you did. For instance, is it more cost-ef-

> *The writing must be clear, sincere, enthusiastic, fresh, eager. Tell the story of your project with brevity and simplicity and avoid library jargon. Foundation executives like proposals that use positive, expressive, action-oriented words in short sentences and paragraphs. Detail what the program will do for its intended audience—not for your library—and how it will meet the goals of the grantmaker...never lose sight of your objectives just to get a grant.*

fective, or quicker to implement, or a proven success elsewhere? Convince the grantmaker that yours is the way to do it. Substantiate your staffing choices by explaining each individual's suitability for the particular assignment, but do it briefly; detailed biographies belong in the appendix.

Timetable. Detail here how your project will proceed, specifying what will be achieved and when. Be sure to allow time for the funding to be in place. If a corporate contributions committee will not make a decision for three months, don't anticipate starting the program in two months.

Future Funding. Grantmakers want the programs they fund to succeed, but they don't want to support them indefinitely. Many foundations only provide support for a maximum of three years; they are not the answer for the long haul. If yours is a self-contained project or a one-time expenditure, future funding may not be involved. But if it is a start-up program or a long-range project, be prepared to accurately appraise where future funding will originate.

If you are confident that a successful demonstration project will secure continuing funds, say so; but if you cannot assure a continuation of the project and plan to seek additional grants from outside sources, indicate that. A funder who believes in your program may be able to suggest other sources for you to approach.

Evaluation. It is important to build a plan that judges your program's effectiveness. Maintain "before and after" statistics. Evaluating appreciation is difficult, but attendance records or circulation statistics are concrete evidence. If feasible, invite the benefactors of your program to assist in its evaluation. If your program will serve as the model for similar programs in other libraries, incorporate professional dissemination through the library press or conference programs.

Budget. Don't pad the budget, but don't think too small, either. What do you realistically anticipate needing to achieve the proposed results? Follow your library's normal budget outline and include the costs of the entire proposal—salaries, benefits, consultant fees, materials and equipment, supplies, facilities, publicity, and indirect costs. Most grantmakers will want copies of the library's overall budget along with your sources of support.

If your library can absorb much of what might be project overhead or administrative responsibility, be sure to state that. If another funder will be assuming part of the costs, clearly delineate who is paying for what. For instance, a foundation may frown on paying for a reception, although you think it essential to the program. But if you are able to line up a corporation to pay for the reception, let the foundation know. This will show how enterprising you are, and how well you understand the foundation's guidelines.

Appendix. Include here all of the facts and figures referred to in the body of the proposal, but which would have interrupted the flow if placed there. For example, latest financial statement, a list of board members and their affiliations, biographies of key personnel, letters of support, photographs/drawings, and a list of other foundations you have or will contact. If you have a fairly respectable record of grants, include that as well. Some fund makers specifically request a copy of your audited financial statement or a copy of your tax return.

Questions Grantmakers Ask

The following list of guidelines from the "Contributions' Policy" brochure of the American Honda Foundation are typical of the scrutiny your proposal will receive. Consider them before sealing the envelope:

- Does the request fall within the scope of the American Honda Foundation's guidelines and grantmaking policies?
- Are the objectives and programs of the organization seeking funding clearly defined and reasonably capable of achievement?
- Does the program have merit?
- What is the specific need of this agency as related to the particular problem it seeks to address compared with the needs of other similar programs?
- Are the organization's objectives and programs supportive of the public and the interests of American Honda Motor Co., Inc.?
- Does the proposed activity serve a needed function, without the creation of undesirable program duplication?
- Where will the program be and what is planned in the next three to five years?
- Has the organization and its leaders demonstrated, by past accomplishment, an ability to fulfill the stated objectives and successfully implement their programs?
- Is the organization both efficiently and ethically managed?
- What is the maturity and competency level of the administrators of the program or agency?
- Who is on the organization's Board of Directors?
- Does the organization have an active governing Board and support from the community?
- What is the financial status of the organization and what are the sources of its income? Does it have a broad base of support?

Proofread the entire proposal carefully for typing errors, incorrect appendix references, and the spelling of names and titles. Foundation executives are annoyed by typos—if you are not exacting with an important proposal, how much attention will you give the project? When the package is completed have everyone involved with it review it. Review it yourself a day or two after you have finished it. Invite critical reading of it; don't be antagonized by questions—if you haven't made a point clear, now is the time to find out.

After the Proposal

Your efforts don't end when the proposal gets into the hands of the potential funder. If there is interest in your proposal, you may be called for additional information or be invited to visit and discuss the project in more detail. The funder may request a site visit—to see the program in action, if it already exists, or to meet with the key personnel on location.

If you get the grant, acknowledge its receipt and determine when you are to receive payment. Be sure to maintain the proper records, since reporting requests are not unusual.

Some funders ask for a narrative report at the end of the year; others want more frequent contact. Your funder will advise what financial reporting is required. Ask about publicizing the grant; although some grantmakers do not want their name mentioned, others have no objection and are eager for public acknowledgment.

Keeping the funder informed about your progress is very important. Send copies of press releases and newspaper articles, invite your contact to any special programs, advise the grantmaker of any problems, such as having to shift funds from one part of the budget to another or encountering higher printing costs than anticipated.

Don't make any major change from the original proposal without consulting your funder, and above all, don't decide after you get the money that you would rather use it for something else! You have a commitment to spend the grant for the purpose for which it was made.

If you don't get the grant, keep trying—you knew the odds were long when you started. If the grantmakers respond with anything more encouraging than a "thanks but no thanks" form letter, maintain your contact. Let them know if you get the project funded elsewhere. Send them an annual report. Most of these grant-making organizations will be around the next time you have a proposal to submit, and next time might bring the right mix to win you that most satisfying of rewards—winning a grant to implement a project for the people your library serves. ▬

Footnotes

1. *GIVING USA*, Annual Report 1986. (New York: American Association of Fund-Raising Counsel, Inc., 1986).

HOW TO LOOK A GIFT HORSE IN THE MOUTH
Saying No to Donations

Kathleen Raab Huston

Librarians often have more reasons to say no to a gift than yes. But saying yes is easier so they often end up with many books they don't need. Or even want.

Why should librarians ever say no? Wouldn't most libraries welcome a copy of a rare first edition? Probably. But most offers aren't so valuable. More common are the humble but plentiful books which are, after all, the staples of our collections. Librarians can say yes to them for many reasons: to build a collection, to replace worn copies of old favorites with fresh copies, to fill gaps with out of print books or to sell them.

But there are also many reasons to say no, and saying no takes more preparation, more diplomacy and more professional finesse than saying yes. In the end, common sense and good judgment must be trusted when the final decision is made.

The following outline should be used only as a guide, because in the area of gifts there will always be exceptions. Among the reasons for saying no to gift books or other items are the following:

Investment of staff time or effort exceeds the value of the gift. As a rule of thumb, the cost of acquisition and processing should not exceed the value of the collection.[1] Library directors and staff must remain vigilant about the hidden costs the gifts may bring with them. When time to sort, check holdings, process, catalog and acknowledge the donation is added up, the cost in staff time and effort may far outweigh the value of the gift.

The gift doesn't meet selection criteria. This, of course, assumes that your library *has* a selection policy with carefully developed guidelines for including or excluding particular types of material.

For example, the director could explain to the potential donor that the library's goal of providing a balanced collection doesn't permit it to have as many books on one religious sect as the donor wants to give.

The gift doesn't fit the library's collection development plan. If your library emphasizes recreational reading, don't accept a scholarly collection of books and manuscripts on the Middle Ages. A collection development plan guides the materials selection policy. It includes the library's mission and lists such pertinent factors as population, community demographics, availability of other resources in the area, and emphasis of the collection.

The proposed gift collection does not mirror community needs. A Midwestern library that has devoted dollars and space to a collection on the Great Lakes may not want a collection about Atlantic passenger ships. For example, the Milwaukee Public Library houses the Wisconsin Marine Historical Society Collection, with thousands of documents and photographs about Great Lakes shipping. When the society was offered more than 200 models of aircraft carriers and ocean going vessels, the library and the society agreed it was not appropriate for the collection. Staff is assisting the donor in finding a more suitable home.

Strings are attached. This may be the most compelling reason not to accept a gift because a web of strings is often sticky enough to be a long-term trap. Donors may ask that the collection be kept intact, housed in a special room with staff and clerical support, or even volunteer their own services to organize the collection. In these cases, the library administration must consider the long-term consequences. There are many sad stories of library directors who have accepted large gifts with housing or circulation restrictions who eventually wished to adjust the terms but found that they were legally bound by the original agreement. Legal advice should be sought in the case of large gifts if there are even minor restrictions.

Other strings may specify display or access. In some cases a donor may request that the material be displayed in a certain area, as did the man who gave the Milwaukee Public Library a large rusty anchor from a sunken freighter. Such requests present space problems. Worse, they require the library to yield its decision-making prerogatives.

In other cases there may be access restrictions: books are not to circulate, or are to be used only by members of the group which donated them. A writer or politician may give papers that may not be used until after the donor's death. If the papers are of value to the library, this restriction—to protect privacy—is neither unusual nor unreasonable. Limits on physical access, however, must be carefully studied, particularly in public libraries which have a tradition of providing open access to all.

The gift doesn't fit the library's long-range plan. If the mission of the library is to meet the informational, educational, cultural and recreational needs of the community, almost any gift would qualify. However, if the library board has identified "improved service to business in the community" as an important goal in the library's five-year plan, an offer of letters and manuscripts from a local poet would not be nearly as attractive as a collection of annual

Saying no takes more preparation, more diplomacy, and more professional finesse than saying yes

reports from a local company.

The age of the collection may be a factor. Librarians should probably decline out-of-date reference books, encyclopedias, travel guides, textbooks and the like.

The material is more appropriate for another library or agency. Even if the donor means well, accepting a gift which belongs elsewhere may result in bad public relations, hurt feelings and inconvenienced patrons. For example, a county historical society in Wisconsin had a collection of letters and papers from a decreased politician. The public library was approached and asked to accept several archival boxes of additional letters and papers. It did. The director of the historical society was furious, the patrons of both institutions were inconvenienced by having to do research in two places, and the donor, well intentioned when he gave his gift, was perplexed.

The political or public relations price is too high. The Grafton Public Library board in Wisconsin recently accepted a $250,000 donation toward a new library building. There was only one string attached: the donors stipulated that the library be named the "U.S.S. Liberty Memorial Public Library," after a U.S. Navy spy ship which was attacked by Israel in 1967. The donors said the gift was a way to honor the 35 men who died in the attack. But because the name had become a rallying symbol of anti-Semitism, it started a community uproar.[2] In this case, the library board might have considered the political or public relations costs too high to accept the money.

The material is in poor condition. All librarians carry damp, moldy books in their olfactory memories. Once a book has been so perfumed, it should be discarded, unless it has very special value. Placed on the shelf, its condition will spread to other, previously uninfected books. Insects are also contagious and books with signs of insect damage—or with the insects visible—should not be accepted. Finally, "brittle" books have become more and more common. Books printed on paper made of wood pulp are acidic and will eventually crumble and flake. There is little point in accepting brittle books unless you plan to photocopy them to preserve the contents before discarding the book. Such action might be warranted when the title or material will supplement a strong collection your library holds. This is especially true in the area of local history. In some cases it may even be wise to employ a deacidification process to prevent further deterioration, though this is expensive.

The collection is too large. Every library has, or eventually will have, space problems. Count shelves, figure the consequences of having to shift other parts of the collection, and be aware that a large gift may also require additional file cabinets, shelving units or map cases—equipment which may need to be purchased from an already strained budget. Apply selection criteria and consider the collection development plan before accepting Mrs. O'Brien's 800 cookbooks.

The library doesn't need the gift. National Geographic magazines may be high on this list. Best sellers from five years ago in Book-of-the-Month Club binding and condensed books may be a close second. Certainly these items could be welcome if you regularly sell books. But if your fiction librarian already has two decent copies of *The Robe*, don't add another.

How to Say No

All the public relations skills you or your staff can call upon may be needed when turning down a gift. If your library has made it known that you welcome donations, it may be difficult to turn away a patron bearing boxes overflowing with unwanted books. In some cases it might be necessary to accept an unwanted gift, ask the donor to sign the Gift Form (more about this later), and then quietly enforce your right to dispose of the gift.

It is important to say something positive about the gift while turning it down gently. One approach might be to begin by saying something like, "Why thank you, Mr. Coover, this is a marvelous collection of Harvard '37 textbooks. You know, unfortunately, the library just isn't able to accept any more textbooks, but we would certainly like to have them for our sale shelf." Mr. Coover, who can't bear to throw a book away, is happy. You've acted as the intermediary between Mr. Coover and the patron who buys the book, who presumably will also be pleased. If no one buys the books, the library can discard them after a suitable length of the time.

In refusing a gift, be polite and be direct and be sure to give the patron the opportunity to save face. Be sure, also, that in refusing today's National Geographics you don't also refuse next year's gift of a first edition. Have ready a list of agencies in your community which accept gift books. Hospitals, nursing homes, senior centers, and jails or prisons come to mind. Used book dealers, auction houses and agencies such as St. Vincent De Paul and Goodwill Industries are others. Special libraries, historical societies and academic libraries are further possibilities.

Also, be ready to negotiate. You may wish to say yes *and* no—yes to part of the gift, and no to another. A box with scrapbooks, photo albums and a set of Civil War books may yield a welcome addition to your U.S. history shelves while the local historical society may be pleased to have the scrapbooks and albums.

Consider the psychology of the donor. In most cases, a donor is interested in disposing of the books for one or more of the following reasons:

1. The books are no longer needed or of interest.
2. The donors need space.
3. The donors have recently inherited a collection they don't want but can't bear to throw away.
4. The donor wants a tax deduction.

In most cases, the donors don't want the material and won't be offended if the library helps them get

Librarians should probably decline out-of-date reference books, encyclopedias, travel guides, textbooks, and the like

rid of it gracefully or, at least, without guilt.

Above all, don't offend donors. Some time in the future, the donors may have something to give that you'll really want—perhaps money—and it is important that they remember their experience with you and the library favorably.

Who Says No

It is very important to have one person in charge of making the final decision about large gifts. It may be the branch manager or head of branch libraries. In a community with just one library, it is likely to be the director. In an urban library system, it may be the acquisitions librarian, the director, or the head of the central library. Many members of the staff, however, may become involved in the decision process. Subject specialists should be consulted about materials which fall within their area of expertise. Those who make the decisions should be familiar with the library's mission, its selection policy, its space and staff limitations and its long-term goals.

Large or significant collections should be brought to the attention of the library board for consideration, because there may be expensive consequences to consider. When the Milwaukee Public Library accepted the archives of the bankrupt Chicago, Milwaukee, St. Paul and Pacific railroad, much thought was given to such issues as where in the building the collection would be located, how it would be stored and who would process and index the thousands of papers, photographs, business records and memorabilia which measured more than 2,000 cubic feet. All those issues had to be

resolved before the library board granted approval.

A written gift policy is crucial when gifts are rejected. Such a statement might read:

Gifts of materials are accepted by the library with the understanding that the disposition of such items is a prerogative of the library. At the discretion of the Board of Trustees, the library may occasionally accept some gifts with restrictions imposed. Gift books are added to the collection if they meet the selection criteria established for purchased books and have some merit in the collection.[3]

When deciding whether to say yes or no, ask the following questions:

1. Is it needed?
2. Is it wanted?
3. Will it be used?
4. Will it enhance the collection?
5. Does the value exceed or offset the cost of adding it?

If the answer to all five questions is yes, then accept it. If the answer to any of the questions is no, consider carefully.

As library director, you may want a collection of books on antiques because antiques are your personal passion. However, the library may not need the collection, it won't be well used and won't enhance the rest of the collection, and your bias will be obvious to your staff. It is probably better to say no.

Sometimes patrons don't give the library a chance to say no. Often books are "donated" in a book drop. A patron may leave a grocery bag full of paper-back romances at the

A simple gift form such as this one should be signed by the donor and kept by the library when a gift is accepted.

MILWAUKEE PUBLIC LIBRARY

Gift Presentation Form

These printed materials are presented to the Board of Trustees of the Milwaukee Public Library to be used at their discretion.

Donor's signature _____

Name _____

Address _____

Phone number _____

No. of boxes _____

Agency where donation was received

_____ Date _____

circulation desk. In such cases the library can do whatever it pleases with the books.

Proud authors, particularly vanity press authors, may mail in unsolicited copies of their books. A library has no obligation to add, or even to acknowledge, such gifts.

Saying Yes

There are also right ways to say "yes."

Once again, have a selection policy, collection development plan and gift policy in place.

Have a donor form and use it. File it and give the donor a copy. The form can be very simple (see illus.). It should include the donor's name, the date of the gift, and a description of the items donated. Most importantly, it should include a statement signed by the donor which gives the library full rights to use or dispose of the material.

Do not attempt to place value on the gift. If the collection is substantial and the donor wishes to take a tax deduction, the donor should retain an appraiser. Evaluating for tax purposes is complicated. The library should limit its role to accepting the gift. Tax laws change often, and if a gift has significant value the donor may wish to consult an attorney or the Internal Revenue Service. The IRS has recently issued two publications dealing with this issue: "Charitable Contributions" (Publication 526, Revised November, 1987) and "Determining the Value of Donated Property" (Publication 561, Revised December, 1987). According to the latter: "The value of books is usually determined by selecting comparable sales and adjusting the difference between the comparable sales and the item being evaluated. This is difficult to do and, except for a collection of little value, should be done by a specialized appraiser."[4]

Follow up with a letter of acknowledgment and thanks to the donor. File a copy. Again, this letter may be quite simple but should be inclusive. Written on the library's letterhead, the letter should identify the donation, indicate its usefulness to the collection and say thanks for the donor's generosity. The donors may also be acknowledged with a book plate if their items or collections merit one.

Gifts to libraries are important for collection development, to supplement the book budget and to encourage community interest and involvement in the library's mission. While conventional etiquette dictates that one shouldn't look a gift horse in the mouth, it is only prudent for the library staff to examine carefully all the consequences of any gift. Otherwise, the so-called gift may become an expensive, unwieldly or unwelcome acquisition. ▬

References

1. Dole, Wanda V. "Gifts and Block Purchases: Are They Profitable?" *Library Acquisition: Practice and Theory*, 7(3), 1983, pp. 247–254.
2. "Petitions Oppose Proposed Name for Grafton Library," The Milwaukee Journal, May 23, 1988, p. 3.
3. Milwaukee Public Library, Collection Development Policy, 1988, p. 4.
4. Department of the Treasury. Internal Revenue Service. "Determining The Value of Donated Property," Publication 561, (Revised December 1987), p. 6.

SALARIES
MATTER

SALARY MATTERS

Betty J. Turock

A "gloomy career" is how the July 1986 issue of *Working Woman* describes librarianship, citing it as one of the 10 worst careers for women in 1986. Over 100 years ago, women were encouraged to enter the library profession as a source of plentiful, educated, cheap labor. Half a century ago, *Library Journal* first chronicled the issue of competitive salaries. Today, we are still facing the dilemma of how to recruit and retain library professionals given the depressed salaries paid to MLS graduates.

Nancy Van House has documented that the return on the investment in an MLS degree does not generate enough income to balance its cost. If the MLS were purely a financial investment, she concludes, students would do better to bank the money and go into another line of work. Try to argue that these findings show that librarians are not concerned with income and Van House demonstrates in another study that the number of MLS graduates is a function of starting salaries. While many librarians may enter the profession for reasons other than salary, low salaries do reduce the total benefits of being a librarian, which in turn affects recruitment and retention.

Salary comparisons put the final clincher on the urgency of the issue. According to *The New York Times'* 1986 annual occupational supplement, earnings of librarians with five years' experience are lower than the beginning levels for new graduates with *bachelors'* degrees in mathematics or science. While these graduates inch closer to a $30,000 beginning salary, new MLS graduates are making $19,753.

It is easy to see why math and science majors are not attracted to librarianship. It's also becoming clear why we cannot find sufficient numbers of children's librarians and catalogers to fill job vacancies.

If you think the importance of beginning salaries has been magnified unreasonably, let me share a personal survey with you. At the beginning of each semester I gather some data on my students to find out where they see themselves in 10 years. One question asks them what career in librarianship they want to pursue and why.

Over the past three years the answer that was first a whisper (8% of the students) is now a shout (over 50%): the primary career choice is the information profession *outside* of librarianship. The reason: better salaries.

Our profession is losing some of our best and brightest. These students cannot be dismissed as yuppies who are uninterested in upholding our long history of dedicated professional service. Theirs are voices that must be reckoned with.

Herb White points out an escalating impatience with salary levels among working librarians as well. Librarians are agreeing as never before, he assures us, that salaries—the ultimate validation of the esteem in which we are held—undervalue our profession and its contribution to the fundamental fabric of American life.

In the latest membership survey to determine priorities for ALA's action agenda, salaries were a top priority for 72 percent of those responding. There is certainly general agreement that salaries are too low, but solutions seem hard to come by.

Setting a minimum salary is one proposed corrective—albeit controversial. Thought by many to be a compelling course of action, it has been stalled and stalled again within ALA. The latest effort at the 1985 Midwinter Conference brought with it a rehash of old arguments and added some new bromides to give the ALA Council enough ammunition to reject the approach one more time.

The reasons for and against a minimum salary have been equally devoid of factual underpinnings. Although there is a common feeling that "something" must be done, like setting guidelines, there has been no agreement that ALA should assume this responsibility. Failing to find a common point for action, Council passed the buck back to the state chapters. Since then, six states have adopted recommended minimum salaries: Connecticut, Iowa, Massachusetts, New Hampshire, New Jersey, New York, and Vermont.

This hardly represents a ground swell. Why the lack of minimum salary recommendations? It is obviously not the result of disinterest or ignorance of the historical and theoretical implications. Rather, it indicates the need for workable guidelines. Even New York, with the best of intentions, did not think through the process wisely. The state has tied its minimum to that of teachers even though there is ample evidence that accepting teachers' salaries as a standard is not very different from using the high-end of current librarians' income. Since both professions are gender-typed, their salary standards are influenced not only by market forces but by the culturally determined patterns of unequal compensation in those occupations where women predominate. In the long-run the comparison will very likely *perpetuate* lower salaries in New York.

ALA must accept responsibility on this basic economic issue. If the states are to be a point of action for effecting change in librarians' salaries, they need leadership in finding the basis for an equitable standard. The six states that have set minimums can supply substantive evidence on the consequences. They are fertile ground from which to find answers to such questions as: What constitutes a good minimum? How does it affect librarians' salaries? Where does the money come from when higher salaries result? Does comparison with other professions induce greater pay equity? With what profession should we compare ourselves? How can we insure that minimum salaries are kept up to date? How can we document the need for a minimum salary to our constituents?

We must end the cyclical debate and begin rational progress toward pay equity. Since ALA's membership has decided to invest its resources in working to raise the salaries of librarians we had better do it right—before the future of the profession is seriously jeopardized.

THE FISCAL IMPACT OF PAY EQUITY

Helen Josephine

For most working women, being in the job market doesn't pay. Women earn the most in professions where men predominate—operations research, law, engineering, medicine—but they earn less than their male colleagues. Women predominate in the low-paid occupations—clerical, retail sales, health services—and yet, even in these lower-paid occupations, they still earn less than men.

Stanford University economist Victor Fuchs in an article on sex differences and economic factors concludes that "for women to earn as much as men they would have to behave like men with respect to subjects studied in school, choice of jobs, post-school investment and commitment to career."[1]

The major changes in public policy that would help narrow the earnings gap between men and women—subsidized child care, allowances for women who have children, comparable worth programs, and paid maternity leave—have not been fully implemented. Comparable worth programs are probably the most controversial. And, it is in the professions where women predominate—like librarianship—that the issues are most crucial.

Pay equity, comparable pay for work of comparable value, and comparable worth are all terms used interchangeably to describe the concept of setting salaries not by the predominant gender of workers in a field, but by the experience, responsibility, education, and skill required to perform the job.

What are the choices for those who have already invested themselves and their education in a career in librarianship? How much does it really cost to implement comparable worth? How much does it cost not to?

To realize the full fiscal implications of pay equity, costs must be calculated in three ways to determine: the actual dollar amount needed to raise salaries to equitable levels; the cost of litigation, back pay adjustments, and possible union actions if pay equity is achieved through legal channels; and the loss to the profession of the best and the brightest as qualified professionals seek employment in other fields.

The earnings gap between women and men persists despite enactment of the Equal Pay Act of 1963 and subsequent executive orders. The problem is the result of gender-based occupational segregation and sexually discriminatory salary-setting procedures. The Equal Pay Act covers only those positions where men and women are doing exactly the same work but are being paid differently. Occupational segregation and gender bias in salary setting are much more subtle and much more difficult to document. But their effects are not germane to women alone. They are felt as much by men as by women in librarianship because the wages of *all* workers in female-dominated professions are lower than those where males have historically formed the bulk of the workforce.

Legislate, Litigate, Negotiate

The three main methods for achieving comparable worth are litigation, legislation, and negotiation. It takes an average of five years for a lawsuit to be heard by the courts; before any salary adjustments are made, one side usually appeals the decision, adding another three to five years to the process.

In those cities and states where comparable worth is part of a negotiated contract, the time between the introduction of the concept into the collective bargaining process and the implementation of adjustments is usually less than two years. Historically, when comparable worth has been legislated, the time between the introduction of legislation and its implementation is also less than two years.

Regardless of the jurisdiction, the process of achieving pay equity in the public sector has some common elements. The first step often involves conducting a job evaluation. This kind of study is frequently spearheaded by a state commission on the status of women, or by a labor union or employee association. (The state of New Mexico is an exception. There, $23 million was appropriated to upgrade the lowest paid job titles in the state government workforce without first having completed a job study.)

One of the first steps in designing a job evaluation study is to set up a joint labor-management advisory committee to monitor the process and review the results. The second step is implementation, which usually requires that employees pressure management to accept the results of the study and to negotiate for salary adjustments. In some cases, litigation (Washington State, Los Angeles, and Connecticut) and union actions (San Jose, California) have been used as pressure tactics.

In general, comparable worth adjustments are phased in over a period of several years. Gradual budget adjustments provide time for program review and allow for changes in the implementation process. Further negotiations for subsequent adjustments can be made once the contract term expires.

The Comparable Worth Project has estimated that 19 cities and school districts and 37 states have initiated some form of comparable worth action.[2] In many cases lengthy job evaluation studies were performed, in other cases lawsuits or EEOC actions were filed, and in still other cases labor union strikes were called or the issue was part of collective bargaining.

Laws have been passed, court decisions have been rendered — but are we any closer to comparable worth as an accepted principle?

A study sponsored by the National Committee on Pay Equity (NCPE) attempted to assess the cost to public and private employers of implementing pay equity; it shows that, for the most part, private industry has adopted a wait-and-see attitude.[3] The NCPE identified six private employers who have implemented pay equity as a result of lawsuits or lawsuit-related settlements and 56 companies that have implemented pay equity as a result of collective bargaining. None of the six private employers were willing to cooperate with the NCPE study, and only one company representative of the collective bargaining settlements was included. Based on interviews with 15 private employers, this report shows that companies are committed to paying fairly as a good business practice only if they can remain "competitive" in the marketplace.

The report also shows that in some instances, private employers don't want to admit that a bias exists in their salary-setting policies for fear of future litigation. Others are concerned about internal equity—paying fairly within the organization, and external equity—paying fairly in the context of the marketplace. Some believe that comparable worth will be federally legislated eventually, but prefer to achieve equity in salaries by fully integrating job classes through recruiting and training of women and minorities. Overall, accurate cost estimates for pay equity implementation in the private sector are not available because companies are unwilling to share information about salaries and salary-setting policies.

Led by women, workers in the public sector have been organizing and demanding salary adjustments based on comparable worth for over ten years. The comparable worth issue made front page news when city employees in San Jose, California,

went on strike in 1981. After the state of Washington lost a comparable worth case to the American Federation of State, County and Municipal Employees (AFSCME) in 1983, and was ordered to pay back-wages as well as make salary adjustments, comparable worth became a well-known phrase. With less notoriety, Minnesota passed legislation in 1982 that included a timetable for implementation of comparable worth and a process for increasing salaries. And in 1985 the city of Los Angeles negotiated a precedent-setting agreement which used comparable worth as a basis for setting wages for city employees.

The Minnesota Example

The history of Minnesota's success in achieving pay equity begins with the studies and reports on the status of working women issued by the state's Commission on the Status of Women. In 1981 the commission became an official legislative advisory body—the Council on the Economic Status of Women—and included state legislators, representatives of employee unions and associations, and prior to 1983, the public. The pay equity recommendations made by the council resulted in passage of comparable worth legislation in 1982 which included a timetable and process for implementation. Documentation for the wage disparities came from a job evaluation system developed by Hay and Associates and the state's Department of Employee Relations.

The procedure established by law for making the required pay adjustments involved four steps[4]:

1. By January 1 of odd-numbered years, the Commissioner of Employee Relations submitted a list of female-dominated classes in which salaries are less than other classes with the same number of Hay points. Also submitted was an estimate of the cost of full salary equalization.

2. The Legislative Commission on Employee Relations recommended an amount to be appropriated for comparability adjustments to the House Appropriations Committee and the Senate Finance Committee.

3. Funds for comparability adjustments were appropriated through the usual legislative process. These funds were within the salary supplement, but were only used for salary equal-

ization according to the job classes on the list submitted to the commissioner. Any funds not used for this purpose reverted back to the state treasury.

4. The funds were assigned to bargaining units based on the number of underpaid classes they represented. The actual distribution of salary increases was negotiated through the usual collective bargaining process.

Implementation of pay equity in Minnesota was phased in over four years by increasing the state's payroll budget by one percent each year. Initially $21.7 million was appropriated to cover the first two years. In addition, the usual cost-of-living increases were given to everyone.

Inaction in Washington

In contrast to Minnesota's efforts, inaction by the legislature in Washington has cost the state more than four percent of its annual payroll budget to correct salary inequities. In 1974, the state commissioned a comparable worth study of 121 selected job classes. Performed by an outside consultant, Willis and Associates, the study found that employees in classes where women are predominant were paid about 20 percent less than those in comparable predominately male classes. Each time the study was updated (1974, 1979, and 1980) the findings were reconfirmed. However, no steps were taken by the state legislature to correct the inequities. In 1983, nine years after the completion of the original study, and only after AFSCME had filed a lawsuit against the state under Title VII of the Civil Rights Act, the state legislature appropriated $1.5 million to *begin* wage corrections and gradual implementation over ten years. Workers whose jobs paid at least 20 percent less than the average rate of compensation received $100 ($8.33 per month) for the year July 1984–July 1985.[5]

In September 1983, Federal District Court Judge Jack Tanner found Washington State guilty of "direct, overt, and institutionalized" discrimination against employees in the predominately female job classes. Judge Tanner further ruled that the court could not adopt the 1983 action by the Washington state legislature as the appropriate remedy.[6] In its appeal, the state estimated the decision could cost $838 million to cover immediate wage corrections to employees, pay adjustments retroactive to September 1979, and increased costs for pensions and other benefits that vary with pay levels.

While Judge Tanner's decision was under appeal, AFSCME prodded the state legislature into appropriating $42 million in June 1985 for implementing pay equity. After the judge's decision was overturned and AFSCME decided to appeal, the state agreed to begin negotiation. A $106.5 million settlement was agreed to on December 31, 1985—12 years after comparable worth was first raised as an issue in Washington State. Under the terms of the settlement, employees in specified classifications will receive $46.5 million between April 1986 and July 1987 and an additional $10 million each year thereafter through 1992.

Negotiation in Los Angeles

The struggle for pay equity in Los Angeles began in 1981 when EEOC charges were filed by AFSCME alleging wage discrimination against female employees in the city's salary structure. The union did a preliminary study of salaries in 1982 which documented a high level of sex-segregation and wage disparity in the city's workforce. After a year of negotiation, the city and AFSCME reached an agreement in May 1985 on pay equity adjustments averaging 26 percent over a three-year period.

The contract includes pay equity adjustments for clerical classifications ranging from 10 percent to 15 percent, to be paid in four adjustments: April 1, 1985; July 1, 1985; July 1, 1986; and July 1, 1987. Annual salary increases for clericals averaged $5,000 per year and for librarians $6,000 per year. The salary increases cost the city $12 million — one-half of one percent of its annual $2.1 billion budget.[7]

The Cost to Implement

The costs of salary adjustments based on comparable worth vary considerably depending on differences in numbers of employees, recommended adjustments, and the timetables for implementation. However, the overall figure is clearly higher if a lawsuit is filed and employees are awarded back-pay as well as future salary adjustments. For example, Minnesota's implementation costs are an estimated 1.25 percent of the personnel budget for the 1983–85 biennium, while in Washington State, the cost for back-pay and current adjustments is estimated at over 25 percent of the state's payroll. Implementation costs for Los Angeles are .05 percent of the city's total annual budget.[8]

The costs of achieving comparable worth in libraries is similar to those for jobs in other classifications. Most library employees—both professional and support staff—are women. Wages in these classes are 20 percent less than comparable classes where men predominate. Once established, comparable worth policy must remain part of the salary-setting process or all gains will be lost when negotiated contracts expire.

Pay equity adjustments are usually negotiated as an addition to cost-of-living adjustments. In the public sector, they have ranged from 14 percent (Berkeley Public Library) to 19.2 percent (Chicago Public Library). Adjustments are occasionally made over a two-year period ranging from 12 percent (Los Angeles Public Library) to 15 percent (San Jose Public Library).

Events at the University of Connecticut illustrate pay equity adjustments in academic libraries. Librarians there are among the non-faculty professionals' bargaining unit, represented by the University of Connecticut Professional Employees Association. Library assistants, archivists, computer programmers, student service personnel, nurses, and other employees are included in this unit. A job classification plan was first proposed in 1979 to create an entirely new system of payroll titles and an equitable pay system. The study, completed in 1983, was based on recommendations outlined by Douglas MacLean in "Development of a Classification Plan and a Related Pay Plan," and the criteria established by Hay Associates—skill, responsibility, effort, and working conditions.[9] After further adjustments, including a review of library positions, equity salary increases were announced.

In July 1984, almost half of the library staff received an equity increase; other library staff were reclassified or promoted. Most increases ranged between $1,000 and $2,500, although some were as high as $3,500. A total of 131 employees received equity adjustments. The university's new salary schedule has 12 groups; library classifications fall between group one, University Library Assistant 1 (starting salary $14,000) and group ten, University Assistant of Associate Librarian (starting salary $27,026). Group ten also includes computer programmer analysts and engineers.

To alleviate the problem of salary compression — employees with years of experience but now at the minimum level of their salary group — an additional $200,000 in salary increases was distributed. Those with more than 10 years of service received 69.1 percent of the total money available. In all, 130 women and 29 men received adjustments, with maximum increases of $2,000.

The bargaining power of UCPEA and the inclusion of all nonteaching faculty in the same unit to create a larger base for the study accounts for the success of the university's salary adjustment and job reclassification plan. Helen Lewis, president of the UCPEA, noted that during the scoring of library positions for reclassification, librarians had to explain the nature of library work and overcome the stereotypes and assumptions associated with libraries and librarians.[10]

Based on prior cases in public and academic settings, we can come up with a scenario for a comparable worth salary adjustment in a large library with a total operating budget of about $5 million (excluding expenditures for acquisitions). By increasing the total operating budget by $600,000—less than 10 percent—the salaries of 200 professionals and classified staff could be raised. All staff members would receive a $1,000 comparable worth adjustment added to their base salaries, bringing salaries closer to comparable job classifications. An allocation of $300,000 would allow for a $500 cost-of-living adjustment and a $1,000 comparable worth adjustment; or the implementation could be phased in over two years.

The cost of not implementing pay equity is growing daily. In most areas librarians are receiving cost-of-living increases, but these are added to a base salary that does not reflect the education, experience, or expertise required in the position. The result is a continued depression of salaries for librarians. Increasingly, library administrators are finding it difficult to hire qualified candidates, and enrollments at many library schools are down.

In *Library Journal*, Herbert White poses the question, "Why don't we get paid more?"[11] Although he is not convinced that achieving pay equity

---

PAY EQUITY RESOURCES

Comparable Worth Project
Center for Labor Research and Education
University of California, Berkeley
Berkeley, CA 94720

National Committee on Pay Equity
1201 Sixteenth St., N.W., Rm. 422
Washington, DC 20036

Office for Library Personnel Resources, ALA
50 E. Huron
Chicago, IL 60611

Pay Equity Trends
A National Newsletter on Pay Equity Developments
Hubbard & Reno-Cohen, Inc.
1810 Michael Faraday Dr., Suite 101
Reston, VA 22090

---

through legal action or threat of legal action is the best strategy, he does concede that "if the drive for legal solutions to our pay dilemma has a particular positive emphasis it is that it disposes once and for all the myth that we are paid so little because our employers cannot afford to pay us more." White goes on to say that while "nobody is required to hire librarians, or for that matter to have libraries . . . if they do, then those with fund-raising authority have the responsibility for finding the money."

The responsibility for convincing those with fund-raising authority to raise salaries lies with librarians—we must work to change the perception of libraries and librarians. As White says, "We will change the perception when we take ourselves and our roles more seriously, and when we concentrate on economic issues just as other professions do."

Librarians are beginning to discuss the shortage of professionals in their field in articles and letters to the editors of the library literature. Librarians who once filled the ranks of children's specialists have found that other fields are now open to them, most of which pay $2,000 to $5,000 more per year if they invest in a master's degree. Catalogers, science reference/subject specialists, and business reference/subject specialists are becoming more difficult to find for the same reason. The special expertise required in these positions is liberally rewarded and valued in other institutions where the jobs no longer have the title of librarian attached to them.

As positions remain unfilled, what are the options? Will administrators tough it out until a candidate is found or will they, as White suggests, lower their requirements and hire whoever they can get for the salary offered? What must we do to improve the salaries of librarians?

As administrators, we should make equitable salary ranges our first priority. As librarians, we must bring the issue of salary inequities to the public and make them aware that attracting the best and brightest to library service is to their advantage. How much an institution—whether public or private—is willing to pay librarians is directly influenced by the value they assign to their services, which in turn is influenced by the value librarians place on their professional worth. How willing are we to make equitable salary treatment a priority for action? ▬

References

1. Victor Fuchs, "Sex Differences in Economic Well-Being," *Science* 232 (25 April 1986), pp. 449–464.
2. *Who's Working for Working Women?: A Survey of State and Local Government Pay Equity Initiatives* (Washington, D.C.: National Committee on Pay Equity, 1984).
3. *The Cost of Pay Equity in Public and Private Employment* (Washington, D.C.: National Committee on Pay Equity, n.d.).
4. *Pay Equity and Public Employment* (Minnesota Council on the Economic Status of Women, Task Force on Pay Equity, 1982).
5. Helen Remick, "An Update on Washington State," *Public Personnel Management Journal* 12 (Winter 1983), pp. 390–394.
6. *Pay Equity and Comparable Worth* (Washington, D.C.: The Bureau of National Affairs, 1984).
7. Helen Mochedlover, "Special Issue on Pay Equity," *Communicator* 18 (May–June 1985).
8. Karen Shallcross Koziara, "Comparable Worth: Organizational Dilemmas," *Monthly Labor Review* 108 (December 1985), pp. 13–16.
9. Douglas MacLean, "Development of a Classification Plan and a Related Pay Plan," *Journal of the College and University Personnel Association* (February 1968).
10. Helen Lewis, "Job Evaluation: The University of Connecticut Experience," *Connecticut Libraries* 27 (October 1985), pp. 1–7, and other documents from the University of Connecticut Professional Employees Association.
11. Herbert S. White, "Why Don't We Get Paid More," *Library Journal* 111 (March 1, 1986), pp. 70–71.

VIEWPOINT: COMPARING LIBRARIAN AND TEACHER SALARIES *IS* VALID

Frank William Goudy

Some would have us believe that tieing librarians' salaries to teachers' salaries does not help librarians (see Betty Turock's editorial in *The Bottom Line* 1/1). She contends that since both professions are gender-typed, with salary standards influenced not only by market forces but by the culturally determined patterns of unequal compensation found in occupations where women predominate, we would be better off forgetting teachers' salaries as benchmarks in our salary negotiations.

I could not disagree more. If we are not even up to salary level of other female-dominated professions, isn't that a most persuasive factor in bringing home the unacceptable level of our current salaries?

Teacher's Salaries Get Attention

First a little background. The past few years have witnessed increasing print and media attention to the low salaries that public school teachers receive in this country. *A Nation At Risk* warns that society's educational foundations are being eroded by a "rising tide of mediocrity." And although there are many complex reasons for this national problem, the low salaries of teachers is a key factor in the dilemma; the nation is not recruiting its better college students to teach in the nation's classrooms. David Gardner, chair of the national commission that wrote this report, notes that starting salaries need to be from $22,000 to $25,000 a year, up from what was the $17,000 a year 1985 national average.[1]

More recently, the Carnegie Forum on Education and the Economy also has noted many of the glaring deficiencies of our educational system and again very strongly claims that low salaries in the teaching profession are a hindrance in both recruiting and keeping good teachers. This report advocates a "norm" of approximately $35,000 for teachers with certain "lead teachers" earning up to $72,000 for a 12-month contract.[2,3,4] These salaries should be possible without promotion into the administrative ranks so that good teachers could be sufficiently rewarded and remain in the classrooms where they are needed.

How does the library field compensate its professionals relative to the teaching field? Both have similar educational backgrounds. Both are involved in the educational process and activity of the communities they serve and both suffer problems of recruitment and retention stemming from meager salaries. The comparisons made here are based on the most-up-to date ALA salary survey data and statistics on teachers' salaries for the same period.

Salary Comparisons

It is not uncommon for most school districts to add $1,500 to $2,000 more for an MA to the $17,000 salary of a beginning teacher. Superficially, this 1985 figure appears to compare somewhat favorably with data from the 1986 ALA Survey of Librarian Salaries (see Table 1 for the following discussion) in that most of the entry level positions ranged from $17,649 for a children's librarian to $19,894 for a government documents librarian; most of the other beginning, nonadministrative positions are in the $18,000+ range.

Although the dollar amounts may be roughly equivalent, it is also true that most public school teachers are on nine-month contracts which usually range from 180 to 190 days. The overwhelming majority of librarians are on 12-month contracts which comprise from 230 to 240 work days a year. In effect, most librarians work approximately 25 percent to 30 percent more days to earn the same or even less salary.

If one considers the average 1985–86 pay for teachers of $25,257 and then compares that to the the mean of salaries paid for various nonadministrative librarian positions, a similar pattern can still be seen. For instance, the mean salary for a children's librarian is still only $20,736 while the average pay of a government documents librarian is $24,011. Most of the other positions are in the $23,000+ category.

It would appear from these data that experienced, nonadministrative librarians actually lose monetarily compared to experienced teachers who earn more while working significantly fewer days. I can only conjecture that this is the result of teacher salary schedules often being quite higher at the maximum end of the salary schedule while librarian salary schedules are often more compressed with fewer steps recognized.

The last point of comparison is the mean of scheduled maximum salaries. The data compiled by the 1986 ALA Survey indicate a range of from $23,933 for a children's librarian to $29,887 for the government documents librarian with other nonadministrative positions in the $25,000 to $28,000 range. Although no equivalent national data exist for public school teachers, such data were available for the state of Illinois.

In Illinois, those schools with enrollments of 3,000 and over had a median maximum salary of more than $31,000 for an MA only and

TABLE 1
SALARY COMPARISONS BY TITLE*

Title	Scheduled Starting Salaries	Mean of Salaries Paid	Mean of Scheduled Maximum Salaries
Director	28,868	36,152	41,275
Deputy/Associate Director	25,031	31,299	34,896
Assistant Director	25,026	31,722	36,359
Coordinator, Adult and/or Young Adult and/or Children's Services	21,426	26,983	29,583
Department Head/Branch Head	20,028	26,347	29,178
Government Documents Librarian	19,894	24,011	29,887
Subject Specialist/Bibliographer	19,780	26,748	30,612
Audiovisual Librarian	19,018	23,245	28,076
Adult Services Librarian	18,808	22,886	25,375
Serials Librarian	18,763	22,821	29,528
Cataloger and/or Classifier	18,346	23,201	27,481
Reference/Information Librarian	18,262	23,552	27,355
Children's and/or Young Adult Services Librarian	17,649	20,736	23,933

Source: ALA Survey of Librarian Salaries, 1986

TABLE 2
PUBLIC SCHOOL/PUBLIC LIBRARY SALARY COMPARISONS – NONADMINISTRATIVE POSITIONS

Public Schools	*Public Libraries*
Pittsburgh MA: $16,500–$35,580 10 Steps (189 days)	*Carnegie Library of Pittsburgh* Staff Librarian: $16,079–$24,119
Atlanta MA: $22,464–$31,956 14 Steps (190 days)	*Atlanta-Fulton Public Library* Librarian I: $17,184–$25,524 10 Steps
Denver MA: $19,902–$33,941 13 Steps	*Denver Public Library* Librarian: $19,932–$26,040 12 Steps
Decatur MA: $19,111–$31,939 15 Steps (182 days)	*Decatur Public Library* Librarian: $23,908–$29,059 5 Steps
Little Rock MA: $15,817–$22,694 13 Steps (9¼ months) MA: $20,445–$29,334 13 Steps (12 months)	*Central Arkansas Library System* Librarian I: $15,703–$20,507
Des Moines MA: $16,610–$28,312 16 steps	*Public Library of Des Moines* Librarian: $10,125–$12,120

$34,000+ for an MA + 30 hours. The smaller schools (500–999 students), however, averaged only $25,159 for an MA.[6] Again, it appears that librarian salaries are indeed less for this comparable category, although Illinois public school salaries were nearly eight percent higher than the national average. And again, most librarians work 12 rather than nine months for this lesser salary.

TABLE 3
PUBLIC SCHOOL/PUBLIC LIBRARY
SALARY COMPARISONS—
ADMINISTRATIVE POSITIONS

Public Schools	*Public Libraries*
Pittsburgh Coordinating Supervisory Instructional Program Specialist: $39,732–$48,480 205 days	*Carnegie Library of Pittsburgh* Division Head: $20,822–$31,232
Denver Assistant Principal: $36,286–$43,882 40 weeks	*Denver Public Library* Branch Manager: $27,228–$35,592
Des Moines Secondary Vice Principal: $36,523 at 5th Step 10½ months	*Public Library of Des Moines* Department Head: $13,623–$16,430

Regional Differences

In addition to the this macro comparison of teacher and librarian salaries, it is also useful to analyze specific cities and consider the salaries paid in the same area. Nine different cities from across the country were asked to supply the pay schedule for the public school teachers and the public librarians in each city or geographical area. Six different school systems and public libraries covering the same area responded. All salary data were effective for 1986. In all cases the librarians were required to have an MLS. And, unless otherwise noted, librarians were on 12-month contracts and teachers were on nine-month contracts.

In Pittsburgh, the beginning librarian salary is 16,079 and rises to $24,119, while the teachers pay schedule for an MA is from $16,500 to $35,580. The Denver Public Library salary schedule is from $19,932 to $26,040. Decatur, Illinois, appears to have the most comparability between librarians and teachers: the librarian entry level position for cataloging is $23,908 to $29,059 while public school teachers with an MA earn from $19,111 to $31,939. Of course, it must be cautioned that a twelve-month employment period is required for a librarian in Decatur, Illinois, while the teachers have a nine-month contract. One of the shocking differences appeared in Des Moines, Iowa, where teachers earn from $16,610 to $28,312 and librar-

ians earn only $10,125 to $12,120, with department heads in the library earning a top of $16,430. (See Table 2 for more detailed information.)

It is somewhat more tenuous to compare different public school administrative titles with that of library administrative titles. Nevertheless, it proves interesting and serves as a beginning point for further discussion. For example, a coordinating supervisory instructional program specialist in the Pittsburgh public schools earns from $39,732 to $48,480 while a division head in the Carnegie Library of Pittsburgh earns $20,822 to $31,232. Similarly, in Denver, an assistant principal earns $36,286 to $43,882 for 40 weeks of employment while a branch manager of the Denver Public Library earns $27,228 to $35,592. And in Des Moines, Iowa, a secondary vice principal is paid $36,523 after five years for a 10-month contract while a department head in the public library earns $16,430 after five years for a 12-month contract. (See Table 3 for more detailed information.)

This analysis is not designed to be an authoritative statement on the similarities or differences of all public school and public library salaries across the country. However, glaring differences are evident. The data from the individual institutions, combined with the national average data for librarians and teachers at various career stages, demonstrate that librarians have a long way to go

to catch up to school teachers of equivalent educational backgrounds.

It is true that there is not only a national market for salaries in a given field but also a regional and even local market to consider. Nevertheless, I recommend that the library profession have as its goal to establish an overall salary standard for an MLS ranging from approximately $23,000 at the entry level to not less than $37,000 after 12 years for an experienced nonadministrative librarian employed for 12 months. Administrative librarians would be paid appropriately more, depending upon the nature of their responsibilities. Naturally, different areas of the country might pay more or less with urban areas drawing higher salaries. Librarians and library administrators should carefully compare their salaries with those of the teaching professionals in their communities with similar educational and experience backgrounds in formulating an equitable salary schedule.

This proposed national average of $23,000 to $37,000 only places the librarian at a basic salary equity with public school teachers working today. If teachers are to receive greater rewards as has been proposed by such groups as the Carnegie Forum, then the library profession should follow suit. If we don't we will surely drive away many capable individuals who would choose librarianship as a career but who for financial reasons will not be able to do so. Increasingly, this will become a field for those who have already served many years and cannot readily exit and for those of lesser ability. We have to begin somewhere—why not salary parity with teachers? ===

References

1. "America's School System Still 'At Risk'", *U.S. News & World Report*, May 5, 1986, p. 64.
2. "Putting Teachers Up On Top," *Time*, May 26, 1986, p. 58.
3. "Teaching in Trouble," *U.S. News & World Report*, May 26, 1986, pp. 52–58
4. Carnegie Forum on Education and The Economy, *A Nation Prepared: Teachers for the 21st Century; The Report of the Task Force on Teaching as a Profession*, Carnegie Forum on Education and the Economy, Washington, D.C.: 1986.
5. Illinois State Board of Education, *Illinois Teacher Salary Schedule, 1985–1986*, Springfield, Ill.: Illinois State Board of Education, 1986.

RESPONDING TO THE LABOR MARKET: Matching Salaries and Paying for Training

Malcolm Getz

The library manager is faced with innumerable personnel policy issues. Two questions that are impacted by labor market considerations are:

If a valued professional receives an attractive offer from a competing institution should you match the offer?

To what extent should training and professional development activities be paid for by the library, and to what extent should the employee bear the cost?

Do We Match The Salary?

When a library's salary level for a skilled position is well below the going rate, you can expect a more rapid staff turnover, especially among the most marketable, mobile personnel. In addition, you will receive few qualified applicants for the library's openings. The next-best available opportunities to workers set a lower bound on salary levels in any given library. Available external positions, then, set a lower bound.

Conversely, when a library's salary level is at or above the going rate, you will have a variety of well-qualified applicants from which to choose. In fact, you should find a surplus of applicants for the library's openings. Available external applicants, then, set an upper bound.

The External Market

The external market defines a band with upper and lower limits wherein a library normally offers salaries for a given position. You may easily find that it is at its lower limit for some positions—perhaps those with rapidly increasing salaries, and at upper limits for others—perhaps those with declining demand in the industry.

Figure 1 presents this idea in schematic form for a particular skill level. Since we are dealing with the short-run managerial goal of keeping authorized positions filled, the demand curve D, for workers, is vertical.

The figure shows two supply curves: S_H applies when the librarian wants to hire new workers; S_L shows the salary level at which workers will leave. The salary level where D intersects S_H is the upper boundary on salaries for this skill level, as defined by the external market. The salary level where D intersects S_L is the lower boundary on salary level, also defined by the external market.

The upper and lower bounds are usually closer together in a large metropolitan area where the cost of changing position may be less than if a worker must also move to a different city to find a comparable job. Job holders are less likely to move for a given salary differential if the cost of moving is larger. (The limits are closer together for those positions not specific to libraries because of the larger number of alternative positions and applicants available.)

The external bounds on salaries are likely to be farthest apart for those positions that are unique to a particular class of librarians, for example, reference librarians with specialization in anthropology. With fewer competing positions, an employee will find the cost of finding an alternative position to be higher, and so he or she will be less likely to move. At the same time, you may have to offer a significantly higher salary to draw the attention of the small pool of potential applicants for an opening.

The Internal Market

The internal labor market is defined by the library's salary policy and reflects the institution's goals and its attitude toward management. Within the limits of external market forces, librarians can define a salary policy to achieve those institutional goals. The internal salary policy can be structured and formal, informal and flexible, or somewhere in between.

One way to assure fairness is to adopt a set of formal salary guides. This would include objectively observable attributes of employees and positions. For example, specific salary levels can be formally linked to years of seniority and formally established salary increments can be tied to a specific degree or other credential.

A library with a strong civil service system and a rigid job classification system is more likely to have its salaries for different positions bumping both limits. In such environments all salaries have a strong tendency to move together: all stagnant or increase at the same pace.

In settings with formal salary structures, the internal market is highly structured. The formal structure may cause staff shortages in some positions and surpluses in others.

Take, for example, a salary scale tied primarily to number of years of schooling completed and years of experience. You are likely to find a surplus of persons oriented toward lower-demand fields, say, literature and religion, and a shortage of scientific and technical staff. These relative differences arise because the internal salary scale is constructed with minimum attention to external markets.

An alternative, less formal salary policy could include a program of performance evaluation with merit evaluations influencing raises. Since there will probably be higher salaries in skill positions that are in higher demand in external markets, salaries will have a lower correlation with such attributes as seniority and credentials.

FIGURE 1
UPPER AND LOWER BOUNDARIES
ON SALARIES

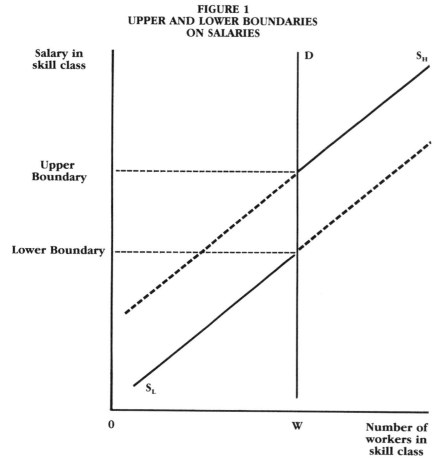

There is the danger, however, that an informal salary policy will have too little link to either performance or observable credentials and so be unfair. An informal policy that gives more managerial discretion only works well when management is attentive.

And so, given the external and internal markets, how do you deal with competing institutions? If the offer is for a significant move up a career ladder, you probably will not make a counter offer. If you have a vacancy in a comparable position, then an offer of an internal promotion might be appropriate. However, such a circumstance is usually rare.

In an institution with a formal internal salary schedule, you may have no discretion to match an external offer, and so the question is moot.

If the offer is for a comparable position and your library's internal salary scale is significantly below your competitor's, then you might consider a significant increase. However, you'll now have to see the counter offer as a first step in raising the whole salary scale. If the institution cannot afford to raise its salary scale or has some other policy reason for maintaining its scale, then you cannot counter the offer.

In a fourth circumstance, suppose your library has an informal internal salary policy and the employee considering the external offer for a similar position is near the lower salary boundary. In this situation, matching the external offer may make considerable sense if the employee's performance warrants such action. The external offer then serves as a useful source of information for adjusting the salary program.

If the incumbent's present salary fits well in the overall salary pattern and the pattern is carefully positioned with respect to external markets, then a counter offer will not make sense.

A salary policy then acts as a barometer to both external and internal circumstances, reflecting the potential for career paths. Whether it is informal, and so managerially oriented, or formal, you should counter offers in light of your library's salary policy.

Do We Pay For Training?

A library can enhance its position in the labor market by emphasizing the training value of its positions. Just as young lawyers accept low salaries for the privilege of serving as law clerks, so too will young librarians accept low salaries to receive significant learning experience on the job.

A library, then, could create a set of positions with a very heavy training component and an expectation of high turnover, but with low salaries. Of course, the quality of the training and experience must be significant if this strategy is to work well.

In this situation you will make budgetary outlays for training, perhaps maintaining a somewhat larger staff to allow time for it. This is compensated by the lower salary levels. In effect, new workers pay for the training by accepting the lower salaries.

Training at entry level is oriented toward the external labor market. The skills are those that other firms, as well as other libraries, value. The value of the training is not primarily to the individual library served. It is of significant value in a career that could span several institutions. In this case, the individual worker should be willing to pay for the training, either by the lower salary or by paying tuition.

When training is specifically for the job at hand, learning the practices of your library, then you must pay. Since the skill learned may have little value to the employee in another setting, it is not marketable.

Many kinds of training and skill enhancing job experiences create some mixture of marketable and non-marketable skills. In this case, the library and the worker should share the costs.

Some payments are essentially a part of the library's compensation program, that is, a fringe benefit, for instance, underwriting tuition in a degree-oriented graduate program. However, be aware that when a worker attains a new skill or credential, you are going to be paying a salary above the lower limit for the new skill level or lose the employee to an institution that *will* pay at the upper boundary. Because you can hardly hope to recoup the expense of the general training by getting a given set of skills at lower cost, you should not view general skill development as an investment when you support it. ▬

HIGH DEMAND/LOW SUPPLY IN LIBRARY FINANCIAL MANAGEMENT CAREERS

Margaret Myers

As libraries and information centers grow in complexity and, in many cases, become big business, financial management skills take on increased importance for librarians and other information workers. External and internal pressures like reductions in library budgets, escalation of costs faster than revenues, pressures from outside agencies for increased productivity, accountability, organizational efficiency and effectiveness have all pushed librarians to expand their competencies in the financial arena.

There is little on career options relating to financial management in the library and information field in the library literature. Beyond the librarians who earn an MBA and leave the library and information world to use their business administration background in some other setting, career paths for those interested in financial management are primarily found in four areas. These are: as part of generalist management positions, in specialist positions as budget or financial officers, as information entrepreneurs, and as librarians in business libraries.[1]

Management Positions

What can be seen in the increased number of articles and books appearing in library literature is that fund raising, budgeting, cost analysis, and financial planning have expanded the role for library and information managers. However, as indicated by Betty Turock, library managers—like their counterparts in other segments of the nonprofit arena—have "rarely been noted for their financial experience or acumen."[2] Ann Prentice thinks the image of people working in nonprofit service agencies as unskilled in management of financial resources is due in part to the dual responsibilities of public services administrators: They

must be both professionals in the services performed and managers of the resources supporting those services.[3]

Since librarians tend to enter library management positions from a professional career path, they have to learn management skills on the job or through additional formal education or continuing education courses. A number of people entering the profession do have a second master's degree, but it is not known how many of these are MBAs. Most likely it is a small number—the field is *not* known for attracting people with mathematical or business backgrounds. One possible reason is that the low salaries generally offered librarians can't compete with the more lucrative compensation in the business world.

That financial management awareness and expertise are needed in a variety of library and information careers is clear. Robert Hayes has outlined a range of management decisions that depend on accurate, reliable data about cost and performance. This includes the need for managers to support proposed budgets with concrete data concerning costs, develop and submit proposals for grants to carry out special projects, maintain budget projections and control these once established, relate costs to performance, allocate resources among alternatives, and evaluate costs and fees for services.[4]

Additional competencies in financial management include the ability to develop financial policies and procedures in keeping with library overall financial operations, establish costs for services if appropriate, determine the cost of inhouse vs. contract processing and services, and supervise the deposit of any funds received.[5]

Most fiscal management responsibilities take place at the top ad-

ministrative level. But staff at other levels can also be involved in financial management activities, particularly in helping to prepare and monitor budgets for their own departments or in developing proposals for outside funding for special programs or projects. Financial awareness of how the library's budget fits into the overall administrative unit—whether this be the city, county, campus, or corporation—is essential knowledge for all librarians, regardless of level of responsibility.

While libraries have traditionally hired a business manager to oversee bookkeeping and accounting operations, it appears that more financial management responsibilities are being assigned to professional librarians in top administrative positions. Perhaps this is a result of recognizing that budgetary implementation goes hand-in-hand with planning and evaluating library services. In larger libraries, the assistant or associate director position often is assigned responsibility for the budget, along with other areas such as administrative services, personnel, planning systems, and coordinating public or technical services.

A survey by the Association of Research Libraries (ARL) on the assistant/associate director (AD) positions in ARL libraries found that most of these persons function as executive or operations officers. They oversee day-to-day activities in a variety of units at the department or branch levels and carry out specialized staff—as distinct from line—duties. The survey shows that the number of AD positions has increased with the expanded complexity of research library management. Out of the 46 responding libraries, 33 indicated this position had responsibilities for budget preparation and fiscal control.

While advanced degrees were rated highly desirable in recruiting for the AD positions, it is clear that qualitative criteria were equally important: interpersonal, group leadership, and analytical skills. Respondents ranked general management ability highest among the specific skills required for AD positions. Skills in finance and technology were also rated highly, along with skills in interpersonal relations. Candidates for AD-level positions were expected to be fully prepared for their responsibilities without further training. It was pointed out, however, that developmental training geared for top level staff is scarce.[6]

Specialist Positions

Technical and managerial specialists, including fiscal officers, are often found in large libraries. Little data exist regarding the educational and experience backgrounds of these specialists. Nor does there seem to be a fast rule that libraries follow in hiring. Some libraries hire primarily those with nonlibrary related qualifications; others require an MLS in addition to the specific subject expertise. ALA's policy on "Library Education and Personnel Utilization" in recommending levels of library staffing does provide a career ladder for a category of specialists without the MLS. It recognizes that skills other than those in librarianship also have an important contribution to make to the achieving of superior library service.[7]

In a survey of specialty positions in ARL libraries, the 60 out of 80 libraries responding reported 123 specialty positions involving a wide range of activities. Twenty-six of these were positions in budgeting, fiscal planning, or business management with titles ranging from library budget officer to assistant director for budgeting and administrative services to director of fiscal affairs. Sixteen of the positions reported directly to the director. Fourteen of 20 persons in these positions held a BA or MA in a business-related area; four held MLS degrees.

Half of the positions had seen major changes take place in their duties and responsibilities. Primarily these included more involvement in decision making and consolidation of budget-related responsibilities, such as combining all revenue-producing activities under the supervision of the individual. One of the positions was characterized as having line responsibility, ten were seen as a staff responsibility, and the remaining were some combination of line and staff. Supervision by these fiscal specialists averaged six persons, but the range was from zero to 30 persons.

Two-thirds of all the specialist positions did not require the MLS although 56 percent were MLS-holders. It is not known if the specialists received the MLS after hiring or had it prior to their appointment.[8] ARL predicted an increasing number of specialist positions to be created as the complexity of library operations increases.

In the ARL SPEC Kit, reporting on the survey, a number of specialist positions are described. Budget responsibilities are sometimes combined with other functions, such as personnel, planning, public relations, administrative services, fund raising or development. A sample job description for seven budget officers includes responsibilities for:

- preparing, analyzing, and interpreting a variety of financial statements for the library administration
- auditing and supervising preparation of staff and student payrolls
- serving as liaison to university financial officer
- preparing monthly reports on the status of all funds
- keeping current with the rules, regulations, and laws pertaining to fiscal responsibilities
- developing cost studies and proposals for library programs, equipment, and furnishings
- reporting statistics and budget data to state and federal agencies.[9]

The major activities of a "chief fiscal officer" have been described as including developing a system of recording financial transactions, assuring compatibility between internal monetary allocations and organizational priorities, and identifying significant deviations in the use of resources. The planning and evaluation roles are equally important as the budgetary implementation.[10]

Information Entrepreneurs

Financial management has also become a vital area for special attention for librarians moving into consultant, freelance, or information broker jobs and establishing contract services or small companies on their own. As they move into entrepreneurial, profit-making enterprises, librarians must be able to create a business plan, project the need for capital investments, estab-

lish pricing policies, understand their cash flow situation, determine the effect of advertising, etc.[11] Many librarians moving into an entrepreneurial situation think primarily in terms of how they can best offer their information expertise—thus do not recognize the need for business, public relations, and promotional skills.

In the book *New Options for Librarians: Finding a Job in a Related Field*, a survey reports on 487 librarians who have moved into nonlibrary situations but still are using their information skills. Fifty-four (11%) were self-employed, owning their own business. Another 43 (9%) were self-employed, working in freelance situations. Of the 487, only 12 (2%) had an MBA.[12]

Running a fee-based information service is like running any other business. One advantage is that it can be started with less capital investment than most businesses. It appears that the failure rate for information services is less than small businesses in general, where 80 percent fail in the first three years. However, cash-flow problems are often a chronic condition, especially in the first several years.[13]

Business Librarians

Special libraries within the corporate setting have often tried to recruit persons with business backgrounds in order to use their subject expertise as well as skills in librarianship. There is a shortage of individuals with this background. As a result, many business libraries accept persons with at least a knowledge of business literature and skills in online searching of business databases.

Eddison and Daniel advocate that special librarians should move into the role of corporate vice presidents for information services. This is a position which usually oversees the library information center and records management and data-processing departments. Although there is a need for effective management of all information services resources within a company, the role of librarians and their availability for promotion into these top level, administrative corporate positions is seldom acknowledged.

Eddison pictures the ideal chief information officer in a company as a professional with training in special libraries, records management, data-processing management, systems analysis, business administration, corporate finance, and marketing strategies.[14] Librarians need to increase the visibility of their role in information management so they *will* be considered viable candidates for top corporate positions.

Nonlibrary Fiscal Workfields

A survey of 1,641,000 information professionals working outside of libraries identified a variety of "workfields" or areas of work activity in which persons were grouped according to the nature of the work they do, independent of institutional affiliation. The financial workfield accounted for 69,100 (4%) of the information professionals. (The library workfield represented 10 percent.) Of the approximately 1,500 unique occupational titles reported, 121 were found in the financial management and analysis, accountancy, and budget control areas. However, it's not likely that a move by librarians into these other areas would be possible without specific business training—in spite of the fact that these are considered positions with information functions.[15]

Salaries and Education

Little is known about salaries for financial officers in libraries. These positions are not usually singled out in existing salary surveys. A 1984 salary survey of public libraries provides some data for business manager positions in relation to other salaries. Business manager salaries ranged from $17,113 to $64,032, with a minimum median of $26,400 and a maximum median of $34,092. Business officer positions ranked higher than professional librarians in the survey except for those in top administrative positions. Here business managers were described as directing accounting, personnel, purchasing, and related staff services. Typically required was a BS degree in accounting or business administration and five years of responsible accounting experience.[16]

In its annual survey, the Association of Research Libraries collects and publishes data on a variety of positions. These include the functional specialist positions into which budget officers fit. The average functional specialist salary in fiscal year 1987 was $29,663. Department and branch heads and other top administrative positions generally earned more than the functional specialists.[17]

Some salary data for entrepreneurs are included in the *New Options for Librarians* survey. Salaries for the 58 persons surveyed who own their own businesses and were engaged in free-lance work as entrepreneurs showed 35 earned less than $25,000, ten earned between $25,000 up to $40,000, and seven earned $40,000 and above.[18]

Although fiscal officers often come to specialist positions in libraries from a nonlibrary background, it may be that the combination of the MLS and some type of financial management training will become the norm—combining the best of both worlds. In the tight job market of the late 1970s and early 1980s, a number of librarians talked about obtaining an MBA, thinking it would help advance them into management positions. While the value of the MBA for librarians has been discussed in the literature,[19] there are no data on how many have obtained the degree or if it has helped in promotion to management positions. Because the library job market has improved somewhat in the last few years, individuals can probably move more easily into management positions without it.

Some academic libraries do require a second master's for initial employment or for promotion and tenure once they are on the job. However, there is no agreement in the academic librarian community as to whether the subject master's is necessary. Some feel that it serves as an indicator of commitment to scholarship. Others feel that persons with a second subject master's will be given preference in hiring.[20]

Hayes raises a number of issues relating to how librarians should acquire education in financial management. For instance, should an educational program related to managerial accounting be a requirement for all students or just recommended? The difficulty in finding time for such programs in the MLS program is a real drawback, as well as dealing with the aversion to quantitative courses on the part of students. Where should instruction take place? Within the library school? Through some type of self-paced instruction program?

The UCLA library school offers a managerial accounting course (required for the MLS, recommended for others) based on the needs and interests of library school students with examples from library programs. It is taught by faculty from the graduate school of management.[21]

Should financial management be taught within the MLS program or as a continuing education activity? Perhaps the best answer is to design a curriculum which exposes MLS students to the need for financial awareness in a variety of library and information positions and introduces some of the basic concepts. Then as individuals move more directly into management, specialist, or entrepreneurial positions where these skills are essential for effective performance, they can gain a more in-depth education through a variety of continuing education opportunities.

There is an increasing need for financial management skills in libraries. Librarians able to take on these responsibilities are in demand—albeit still in short supply. We may be experiencing a situation similar to that of library automation. In the early days of automation, computer experts were hired who had little knowledge of libraries. Gradually, automation courses were integrated into library school curriculums and library automation continuing education courses became popular across the country. Today, librarians with both computer knowledge and professional background are sought after as systems analysts and heads of automation projects.

Perhaps we can learn from that experience. Librarians now largely control technology in libraries. Is the financial management of our institutions any less important? ==

References

1. For a discussion on placements and salaries of new masters in business administration, see "MBAs Shift Away from Consulting as Investment-Banking Pay Rises," *Wall Street Journal* (July 30, 1985): 2,1.
2. Betty Turock, "Productivity, Financial Management and the Public Library," *Public Library Quarterly* (Winter 1984): 3.
3. Ann Prentice, *Financial Planning for Libraries* (Metuchen, N.J.: Scarecrow, 1983), p. 205.
4. Robert M. Hayes, "Managerial Accounting in Library and Information Science Education," *Library Quarterly* (July 1983): 343.
5. Jose-Marie Griffiths and Donald W. King, *New Directions in Library and Information Science Education* (White Plains: Knowledge Industry Publication, 1986).
6. Association of Research Libraries, Office of Management Studies, *The Assistant/Associate Director Position in ARL Libraries*, SPEC Kit #103 (Washington, D.C.: ARL, 1984), p. i-ii.
7. American Library Association, *Library Education and Personnel Utilization* (Chicago: ALA, 1970), p. 2.
8. Association of Research Libraries, Office of Management Studies, *Speciality Positions in ARL Libraries*, SPEC Kit #80 (Washington, D.C.: ARL, 1982), p. ii.
9. Ibid., pp. 29–52.
10. Turock, "Productivity," p. 4.
11. Hayes, "Managerial Accounting," p. 353.
12. Betty-Carol Sellen and Susan J. Vaughn, *New Options for Librarians: Finding a Job in a Related Field* (New York: Neal-Schuman, 1984), p. 5 Summary article "Librarians in Alternative Work Places" was published in *Library Journal* (Feb. 15, 1985): 108–110. See also Alice Sizer Warner, *Mind Your Own Business* (New York: Neal-Schuman, 1987).
13. Lorig Maranjian and Richard W. Boss, *Fee-Based Information Services: A Study of a Growing Industry* (New York: R.R. Bowker, 1980), p. 59.
14. Elizabeth Bole Eddison, "Who Should Be In-Charge?" *Special Libraries* (April 1983): 107–109 and Evelyn Daniel, "Special Librarian to Information Manager," *Special Libraries* (April 1982): 93–99.
15. Anthony Debons, et al., *The Information Professional: Survey of an Emerging Field* (New York: Marcel Dekker, 1981), pp. 54, 194–198.
16. "Salary Surveys," *Public Library Quarterly* (Winter 1984): 72–73.
17. Association of Research Libraries, *ARL Annual Salary Survey 1986* (Washington, D.C.: ARL, 1987), p. 34.
18. Sellen and Vaughn, *New Options for Librarians*, p. 8.
19. Joanne Euster, "The MBA in Library Land," *Louisiana Library Association Bulletin* (Spring 1979): 80–81.
20. "Forum: The Second Master's Degree in Academic Librarianship," *Tennessee Librarian* (Winter 1978): 26–30.
21. Hayes, "Managerial Accounting," pp. 354–57.

EMPLOYEE BENEFITS
Emerging Trends for Librarians

Marjorie Watson

Employee benefits — nonwage payments and services made to employees in addition to salary compensation — are commonly taken for granted by employees. They are, however, a relatively new phenomenon. As recently as the 1930s, many workers took vacations without pay and some employers provided only a turkey at Christmas. Today, employee benefits come in many forms. When initiated by the employer, they are thought to enhance the employee's well-being physically and psychologically and so increase productivity. Initiated as the result of collective bargaining between an employer and a union, they are expected to bring credit to the union and to better the membership's lot. When benefits are required to be paid or offered as a result of social legislation, the picture becomes crowded with politicians, taxpayers, and the

workers.

The Bureau of Labor Statistics has reported that over 177,000 librarians are employed in the labor force,[1] and receive employee benefits. As their varied job assignments are examined, however, it becomes apparent that this small group does not fit neatly into any one employment category. Rather, they range from large industrial firms, where compensation and benefits plans are carefully managed, to small, nonprofit organizations, where employee benefits are few or lacking because of financial constraints.

Librarians and Benefits — A Survey

This was found to be the case in New Jersey, where a survey was undertaken to determine the general availability of basic benefits for librarians. The 222 special and public librarians who responded receive traditional benefits to the same degree as in the public and private sectors. However, innovative benefits were located more often in the private arena, where librarians enjoy a level of benefits equal to or higher than those reported by the Bureau of Labor Statistics[2] and the U.S. Chamber of Commerce.[3] Most of the librarians reporting from the public sector were in benefits programs similar to those offered New Jersey state employees. There were some exceptions; for example, in small municipalities where few or no benefits were offered.

Some surprising findings emerged concerning flexible benefits and health care. Few librarians reported receiving flexible benefits, and private-sector librarians reported diverse health care plans and an unexpected pattern of payment for basic plan premiums. It is generally believed that employee benefits in the private sector are richer because employers contribute in full, but this was not true in the case of basic health plans for librarians in New Jersey. This finding probably reflects the national trend to control employer costs in the private sector.[4,5]

Since it is reasonable to believe that the pattern found here exists elsewhere, after giving a capsule summary of the survey findings for each of the benefits — cafeteria plans, daycare or child care, flextime, and health care — this article will define and describe that benefit, set it in an historical perspective, and suggest some guidelines for instituting it more broadly in the library community.

Cafeteria or Flexible Benefit Plans

The librarians who reported cafeteria or flexible benefits were a minority of the special librarians employed by large national or international firms. The term cafeteria benefits is derived from Section 125 of the Internal Revenue Code entitled "Cafeteria Plans." In popular usage, the term has become synonymous with flexible benefits. However, one expert has defined cafeteria plans as meaning that employees are allowed to pick and choose the elements of their own programs, while flexible benefits give employees a certain amount of latitude in determining some levels of benefit coverage, with the capacity to trade off between benefits, or between cash and benefits.[6] The plans have become popular for several reasons:

Changing Labor Force. Many employees are members of two-income households; others are working single parents. Options help satisfy their diverse needs and ease the pressure for additional benefits. In a study of small midwestern firms which had implemented cafeteria benefits, Cockrum showed that women were especially enthusiastic about them. The plans enable them to bring additional benefits into two-income households or otherwise make choices to their advantage.[7]

Company Image-Employee Relations. These plans are useful recruiting tools because they can appeal to a wide range of prospective employees and so enhance the organization's image. A mirror effect develops in promoting employee good will, because regular workers have the option of choosing those benefits they deem important.

Cost Containment. The plans are seen by many as a means of containing the costs of an increasingly expensive component of the total wage package. IF costs continue in their present pattern, by 1990 the ratio of benefits to salary could reach 60 percent.[8] When benefits are offered, one of the primary objectives is to obtain the best use of money. Standardized benefits waste a lot of employer dollars for, in spite of the fact that more and more money is spent, the needs of most employees are served only partially.[9]

An employer wishing to consider one of these plans in a library should first examine the institution's existing benefits program and its goals to determine exactly what is being provided; then find out how much employees really know about the program and what they dislike about it; and analyze the efforts of other organizations to learn why they adopted plans and how they implemented them.

American Can, a pioneer in this area, started its program early in 1978 with a small group of employees. After the initial problems were worked out, services were gradually expanded to include all of the company's employees. Pepsico and North American Van Lines followed a similar course. TRW and Educational Testing Service had plans established by 1976.

Heavily sought after since the Great Depression, health insurance has become one of the most common employee benefits offered by U.S. employers.

Although cafeteria or flexible benefits are seldom found in public libraries, at present, they are needed for the same reasons that they are needed in the corporate world. And what about the small library? In Cockrum's survey of firms so small there were no designated personnel administrators, these companies managed to set up flexible plans, the majority of which were unique to an organization and varied from quite simple to very complex.[10]

There are several approaches to establishing these plans. One is to set basic levels of pay and benefits for all and provide a supplemental allowance that the employee allocates according to need. This is sometimes offered as a reserve of flexible credits.

Existing coverage levels might be shrunk to a core that meets the objectives of the organization. The value difference between the new core and the former program is made available to plan participants in the form of a flexible allowance to be used for the purchase of optional benefits. The employer may not add options at additional expense or dollars to the flexible account pool at will. Some plans allow unused money credits to be put into a capital accumulation plan or taken as cash. Cash, of course, is taxable.[11]

Another approach permits more flexibility. It involves coordinating a flexible plan with a cash or deferred profit-sharing plan. Employees would have a choice of deferring account dollars, electing to receive a portion in cash or assigning a portion for reimbursement expenses. They could utilize IRAs and 401 (k) cash or deferred profit-sharing plans, since Section 401 (k) of the Internal Revenue Code permits the conversion of pay into compensation which is tax-deferred. Under Section 125 (d) of the Internal Revenue code, which deals with cafeteria plans, the employer can pay out costs for employees out of before-tax dollars with a full deduction as an employee expense. Some of the items which could be covered include major medical co-insurance and deductible, noncovered medical, dental, drug and vision care expenses, certain legal and employee education costs, day and other dependent care and adoption expenses.[12] The employee also may take cash, but this would be taxable.

What are some of the drawbacks to flexible benefits plans?

Administrative expense is the most frequently cited problem, not only because of start-up costs, but because of the recordkeeping involved. Computerized personnel information systems are expected to overcome many of the difficulties, but management will still be responsible for maintaining good operating policies.

A good **communications program** is imperative so that employees fully understand what is being offered and its value to them; it must be initiated before the plan is put into effect.

Employer costs must be calculated carefully and early. Employee expectations can not be permitted to rise beyond the employer's capability to provide.

Equity and how credits are distributed among single employees and those with dependents can impact on the success of the program.

Employee input is recommended before the decisions are made.

Typically, **adverse selection** destroys the concept of group insurance in that only those needing a benefit will choose it and costs will soar. One specialist has advised avoiding multiple health benefits offerings for this reason.[13]

It takes expert planning to deal with all the facets of these plans, but employee satisfaction may be worth the significant cost. At a meeting of the Western Pension Conference, one of the speakers described the traditional benefits package as an "invisible paycheck" that is becoming more visible as flexible benefits plans offer employees a greater voice in choosing their benefits and help them understand the cost of benefits.[14]

Daycare/Child Care

In the New Jersey survey few librarians replied that they had access to childcare facilities provided by their employers. Those that did were employed in the private sector. Many indicated that it would be desirable.

As early as 1910, daycare was reported as a benefit initiated by employers in the United States. Why has a resurgence of interest in child care occurred on the part of employers? Economic and demographic conditions have undergone drastic changes. Inflation and a wave of individual awareness have brought women back into the labor force. In 1978, there were 42 million working women in the country, a participation rate of 40 percent. By 1990, it is expected that 44.8 percent of all preschool children will have mothers who work outside the home, in contrast to 37.6 percent in 1977.[15]

A study conducted for the U.S. Women's Bureau in 1980 noted that 74 percent of the parents utilizing child care centers were skilled and professional employees. Unskilled, single mothers, so often considered clients for these services, ranked low as users.[16]

The present need is obvious but a solution has not come from the public sector. Despite certain efforts by the federal government, which has provided varied funding for child care through such legislation as Head Start, CETA, the Elementary and Secondary Education Act, the SSA Title IV series, and Title XX Social Service Grants to the States, no federal policy

exists. This was highlighted in the concluding statements of a report published by the U.S. Commission on Civil Rights. The document noted that we have "no well-articulated or cohesive federal child care policy."[17]

The problem has not escaped the notice of labor unions, especially those representing large numbers of women. Haddad's 1979 booklet, *Local Union Guide for Establishing Child Care Centers,* published by the School of Labor and Industrial Relations at Michigan State University, included suggestions for financing these projects.[18] Other labor groups such as the Coalition of Labor Union Women, the United Federation of Teachers, and the Amalgamated Clothing and Textile Workers Union have been active in their support. But to date, very few collective bargaining agreements contain provisions for child care.

With the passage of the Employment Recovery Tax Act of 1981, the Congress allowed a tax incentive to provide this benefit for both on-site and referral subsidies. However, even with an incentive, the $100,000 estimated start-up expenditure for an on-site daycare center is prohibitive for most employers. In addition to a large capital outlay, the sponsor is faced with administrative reponsibility and program development. If demand for these services drops or economics change, the center may have to be converted for other purposes.

There are other less imposing choices. Some are expensive and others are within the reach of a small employer. This is one area where innovation and imagination can be exercised. What can be done?

- Offer direct support to family homes providing day care off-site.
- Establish a voucher system through which employees purchase their own child care services. One firm, for example, pays between five and 85 percent of the costs in licensed homes for employees who earn less than $20,000 a year.
- Support the existing child care community by making in-kind contributions. Purchase slots at local centers.
- Offer information and referral services inhouse or through an agency as Steelcase, Mountain Bell, and Honeywell currently do.

- Sponsor parent education seminars at the workplace.
- Offer daycare as part of a flexible benefits plan. This eliminates the problems of equity.
- Consider scheduling arrangements such as job-sharing, a compressed work week, and flextime.[19]

Flextime

Flextime is a concept that is growing in popularity throughout the country, although it was seldom reported by New Jersey librarians. When it was, it was — once again — by those in the private sector. While its use has been limited by the overtime provisions in legislation such as the Walsh-Healy Public Contracts Act, the Federal Pay Act, and the Fair Labor Standards Act, flextime is encouraged by the whole body of legislation affecting affirmative action.[20] When it has been well-planned, a flextime program has not cost the employer additional money. What are its advantages and disadvantages?

Advantages

- Increased productivity.
- Less tardiness and absenteeism.
- Enhanced recruitment opportunities.
- Improved morale.
- Longer business hours.
- Reduced overtime costs.
- Easier commuting for workers.

Disadvantages

- Supervisors feel lack of control.
- Increased tension between management and unions.
- Workers may have to learn new tasks and substitute for each other.
- Workers on traditional schedules may resent those on flextime.

Before instituting flextime, library administrators need to develop clear plans of action with targeted jobs tested to determine what the specific effects might be. This type of schedule requires flexibility on the part of managers as well as staff. It won't work in an organization hostile to innovation.

Health Benefits

Librarians in New Jersey, from both the public and private sectors, reported having health benefits. Several in the private sector included this benefit as part of a flexible plan. Although almost all members of both groups receive health coverage, differences in the method of payment were evident.

Basic Health Plan Premiums

Public Sector

Employee Co-pay?		Dependent Co-pay?	
(N=135)		(N=120)	
Yes	No	Yes	No
17	118	29	91

Private Sector

Employee Co-pay?		Dependent Co-pay?	
(N=87)		(N=72)	
Yes	No	Yes	No
46	41	50	22

In the public sector, only 13 percent of the responding employees contributed, while in the private sector, 53 percent of the total contributed as employees. In the case of dependents, 24 percent of the public sector librarians answering the question contributed for dependents, while 69 percent of the private sector respondents did.

Dental plans, a relatively new offering popular with employees, were provided for 42 percent of 165 respondents from the public sector and for 93 percent of 74 respondents from the private sector.

Basic Dental Plan Premiums

Public Sector

Employee Co-pay?		Dependent Co-pay?	
(N=60)		(N=53)	
Yes	No	Yes	No
20	40	22	31

Private Sector

Employee Co-pay?		Dependent Co-pay?	
(N=74)		(N=54)	
Yes	No	Yes	No
45	29	35	19

In the public sector, 33 percent contributed for employee benefits and 42 percent for dependents. Among private sector respondents, 61 percent contributed for employee benefits and 65 percent for dependents' benefits. The number of public employees contributing to premiums for this newer health benefit may be the result of a move on the part of employers to control costs.

At the end of 1983, 61 percent of the population was covered by a health insurance plan related to current or past employment, theirs or that of another family member.[21]

Heavily sought after since the Great Depression, health insurance has become one of the most common employee benefits offered by U.S. employers. It has also become one of the most costly. Major employers are taking steps to reduce some of these costs, or at least to bring them under control. The differences noted in contributory payments by librarians reporting from the private sector may reflect this.

B. F. Goodrich has seen its health care costs triple to $64,000,000 in the last decade, and Caterpillar Tractor Co., in spite of layoffs, has seen its medical benefits costs double since 1979.[22] To alleviate this, employees, represented by their unions, are being faced with having to make cost-effective decisions regarding medical care usually through increased deductibles and copayments.

Why are costs so high? There are five basic reasons with no simple answers.

- The employer purchases medical care, but has no control over the services provided to the employees. Hospitals and physicians have little inducement to lower prices.
- Most medical plans emphasize hospitalization.
- The cost of hospital care is increasing.
- Advanced medical technology is expensive and raises costs.
- Defensive medicine is practiced more and more by the medical community.[23]

Two health plans give employees the option of accepting a higher degree of risk for greater medical coverage. One is a comprehensive plan for which no monthly premium is charged and which pays up to $1,000,000 in medical benefits annually for each individual covered. When medical services are used, the employee contributes by means of copayments and deductibles. Out-of-pocket expenses are limited to $1,000 for an individual and $2,000 for a family. A $200 deductible is taken for inpatient surgery, doctor's visits, therapy, and other procedures, but there is no deductible for the use of extended care facilities, hospices, approved home health care, x-rays, tests, and second opinions.[24]

The other plan allows four options. Three have annual deductibles and limits which go from low to high on a sliding scale. The fourth option allows membership in a company-approved health maintenance organization (HMO). After meeting the deductible, the employee pays 20 percent of the charges. For example, with the highest deductible/limit option, a single person's deduction would be $400, and a copayment of 20 percent of the $5,000 limit would be $1,000.

What are some of the other strategies being used to reduce corporate costs that might also be applied to libraries?

- Relate the employees' cost for medical coverage to the amount of the claims paid. The use of benefits changes the cost reflected in the premiums paid by employees.
- Increase contribution rates according to the number of individuals covered. In one corporation, the rate rose 25 percent for a single person to 43 percent for those with dependents.
- Demand second opinions. Many plans will not pay the full cost incurred without one.
- Require precertification. Hospital confinement accounts for more than one-half of total medical costs. Savings have been reported by decreasing the number of afternoon and weekend admissions before surgery.
- Provide financial incentives. New plans do not penalize those using outpatient services and extended care facilities.
- Encourage preventive care. One firm's dental plan, oriented toward prevention, saved it $600,000 in 1983.
- Make home health care a viable plan feature.
- Implement a personal-time bank. This has been particularly successful in reducing sick leave abuse and absenteeism. The employee has control over all the leave time for which he or she is eligible. Use is discretionary with a possible exception of taking a certain number of days consecutively each year.
- Institute a well-pay plan. The employee is offered a financial incentive to stay well. One plan offers a bonus to employees who stay well for four weeks. No sick leave is accrued and no pay is given for the first eight hours of absence. The

firm pays for illness time beyond the first eight hours until disability pay begins, if that is necessary.

- Set up flexible reimbusement accounts. These accounts, usually containing between $300 to $500, are set up for each employee to pay for initial medical expenses. Unused funds are paid at the end of the year or held in an interest-bearing account. A variation allows employees to reduce their salaries monthly to pay health benefits premiums. The excess is set aside to pay for deductibles, copayments, and other uncovered needs.

In January 1985, Wells Fargo and Company offered a new flexible benefits plan that includes selections in health, life, and disability coverage. Employees also have the option of purchasing additional health care coverage. An IBM package encourages preventive medicine. A $200 a year personal health account is available to employees and their families to help pay for items not included in the health plan such as immunizations, hearing care and prenatal care. The account pays 80 percent of these expenses.

The search for innovative costs containment is not limited to management. Concerned about the impact of rising health care costs on their members' incomes, such unions as the Teamsters (IBT), the Autoworkers (UAW), the Communications Workers (CWA), and the Service Workers International Union (SEIU) have negotiated contracts with management which reflect cooperative efforts to control health care costs. Further, the trend toward cost cutting is reflected vividly in data from the Bureau of Labor Statistics' 1984 survey of private firms. From 1983, coverage for treatment in extended care facilities has risen from 58 percent to 62 percent; for home care, from 37 to 46 percent.

Hospice care appeared for the first time in 1984 as being available to 11 percent of the employees covered.[25]

Future Benefits for Librarians

It has become evident that employers and employees both gain from well-managed and well-presented benefits programs. There is no reason to believe that the two cannot continue to work together to improve these offerings, especially in the public sector. This survey showed that only in the area of health benefits did librarians employed in the public sector achieve any kind of parity with those employed in the private sector. It was the librarian in the large corporate environment who had access to the broadest range of services. Except for health and dental plans, daycare, cafeteria or flexible benefits, and flextime were far less frequently part of the benefit package.

Clearly, librarians in public employment need to work to bring their benefit packages up-to-date. Using some of the suggestions for cost containment reviewed in this article, there is no reason why librarians cannot enjoy benefits responsive to their current needs without jeopardizing the fiscal health of the organizations that employ them.

References

1. U.S. Bureau of Labor Statistics, *Labor Force Statistics Derived From the Current Population Survey: A Databook, Volume I,* Bulletin 2096, September 1982, p. 664.
2. U.S. Bureau of Labor Statistics, *Employee Benefits in Medium and Large Firms, 1983,* August 1984, Bulletin 2213.
3. 118 *Labor Relations Reporter* 275, December 3, 1984.
4. Phillip M. Alden, Jr., *Controlling the Costs of Retirement Income and Medical Care Plans* (New York: AMACOM, 1980), p. 55.
5. 117 *Labor Relations Reporter* 275, December 3, 1984.
6. *Flexible Benefits: Will They Wrok For You?* (Chicago: Commerce Clearing House, 1983), p. 7.
7. Robert B. Cockrum, "Has the Time Come for Employee Cafeteria Plans?" *Personnel Administrator,* July 1982, p. 68.
8. Carson E. Beadle, *Flexible Compensation and Benefits: Innovations and Issues for the 80s* (New York: William M. Mercer, Inc., 1983), p. 4.
9. John Perham, "New Life for Flexible Compensation," *Dun Review,* September 1978, p. 66.
10. Cockrum, p. 67.
11. Greenberg, K. and M. Zippo, "Roundup Flexible Compensation Cuts Costs and Meets Employee Needs," *Personnel,* March-April 1983, p. 48.
12. Beadle, p. 13.
13. *Flexible Benefits,* p. 32.
14. 113 *Labor Relations Reporter* 289, August 8, 1983.
15. Center for Public Resources, "On the Fringe of Benefits: Working Parents and the Corporation" (New York: Center for Public Resources, 1980), p. 3.
16. U.S. Women's Bureau, *Child Care Centers Sponsored by Employers and Labor Unions in the United States,* by Catherine S. Perry (Washington, D.C.: Government Printing Office, June 1980), p. 6.
17. U.S. Commission on Civil Rights, *Child Care and Equal Opportunity for Women,* Clearinghouse Publication No. 67, Washington, D.C. Government Printing Office, June 1981, p. 51.
18. Carol Haddad, *Local Union guide for Establishing Child Care Centers* (East Lansing: Michigan State University, 1979).
19. *On the Fringe,* pp. 17-18.
20. Ibid., p. 11.
21. U.S. Bureau of the Census. *Economic Characteristics of Households in the United States: Fourth Quarter, 1983,* February 1985. (Series p-70-83-4).
22. Gerard Tavernier, "Companies Prescribe Major Divisions in Medical Benefits Programs to Cut Soaring Healthcare Costs," *Management Review,* August 1983, p. 9.
23. Alden, p. 48.
24. Tavernier, p. 11.
25. 118 *Labor Relations Reporter* 256, April 1, 1985.

FRINGE BENEFITS

Malcolm Getz

Nineteen eighty-nine is the year of fringe benefits. The Tax Reform Act of 1986 introduced a series of rules that have forced employers to adopt fringe benefit regimes that do not discriminate in favor of highly compensated employees if the benefits are to remain exempt from federal income tax. Recent regulations require compliance by the end of calendar year 1989. The test for nondiscrimination applies to health, retirement, dependent care, and educational benefits, among others.

The changes in fringe benefit programs induced by the tax code create an opportunity to consider fringe benefits more broadly. The general officers of many profit-making and not-for-profit establishments, including libraries, put considerable energy into designing fringe benefit programs that employees will find attractive, that the employer can afford, and that satisfy the demands of the Internal Revenue Code. This column will not provide a detailed discussion of the many rules and alternatives in fringe-benefit programs. Rather, it affords a context for understanding the nature of fringe benefits, their goals, and their problems.

Fringe benefits averaged about 25 percent of total compensation for white-collar workers in the private sector.[1] Legally mandated expenditures, including the employer's contribution to social security, and the cost of unemployment insurance and worker's compensation, amounted to 7.2 percent of total compensation; pensions and savings, 3.7 percent; insurance, 4.9 percent; paid leave, 7.7 percent; and other benefits, 1.9 percent.

In light of the substantial cost of fringe benefits, both employers and employees want to assure that benefit programs are well-designed and well-managed. The Internal Revenue Code requires that plans be defined in writing and that employees receive an annual statement describing their benefits. Employers should let their staff know how much benefits cost, so that employees have a sense of their total compensation. It is also advisable to budget fringe benefits in a decentralized manner so that line managers can appropriately identify the total cost of labor. (Training and supervision are additional costs for maintaining a labor force.)

Why Fringes?

Why should both employers and employees desire that a significant part of the total compensation package be in the form of in-kind services? If compensation were solely monetary, employees would be able to shop for services for themselves and allocate their compensation to meet their own needs.

Several advantages of fringe benefits are obvious. First, with implicit long-term contracts with their employees, employers can compensate them according to their needs: varying with illness, death, dependency, education, and retirement. Employees give up a measure of control of their consumption choices in order to have compensation levels that vary with their life circumstances.

Second, employers can shop more effectively for certain services for the employees as a group than the employees can shop individually. For example, the transaction costs involving each employee seeking life insurance may be significant. Insurance is a complex commodity with high transaction costs.

Third, the costs of certain benefits may be lower when the employer buys. For example, because the employer has screened employees in hiring and retaining them, that group may differ from the rest of the population. The screening process may change the insurance risks, perhaps unintentionally, in ways that insurers may recognize in a group contract.

Fourth, fringe benefits may not be subject to income tax. Significant rates for income tax emerged during World War II. Fringe benefits were probably excluded from the tax base because of the difficulty of tracking their value. With higher tax rates, interest in seeing a larger proportion of compensation come in the form of tax-exempt benefits.

Finally, although fringe benefits are sometimes associated with unions and collective bargaining, they are increasingly used by occupational groups little affected by union activity. And so, the net effect of union activity in increasing benefits may be hard to establish.

Fringes and Income Taxes

The tax reform efforts of the 1980s have reshaped fringe benefits to a degree. Since Congress now understands benefits to be part of total compensation, fringes are part of the total income base that might be subject to taxation. The higher the marginal tax rates, the greater the distortions of incentives created by the existence of taxation. Therefore, tax reformers have sought to widen the tax base to allow a comparable level of revenue to be collected on lower rates. Including fringe benefits in the base for income tax would help in this goal. Such a change in the tax law would also reduce the bias toward compensation in-kind as opposed to monetary compensation. The willingness to consider taxation of fringe benefits has played a part in the more aggressive regulation of fringe benefits under the Internal Revenue Code.

Of course, the 1980s brought not only lower marginal tax rates, but also significant and persistent deficits in the federal budget—deficits that were specifically advocated by the President as a strategy to reduce the scope of federal expenditure programs. As new or expanded direct expenditure programs were foreclosed as ways of meeting social goals, taxation and regulation drew attention as alternative methods. Mandated private retirement and health plans drew particular attention. Just as tax and expenditure programs are used to redistribute income to lower-income households, so fringe benefit programs are now regulated so that employers may no longer offer fringe benefits that discriminate in favor of highly compensated employees. Even if all employees are eligible for a voluntary program, highly compensated employees may not participate at a much higher rate than non-highly compensated employees or the plan may violate the new rules against non-discrimination.

In adjusting plans to meet the non-discrimination tests, employers can either adopt changes that provide smaller benefits to highly compensated employees, thus providing higher benefits to non-highly compensated employees, or employers may increase expenditures on benefits to extend benefits to lower-paid employees.

If we believe that levels of total compensation tend to be determined by competition in markets — with persons of relatively scarce skills being more highly compensated — then we might expect monetary compensation to adjust around the mandated changes in fringe benefits, leaving the pattern of total compensation unchanged. Should this, in fact, be the result, then lower-income workers will find a growing proportion of their compensation coming from fringe benefits, while highly compensated employees will see more cash.

In contemplating the modification or addition of a new benefit, an employer will be keenly interested in how the IRS will view the change. With the new rules governing non-discrimination, it will take years of IRS rulings and of case law before the area will be fully settled.

Retirement Plans

Retirement and health care benefits are very important elements of most employee benefit programs. They are complex and expensive enough to merit separate comment here. For retirement, the central issues are: How large should contributions be and at what age should benefits begin?

The Social Security Act of 1935 identified age 65 as the time when full benefits might begin. In the 1950's, as life expectancy increased, adding to the number of years after age 65 in which one might expect to live a full and active life, many more individuals came to plan for retirement. Our society, then, invented the concept of retirement as

a mass phenomenon in this century. Employers in larger numbers began to establish programs beyond Social Security to provide financial support for retirement. For example, Teacher's Insurance and Annuity Association and the College Retirement Equities Fund (TIAA/CREF), the most common retirement programs for university faculty, were founded in 1918 and 1952 respectively.

The employer's financial contributions toward employees' retirement is a form of deferred compensation. The work effort that merits compensation occurs at a given time, but the employee receives the benefit at certain periods in the future.

Retirement plans are of two forms. In the defined contribution form, the employer deposits an amount in the employees name in a retirement fund as the work is performed. Deposited funds earn interest until retirement. At retirement, the balance in the employee's name is available for the employee to use to purchase annuities that will provide payments until death. The employee typically knows the balance in the retirement account at any point in time, knows the rate of interest earned, and is aware of the various financial risks that shape the value of the fund at retirement.

The second form of retirement plan is called defined benefit. For this plan, the employer typically guarantees a payment at retirement that will continue until death. This payment depends on the number of years of employment and on earnings during the final years of employment. The payment may be defined inclusive of the Social Security benefit, so that the employer plan effectively tops up the Social Security benefit. With a defined benefit plan, the employee may make annual contributions to a retirement fund as work is performed. If so, the plan is called "funded." The Employee Retirement Income Security Act (ERISA) of 1974 requires that pension plans be funded and establishes rules for funding. However, prior to ERISA, many employers had not built funds to pay for retirement plans and simply paid benefits to current retirees from current operating funds. Such pension plans are called "unfunded," and employees with unfunded plans can be left with no benefit if the em-

ployer's business fails. In time, ERISA rules should minimize this risk.

Employees may not be eligible for retirement benefits until they have completed a certain number of years of service. At the point when the employee becomes eligible for retirement benefit, the benefit is "vested" in the employee. If the employee leaves employment, he or she will be eligible for at least some retirement benefit. In some cases, this may be a lump sum payment; in other cases, the employee receives some level of retirement payment at the retirement age.

The critical issue for employers and employees is at what level to contribute to the retirement fund. With the new requirement that the plan not discriminate, firms must consider the issue carefully. For defined contribution plans like TIAA/CREF, which is important in many libraries, the issue is the level of contributions to be made annually during the working years. The rate is usually expressed as a percentage of salary. For defined-benefit plans, the level of benefit that employers offer must be translated into annual funding commitments under ERISA rules. The annual financial commitment to funding future retirement benefits is then comparable under the two regimes.

A typical goal for a retirement plan is to provide a retiree with 65% to 75% of the salary level in the final years of employment for a person who has worked steadily for the employer over a period of 25 to 35 years. In the following discussion, I assume a goal of 75% of replacement of salary. What rate of annual contribution is necessary to meet this goal? Table 1 addresses this question. There are three important factors.

First, what rate of interest are we willing to assume the fund will earn, net of inflation? If we are willing to assume higher rates of return, then lower levels of contribution will be necessary. Second, how many years of contribution will we require to meet the 75% of salary replacement goal? The longer the period of contribution assumed, the lower the level of contribution will be necessary. Third, for how many years of retirement must our plan provide? Actuaries make careful calculations of life expectancy in determining the likely number of years of survival in selling annuity contracts. For our calculation, the issue is more a matter of the age at retirement. The later the age at retirement, the fewer the years of retirement, the lower the level of contribution required during working years. At age 60, the average life expectancy is about 20 years. At age 67 (where changes in the Social Security system are moving the retirement age), life expectancy is about 15 years.

Table 1 simplifies the actuarial issue by assuming that people all live the same number of years in order to focus on the financial issue. If the retirement fund will earn 4% above the average rate of inflation and we assume an employee must work 25 years to achieve "full benefit," and we assume the retirement age is such as to yield 15 years of expected retirement, then the annual rate of funding must be 20% of salary during the working years. Contribution rates required for other interest rates, years of contribution, and years of retirement are shown in Table 1.

Employer and employee contributions to Social Security amount to about 15% of salary up to a ceiling. Social Security benefits are calculated in such a manner to yield a higher ratio of salary replacement for lower-income employees—that is, it tilts toward lower-income people. For a married couple with two earners at a minimum level of earnings, Social Security alone will replace about 80% of earnings. For a couple with average earnings Social Security will replace about 63% of earnings. For a couple contributing to Social Security at the maximum level, Social Security will replace about 42% of earnings.[2] If the target for funding retirement is to replace about 75% of pre-retirement average salary, then higher earning employees will need to contribute more to offset the low income tilt of social security benefits. Employers will find, however, that the non-discriminatory rules of the Tax Reform Act of 1986 may make that somewhat more difficult.

What rate of contribution to retirement may be desired? If an employer has a significant number of highly compensated employees, and is willing to assume that a 4% to 5% rate of interest will be earned on the retirement fund over and above inflation, then annual contributions to

TABLE 1
INCOME REPLACEMENT

Unit Income Replacement
Earn salary 1.0 for x years
Retire for y years at replacement rate: 0.75
Retirement fund earns real rate of interest r (net of inflation)
Implies required rate of contribution z during working years

z is the percent of salary to be saved for retirement

r Real Rate of interest	x Years of contribution	y Years of Retirement	z rate of contribution
4.0%	25	15	0.200
	30	15	0.149
	35	15	0.113
	25	20	0.245
	30	20	0.182
	35	20	0.138
5.0%	25	15	0.163
	30	15	0.117
	35	15	0.086
	25	20	0.196
	30	20	0.141
	35	20	0.103

the retirement fund might run in the 5%-10% range (total for employer and employee contributions, if any). Employees who wish to defer more compensation than the employer's mandatory plan may make additional contributions or use other financial vehicles to accumulate wealth in support of retirement. Some of these may postpone income taxation until retirement. Mandatory contributions that total over 10% for all employees are probably unwise when the work force includes many lower-income employees who are more generously treated by Social Security. Lower-income employees have other important needs and are likely to value more current income instead.

Health Care

The primary issue in health care

is the rapid escalation of costs. Health care now constitutes 11% of Gross National Product, and health care costs increased at 7% in 1987-88—the most rapid increase in prices over the last decade of all sectors of the economy. As an element of total compensation, it is clearly impinging on other forms of compensation, holding down salary levels, crowding retirement contributions, and limiting employer flexibility in designing compensation programs.

As long as the health care benefit insulates the employee from price considerations in deciding on the consumption of health care, we can expect the cost of health care benefits to continue to grow unabated. However, many employers are now providing "cafeteria" plans that allow employees to choose among a number of alternatives with different prices. Although the menu may extend beyond health care, health care cost containment is often a principal goal.

To have maximum effect in controlling costs, the employer should support several alternative health care plans, each of which provides an adequate level of physician and hospital services. These might include preferred provider groups as well as health maintenance organizations. The menu might provide different levels of deductibles and co-insurance. We might expect the employer to provide some standard dollar level of benefit that might cover the cost of the lowest or next to lowest plan. Employees who wish to choose a higher cost plan could pay the additional cost. Employees who choose a plan that costs less than the employer's standard might have the difference deposited in a flexible reimbursement account that could be drawn for use in paying de-

ductibles, co-insurance, and in purchasing non-covered items like routine eye examinations or dental bills. We can expect that those families who expect to make the largest use of health care services will elect plans with lower deductibles. However, they may also choose lower cost providers so as to minimize the effect on their household budgets. Such a benefit regime invites employees to reveal their individual preferences among health care systems that come at different costs because the dollars saved are their own. Such a regime will also create an incentive for providers to control costs. Such programs, however, must pass the IRS non-discrimination tests.

Summary

Fringe benefits are an important part of total compensation in most institutions in our society including libraries. Changes in the federal income tax law have caused most in-

stitutions to review their fringe benefit programs and 1989 is a pivotal year for many. In addition, the continuing growth in health care costs poses additional challenges. Thoughtful design of fringe benefit programs can yield compensation programs that give a high degree of employee satisfaction, yet remain affordable for employers. =

References

1. Felicia Nathan, "Analyzing employers' costs for wages, salaries, and benefits," Monthly Labor Review, October, 1987, pp. 3–11, Table 2. Robert M. McCaffery, Employee Benefit Programs: A Total Compensation Perspective, (Boston: PWS-Kent Publishing Company, 1988) Table 5.1, p. 111. Source: Office of the Actuary, Social Security Administration, U.S. Department of Health and Human Services.

HOW THE PROFESSIONAL LIBRARIAN FARES UNDER THE 1986 TAX ACT

William J. Walsh, CPA

The Tax Reform Act of 1986, signed into law by President Reagan on October 22, 1986, makes the most sweeping changes to our tax system that we have experienced in over 30 years. Virtually every individual in the United States will feel its impact. In fact, the reverberations began late last year even though most of the law's provisions did not take effect until January 1 of this year.

There is good news — and there is bad news — relating to how librarians conduct both their professional and personal lives.

THE GOOD NEWS

The basic premise of the new tax code is to lower tax rates while at the same time removing the myriad of loopholes and deductions that taxpayers have used to lower their taxable income. The lower tax rates will be phased in between this year and next. For 1987, the tax rate will drop only to 38½ percent; by 1988, the top rate on personal income will have dropped from a high of 50 percent to 28 percent. The majority of changes in deductions were effective January 1.

The amount you can claim as personal exemptions increases from $1,080 in 1986 to $1,900 in 1987, $1,950 in 1988, and $2,000 in 1989. In addition, the standard deduction has been increased to $5,000 for married people filing jointly, $2,500 for married people filing separately, and $2,540 for single people. The new code also provides an extra $600 deduction for taxpayers over the age of 65 and for those who are blind.

The overall effect of the new tax law on the majority of librarians will be a slightly lower tax rate and taxable income in 1987, with a significant change in 1988. For taxpayers who do not itemize, the new law will be a real boon — lower tax rates and higher exemptions. For the taxpayer who is accustomed to itemizing there may be a different story. Whether or not you fare well under the new law will depend on how much the changes in deductions affect your taxable income.

THE BAD NEWS

The down side of the new lower rates and higher exemptions is the severe limitation on deductions being imposed by the new tax law. The two areas where librarians might be most affected are the limitations on Individual Retirement Accounts (IRA's) and the 2 percent floor on unreimbursed business expenses.

Possibly the most far-reaching effect is the 2 percent limitation on miscellaneous deductions. Under the old law, the majority of your nonreimbursed business and educational expenses were fully deductible. According to the 2 percent limitation, unless your miscellaneous expenses exceed 2 percent of your adjusted gross income, they cannot be deducted. Deductible expenses commonly used by librarians that are now subject to the 2 percent limitation include:

- dues to professional organizations
- employment-related education
- conference expenses (e.g., registration fees, hotel and meal costs)
- work-related travel expenses
- job-hunting expenses
- home-office expenses
- subscriptions to professional journals, newsletters, magazines, and other periodicals
- union dues and fees
- business entertainment expenses
- legal and accounting fees
- investment counseling fees

Here is an example of how the limitation works. Mary F. is a librarian earning $30,000 a year. She files jointly with her husband Kim, a gift-shop owner, who earns $60,000 a year. Mary has $1,000 in nonreimbursed miscellaneous expenses for continuing education courses, association dues, and three subscriptions. The couple's 1987 adjusted gross income is $90,000. Mary therefore cannot deduct these expenses since 2 percent of $90,000 is $1,800. In fact, even if Mary had $1,900 in expenses, she would only be allowed a $100 deduction.

In addition to the 2 percent limitation, there is a limitation on deductions for business-related meals and entertainment. Only 80 percent of these expenditures are allowable as a deduction. In Mary F.'s case, this means that if $100 of her expenses were for meals or entertainment, she would first have to reduce that amount by $20 before applying the 2 percent rule.

EXAMPLE:

Nonreimbursed expense	$1,000
Less 20% reduction of $100 in meals and entertainment	− 20
Nonreimbursed expense subject to 2 percent rule	$ 980
2% limitation (2% of $90,000 gross income)	1,800
Amount deductible	$ − 0 −

The new IRA provision will certainly have significant impact on your financial planning since many of you are covered by your institution's pension plan *and* have IRA's Under the old tax law, you were allowed to open IRA's even if you were enrolled in a company/institution pension plan. According to the new law, if a taxpayer is covered by an existing pension or profit-sharing plan, and has $50,000 in taxable income if married or $35,000 if single, he or she is no longer allowed a tax deduction for putting money into an IRA (even if separate returns are filed). Even if only one spouse is covered by a plan, neither is allowed the deduction. But, if you or your spouse is covered by a pension plan you can claim a full IRA deduction if your adjusted gross income is below $40,000 on a joint return or $25,000 on a single return. For couples with incomes between $40,000 and $50,000, and for single individuals with incomes between $25,000 and $35,000, a partial deduction (reduced proportionately over the $10,000 range) is allowed.

OTHER PROVISIONS

A number of other provisions of the new tax code will impact on the individual librarian. One that may very well have a ricocheting effect on the institutions for which they work is the elimination or reduction in deductions for charitable contributions. After 1986, the contributions of taxpayers who do not itemize—estimated to be 65 percent of all taxpayers—are no longer deductible. As the standard deduction is raised, more taxpayers probably will fall into this category. As for those who do itemize, the itemized contributions will be worth less this year and even less from 1988 on because of the scheduled reduction in tax rates. We can only surmise what effect this will have on libraries that receive individual donations.

Those tax law provisions you should also be aware of are:

1. The elimination of favorable capital gains treatment: Up until 1986, taxpayers were only taxed at 40 percent of their gain from the sale of stocks, bonds, land, or other capital assets. Now, 100 percent of the gain is taxable.

2. The elimination of the consumer-loan interest deduction: You will no longer be able to deduct the interest on loans for such items as boats, cars, and credit card purchase. This provision will be phased in over a five-year period. The chart below shows the progression:

Year	Amt. of Interest that Can be Deducted
1987	65%
1988	40%
1989	20%
1990	10%
1991	nondeductible

3. The elimination of the deductibility of tax shelter losses: Under the old law, a taxpayer with high taxable income could invest in such things as real estate syndications, in which they were limited partners. The "paper" losses generated from these investments were used to offset income from other sources, such as salary, dividends, or interest. Under the new law, these activities are severely restricted and investors in such shelters should consult their professional advisors. This provision will be phased in over a four-year period.

STRATEGIES

In light of the 2 percent and IRA limitations, as well as the other provisions of the new tax law, librarians should reassess their financial situations. A good example of how to deal with your reimbursables is travel expenses. If you cannot be fully reimbursed—and that, of course, would be the best solution—you should encourage your employer to institute a fixed per diem rate whereby you are paid so much per day up to $75, the current government maximum, for work-related travel, lodging, and meal expenses.

For example, Mary F. attends an overnight conference in Buffalo every year. If next year she and her employer agree on the $75 per diem rate, and as long as Mary F. provides her employer with a record of time, place, and business purpose, then she will not have to report either the reimbursement nor the expenses on her tax return.

Since many of you will no longer benefit from nonreimbursed business expenses because of the 2 percent limitation, there will have to be a meeting of minds between you and your employer over what is reimbursed and what is not. And if you are given the choice of a per diem or using the 2 percent limitation, you will have to look at your personal financial situation very carefully. You might suggest to your employer an annual budget for these business expenses. It will then be up to you to decide which activities and expenditures are the most important and worthwhile. If you have been paying for these business expenses on your own, you are going to find that they cost you more because of the new law. You may have to reexamine your current memberships and subscriptions and choose to maintain only those from which you derive the greatest benefit.

In the case of IRA's, you should consider deferring more income into your existing pension plan or negotiating with your employer for a larger contribution to offset the loss of the IRA. In addition, even though the contribution to an existing IRA is not deductible, the income is still tax-deferred, which may make a case for continuing to fund it.

Generally, how you will fare under the Tax Reform Act of 1986 depends on your individual circumstances. While it is difficult to draw generalized conclusions overall, two are obvious. If you are a married taxpayer covered by a pension plan, with high consumer debt, joint income over $50,000, and nonreimbursed business and educational expenditures, you will probably not fare very well. If, on the other hand, you benefit from the lower rates and do not lose significant deductions, you should do just fine. (See Figure 1 for a three-year comparison of an unmarried taxpayer's tax returns.)

One thing is certain: 1987 will be a complicated year for all taxpayers. Now is the time for you to carefully review your situation with your tax advisor and to discuss strategy with your employer so that both you and your institution can gain the advantage.

FIGURE 1
Three-Year Comparison of Tax Returns
of Single Taxpayer Blair Libris

		1986	1987	1988
Salary		$30,000	$30,000	$30,000
Adjusted Gross Income	(a)	30,000	30,000	30,000
Itemized Deductions:				
Charitable contributions		100	100	100
Taxes:				
State and local income tax		750	750	750
Sales tax		275	0	0
Property tax		1,000	1,000	1,000
Interest Deduction:				
Mortgage		4,000	4,000	4,000
Consumer interest	(b)	350	227	140
Miscellaneous Deductions:				
Professional dues		250	0	0
Subscriptions		200	0	0
Tax return preparation fee		150	0	0
Total Itemized Deductions		7,075	6,077	5,990
Zero Bracket Amount (c)		− 2,480	0	0
		4,595	6,077	5,990
Exemptions (1)		1,080	1,900	1,950
Taxable Income		24,325	22,023	22,060
Tax	(d)	− $ 4,172	$ 3,910	$ 3,857

(a) 2% of $30,000 or $600 is the floor for the miscellaneous deductions. Because Blair's miscellaneous deductions equalled $600 ($250 + $200 + $150) she received no deduction in 1987 or 1988.

(b) Her deduction for consumer interest was reduced to 65% of the amount in 1987 and was reduced to 40% of $350 in 1988.

(c) Eliminated under the new law.

(d) Even though Blair lost some deductions in 1987 and 1988, she will pay less tax due to higher exemptions (2,000 vs. 1,080) and the reduction in rates.

INDEX

LIST OF
CONTRIBUTORS

Virgil L.P. Blake is Assistant Professor of Library and Information Studies, Queens College, N. Y. "Library and Municipal Officials: The Great Divide" was originally published in Vol. 3, No. 2, pp. 28–31.

Daniel J. Bradbury is Director, Kansas City Public Library, Missouri. "Seven Strategies for Effective Fund Raising" originally appeared in Vol. 2, No. 4, pp. 11–14.

Clifford D. Brown is Accountancy Professor, Bentley College, Waltham, Mass. "Fund Accounting Basics" originally appeared in Vol. 3, No. 2 pp. 32–33.

Robert Burgin is an Instructor, School of Library and Information Sciences, North Carolina Central University, Durham. "Creative Budget Presentation: Using Statistics to Prove Your Point" was originally published in Vol. 1, No. 1, pp. 13–17.

Carol A. Cameron is a Title VI Program Officer at the Office of Educational Research and Improvement of the U. S. Department of Education, Washington, D. C. "Funding Library Literacy" originally appeared in Vol. 4, No. 4, pp. 9–12.

Edwin S. Clay III is Director, Fairfax County Public Library, Fairfax, Va. "Fund Raising by Strategic Design" appeared in Vol. 1, No. 3, pp. 25–27.

Thompson R. Cummins is Planning and Evaluating Librarian, Miami-Dade Public Library, Miami, Fl. "Cost-Benefit Analysis" originally appeared in Vol. 3, No. 2, pp. 18–21.

Barry Devlin is Head of Technical Services, Rockwood Memorial Library, Livingston, N. J. "Basic Budget Primer" was originally published in Vol. 2, No. 3, pp. 20–24.

Walter E. Doherty is a Library Consultant in Phoenix, Ariz. "How to Turn a Library into a Profit Center: The Law Library Example" originally appeared in Vol. 2, No. 4, pp. 28–29.

Ralze Dorr is Director, Office of Planning and Administrative Services, University Libraries, University of Louisville, Ky. "Planning Photocopy Services" originally appeared in Vol. 3, No. 1, pp. 21–26.

Richard M. Dougherty is Professor, School of Information and Library Studies, University of Michigan, Ann Arbor. "Are Libraries Hostage to Rising Serials Costs?" originally appeared in Vol. 2, No. 4, pp. 25–27.

Gary J. Egan is Assistant Controller, Georgetown University, Washington, D.C. "Harnessing Accounting Theory: Scrupulous Coding Can Revitalize University Library Systems" originally appeared in Vol. 3, No. 3, pp. 21–24.

Judith Foust is Deputy Director, Brooklyn Public Library, N. Y. "Economic Vitality: How Libraries Can Play a Key Role" was originally published in Vol. 3, No. 1, pp. 18–20.

Brinley R. Franklin is a Library Consultant for Peat Marwick Mitchell and Co., Washington, D.C. "Harnessing Accounting Theory: Scrupulous Coding Can Revitalize University Library Systems" originally appeared in Vol. 3, No. 3, pp. 21–24.

David R.L. Gabhart is Professor of Accountancy at Bentley College, Waltham, Mass. "There's Depreciation in Your Future" originally appeared in Vol. 2, No. 2, pp. 27–28.

Alice Gertzog is a Library Consultant in Meadville, Penn. "Gathering Grants: Boom or Bust?" was originally published in the Charter Issue, pp. 17–20.

Malcolm Getz is Director of Libraries, Vanderbilt University, Nashville, Tenn. He is a regular columnist for *The Bottom Line*.

Pete Giacoma is Assistant Director, Davis County Library, Farmington, Ut. "User Fees: Pros and Cons" originally appeared in Vol. 3, No. 1, pp. 27–30.

Frank William Goudy is Professor, Western Illinois University Libraries, Macomb, Ill. "Viewpoint: Comparing Librarian and Teacher Salaries *Is* Valid" originally appeared in Vol. 2, No. 1, pp. 17–19.

Sherman Hayes is Director, Solomon R. Baker Library, Bentley College, Waltham, Mass. He is a regular columnist for *The Bottom Line*.

Barbara A. Humes is a Title VI Program Officer at the Office of Educational Research and Improvement, U.S. Department of Education, Washington, D.C. "Funding Library Literacy" originally appeared in Vol. 4, No. 4, pp. 9–12.

Kathleen Raab Huston is Assistant City Librarian, Milwaukee Public Library, Wis. "How to Look a Gift Horse in the Mouth: Saying No to Donations" originally appeared in Vol. 3, No. 1, pp. 14–17.

M.E.L. Jacob is a Library Consultant in Columbus, Ohio. "Costing and Pricing: The Difference Matters" was originally published in Vol. 2, No. 2, pp. 12–14.

Helen Josephine is the Manager of FIRST (Fee-Based Information Research Team), Arizona State University Library, Tempe. "The Fiscal Impact of Pay Equity" originally appeared in Vol. 1, No. 2, pp. 18–24.

Lawrence A. Klein is Associate Professor of Accountancy, Bentley College, Waltham, Mass. "Cost Accounting Basics" was originally published in Vol. 2, No. 1, pp. 29–30.

Paul Little is Chief of Planning Services, Metropolitan Library System, Oklahoma City, Okla. "Managing Overdues" originally appeared in Vol. 2, No. 2, pp. 22–25.

Sandra Bokamba Lockett is the Extension Services Coordinator, Milwaukee Public Library, Wis. "Adult Programming on a Shoestring" originally appeared in Vol. 3, No. 3, pp. 25–28.

Donald MacIntyre is Assistant Professor of Marketing, Bentley College, Waltham, Mass. "Accounting for Marketing Costs" originally appeared in Vol. 3, No. 1, pp. 31–34.

Murray S. Martin is Professor of Library Science and Special Assistant to the Provost for Library Planning and Development Tufts University Library, Medford, Mass. "Stagnant Budgets: Their Effects on Academic Libraries" was originally published in Vol. 3, No. 3, pp. 10–16. "Financing Library Automation" is from the Charter Issue, pp. 11–16.

Gail McGovern is Funding Source Consultant, California State Library, Sacramento. She was a regular columnist for *The Bottom Line*.

Irene E. Moran is a Library Consultant in Modesto, Calif. "Writing a Winning Grant Proposal" originally appeared in Vol. 1, No. 2, pp. 13–17.

Jane Morgan is a Trustee of the Richton Park Public Library District, Richton Park, Ill. "Holding a Successful Referendum" was originally published in Vol. 2, No. 2, pp. 18–21.

Elizabeth Mueller is Consulting Services Director, Suburban Library System, Burr Ridge, Ill. "Holding a Successful Referendum" originally appeared in Vol. 2, No. 2, pp. 18–21.

Christine M. Murchio is a Research Manager, AT&T Consumer Communications and Services, Murray Hill, N. J. "A Circulation System Cost Profile" originally appeared in Vol. 1, No. 3, pp. 20–24.

Margaret Myers is Director, Office for Library Personnel Resources, American Library Association, Chicago. "High Demand, Low Supply in Library Financial Management Careers" originally appeared in Vol. 1, No. 2, pp. 4–8.

W. David Penniman is the Director of Libraries and Information Systems, AT&T Bell Telephone Labs, Murray Hill, N. J. "On Their Terms: Preparing Libraries for a Competitive Environment" was originally published in Vol. 1, No. 3, pp. 11–15.

Mark Reidell is Public Information Officer, St. Paul Public Library, Minn. "The Joy of Staging Special Events" originally appeared in Vol. 1, No. 4, pp. 21–24.

Catherine R. Reilly is Vice-President and Administrator, The Information Center, Chase Manhattan Bank, New York City. "Productivity Measurement for Fiscal Control" originally appeared in the Charter Issue, pp. 21–28.

Elizabeth Richmond is Library Consultant and Co-Owner of the Rick Richmond Information System, Eau Claire, Wis. "Cost Finding: Method and Management" originally appeared in Vol. 1, No. 4, pp. 16–20. "Cost Finding: The Wisconsin Experience" is from Vol. 2, No. 1, pp. 23–28.

Betty-Carol Sellen is a Library Consultant in New York City.

Erica Steinberger is Head of Marketing and Library Systems, General Research Corporation, Santa Barbara, Calif. "The Balance Sheet: How to Read It and How to Use It" originally appeared in Vol. 2, No. 1, pp. 20–22.

Deanna K. Suter is the Head of Business and Accounting Services, Fort Vancouver Regional Library, Vancouver, Wash. "How to Write an Award-Winning Financial Report" originally appeared in Vol. 2, No. 4, pp. 15–20.

Betty J. Turock is Editor, *The Bottom Line*, and Chair of the Library and Information Studies Department at Rutgers University, New Brunswick, N. J.

Michael Vinson is Reference and Collection Development Librarian, DeGolyer Library, Southern Methodist University, Dallas, Tex. "Cost Finding: A Step-by-Step Guide" originally appeared in Vol. 2, No. 3, pp. 15–19.

William J. Walsh is a CPA for Walsh & Company, Certified Public Accountants, Canandaigua, N. Y. "How the Professional Librarian Fares Under the 1986 Tax Act" originally appeared in Vol. 1, No. 1, pp. 5–6.

Marjorie Watson is Reference Librarian, Dana Library, Rutgers University, New Brunswick, N.J. "Employee Benefits: Emerging Trends for Librarians" was originally published in the Charter Issue, pp. 29–32.

Frances K. Wood is Program Director, Information Services Division, Kurt F. Wendt Engineering Library, University of Wisconsin, Madison. "When Do Dollars for Information Services Make Sense?" originally appeared in Vol. 1, No. 4, pp. 25–27.

Blue Wooldridge is Associate Professor for the Department of Public Administration, Virginia Commonwealth University, Richmond. "Revenue Planning: A Vital Tool for Public Libraries" was originally published in Vol. 1, No. 1, pp. 29–33.